Deadly Connections

Thousands of people have died at the hands of terrorist groups that rely on state support for their activities. Iran and Libya are well known as sponsors of terrorism, while other countries, some with strong connections to the West, have enabled terrorist activity by turning a blind eye. Daniel Byman's hard-hitting and articulate book is the first to analyze this phenomenon. Focusing primarily on sponsors from the Middle East and South Asia, it examines the different types of support that states provide, their motivations, and the impact of such sponsorship. The book also considers regimes that allow terrorists to raise money and recruit without providing active support. The experiences of Iran, Pakistan, Afghanistan, Syria, Saudi Arabia, and Libya are detailed here, alongside the histories of radical groups such as al-Qa'ida, Hizballah, and HAMAS. In conclusion, the book also assesses the difficulties of forcing sponsors to cut ties to terrorist groups.

DANIEL BYMAN is an Assistant Professor in the Security Program of the Edmund A. Walsh School of Foreign Service at Georgetown University. He has published widely on issues related to terrorism, Middle East politics, and national security. He is the author of *The Dynamics of Coercion: American Foreign Policy and the Limits of Military Might* (2002).

Deadly Connections
States that Sponsor Terrorism

DANIEL BYMAN

Security Studies Program of the Edmund A. Walsh School of Foreign Service at Georgetown University

and *Saban Center for Middle East Policy at the Brookings Institution*

CAMBRIDGE
UNIVERSITY PRESS

Hartness Library
Vermont Technical College
One Main St.
Randolph Center, VT 05061

CAMBRIDGE UNIVERSITY PRESS
Cambridge, New York, Melbourne, Madrid, Cape Town, Singapore, São Paulo

CAMBRIDGE UNIVERSITY PRESS
The Edinburgh Building, Cambridge CB2 2RU, UK
Published in the United States of America by Cambridge University Press, New York

www.cambridge.org
Information on this title: www.cambridge.org/9780521

© Daniel Byman 2005

First published 2005

Printed in the United States of America

A catalogue record for this book is available from the British Library

Library of Congress cataloguing in publication data

ISBN-13 978-0-521-83973-0 hardback
ISBN-10 0-521-83973-4 hardback

Contents

Tables

Acknowledgments

As in all of my work, I have relied heavily on my friends and colleagues in writing this book. To five friends I owe a particular debt. David Edelstein helped me struggle through my early conceptualizing as well as scouring the final drafts. Kenneth Pollack encouraged my initial focus on this topic and provided a detailed and constructive review of the manuscript. Jeremy Shapiro and Brent Sterling also reviewed major portions of the manuscript, offering extremely useful criticism which has made the final version much stronger. Last, but certainly not least, Andrew Amunsen served both as a research assistant for this project and as a peer, offering me his unvarnished criticism as well as his constant assistance. I am confident that Andy and other members of the next generation of terrorism scholars will bring far greater rigor and clarity to what is for now an undeveloped field of social science and policy analysis.

Many scholars and experts kindly gave of their time and expertise, reading sections of the manuscript, guiding me to the best sources, or otherwise offering their insights. My thanks go to Shaul Bakhash, Daniel Benjamin, Michael E. Brown, Seymour Byman, Peter Chalk, Steve Cohen, Rebekah Kim Cragin, Martha Crenshaw, Emile El-Hokayem, Christiane Fair, Robert Gallucci, Mark Gasiorowski, F. Gregory Gause III, Sumit Ganguly, Bruce Hoffman, Martin Indyk, Robert Litwak, Mohsen Milani, Paul Pillar, William Rosenau, John Paul Sawyer, Shibley Telhami, David Tucker, Paul Wallace, and Tamara Cofman Wittes. An anonymous reviewer at Cambridge University Press also provided extremely helpful comments.

Acknowledgments

Georgetown's Security Studies Program and Center for Peace and Security Studies proved an extremely congenial location for writing this manuscript. My thanks to Michael E. Brown and Robert Gallucci for their support. Elena Schweiger, Sara Yamaka, and Sarah Yerkes all assisted in the research and administrative tasks that come with transforming a manuscript into a finished work.

Finally, I would like to thank Marigold Acland, my editor at Cambridge University Press, for her constant encouragement and support.

Acronyms

ADF	Allied Democratic Forces
AIAI	Al-Ittihad al-Islami
AIG	Armed Islamic Group
ANO	Abu Nidal Organization
ASALA	Armenian Secret Army for the Liberation of Armenia
ASG	Abu Sayyaf Group
BJP	Bharatiya Janata Party
CIA	Central Intelligence Agency
CRD	Congolese Rally for Democracy
DFLP	Democratic Front for the Liberation of Palestine
EIJ	Egyptian Islamic Jihad
ELN	National Liberation Army
ETA	Basque Fatherland and Liberty
ETIM	Eastern Turkistan Islamic Movement
FARC	Revolutionary Armed Forces of Columbia
FBI	Federal Bureau of Investigation
FoSF	Friends of Sinn Féin
FTO	Foreign Terrorist Organization
GCC	Gulf Cooperation Council
IDF	Israeli Defense Forces
IG	Al-Gama'a al-Islamiyya (Islamic Group)
IIRO	International Islamic Relief Organization
ILSA	Iran–Libya Sanctions Act
IMU	Islamic Movement of Uzbekistan

List of acronyms

IRA	Irish Republican Army
IRGC	Iranian Revolutionary Guard Corp
ISI	Inter-Services Intelligence
JKLF	Jammu and Kashmir Liberation Front
JRA	Japanese Red Army
JUI	Jamiat-e Ulema Islam
	Jamiat-ul-Ulema-e-Islami
LRA	Lord's Resistance Army
LTTE	Liberation Tigers of Tamil Eelam
MAK	Maktab al-Khidmat – Bureau of Services
MEK	Mujahedin-e Khalq
MNLF	Moro National Liberation Front
MUF	Muslim United Front
NATO	North Atlantic Treaty Organization
NIF	National Islamic Front
NGOs	non-governmental organizations
NORAID	Irish Northern Aid Committee
NPA	New People's Army
NPA/CPP	New People's Army/Communist Party of the Philippines
N17	Revolutionary Organization November 17
PA	Palestinian National Authority
PASOK	Panhellenic Socialist Movement
PDFLP	Popular Democratic Front for the Liberation of Palestine
PFLP	Popular Front for the Liberation of Palestine
PFLP-GC	Popular Front for the Liberation of Palestine–General Command
PIJ	Palestine Islamic Jihad
PIRA	Provisional Irish Republican Army
PKK	Kurdistan Workers' Party
PLF	Palestine Liberation Front
PLO	Palestine Liberation Organization
PSF	Popular Struggle Front
RUF	Revolutionary United Front
SALSRA	Syrian Accountability and Lebanon Sovereignty Restoration Act
SCIRI	Supreme Council for Islamic Revolution in Iraq

SPLA	Sudanese People's Liberation Army
SPLM/A	Sudan People's Liberation Movement/Army
SSP	Sipah-e-Sahaba Pakistan
Tamil Tigers	Liberation Tigers of Tamil Eelam
UN	United Nations
UNICEF	United Nations Children's Fund
WMD	weapons of mass destruction

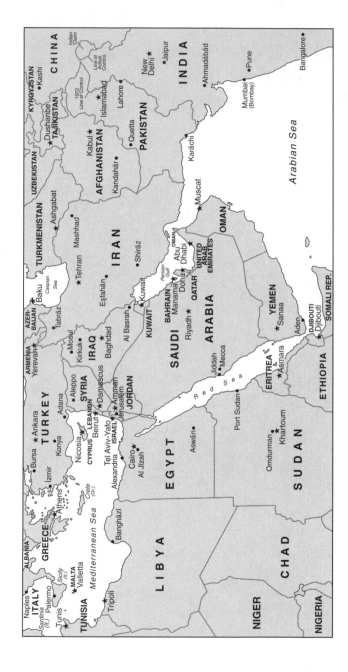

The Middle East and South Asia

I

Introduction

States and terrorist groups have long had a deadly relationship. During the 1970s and 1980s, almost every important terrorist group had some ties to at least one supportive government. Iran backed the Lebanese Hizballah, India aided the Liberation Tigers of Tamil Eelam (Tamil Tigers), and the Palestine Liberation Organization (PLO) (as well as its rivals) drew on support from a host of Arab states. At times, these connections were far-flung and seemingly bizarre. Libya, for example, helped arm the Provisional Irish Republican Army (PIRA), and Damascus had links to the Japanese Red Army (JRA). The Soviet Union and several Eastern European states backed Palestinian and Western European terrorist groups, among others. East Germany's last interior minister declared that his country had become "an Eldorado for terrorists."[1]

These links between governments and terrorists have lethal consequences. Chris Quillen finds that states are at least indirectly responsible for several thousand deaths at the hands of terrorists, a staggering figure that I believe may understate the scale of the violence. More generally, Quillen finds that "state-sponsored terrorists would appear both more able and more willing to kill in large numbers" than terrorists who lack ties to states.[2]

With the end of the Cold War, one of the major sources of state sponsorship – the communist government in the Soviet Union and its

[1] Andrew and Mitrokhin, *The Sword and the Shield*, p. 298.
[2] Quillen, "A Historical Analysis of Mass Casualty Bombers," p. 285.

puppet regimes in Eastern Europe – ended. The severing of the link between the US–Soviet competition and terrorism decreased the strategic importance of fighting terrorism in the eyes of many observers, as did the decline or collapse of many Marxist groups whose credibility fell along with the Soviet regime.[3] While the importance of terrorism grew again in the 1990s and skyrocketed after al-Qa'ida's devastating September 11, 2001 attacks, the focus on state sponsorship continued to decline. Indeed, in the wake of the September 11 attacks, pundits and policymakers alike made much of al-Qa'ida's non-state nature and derided a focus on states as unimportant or "old think."

Such a dismissal, however, suggests a superficial understanding of terrorism in general and of al-Qa'ida in particular. The Lebanese Hizballah, HAMAS, and the Kashmiri Hizb-ul-Mujahedin are only a few of the many successful terrorist groups active today that maintain close links to states and work with them in a variety of ways to advance their goals. Even al-Qa'ida itself relied heavily on states, first working with the Islamist regime in Sudan and then in 1996 becoming closely intertwined with the Taliban's Afghanistan. Investigations of the September 11 attacks suggest that an operation of such scale and lethality would have been far more difficult for al-Qa'ida to pull off had it lacked a haven in Afghanistan.

It is more accurate to say that the dynamic between states and terrorist groups may be changing but has become perhaps more important. With the robust global market in small arms, access to a state's arsenal is no longer necessary if a group wants to use violence. Nevertheless, money, training, diplomatic support, a sanctuary, and other forms of aid are still vital. Even al-Qa'ida's experience after being ousted from Afghanistan suggests the importance of states. No government today openly backs al-Qa'ida, but some governments look the other way as the group recruits or raises money on its territory, while others try to exploit the presence of the group on their territory to extract concessions from the United States.[4]

State sponsorship still plays a major role for many terrorist groups today. Of the thirty-six terrorist groups designated as foreign terrorist

---

[3] Tucker, "The United States Government and Counterterrorism," pp. 2–3.

[4] Iran, for example, in 2003 arrested several high-level al-Qa'ida leaders. It appears to have offered to surrender them to US allies, but only in exchange for several concessions from the United States.

organizations by the Secretary of State in 2002, for example, twenty had enjoyed significant state support at one point in their history, and nine still do today.[5] These numbers exclude the important, but more difficult to assess, informal backing that states can provide by looking the other way as a terrorist group raises money, recruits, or otherwise sustains its organization from the state's territory. Terrorist groups that received these states' support flourished, becoming more deadly and less vulnerable to arrest or disruption.

States can provide a wide range of backing to radical groups. Iraq offered sanctuary and arms to anti-Iranian and anti-Turkish groups. Libya sent funds and weapons to numerous Palestinian groups, the Provisional Irish Republican Army, and other violent radical causes. Arab states consistently championed the PLO in the 1970s in international fora, even as it regularly carried out terrorist attacks as part of its struggle against Israel. As a result, the PLO enjoyed widespread diplomatic recognition.

Policymakers have recognized this convergence between states and terrorists in their rhetoric at least. In his historic speech to Congress in the wake of the September 11, 2001 attacks, President Bush declared, "Every nation, in every region, now has a decision to make. Either you are with us, or you are with the terrorists. From this day forward, any nation that continues to harbor or support terrorism will be regarded by the United States as a hostile regime."[6] This logic was used to justify the 2001 invasion of Afghanistan. Moreover, President Bush's linkage of terrorist groups and their sponsors established what many called "the Bush Doctrine." However, policymakers still are unsure how to confront

---

[5] By my assessment, the Abu Nidal Organization (ANO), the Basque Fatherland and Liberty (ETA), Al-Gama'a al-Islamiyya (Islamic Group), Al-Jihad (Egyptian Islamic Jihad), Armed Islamic Group, Liberation Tigers of Tamil Elam, National Liberation Army (ELN), Kurdistan Workers' Party (PKK), Mujahedin-e Khalq, al-Qa'ida, and Revolutionary Armed Forces of Columbia (FARC) all at one point enjoyed significant, deliberate, and direct state assistance but no longer do. However, HAMAS, Harakat-ul-Mujahedin, Hizballah, Jaysh-e-Muhammed, Lashkar-e-Tayyiba, Palestine Islamic Jihad, Popular Front for the Liberation of Palestine, and the Popular Front for the Liberation of Palestine–General Command still enjoy significant support. For a comprehensive review of the groups on the list, see Audrey Kurth Cronin, "Foreign Terrorist Organizations." *Congressional Research Service*, February 6, 2004.

[6] President George W. Bush, "Address to a Joint Session of Congress and the American People." Washington, DC, September 20, 2001.

sponsors like Iran, Pakistan, or Syria and how to address the complex issue of "passive" support from friendly regimes like Saudi Arabia, which at times looked the other way at terrorist activity in their country.

As this policy confusion suggests, despite the continued importance of state sponsorship, we lack tools for understanding it. The process by which the United States and other governments designate a terrorist sponsor is highly politicized, leading to poor conceptualization of the overall problem. Non-government analysts, for their part, have offered little clarity beyond government categories. Indeed, analysts have provided only limited insight into broader questions about the impact of sponsorship and the reasons it ends. By failing to recognize the many varieties of sponsorship, progress is often ignored. Sudan, for example, no longer works closely with radical groups against Western targets, but it is still lumped into the broad category of state sponsorship because it still hosts several radical Islamist groups. In addition, states may provide one form of support, such as diplomatic backing, even as they try to limit a group's military capabilities.

The question of state sponsorship in all its complexity deserves serious scholarly attention. States work with terrorist groups for a host of reasons, and the effects are often varied. Some terrorist groups become far more deadly and active, while others actually become weaker or more restrained. Understanding why and how states support terrorism will make it easier to recognize the risks state-backed groups pose to governments and citizens around the world. Better understanding can also improve efforts to coerce sponsors into halting their support, or even to turn against their former proxy – vital steps for stopping the scourge of terrorism.

This book is an attempt to offer a more nuanced and comprehensive picture of state sponsorship of terrorism. Understanding this dynamic, and designing policies to stop or reduce state support for terrorism, requires recognizing its many dimensions.

Key findings

States sponsor terrorists as their proxies for a variety of reasons. The most important is often strategic interest: terrorists offer another means for states to influence their neighbors, topple a hostile adversary regime, counter US hegemony, or achieve other aims of state. Pakistani-backed radical groups have undermined the governance of Kashmir and tied down hundreds of thousands of Indian Army forces. Iran helped disrupt the Middle East Peace Process by backing the Lebanese Hizballah, HAMAS, and other radical groups. This influence was possible even though Iran is hundreds of kilometers from Israel and does not have the military or economic influence to otherwise affect the conflict. Support for terrorism is cheaper than developing conventional military capabilities, and it can allow states to influence events far beyond their borders.

Backing terrorists also can serve a broader range of regime objectives, including domestic and ideological ones. The Taliban gave al-Qa'ida a haven in Afghanistan out of ideological sympathy and to gain allies in their civil war against the Northern Alliance. Iraq and Iran used terrorists to kill dissidents overseas. Saudi Arabia provided aid to Palestinian radicals in an attempt to buy them off and turn their guns elsewhere. Syrian leader Hafez al-Asad also helped a range of Palestinian groups in order to demonstrate his Arab nationalist bona fides.

Whatever the motive, state support can transform a radical group. Iran helped change the Lebanese Hizballah from a disorganized and rag-tag collection of fighters to one of the most formidable guerrilla and terrorist groups in history. Libya's weapons shipment to the Provisional Irish Republican Army enabled the organization to sustain its fight against Britain at a time when arms supplies from the United States and elsewhere were disrupted. Perhaps most important, terrorists enjoying state support are far less vulnerable to their target regime's countermeasures. The victim state is less able to deal a knockout blow to the terrorist group, disrupt its logistics, discredit its cause, or otherwise defeat it.

Some groups, however, acquire new limits on their activities as a result of state support. State sponsors fear risking all-out war or other punishments and thus want their proxies to limit their attacks. Pakistan modulated the activities of various Kashmiri groups in response to US pressure and the growing danger of an all-out conflict with India. Some groups lose touch with their constituents as a result of state sponsorship, making them far less effective over time.

The relationship between states and their proxies is thus a dynamic one, and the end result often harms both the terrorist group and its cause. In general, state support almost always increases the capabilities of individual terrorist groups. However, it often forces the group to restrain its activities to accord with the interests of the sponsoring state. In addition, the sponsor often seeks to control the terrorist group and the cause it represents, a desire that may lead the sponsor to support competing groups or otherwise weaken the opposition to a target state as a whole.

In addition, many terrorist groups are not puppets of their sponsor, and some groups even turn against their supposed masters. This lack of loyalty is more than repaid by sponsoring governments. Sponsors are notoriously fickle: for example, Libya and Iraq both alternately supported and expelled radical Palestinian groups such as the Abu Nidal Organization.

Support for terrorism can be exceptionally difficult to stop, particularly for the most committed sponsors. Sponsors often anticipate the punishment that they may receive for backing terrorists and nevertheless choose to provide support, believing they can endure or avoid the pain. In addition, the stakes involved for the sponsoring state are often much higher than those for the victim of the terrorists. The sponsoring state may also feel it has few options for achieving its goals besides backing terrorists. Ideologically driven states are particularly hard to influence, as their goals are often resistant to standard forms of coercive pressure. The coercing state's poor understanding of the problem often compounds these difficulties.

States reduce or end their support for terrorist groups due to changes in their own goals, because of outside pressure, or (more rarely) because the terrorist group itself changes. As Iran's revolutionary ardor dimmed, so too did its support for radical groups dedicated to overthrowing regimes in the region. Other regimes have responded to outside pressure. To gain the goodwill of the United States after September 11, 2001, Pakistan put its Kashmiri proxies on a shorter leash. A combination of multilateral economic sanctions and diplomatic isolation has led Libyan leader Moammar Qaddafi to surrender the architects of the Pan Am 103 bombing over Lockerbie and to cut his ties to various terrorist groups. Palestinian leader Yasir Arafat lost the support of several hard-line Arab leaders who rejected his willingness to make concessions to Israel.

Military strikes – particularly limited ones – often backfire. The 1998 cruise missile attack on Afghanistan and the 1986 bombing of Libya both appear to have hardened these regimes' support for radicals. Israeli efforts to force neighboring states to stop sponsoring groups have met with some success, but they too have at times backfired or even escalated into all-out war. The fall of the Taliban to US-backed Afghan militia groups, of course, suggests that military force remains a necessary option for ending state sponsorship once and for all. However, the sheer scale of the operation also indicates that it is not one to be undertaken lightly.

Definitions and their limits

The terms "terrorism" and "state sponsor" are widely used but little examined. Both terms are ideologically and morally loaded. As Brian Jenkins, a leading terrorism expert with the RAND Corporation, noted over two decades ago, "Terrorism is what the bad guys do."[7] Governments often denounce any sort of political activity as "terrorist-related," while violent groups try to brand the governments they oppose as "terrorist regimes." The concept of state sponsorship further muddies these already murky waters. US support for Israel is regularly denounced in the Arab media as a form of sponsorship of terrorism, while the United States has formally branded several governments – most of them in the Middle East – as state sponsors of terror, singling them out for economic and political punishment.

The debate about terrorism's definition or the true role of a state behind the group is often dismissed with the wave of a hand. Some critics claim that terrorism is easy for any clear-headed individual to understand, with the focus on definitions little more than an exercise for intellectuals that detracts from the horror of terrorism. Others dismiss the idea of defining terrorism as hopelessly relativistic, repeating the adage that one man's terrorist is another man's freedom fighter. Still others find any role that states may play in abetting terrorism to be illegitimate, making any nuance irrelevant.

A lack of a definition, however, creates more problems than it solves. Labeling an act as terrorism quickly becomes meaningless. Depending on the speaker, terrorism becomes a synonym for crime, for peaceful political activity, for state repression, and for other phenomena – both desirable and horrid – that are quite different in purpose, nature, and impact. Similarly, by lumping all state actions with regard to terrorism into one category, we lose the opportunity to recognize different motivations and, more importantly, to craft more effective solutions that require a nuanced understanding.

---

[7] Jenkins, "The Study of Terrorism," p. 3.

This section asks two basic, but fundmental, questions: what is terrorism? And what is state sponsorship? The answers to these questions shape the empirical and analytic sections in the remainder of the book.

WHAT IS TERRORISM?

Rather than revisit the entire debate on terrorism, this book will build on one of the most carefully considered definitions of terrorism – that of Bruce Hoffman, perhaps the world's leading analyst of international terrorism. Hoffman defines terrorism as having five distinguishing characteristics: (1) "ineluctably political in aims and motives"; (2) "violent – or, equally important, threatens violence"; (3) "designed to have far-reaching psychological repercussions beyond the immediate victim or target"; (4) "conducted by an organization"; and (5) "perpetrated by a subnational group or non-state entity."[8] To Hoffman's five criteria I add a sixth: the attack deliberately targets non-combatants.

Although these criteria seem straightforward, it is important to note what is excluded. Attacks conducted for financial gain, such as violence linked to narcotics trafficking or revenge, would be excluded as non-political even if they involved political leaders. In practice, many terrorist groups finance themselves through crime and narcotics trafficking, making it difficult to disentangle a group's effort to finance itself and simple robbery. Acts perpetrated by individuals are excluded, as the definition focuses on groups. Non-violent acts such as drawing graffiti would be excluded, unless it explicitly threatened violence.

A particularly important exception for the purposes of this book is a state's use of its own intelligence, paramilitary, diplomatic, or other agents to carry out "terrorist-like" attacks. Thus, if Iranian government agents try to assassinate a dissident or blow up an embassy, this would be excluded from my definition as the actor is a state, not a terrorist group. Libya's 1986 bombing of La Belle discothèque was directly carried out by state agents, not by a non-state group,[9] and as such is excluded from my study. Many studies of state sponsored terrorism include these acts. However, this book focuses on the nexus between terrorist groups and state sponsors – the actions of the state, by itself, are essentially covert acts of war and are not necessarily part of its relationship to terrorist

---

[8] Hoffman, *Inside Terrorism*, p. 43.
[9] Stanick, *El Dorado Canyon*, p. 143.

groups. As such, traditional covert action programs, where states try to hide their hand while exerting influence, are excluded if only a state's own agents are used.

The sixth criterion I have added muddies these already dark waters but is vital nonetheless. Although "non-combatants" seems straightforward, in reality there is no widely accepted definition. For example, the United States State Department includes military personnel who are on duty but are not immediately engaged in combat as non-combatants for the purposes of terrorism.[10] Thus, al-Qa'ida's attacks on USS *Cole* that killed seventeen seamen in October 2000 and the Lebanese Hizballah's bombing of the Israeli Defense Force barracks in Tyre in 1983 that killed 141 people both qualify as terrorism, even though the targets would be legitimate if an actual state of hostilities existed. The picture is made even cloudier if policemen, intelligence agents, and other non-military personnel, who are often the point of the spear in counterterrorism, are included as non-combatants.

In truth, "non-combatant" status can be painted as a spectrum, particularly from the point of view of a terrorist group. At the upper end are obvious combatants such as soldiers, intelligence personnel, and political leaders who are directly engaged in fighting terrorists and responsible for security. Farther down but still high are government officials such as diplomats or police whose actions have a tremendous influence on counterterrorism but who themselves are not part of the immediate fray. Still farther down are other public officials whose employer makes them symbols of the state but who, themselves, are not involved in counterterrorism beyond helping provide good government. Private citizens whose jobs are linked to counterterrorism, such as arms manufacturers, are the next stop. Lowest on the list are citizens whose jobs have nothing to do with counterterrorism, such as construction workers, office administrators, or businessmen.[11]

I define non-combatants as personnel not directly involved in prosecuting war or counterterrorism operations. Thus, a soldier remains

---

[10] United States Department of State, *Patterns of Global Terrorism 2003*, p. xii including footnote 1.

[11] See, for an illustrative example, Ayla Schbley, "Religious Terrorists," pp. 237–241. Schbley provides a review of Hizballah members' ranking of targets based on her interviews.

a combatant, as would an intelligence operative. However, a policeman whose "mission" is preventing crime would be considered a non-combatant, even though he is nevertheless a symbol of the state. Also included as non-combatants are ordinary diplomats, bureaucrats, and aid workers even though their actions are indirectly vital to many counterterrorism efforts.

By my definition, the al-Qa'ida attack on USS *Cole* would *not* be terrorism. Contending such an attack is not terrorism, however, is by no means to condone it. Any group that attacks a country's soldiers would still be rightly seen as a dangerous enemy to be opposed.

WHAT IS SPONSORSHIP?

I define state sponsorship of terrorism as a government's *intentional assistance* to a terrorist group to help it use violence, bolster its political activities, or sustain the organization. Common types of assistance are detailed in Chapter 3.

The question of intention, however, is complex. Leaders of Iran and the Taliban's Afghanistan, for example, at times openly boasted of their support for terrorist groups. Other government leaders are less enthusiastic about their regimes' ties to terrorists and often try to hide the level of support. Posing yet another wrinkle when examining intentions, the citizens of some states, such as Saudi Arabia, often support terrorist groups with little government interference. In such cases, the governments may have knowingly turned a blind eye to radical activities, but this is a far cry from open support – a difference I examine in detail in Chapter 8.

A spectrum of support

The nature of state support for terrorism is every bit as confusing as the definition of terrorism itself. Although there are occasional clear cases of support, the concept of state sponsorship is plagued with inconsistencies and ambiguities. State support can range from Iran's massive program of assistance to the Lebanese Hizballah to Canada's tolerance of fundraising by the Liberation Tigers of Tamil Eelam. The very concept of sponsorship focuses on funding, training, and other visible and active forms of support. However, many states support insurgent groups that in turn use terrorism. The state's support, however, is focused on the group's guerrilla activities, not its occasional use of terrorism. Similarly, the role

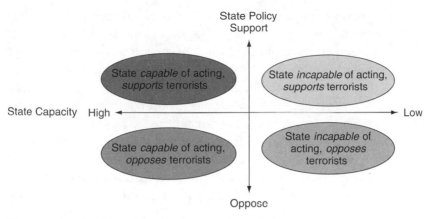

Figure 1.0 A notional spectrum of state support

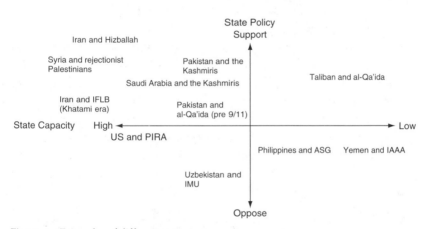

Figure 1.1 Examples of different state sponsors

of a country like Thailand, which fails to police its borders, is often neglected under definitions that focus only on deliberate government action. Including this vast range in the definition helps us understand the full complexity of this issue, but – if these distinctions are not recognized when designing countermeasures – it can also easily lead to oversimplification and confused policy recommendations.

Figures 1.0 and 1.1 offer a notional way of thinking about state support. As these two figures suggest, state support can be judged both by the degree of support for the terrorists as part of government policy and by the regime's capacity for supporting or halting terrorism.[12]

These figures try to capture the range of support to identify important gradations and variations. Some states actively support terrorists, providing them with considerable assistance in the form of arms, money, a haven, or other backing. Other regimes may support terrorists, but less enthusiastically. Of course, a state's enthusiasm for counterterrorism also varies. Before the September 11 attacks, for example, all Western European governments opposed al-Qa'ida, but some were far more energetic in their opposition than others. Their legal codes, level of police and intelligence attention, and other parts of their counterterrorism apparatus reflected this concern.

A second way of characterizing regimes is by their capacity. Some states, such as Iran and Syria, have considerable resources to offer terrorists. Others, such as the Taliban, have far less to offer. Counterterrorism capacity often varies as well. Some states, like Tajikistan, are close to "failed states" and do not truly control their own territory.

The capacity required to provide significant support for a terrorist group is usually far less than that required to suppress it. Offering groups a haven, perhaps the most important form of support, simply requires possessing territory. Shutting down the haven, on the other hand, may demand greater military and other resources than many regimes possess. Thus, the Taliban were one of the world's most active supporters of terrorism, while the government of the Philippines, which was far stronger by most measures of state capacity, was not able to shut down various terrorist groups it fought.[13]

A country can appear at multiple places in such a chart if it has different attitudes toward different groups. Pakistan, for example, has long been a leading and open sponsor of Kashmiri terrorist groups.

[12] One weakness of Figure 1.0 is the middle area of the supportive–hostile "Y" axis. This range not only includes cases where there is open support or open hostility, but also instances where a government has only lukewarm enthusiasm for the terrorists, where the regime is at times hostile but provides support in part to control the overall cause, and where the society in question backs the terrorists but the government does not. These intermediate categories do not neatly follow a progression from support to hostility.

[13] For an insightful study on the nature of state capacity today, see Tellis *et al.*, *Measuring National Power in the Postindustrial Age*.

For many years in the 1990s, it allowed al-Qa'ida members to organize, plan, and recruit in Pakistan but did not directly fund or otherwise direct their activities. Figure 1.1 tries to capture such variations.

The figures above cover not only the most active state sponsors, such as Iran, but also more passive ones like Saudi Arabia. Passive support, as described in more detail in Chapter 8, includes regimes that deliberately turn a blind eye to the activities of terrorists in their countries but do not provide direct assistance. There are many instances where a regime is nominally, or at times actively, hostile to a terrorist group or its cause while parts of its population are sympathetic to it.

The figures thus encompass a huge but neglected area between terrorists' active, major supporters and staunch opponents. Terrorism expert Paul Pillar, whose book offers a nuanced description of the variance among state sponsors, pointed out that "the role of states in international terrorism is not a matter of clear distinctions between the good and the bad, between those that sponsor terrorism and those that oppose it."[14] He labeled this category terrorism "enablers." Similarly, the National Commission on Terrorism (The Bremer Commission) noted in 2000 that some states "have relations with terrorists that fall short of the extensive criteria for designation as a state sponsor, but their failure to act against terrorists perpetuates terrorist activities."[15] Both Pillar and the National Commission singled out Greece and Pakistan as countries falling into this category.

Also in these figures are regimes that often host terrorist groups despite actively trying to stop them. For example, the Islamic Movement of Uzbekistan (IMU) menaces Uzbekistan (and the regime fights it ferociously), but Tashkent's counterterrorism capabilities are limited. Similarly, the Philippines has tried to counter the Abu Sayyaf Group (ASG) (though less determinedly and less brutally than Uzbekistan has countered the IMU) but has only limited capabilities to do so. Indeed, almost every state which is a victim of terrorism is likely to suffer at least a minimal presence of the terrorist group it opposes on its territory. Such states should not be included as "sponsors" of terrorism

---

[14] Pillar, *Terrorism and US Foreign Policy*, pp. 178–179. Pillar offers three types of states: "sponsors," "enablers," and "cooperators." I draw on his typology in presenting my own.

[15] National Commission on Terrorism, *Countering the Changing Threat of International Terrorism*, p. 23.

but rather as victims given that they lack the means, not the desire, to end the terrorist presence in their country.

Complicity is often correlated with the level of support, but this is not always so. A high level of complicity would involve a consensus among all of a country's senior government officials and much of the political elite. Various Kashmiri insurgents, for example, have long enjoyed widespread support among Pakistan's senior military and political leadership, and the cause in general enjoys widespread popular backing. Lower on the complicity scale would be support by some elements of a regime. Many reformists in Iran do not appear to support radical groups elsewhere in the Gulf, but more revolutionary elements in Iran's intelligence and security services still maintain contacts with them. Still farther down is a regime's decision to turn a blind eye to support by domestic actors, ranging from political parties to supportive citizens – a position that Saudi Arabia took until 2003 regarding many *jihadist* groups not linked to violence in the Kingdom, such as Chechen radicals. Some governments may also provide support indirectly by refusing to enact legislation that would ban terrorist activity, using legal technicalities to avoid cooperation, and otherwise trying to dodge responsibilities to stop terrorism.[16]

What constitutes a government is also important when weighing intention and complicity. If an individual government member abets a terrorist group that is not the same as saying that a government supports it – unless that individual acts on the behest of the country's leadership. This book both includes cases where government leaders deliberately support terrorism and also examines instances when they knowingly allow terrorism to flourish. It excludes instances where the support occurred without the government's knowledge or when the government unsuccessfully opposed the assistance.

A dynamic that is difficult to describe graphically but is nevertheless vital for understanding state support is the poisonous nature of some states' relationship to their erstwhile proxies. Some states support a terrorist group but also seek to control it and weaken the overall cause. Both Pakistan and Syria, for example, have at times turned against their respective Kashmiri and Palestinian proxies, weakening the overall opposition to the target state even as they strengthen particular movements within it.

[16] Mickolus, "How Do We Know We're Winning the War Against Terrorists?" p. 156.

As Figures 1.0, 1.1, and the above discussion suggest, there are several types of state sponsors:

- Strong supporters. These backers are both highly committed to the terrorist group and are able to offer it significant resources. Iran's support for the Lebanese Hizballah exemplifies this category.
- Weak supporters. In this category fall regimes that support the terrorist group but have few resources to do so. The Taliban's backing for al-Qa'ida would be an example of a weak supporter.
- Lukewarm supporters. A regime may favor terrorists or their cause in a general sense but do little to advance it directly. Iran, for example, maintains ties to a number of radical Shi'a groups in the Persian Gulf, but after the 1996 Khobar Towers bombing has done little to advance their cause.
- Antagonistic supporters. Some states support a terrorist group but seek to control it or weaken its cause. Syria's often hostile relationship with several Palestinian groups, including Yasir Arafat's Fatah, typifies such an ambivalent relationship.
- Passive supporters. Some regimes do not directly aid terrorists but knowingly turn a blind eye to their activities, usually because many people in their society favor it. Saudi Arabia, for example, allowed various *jihadists* linked to al-Qa'ida to raise money and recruit in the Kingdom with little interference before September 11, even though the regime did not directly aid Bin Ladin's organization.
- Unwilling hosts. Some regimes are too weak to stop terrorists within their borders or lack the intelligence to do so. These may include failed states like Somalia or weak regimes like the Lebanese government of the early 1970s, which tried but failed to crush the Palestinian terrorist presence on its soil. By my definition, such hosts are not "supporters" of terrorism but rather its victims.

With the exception of Chapter 8, this book focuses on the first four categories – strong supporters, weak supporters, lukewarm supporters, and antagonistic supporters – all of which should be considered active supporters, although the degree of enthusiasm and capability varies considerably. As discussed further in Chapter 10 and in individual cases, the motives of these different types of supporters and the means to coerce them often vary considerably.

Book structure and case selection

The remainder of this book examines different aspects of the problem of state sponsorship of terrorism. Its structure follows a series of basic questions: what does state sponsorship consist of? What impact does it have, both in making the group stronger and in limiting its activities? Why do states sponsor terrorists? Why is it so hard to stop? And, finally, how can state support be reduced?

In essence, this book is divided into three sections. The first assesses the broad phenomenon of state sponsorship, looking across numerous cases and historical examples. This section categorizes the type of support states give terrorist groups, and discusses the impact of their support. It also offers explanations for why states provide, and why they limit, support. The second section offers an in-depth look at several of the most active sponsors of terrorism since the Cold War ended. In part, these cases are meant to put flesh on the overview presented in the first section, offering far more detail on some of the most important instances of state support. These cases also try to offer a more detailed and more nuanced understanding of the phenomenon of state sponsorship, highlighting the limits and risks of state sponsorship as well as the dangers it poses. In the third section, the book concludes by trying to examine these insights in the context of how to stop state sponsorship of terrorism.

Chapter 2 examines the "why" of state sponsorship. It notes the motivations of a wide range of sponsors, presenting the range of reasons that states sponsor terrorism and discusses their relative importance. The chapter also addresses why state motivations change and the reasons why states at times restrain their proxies.

Chapter 3 gives a detailed description of the various types of support that fall under the broad rubric of sponsorship and assesses what impact state support has on terrorist groups' capabilities and motivations. It tries to determine which factors states can and cannot affect with regard to the types of attacks that groups conduct, their success in recruiting, and other basic questions regarding effectiveness. The chapter pays particular attention to how state support can complicate and limit a rival government's counterterrorism effort.

This general discussion is then followed by in-depth case studies of four state sponsors of terrorism: Iran, Syria, Pakistan, and the Taliban's Afghanistan. These four regimes are chosen for several reasons. First, they represent the most active sponsors of terrorism since the end of the

Cold War. States such as Libya essentially ended their backing of terrorism in the mid-1990s, if not earlier. Sudan was quite active in the early 1990s, but it too reduced, and then largely ended, its support for terrorism as the decade wore on. The above four regimes, however, remained active supporters, and one – the Taliban – was removed from power because of its backing of terrorism. Second, I focused on one group or set of groups backed by each state even though almost all of the states sponsored more than one (often many more than one) because this enabled me to illustrate different state motivations. Third, the impact of sponsorship varied considerably across these states. Some states reined in otherwise hyperactive proxies, while others made them far more active and formidable.[17] Fourth, these cases capture three key types of state sponsors – strong, weak, and antagonistic – and thus highlight the many faces of this phenomenon.

As Chapter 4 describes, for many years the Islamic Republic of Iran has been the world's most active sponsor of terrorist groups. Its relationship was and remains particularly close with the Lebanese Hizballah, one of the world's most formidable guerrilla and terrorist groups. Iran's support for the Lebanese Hizballah illustrates the important role of ideology in why states choose to support radical groups. This case also demonstrates how international power politics over time often become increasingly important in how and why states support terrorist groups. In the early 1980s, Iran tried to export its revolution, using terrorist groups as seedlings for creating a larger revolutionary movement and attacking supposed reactionary regimes. As time went on, however, Iran's support concentrated on groups opposed to Israel and the peace process. Chapter 4 identifies Iran's motivations, discusses why they have changed, and reviews the impact on Hizballah.

In Chapter 5, I examine how Syria's support for terrorism, particularly Palestinian groups, has changed over time. Damascus actively promoted terrorism in the 1970s and 1980s, but it has kept its proxies on a short

---

[17] For several of these cases, the regime's involvement in terrorism precedes the end of the Cold War but continues after it ends. I examine the entire period of the current regime's support for terrorist groups, even though the focus of this book is on the post-Cold War era, in order to understand the motivations for the initial support and how they changed over time.

leash since the end of the Cold War. Syria's support for Palestinian groups also demonstrates the importance of power politics, as Damascus ruthlessly exploited the Palestinian cause to further its own interests. The Palestinian cause, however, was also a burden for Syria's leaders, as for domestic reasons they could not renounce it or reject Palestinian groups even when their actions did not suit Syria's interests. This chapter assesses the impact of Damascus' backing on groups, explores Syria's changing motivations to learn their source, and discusses why the Baath regime's support continues. It also offers a comparison with Syria's support for the PKK, which Damascus abandoned in 1998 in the face of military threats from Turkey.

Chapter 6 looks at Pakistan, one of the most active sponsors of terrorism in the 1990s, but one that the United States at least often ignored. Pakistan's support for Kashmiri groups was part and parcel of its broader rivalry with India. Kashmiri groups offered Pakistan's regime a way to bleed India and, at the same time, play to Islamist and nationalist audiences at home. As such, Pakistan's experience illustrates how strategic motivations lead to support for terrorism and the particularly important role that support for an insurgency can play with regard to support for terrorism. This relationship also demonstrates how terrorism for strategic reasons can quickly become intertwined with domestic politics. In the 1990s, Islamabad worked with insurgents who used terrorism in Kashmir. It provided them with arms, money, sanctuary, and at times direct military support – this backing declined (but did not end) after Pakistan sided with Washington in its post-September 11 campaign against terror.

The Taliban's support for al-Qa'ida in Afghanistan, discussed in Chapter 7, represents a completely different logic. Here, international power politics weighed against supporting al-Qa'ida: the terrorist organization carried with it heavy baggage and led to concerted international pressure against the Taliban. On the other hand, the Taliban's Islamist ideology made it sympathetic to the movement. Moreover, al-Qa'ida provided massive financial and military assistance to the Taliban, making it far stronger domestically. The Taliban government was weak compared with the regimes in Tehran, Damascus, and Islamabad. Nevertheless, its activities made al-Qa'ida far more lethal, and the support was wholehearted. Al-Qa'ida, in turn, provided a range of assistance to the Taliban that was unusual for a terrorist group.

As the brief overview of Chapters 4 through 7 indicates, the problem of terrorism today is particularly acute in Central and South Asia and the Middle East. Regimes in these regions have often maintained strong ties to terrorist groups. Although this book focuses on these countries because they offer the most important instances of state sponsorship in recent years, their experiences are in general applicable to countries outside the region. In addition, many of their experiences offer insights which can be useful when confronting the problem of militant Islam, which inspires many (though hardly all) of the world's most lethal and far-reaching terrorist groups today.

Chapter 8 looks at the vexing question of passive support. Often, a state's most important contribution to a terrorist group's activities is turning a blind eye to radical activities within their borders. Saudi Arabia at times bought off terrorists, and the government allowed its citizens to provide financial support to Islamic militants worldwide. Although less egregious, Greece for many years made little effort to arrest the November 17 movement. Similarly, the United States allowed the IRA to raise money in the United States with at most limited interference. The motivations of such tacit sponsors, however, differed considerably from those of more standard supporters of terrorism.

Chapter 9 draws on the above chapters to summarize this book's findings on why the sponsorship of terrorism is so hard to end. It reviews problems inherent in stopping state sponsorship as well as weaknesses with the current US government approach to state sponsorship.

The tenth and final chapter discusses the reasons that states end or curtail their support for terrorist groups. It focuses particular attention on factors that outside powers can shape (such as economic concerns or international reputation). In addition, it addresses the question of why some forms of pressure tend to prove ineffective or even backfire. A particular focus is on various US efforts to counter terrorism, but examples are drawn also from the experiences of other countries.

Together, my examination of these different pieces of the state sponsorship puzzle forms a broader whole that illustrates the many facets of the problem. Although much work remains to be done on this question, my hope is that this book will provide a useful first step for those seeking to understand the relationship between states and terrorist groups.

2

Why do states support terrorism?

Most governments shun terrorists both for their brutality and for the illegitimate nature of their tactics. Terrorism, after all, is murder. Moreover, terrorist groups often enjoy little support among the publics they purport to represent. Nor are terrorists promising horses to back, as they often have little chance of prevailing, particularly at the beginning of their struggles. Supporting a terrorist group also often carries a heavy price, as the group's opponents may seek to punish a sponsor. Not surprisingly, many states turn to diplomacy, economic pressure, or even conventional war before embracing terrorism. Yet despite being such unsavory and unpromising partners for states, many terrorist groups regularly receive state support. This support is forthcoming because the terrorist group can serve the strategic interests of foreign states, gain their leaders' sympathy for ideological reasons, or play a role in bolstering leaders' domestic positions.

Understanding motivations is vital both for predicting when a state might support a terrorist group and for determining how to end this backing. Regimes seeking to spread their ideology, for example, are in general far less amenable to standard forms of coercion or inducement, and such measures may even make them more likely to support terrorists. Regimes that are trying to gain a strategic advantage over their neighbors, in contrast, may be more willing to end their support if the costs become too high.

This chapter first examines why states often choose to support terrorism instead of using more traditional instruments of statecraft and discusses the overlap between supporting a guerrilla movement (or insurgency) and supporting a terrorist group. It then describes the myriad motivations that regimes have in supporting particular terrorist groups. After this review, it examines why states often urge their proxies to exercise restraint as well as to conduct attacks.

Terrorism as one instrument of many

The remainder of this chapter focuses on the many reasons that a state's leaders back a terrorist group. Before this discussion, however, it is worth noting that many leaders with similar ambitions and concerns to rulers who embrace terrorism nevertheless shy away from backing terrorists, preferring instead to use their diplomatic, economic, and conventional military clout to achieve their aims. However, some states lack such clout: their economies are feeble, they have few allies and little prestige, and their conventional military forces are weak, obsolete, and outclassed by their adversaries. For many leaders terrorism offers a lever of influence that, while far from ideal, has far more potential than other means available. Such an argument, of course, at times becomes self-fulfilling. Iran's and Libya's backing of terrorists contributed to their isolation, and as such weakened their diplomatic influence and, through sanctions, the quality of their military forces and strength of their economies.

Terrorism itself is often considered a "weapon of the weak." As Bruce Hoffman notes, many terrorists argue that the "bomb-in-the-rubbish-bin" is simply a "poor man's air force."[1] This rationale, while of dubious moral force, does have a strategic logic. Many states lack the instruments of national power that Americans, and citizens of other advanced industrial countries, take for granted and thus have few means of achieving their ends. Moreover, using terrorist proxies rather than government agents allows a degree of deniability, which in turn reduces the chances of retaliation from more powerful states that possess stronger economies and militaries.[2]

The "poor man's air force" argument, however, can be taken too far. As discussed in detail below, states often back terrorists for ideological or domestic reasons rather than because they lack other strategic options. Moreover, many states use terrorism in conjunction with other means, seeing it as a way of augmenting, rather than replacing, other instruments of national power.

[1] Hoffman, *Inside Terrorism*, p. 34.　[2] Ibid., p. 27.

However, many state leaders do not support terrorists, considering it an illegitimate instrument of statecraft, despite having strategic or domestic incentives to do so. Terrorism and war crimes have many similarities, the most important of which is the deliberate targeting of non-combatants.[3] States that employ terrorists are in essence knowingly supporting the commission of war crimes (albeit by a non-state actor). While states have committed, commit, and will commit war crimes, many shy away from doing so or at least try to limit such acts to highly unusual circumstances. This may be because of the morality of the leaders themselves, the difficulties of maintaining public support for a cause if it involves innocent suffering, the inevitable decline in international backing that comes with war crimes, or all three. States with robust media may be particularly loath to go down this road, as covert use of terrorists is far more likely to be revealed, thus negating the advantages of deniability.

SUPPORT FOR INSURGENCIES AND SUPPORT FOR TERRORISM

Many states support terrorist groups as part of a broader effort to bolster an insurgent movement – the support they provide helps a group conduct guerrilla operations and, in so doing, enables it to conduct terrorist attacks. Not all terrorist groups are insurgencies, but almost every insurgent group uses terrorism. The overlap between insurgents and terrorism has important implications for understanding state motivations and for effective counterterrorism.

Many of the state-supported terrorist groups are also insurgent groups – there is no clear dividing line, and in fact tremendous overlap exists. Although the exact percentage depends heavily on coding decisions, in my judgment approximately half of the groups listed by the US Department of State as Foreign Terrorist Organizations are insurgencies as well as terrorist groups. Even more important, the majority of the most worrisome terrorist groups in the world today are also insurgencies. The Liberation Tigers of Tamil Eelam (LTTE), the Kurdish Workers' Party, the Lebanese Hizballah, and the Revolutionary Armed Forces of Columbia all use guerrilla war as a major component in their struggles, just as the PLO attempted to do in the 1960s and 1970s. Moreover, several leading analysts consider al-Qa'ida also to be essentially an

---

[3] Ibid., p. 35.

insurgent group.[4] Indeed, many terrorist groups that did not use guerrilla warfare, such as the Provisional IRA and HAMAS, had attempted to do so but found they were not strong enough.

This book uses the definition of insurgencies provided in the Central Intelligence Agency (CIA) pamphlet *Guide to the Analysis of Insurgency*. This definition states:

> Insurgency is a protracted political-military activity directed toward completely or partially controlling the resources of a country through the use of irregular military forces and illegal political organizations. Insurgent activity – including guerrilla warfare, terrorism, and political mobilization, for example, propaganda, recruitment, front and covert party organization, and international activity – is designed to weaken government control and legitimacy while increasing insurgent control and legitimacy. The common denominator of most insurgent groups is their desire to control a particular area. This objective differentiates insurgent groups from purely terrorist organizations, whose objectives do not include the creation of an alternative government capable of controlling a given area or country.[5]

Using this definition, an insurgent group may use terrorism, but not necessarily. It is analytically possible (though empirically rare) for an insurgent group to use only guerrilla war but not to use terrorism. Using the definition of terrorism offered in Chapter 1, a guerrilla group could focus on military targets and others involved in a counterinsurgency campaign. Non-combatants might be killed, but this would not be terrorism if it were a byproduct of a military campaign and thus not intended to send a broader political message.

Groups' organizational structures and preferred methods tend to reflect whether guerrilla war or terrorism is the primary purpose of the

---

[4] See Anonymous, *Through Our Enemies' Eyes*, xviii. The author, an anonymous intelligence officer, notes that Bin Ladin is promoting (and at times directing) a "worldwide, religiously inspired, and professionally guided Islamist insurgency." Much of al-Qa'ida's activities are also designed to establish new or bolster existing insurgencies by providing them with money, supplies, inspiration, and training. Both the PIRA and the HAMAS have elements of an insurgency, though neither "controls" territory in a manner comparable to the Lebanese Hizballah or the FARC.

[5] Central Intelligence Agency, *Guide to the Analysis of Insurgency*, p. 2. The pamphlet was published in the 1980s.

group. For example, groups organized into irregular military units are more likely to pursue guerrilla war, while those with cell structures are probably intending to use terrorism. However, some organizations incorporate different structures. The Lebanese Hizballah, for example, has divided its organization into a component that wages guerrilla war and another that carries out terrorist attacks.

It is particularly important to recognize that atrocities that are part of a guerrilla struggle are not necessarily terrorism. Almost all guerrilla armed forces commit some atrocities against civilians, such as rape, murder, and plunder. Such atrocities may have political ramifications, but if their purpose is not political or intended to influence a broader audience it should not be considered terrorism. However, the same act used to send a political message (such as discouraging collaboration or prompting ethnic cleansing) would be terrorism as well as part of a guerrilla war.

Terrorism offers many advantages for insurgencies, and few will resist its use completely. Terrorism can undermine the ability of the state to rule and gain the group tactical advantages in the broader political-military struggle. For example, attacks on civilians may lead a rival ethnic group to flee a contested area. Strikes on government officials may make an area ungovernable, demonstrating that the government cannot protect its people and provide for their welfare, while convincing other officials to collaborate.[6]

The US government definition of terrorism, which includes military forces not engaged in combat as "non-combatants" and also defines intelligence and law enforcement personnel as non-combatants, effect-ively excludes any possibility of distinguishing between the two. Any inhibitions that insurgent groups might have are further reduced by definitions that lump almost all guerrilla activity under the rubric of terrorism. A group that attacked only soldiers would still be depicted as a terrorist group.

This linkage between insurgencies and terrorism has particular impli-cations for why states support terrorists. Indeed, much of the reason many terrorists receive state support is because they are insurgencies. The support states provide helps a group conduct guerrilla operations and, in so doing, enables it to conduct terrorist attacks. Logistics,

---

[6] See Byman, "The Logic of Ethnic Terrorism," for a review.

recruitment, sanctuary, money, arms, and organizational aid can all be useful when plotting to attack civilians as well as when conducting guerrilla war. As discussed further in Chapter 7, Pakistan's support for many militant Kashmiri groups is primarily (though not entirely) for their insurgent activities. As discussed further in Chapters 9 and 10, whether or not a terrorist group is also an insurgency also has vital implications for counterterrorism. The techniques that would work to halt or destroy a terrorist group often fail or are incomplete against an insurgency.

Thus, it is important to distinguish terrorists groups that are also insurgencies from those that are not. Some groups, such as the Burundian Hutu marauders, are primarily guerrilla groups, focusing their effort on enemy government forces. Others, like the Liberation Tigers of Tamil Eelam and various Kashmiri militants, use both guerrilla tactics and terrorism simultaneously. Still others, like HAMAS, rely primarily on terrorism to advance their cause. However, it is also important to recognize that this distinction is not a dichotomy: using my definitions it is possible to have a "pure" terrorist group or a "pure" insurgency, but in many instances – and in many cases involving the most dangerous terrorist groups – the actors involved are often insurgent groups that regularly use terrorism as a tactic.

An overview of motivations

Table 2.0 gives an overview of state motivations for backing terrorist groups, breaking down the strategic, ideological, and domestic categories into more specific rationales, which are described in more detail below. The Table loosely codes the weight of different motivations, with a "1" meaning the motivation was a leading concern, a "2" indicating that the motivation was an important concern, and a "3" denoting that the motivation was present, but not vital.[7] Iran, for example, began to actively support Islamist Palestinian groups such as HAMAS and Palestine Islamic Jihad (PIJ) in the late 1990s as a way of undermining the Middle East Peace Process and striking at Israel, both of which

---

[7] Such a coding system, of course, is a touch arbitrary as it is difficult to describe with precision why one number is used instead of another. However, it does help suggest the different weight of motivations, even if others may quibble with some of the numbers presented.

Table 2.0 *An overview of state motivations for supporting terrorist groups, 1991–2003*

State	Group	Start Date	End Date	Destabilize or Weaken Neighbor	Project Power	Change Regime	Shape Opposition	Enhance Int'l Prestige	Export Political System	Aid Kin	Mil. Aid
				Strategic Concerns				Ideology		Domestic Politics	
Afghanistan (Taliban only)	al-Qa'ida	1996	2001						1	3	1
	Chechen groups	1999	2001						1	3	
	Eastern Turkistan Islamic Movement (ETIM) (China)	1999	2001						1	3	
	Islamic Movement of Uzbekistan (IMU)	1998	2001	2					1	3	
	Kashmiri groups	1996	2001						1	3	
Greece	PKK	1981	1999	1							
Iran	Hizballah	1982	present		1	2	2	3	1	2	2
	SCIRI	1982	present	1		2	2		1	2	2
	Palestinian Islamists (HAMAS, PIJ)	1988	present		1			2	3	3	

Table 2.0 (cont.)

State	Group	Start Date	End Date	Strategic Concerns				Ideology		Domestic Politics	
				Destabilize or Weaken Neighbor	Project Power	Change Regime	Shape Opposition	Enhance Int'l Prestige	Export Political System	Aid Kin	Mil. Aid
	Palestinian leftists (PFLP-GC)	late 1980s	present		1					3	
	PKK	1990	present	1							
	Tehrik-e Jafariya-e Pakistan	1979	2002					2		2	
	Bahraini Islamists	1979	present	2				2	1	2	
	Saudi Hizballah	1979	present	2	2 (vs. US)			2	1	2	
Iraq	PKK	1991	2003	1			3				
	ANO, PLF, other leftist Palestinian groups	1970s	2003		2		2	1		2	
	MEK	1987	2003	1							
Liberia	RUF	1991	2001	1		1					3

Country	Group	Start	End						
Libya	Leftist Palestinians (e.g. ANO, DFLP, PFLP, PFLP-GC, PLF)	1987	1999		2	1			1
	PIJ	1994	1997			1			1
	New People's Army (NPA)	1987	1994	1		3			
	IRA	1973	1996	1	1				1
Pakistan	Kashmiri secular (Jammu & Kashmir Liberation Front)	1982	1994	1					2
	Kashmiri Islamist (e.g., Harakat ul-Mujahedeen, Jaish-e-Muhammad, Lashkar-e-Taiba)	1980s	present	1	1				2
	Punjabi groups (e.g., Khalistan Kashmir International)	1980s	present	1					
Sudan	al-Qa'ida	1991	1996 present	1	2	2		1	2 2
	AIAI	early 1990s	1997	1				2	2

Table 2.0 (cont.)

State	Group	Start Date	End Date	Strategic Concerns — Destabilize or Weaken Neighbor	Project Power	Change Regime	Shape Opposition	Ideology — Enhance Int'l Prestige	Ideology — Export Political System	Domestic Politics — Aid Kin	Domestic Politics — Mil. Aid
	Various Algerian Groups	?	2001					2	1		
	Al-Nahd (Tunisia)	1991	1994					2	1		
	Palestinian Islamist groups (HAMAS, PIJ)	1987?	present					2	1		
	Egyptian Groups (IG, EIG)	1989	2002	2				2	1		
	Hizballah	1992	2002					2	3		
	Allied Democratic Forces (Uganda)	1996	1999	1							
Syria	Secular leftist Palestinians (often via Lebanon)										

Group	Start	End								
PFLP (PFLP-GC, DFLP, PLF, PSF)	1970s	present	1			1	2	2	1	
Islamist Palestinians (HAMAS, PIJ)	HAMAS 1991; PIJ 1989	present	1				2			
PKK	1980	1998	1						1	
Hizballah	1983	present	1				2		3	
Total Instances			19	7	3	7	18	18	20	4
Total Leading ("1") Motivations			15	5	1	2	3	14	3	1

Tehran saw as vital strategic interests. Iranian leaders also had a genuine desire to help their fellow Muslims in their struggle, but this sympathy paled before Tehran's strategic interests.[8]

As the table makes clear, there is no single, overarching reason that states support terrorist groups. For different states, there is a different strategic, ideological, and domestic mix. Strategic concerns drove Pakistan to support Kashmiris, but domestic politics played in as well. The Taliban, in contrast, had little strategic interest – but plenty of ideological and domestic rationales – for supporting al-Qa'ida. Iran, however, supported terrorist groups for all three reasons. Not surprisingly, given this potent mix of strategy, ideology, and domestic politics, Tehran proved a major backer of terrorist groups.

Strategic motivations are the most common, perhaps because they – in contrast to domestic and ideological concerns – tend to have a longer shelf-life. In particular, the use of terrorists to destabilize a neighbor is both a very common reason that states support terrorism and is common as a primary motivation for doing so (as indicated by a number "1" coding). The use of terrorists to project power far beyond a sponsoring state's borders is less likely to motivate states, but it remains a common motivation – and one that at times plays a leading role in a state's decision to sponsor terrorist groups. Changing a regime is even less common, but when the motivation is present it tends to be a leading one. Shaping the opposition is also a common goal, though it is rarely a leading motivation.

Exporting an ideology is also a common reason that states support terrorist groups. In the 1990s, this goal was particularly important for the Taliban regime in Afghanistan and, to a lesser degree, the theocracy in Tehran. In these as well as in other cases, the very ideas of the regime's leaders, as well as their strategic goals and political concerns, determined why they supported terrorist groups. Ideological regimes often try to enhance their prestige by backing terrorists, though this is seldom their top concern.

---

[8] Ambassador Martin Indyk argues that Iran's support for terrorism was a means of offsetting the US-led campaign to isolate the clerical regime. By backing Palestinian terrorism, Iran successfully disrupted the Middle East Peace Process, which in turn ensured that it would not be an isolated voice in the region. I would like to thank Ambassador Indyk for his thoughts on this issue.

Domestic politics also explain why many states support terrorists. Such an explanation is particularly common when the regime seeks to demonstrate its support for causes that its own people see as representing their "kin," be they ethnic (e.g. fellow Tamils) or religious (e.g. fellow Muslims). By supporting such groups, the state can demonstrate its goodwill and shore up its own popularity domestically. More rarely, the terrorist group is also used to supplement a state's coercive power against its domestic enemies, swelling the ranks of its armies or assassinating dissidents abroad.

CODING AND CAVEATS

Several important caveats should be recognized when weighing the above coding. Taken together, these caveats suggest that Table 2.0 should be used to gain a rough sense of the overall phenomenon of state sponsorship, not as an exact guide to the level of sponsorship occurring in the past decades.

First, many distinct state–group relationships are lumped together under broader categories. Thus the Abu Nidal Organization, the Palestine Liberation Front, the Popular Front for the Liberation of Palestine (PFLP), the Popular Front for the Liberation of Palestine–General Command (PFLP-GC) and other left-leaning Palestinian nationalist groups are put together under the broad category "leftist Palestinians." In order to avoid overemphasizing the role of states that support many small groups compared with those that back only one larger one, these like-minded but organizationally distinct groups are presented in one category. Thus Iran, which usually tries to unify its proxies into one stronger movement, is not underrepresented compared with Pakistan and Syria, which both have tried to divide the movements they back to ensure more manageable clients.

A somewhat subjective approach, but I hope a consistent one, was used in deciding whether or not to join different terrorist groups into a combined listing. First, the groups in question had to have relatively similar agendas (i.e., Marxist, nationalist, Islamist, and so on). Second, groups operating in different countries were never joined, even if the agenda was similar to that of a group in another country. Thus, though Sudan's support for al-Qa'ida and Islamists in Egypt may have similar motives (and the groups had similar worldviews), they are coded differently.

Such an agglomeration, however, has several limits. Most obviously, the various groups often have slightly different agendas and capabilities, and the states that back them recognize and exploit this. The Palestinian leftist group, the Democratic Front for the Liberation of Palestine (DFLP), for example, is more moderate than the Popular Front for the Liberation of Palestine-General Command but less extreme than the Popular Front for the Liberation of Palestine, though all share the same intellectual heritage and worldview. In addition, different groups in the same cluster may receive different types or levels of support. Iran, for example, provided far more extensive backing to the Palestine Islamic Jihad (PIJ) than it did to the like-minded HAMAS movement. Finally, some groups may be excluded from the overall agglomeration on what seems an arbitrary basis. It may be reasonable to argue that, in contrast to the coding above, Syria's support for PIJ and HAMAS should be seen as part of Damascus' overall support for Palestinian rejectionists regardless of their degree of religiosity. In such a case, the two listings might reasonably be joined into one.

A second caveat is that the level and type of support given to the various groups varies by year, but the coding in question summarizes it for the entire period. Libya, for example, steadily backed away from the Abu Nidal Organization and other radical Palestinian groups as the 1990s wore on. Tripoli went from encouraging them to strike to imposing limits on their activities. Eventually, Libya expelled them. The coding, however, does not capture this variance in consistency. Instead, the table highlights the motivation if it was important for *any* time during the overall period of support.

A third caveat when considering the coding above is that it excludes passive support for terrorism. The Saudi relationship with al-Qa'ida, or Americans' ties to the Provisional Irish Republican Army are not included in the above review of state sponsorship because they do not involve a deliberate government decision to support the group. However, looking the other way as private support is given is an important part of sponsorship today. Because passive support is so important but has a different set of motivations and effects, I discuss it separately in Chapter 8.

A fourth caveat is that this table excludes groups that received support during the Cold War era but not in recent years. India, for example, backed the Liberation Tigers of Tamil Eelam, but this support had ended by 1991. This book does, however, include groups that began to receive support during the Cold War and continued to receive it after it had ended.

A fifth point to note is that Cuba and North Korea are both excluded from the chart, despite being on the US government list of state sponsors of terrorism, because their links to terrorist groups are no longer significant. In the 1970s and 1980s, Cuba was active in providing a range of assistance to various revolutionary groups and causes, including several that embraced terrorism.[9] However, by 1996 the State Department noted that "Cuba no longer actively supports armed struggle in Latin America and other parts of the world."[10] Cuba stopped providing weapons to Columbian terrorist groups in 1990, and it no longer appears to actively back militants seeking Puerto Rican independence.[11] The State Department claimed that it provided "political consultation" to leaders of these groups and provides a safe haven for several wanted leaders. The State Department noted in 2003, however, that Bogotá has apparently acquiesced in their presence in Cuba.[12] Similarly, Havana shelters several Basque Homeland and Liberty (ETA) fugitives, but Spain no longer actively seeks their extradition. The State Department notes that North Korea has not been linked to an act of international terrorism since 1987. It harbors several fugitives from the Japanese Red Army (JRA) who hijacked a Japanese Airlines flight in 1970, but has not assisted the group's operations for many years.[13]

A sixth caveat is the linkage between state support for an insurgency and state support for terrorism. The two phenomena are linked and overlap considerably. At times, however, the group in question may use primarily guerrilla tactics, and the state in question may support it for that reason – not because it uses violence against non-combatants.

With this distinction in mind, Table 2.0 excludes numerous violent substate groups that, in my judgment, do not use terrorism as a

---

[9] For a sample review, see US Department of State, "Cuba's Renewed Support for Revolutionary Violence in Latin America." The report notes that since 1978 Cuba "[e]ncouraged terrorism in the hope of provoking indiscriminate violence and repression, in order to weaken government legitimacy and attract new converts to armed struggle" (p. 209).

[10] US Department of State, *Patterns of Global Terrorism 1995*, electronic version.

[11] Several Puerto Rican terrorists backed by Cuba in the 1970s and 1980s found a sanctuary in Havana. See Lane, "Clinton Pardoned Castro's Terrorists."

[12] US Department of State, *Patterns of Global Terrorism 2001*, pp. 102 and 107 and *Patterns of Global Terrorism 2003*, p. 88. See also Peters, "Cuba, the Terrorism List, and What the United States Should Do."

[13] US Department of State, *Patterns of Global Terrorism 2003*, p. 92 and *Patterns of Global Terrorism 1996* (electronic version).

significant part of their tactical arsenal. For example, the Lord's Resistance Army (used by Sudan against Uganda); the Sudan People's Liberation Movement/Army (used by Uganda, Eritrea, and Ethiopia against Sudan); the Congolese Rally for Democracy (various factions supported by Rwanda and Uganda against the Congo); the Mai Mai (a Congolese group supported by the Democratic Republic of the Congo) are all insurgent groups that, though they often attack civilians, are best seen as guerrilla movements for whom terrorism is at most an ancillary tactic. Similarly, several of Iraq's neighbors have backed the Kurdish Democratic Party and the Patriotic Union of Kurdistan, but these groups use guerrilla war almost entirely.

The table, however, includes groups like the Lebanese Hizballah and various Kashmiri groups, even though these groups also use guerrilla tactics, on the grounds that terrorism remains a tactic they still use considerably.

Motivations

As Table 2.0 details, states support terrorist groups for three general reasons: to advance their international political and strategic position; to further their ideology; and to bolster their position at home. These motivations are complementary, not conflicting. All three categories can and do play a decisive role in a state's decision to support terrorist groups.[14]

STRATEGY

States often support terrorist groups to advance their security and power – core concerns for any state. Support for terrorism becomes war and politics by another means, enabling a state to destabilize, or even topple, its rivals, and to shape politics in a neighboring country or one farther way.

---

[14] As with the coding in Table 3.0, this section draws in part on a RAND study on which I was a co-author. See Byman *et al.*, *Trends in Outside Support for Insurgent Movements*. The study examined outside support for insurgent movements. As many terrorist groups are insurgencies, there is considerable overlap between the questions "why do states support terrorists?" and "why do states support insurgents?" My thanks to my co-authors, Peter Chalk, Bruce Hoffman, William Rosenau, and David Brannan for their insights, which have shaped my thinking of this question.

Weaken and destabilize a neighbor

One of the most common reasons to support a terrorist group is to destabilize a neighbor. Weakening a neighbor is often part and parcel of a brutal competition among states, useful for gaining concessions regarding disputed territory, as punishment for joining a hostile alliance, or as a way of augmenting a conventional military campaign in a war. In nineteen instances, this motivation contributed to a state's decision to back a terrorist group, and in fifteen of these cases it was one of the leading reasons for this decision.

The Baath regime in Iraq's support for the anti-Iranian Mujahedin-e Khalq (MEK) illustrates the power of this motivation. Saddam Husayn's regime had little ideological sympathy for the mix of Marxism, radical Islam, and cult of personality that drove the MEK. But it nevertheless backed the MEK because it weakened its Iranian rival. The MEK in the early 1980s launched a bombing and assassination campaign against revolutionary figures in Iran, including a highly successful bombing of the Islamic Republic Party's headquarters on June 28, 1981, which killed the organization's Secretary General, twenty-seven members of parliament, four cabinet ministers, and other senior officials.[15]

Iran, too, played the terrorist card in order to destabilize its neighbors. After the 1979 revolution, Iran backed Shi'a radicals in several neighboring countries, including Afghanistan, Pakistan, Iraq, Bahrain, and Saudi Arabia. Tehran supported these causes in part to spread its revolution, but also to weaken regimes that had banded together to oppose the revolution.[16] Syria similarly has backed a range of Palestinian groups as a means of fighting Israel.

Pakistan's support for Kashmiri militants illustrates the power of this motivation. As discussed further in Chapter 6, the increasing danger posed by several thousand Kashmiri militants forced India to station several hundred thousand security forces in Kashmir. Fighting Kashmiri insurgents and terrorists diverted these forces from protecting India from Pakistan's conventional military forces and required them to undertake the frustrating tasks inherent in counterinsurgency.

At times, efforts to destabilize a neighbor provoke a cycle of retaliation, with each state aiding terrorists (and often insurgents) against their rival.

[15] Bakhash, *Reign of the Ayatollahs*, p. 219.
[16] Ramazani, *Revolutionary Iran*, p. 44.

Revenge mixes with strategy here, as regimes attempt to demonstrate that they will not tolerate terrorist challenges. Over time, Iran and Iraq both supported numerous proxies against each other not only for strategic reasons but also as a form of revenge. Libya cast its lot with the Provisional IRA after Britain supported the US 1986 "El Dorado Canyon" bombing, allowing it almost unlimited access to Libyan-supplied small arms. Similarly, Libya backed a range of terrorists (and sent out its own operatives) to kill Americans after the 1986 bombing.

Projecting power

Many states seek to affect events well beyond their borders but are powerless to do so. They lack aircraft carriers or other military forces that can deploy thousands of miles away. Their economies are too weak to force far-away countries to heed their demands. And without economic or military might, their political protests go unheeded.

Some states turn to terrorist groups to fill this void. In seven instances noted in Table 2.0, states used a terrorist group to project power beyond their neighboring region, and in five of these instances this motivation was a primary reason the state backed the terrorist group. Both Libya and Iraq worked with the Abu Nidal Organization, enabling these states to attack Israeli and Western targets (and, more frequently, rival Palestinians) around the globe. Iran was long the most extensive user of terrorists to project power, particularly in the Arab–Israeli arena but also against Iraqi targets in Europe.[17] Although many Muslim states and others oppose Israel, Iran's support for the Lebanese Hizballah, and to a lesser degree HAMAS and the Palestine Islamic Jihad, has enabled it to play a spoiler role in the peace negotiations and inflict considerable harm on Israel.

Changing a regime

At times states use a terrorist group to try to topple a neighboring regime, seeing that regime as a threat or simply an impediment to aggrandizing the power of the state sponsor regime. Changing a regime was an important motivation in three instances since the end of the Cold War, but a leading motivation in only one of these cases. The goal in such cases

---

[17] Ibid., p. 37.

is not destabilization, but rather the replacement of one leadership with another that is more sympathetic.

In 1981, shortly after the outbreak of the Iranian revolution, Tehran supported Shi'a radicals of the Islamic Front for the Liberation of Bahrain in an attempted coup against Bahrain's ruling Al Khalifa family. From 1985 to 1989, Libya trained Charles Taylor, who later successfully invaded Liberia and seized control.[18] Taylor, in turn, founded, funded, and directed the exceptionally brutal Revolutionary United Front (RUF), which almost took control of Sierra Leone.

Iran took a similar approach in its support for the Supreme Council of the Islamic Revolution in Iraq. Iran had a visceral loathing of Saddam Husayn's regime in Iraq – a hatred reinforced by Baghdad's execution of several prominent Shi'a religious leaders out of fear that they might support an Iranian-style movement in Iraq itself. Almost immediately after the revolution, Iran began supporting radicalism in Iraq, a decision that contributed to Baghdad's decision to invade Iran in 1980. As the war heated up, Khomeini declared that the path to Jerusalem's liberation went through Baghdad.[19] In November 1982 Tehran organized various Iraqi Shiite groups under the umbrella of the Supreme Assembly for the Islamic Revolution in Iraq (SCIRI).[20] SCIRI was more than just a guerrilla front to weaken Saddam's Iraq: it was also a government-in-waiting. As Iran expert R. K. Ramazani contends, Iran's goal was to "undermine the Hussein regime and pave the way for the establishment of an Iranian-type Islamic government in Iraq."[21]

Using terrorists to change a regime is relatively rare in contrast to the use of insurgent groups to this end. In general, terrorism alone is not effective in toppling a government. However, irregular warfare poses a far graver threat, and states that truly seek to change a government usually back guerrilla groups, some of which may use terrorism but many of which rely primarily on guerrilla tactics.

---

[18] Robinson, "Liberia's Uneasy Peace."
[19] Ehteshami, *After Khomeini*, p. 132.
[20] International Crisis Group, "Iraq's Shiites Under Occupation," pp. 12–13. Branches of the Da'wa party initially joined SCIRI, as did the Organization of Islamic Action. SCIRI accepted Ayatollah Khomeini as its spiritual leader. Iran's attempt to dominate the movement, however, alienated many Da'wa members, leading parts of the organization to leave the movement.
[21] Ramazani, *Revolutionary Iran*, p. 37.

Shaping an opposition

Often, states support a terrorist group in order to have a voice in the opposition to a particular regime. They believe that the opposition's actions are important in advancing the state's broader interests (and often, improving the domestic political position of the sponsoring regime). In seven instances, a desire to determine the nature of the opposition contributed to a state's decision to back a terrorist group, though it was only a leading cause in one instance.

Since Israel's independence, all of its Arab neighbors have supported the "Palestinian cause" in a generic way. However, many saw an independent PLO as a rival – or as an uncontrolled actor that could drag them into a disastrous war with Israel – and actively sought to subordinate it to their will. When this failed, states supported a wide range of rivals to the dominant PLO faction Fatah. Syria created al-Saiqa and backed the Abu Musa faction, both of which at times openly and bloodily warred against the Arafat led PLO. When the PLO refused to heed Saddam Husayn's line, Baghdad hired the Abu Nidal Organization to kill PLO officials.[22]

Such manipulation is particularly common when terrorist groups are opposed to the state's interest in one way or another. The Jammu and Kashmir Liberation Front (JKLF) opposed India's rule over Kashmir, but it refused to accept Islamabad's contention that the disputed state rightly belonged to Pakistan. As a result, the Pakistani leadership began to support a range of Islamist rivals to the JKLF, a decision that sidelined the movement and led to the death of many of its members.

Often a state's intervention is motivated by the interference of a rival state, setting in motion a spiral in which many neighbors pick a favored proxy. The particular composition of the regime in Beirut was not a vital interest for Iraq, Israel, or other neighboring states. However, these and other powers sought to ensure that Syria or other states did not control Lebanon, a concern that led them to support their own proxies.

The effects of patronage meant to control rather than empower an opposition can be disastrous for a terrorist group. A particular problem is that numerous small groups hinder cohesion in the overall movement, push more established groups into attacks that backfire, and in

---

[22] Rubin, *Revolution until Victory?*, p. 52.

general curb the flexibility of leaders. Abu Iyad, a senior PLO official, noted that the PLO lacked a unified opposition, in contrast to guerrilla movements in China, Algeria, and Vietnam. This, he lamented, "practically strangled us."[23]

Outsiders' efforts to prop up rival proxies can be particularly deadly when the supposed sponsor seeks to crush or curb the group. Arab states, not Israel, have inflicted perhaps three quarters of the casualties Palestinian militant groups have suffered.[24] As one Palestinian nationalist lamented, virtually every Arab state "stabbed them in the back at one point or another."[25]

EXPORTING A POLITICAL SYSTEM

Strategy, however, is not the only – and at times not the primary – reason that states link themselves to terrorist groups. Many states seek to export their ideology and political system and use terrorist groups as a proxy to this end. The terrorists are often viewed as a revolutionary vanguard that will bring on the desired Islamic, Marxist, or other revolutionary state.

An ideology explains the world's conditions and offers a blueprint for action. Ideology helps individuals formulate, consider, and respond to political problems. Using the noted anthropologist Clifford Geertz's terminology, an ideology thus offers both a "model of" reality and a "model for" action.[26] Modern ideologies have included Marxism, liberalism, White Supremacism, and fascism, among others.

In twenty-five cases, ideological beliefs contributed to a regime's decision to back terrorists, and in seventeen of these instances it was a leading concern. The most important role of ideology was a desire to export the sponsoring regime's political system. Exporting a political system played a major role in the decision of three major sponsors since the end of the Cold War – Iran, Sudan, and the Taliban's Afghanistan – to support terrorism. Exporting the Islamic revolution was a leading foreign policy goal after the 1979 Iranian revolution, an ambition that led Tehran to work with a range of radicals around the world. As Ayatollah Khomeini declared, "We should try to export our revolution

---

[23] Ibid., p. 36. [24] Ibid., pp. 122–127. [25] As quoted in ibid., p. 123.
[26] Geertz, *The Interpretation of Cultures*, pp. 93–95, 221.

to the world."[27] Mullah Omar and other Taliban leaders also sought to spread the revolution they were fostering at home, working with al-Qa'ida and other radical groups to this end. (The importance of ideology for Iran and the Taliban is discussed in Chapters 4 and 8 respectively.)

Sudan represents an important additional instance where ideology trumped strategic interest and led a state to support terrorism. In the early and mid-1990s, for example, Sudan's government was led by General Omar al-Bashir but heavily influenced by radical Islamist Hasan al-Turabi, who headed the National Islamic Front.[28] In 1993, Secretary of State Warren Christopher designated Sudan a state sponsor of terror, and in 1996 the United Nations (UN) Security Council imposed sanctions on Sudan for its involvement in the failed 1995 attempt of Egyptian militants to assassinate Egyptian President Mubarak. The United States in 1996 and 1997 imposed additional penalties designed to isolate and punish Sudan.[29]

During this time, al-Qa'ida, the Abu Nidal Organization, Hizballah, the Palestine Islamic Jihad, al-Gama'at al-Islamiyya, HAMAS, the Armed Islamic Group, and other movements established a presence in Sudan. Indeed, an al-Qa'ida lieutenant later testified that the government in Sudan went to Bin Ladin to convince him to relocate to the country.[30] This invitation was issued in 1989, and Bin Ladin moved his organization there in 1991.[31] As the US Department of State noted at the time, "Sudan continued to serve as a refuge, nexus, and training hub in 1995 for a number of international terrorist organizations, primarily

---

[27] As quoted in Ramazani, *Revolutionary Iran,* p. 24. See also Roy, *The Failure of Political Islam,* p. 175. Olivier Roy notes, however, that Iran was sympathetic to revolutionary movements in general, paying attention to many non-Islamic revolutionary movements in the third world.

[28] Peterson, *Inside Sudan,* p. 11. For an overview of Turabi's views, see Miller, "Faces of Fundamentalism."

[29] For a review, see O'Sullivan, *Shrewd Sanctions,* pp. 238–239.

[30] Burke, *Al-Qaeda,* pp. 131–133. See also Miller, "Global Islamic Awakening or Sudanese Nightmare?"

[31] National Commission on Terrorist Attacks on the United States, "Overview of the Enemy," in *Countering the Changing Threat of International Terrorism,* p. 2.

of Middle Eastern origin."[32] Sudanese officials also had ties to individuals involved in the New York City "landmarks" plot in 1993.

By its actions, Khartoum made an enemy of governments in the West and throughout the Arab world and was even the subject of a UN Resolution – a price for which it gained little in return. Khartoum was not seeking merely to destabilize a neighbor or to change a regime to favor its interests, rather, it sought to aid like-minded groups, believing that their cause alone made them worthy of support.

An ideological foreign policy is typical of revolutionary states. As Stephen Walt notes, the new regimes thrown up after a revolution tend to believe their revolution will be contagious. They often see their opponents as evil, with conflict inevitable. Moreover, they often believe that victory is inevitable, whether it is driven by God, History (with a capital H), or other ultimate powers. Finally, revolutionary powers believe that their revolutions' meanings go beyond their own state and apply to all humanity, or at least to much of it.[33] Not surprisingly, Walt concludes, such regimes are "prone to support revolutionary efforts abroad."[34]

International prestige

Prestige often motivates states, and this is particularly true if they tie their legitimacy to an ideological agenda. The United States, for example, portrays itself as a champion of democracy and thus has a hard time distancing itself from individuals who call for greater human rights or elections in their countries, even when support for these voices harms US strategic and economic relations.

Exporting a political system is not the only role of ideology. Many leaders have backed terrorist groups in the name of ideology, hoping to exploit this association to enhance their political status at home and their influence abroad. In eighteen cases, a desire to enhance the country's prestige led the regime to support terrorists, though only in three instances was this a leading concern.

Such a concern is particularly likely when state leaders believe their influence abroad and political power at home derive in part from their

---

[32] Peterson, *Inside Sudan,* p. 117 and US Department of State, *Patterns of Global Terrorism 1995*, electronic version.
[33] Walt, *Revolution and War,* pp. 23–28.   [34] Ibid., p. 334.

moral or ideological sway over their neighbors' or others' populaces – thus making prestige a strategic and domestic political concern as well as an ideological one. Egyptian President Gamal Abd al-Nasser, for example, was widely recognized as the voice of Arab nationalism, a position that gave him far more influence than Egypt's rather limited military and economy would otherwise provide.[35] After the 1979 Islamic revolution, both Saudi Arabia and Iran competed to champion Muslim causes as a form of influence.

Prestige is typically a less important motivator than other reasons, but it remains a factor in states' considerations. For example, after the outbreak of the second *intifada*, Saddam Husayn offered financial rewards to the families of Palestinian "martyrs" – a means of demonstrating Iraq's anti-Israel credentials and piggybacking on what at the time was perhaps the most popular cause in the Arab world. Indeed, numerous Arab states have given limited support to the Palestinians to gain prestige and demonstrate their leadership credentials.

To gain prestige, states often try to ally themselves to a popular cause, even when they themselves do not endorse the specific objectives of the group. In other words, states support a terrorist group in order to be seen as supporting the cause – the perception is more important than the reality. Nasser, for example, had little respect for the Palestinian movement or its leaders. Nevertheless, to preserve his image as the pan-Arab leader, he had to support it or risk losing that status to a rival leader.

Terrorists exploit such concerns. Many terrorist groups claim to stand for something larger than their struggle against a particular government. European leftists claimed to speak for the revolution and the workers, while al-Qa'ida and other Islamist groups purport to act in the name of Muslims everywhere. For most terrorists, such a broad mantle is bogus: they often enjoy little support from the community for which they claim to speak. Other terrorist groups, however, are exceptionally popular among a broad community. Fatah and other Palestinian groups were widely lauded in the Arab world, as is the Lebanese Hizballah to this day. States may try to bask in this reflected glory to gain more prestige that in turn enhances their domestic and geopolitical power.

---

[35] See Kerr, *The Arab Cold War*; Aburish, *Nasser: The Last Arab,* and Jankowski, *Nasser's Egypt, Arab Nationalism, and the United Arab Republic* for a review of Nasser's influence and its limits.

States motivated primarily by prestige often provide only limited assistance, largely because their main objectives are met simply by offering some support and thus associating themselves with the radicals. Iraq and Libya were two states in the 1990s that backed several terrorist groups (in these cases Palestinian ones). However, they focused their support on limited, but high-profile, financial and other forms of aid, doing far less with regard to training, operations, or other less dramatic but often more important forms of assistance.

The interplay between ideology and strategy

Ideology is often vital in motivating a state's initial decision to support terrorism. This decision, however, soon brings strategic concerns to the fore. Consider Iran's support for Shi'a militants in Iraq. Iraq's Islamist movement had become increasingly strong in the 1960s and 1970s. The movement had its intellectual origins in the religious seminaries and circles of learning (*hawzat al-ilmiyya*) in the Iraqi city of Najaf, where various luminaries from around the Islamic world regularly met and debated the future course of the sect. In Najaf there was a veritable "who's who" of Shi'a Islam's future leadership that went well beyond the eventual leadership of revolutionary Iran, including Ayatollah Khomeini, Ayatollah Baqir al-Hakim, Shaykh Fadlallah who later inspired many in Hizballah, Hassan Nasrallah who took over leadership of Hizballah, and other senior leaders. They were educated there, took part in the debates, and helped shape the doctrine that they then exported to Iran, Lebanon, and other countries. During the 1960s and 1970s, Najaf spawned several Islamist movements, most notably the Hizb al-Da'wa al-Islamiya (Party of the Call to Islam, hereafter referred to as the Da'wa party) but also other movements such as the Islamic Task Organization and the Jund al-Islam.[36]

To spread its revolution, Tehran provided a range of support to Iraq's Shi'a before the Iran–Iraq war. It gave Iraqi Shi'a guerrilla training, sending them back into Iraq to fight.[37] The Baath responded brutally to the Shi'a resurgence. This was not an idle fear. Ayatollah Mohammad Baqir al-Sadr, the leader of Najaf's Shiites, congratulated Khomeini on his revolution and, in an obvious reference to the Baath, noted "Other tyrants

---

[36] Kramer, "The Oracle of Hizbullah."
[37] Hiro, *Iran under the Ayatollahs*, p. 167.

have yet to see their day of reckoning."[38] Khomeini himself regularly called on Iraqis to rise up, declaring the Baath regime to be apostate.[39]

After war broke out between the two countries in 1980 (a war provoked in part by Iran's support for revolutionaries), Iran's backing of the Da'wa and other groups, such as Iraqi Kurds, was a means to undermine a military competitor and ideally replace the regime with one amenable to Tehran's interests – strategic rationales. In November 1982 Tehran organized various Iraqi Shiite groups under the umbrella of the Supreme Assembly for the Islamic Revolution in Iraq (SCIRI). Branches of the Da'wa party initially joined SCIRI, as did the Organization of Islamic Action. SCIRI accepted Ayatollah Khomeini as its spiritual leader. SCIRI was also a government-in-waiting. (Iran's attempt to dominate the movement, however, alienated many Da'wa members, leading parts of the organization to leave the movement.[40])

The Islamists' increasing power posed a threat to the Baath Party's rule, leading to a steady escalation of arrests, murder, and other forms of repression. In all, perhaps 10,000 Islamists died between 1970 and 1990.[41] Najaf's seminaries went from approximately 7,000 students before the Iran–Iraq war, to around 700 after it.[42] Many Najaf-trained theologians fled or were exiled from Iraq, particularly non-Iraqis. These in turned formed the core of religious movements such as Hizballah in Lebanon.[43]

Iran's support for the Da'wa and other groups illustrates how quickly ideology and strategy become intertwined. In this instance, ideology defined the enemy, led to the initial decision to provoke the regime by supporting dissidents, and determined which of the Baath regime's foes received the most wholehearted support from Tehran. Strategy, however, led Tehran to support all the major opposition groups fighting Saddam's regime and gave added impetus to the various ideological concerns. On a more basic level, it is plausible to argue that having an ideologically sympathetic regime in power is in a competitor state's strategic interest.

---

[38] As quoted in ibid., p. 166.   [39] Ibid., p. 166.
[40] International Crisis Group, "Iraq's Shiites under Occupation," pp. 12–13.
[41] Wiley, *The Islamic Movement of Iraqi Shi'as*, pp. 38–63.
[42] International Crisis Group, "Iraq's Shiites under Occupation," p. 7.
[43] Wege, "Hizbollah Organization," p. 152 and Ranstorp, *Hizb'allah in Lebanon*, p. 27.

Leaders often try to mask strategic concerns in the guise of ideology. Syria, for example, trumpets an ideology of Arab brotherhood to explain its support for the Palestinian cause. However, Damascus has ruthlessly, and repeatedly, crushed Arab nationalist movements if they threaten the regime's power and goals. Ideology's importance, however, can be gleaned by states' actions in other areas as well. For example, the government of Sudan sought to impose Islamic law despite the large number of Christians and animists in the country, a move that suggests the importance of ideological concerns to the government. Similarly, the Taliban imposed extreme restrictions on Afghan women and on playing music, moves that served no strategic purpose but were in accord with the movement's ideological orientation.

The value of prestige also can be geostrategic as well as ideological. At times leaders view their reputation as a form of strategic influence, enabling them to cast a longer shadow.[44] In addition, some states believe they must seek this prestige, either to enhance their influence or to deny their rivals the additional influence that would come with increased prestige.

DOMESTIC POLITICS

Domestic politics can also lead a regime to support terrorism, even when it is not in their state's strategic interests and when the elites' ideological convictions are thin at best. Regimes may desire to aid kin, whether ethnic or religious, who are perceived as oppressed or in jeopardy. This backing in turn bolsters a regime's political position at home by tying it to a popular cause. More rarely, regimes use a terrorist group to gain military aid or other forms of assistance in the state's own struggles in a civil war or against regime dissidents.

Aid kin

States at times aid brethren, whether ethnic or religious, who are perceived as oppressed. By providing the terrorist group with support, the state helps them resist such oppression and otherwise improves their position *vis-à-vis* other groups. In twenty instances, domestic concerns

---

[44] See Markey, "Prestige and the Origins of War." For a broader view of the importance of prestige and other non-material aspects of power, see Nye, *Bound to Lead.*

contributed to regimes' decisions to support terrorist groups, though in only three cases did they play a leading role in shaping the states' decisions.

Domestic politics often blend neatly with ideological motivations and strategic concerns. Iran has provided support to a range of Shi'a Muslim groups such as the Iraqi Da'wa party, the Islamic Front for the Liberation of Bahrain, and the Tehrik-e Jafariya-e Pakistan. An ideological desire to spread the revolution and a strategic concern about influencing Iran's neighbors played important roles in this decision. However, the regime's legitimacy also depended on its self-proclaimed status as the protector of Muslims, particularly Shi'as, worldwide. In such a case, defending Shiism was comparable to defending a well-defined community rather than bolstering a particular worldview. Bolstering this position required clear gestures of support.[45]

The process is not always a bottom-up one. Leaders often manipulate the support they give to terrorists to gain standing at home. Pakistani leaders, for example, have used their support for various guerrillas in Kashmir to shore up support among nationalistic Pakistanis, who regard Kashmir as illegally under India's control. Various governments have also used the Kashmir cause to unite Pakistan's many communities, which are often hostile to one another. Past civilian leaders in Pakistan also supported the Kashmir cause to appease the country's most important interest group – the Pakistani military – which is staunchly committed to undermining India's control over the disputed province.

Regimes that link themselves to a militant cause walk a dangerous line, as the terrorists become a force in the supporting country's domestic politics. The Palestinian movement had some leverage over its state sponsors, being able to brand them as unsupportive, and thus illegitimate. To a lesser degree, Kashmiri militants could use their ties to Pakistani political groups to criticize a government that they did not deem properly supportive.

---

[45] See Ramazani, *Turban for the Crown*, pp. 24–27 and Arjomand, *Revolutionary Iran*, pp. 143–145. In the early 1980s, the once-broad coalition that overthrew the Shah gave way to the dominance of a highly ideological group of religious leaders and their agents and allies among the broader population.

Whether top-down or bottom-up, the power of domestic politics makes the appearance of support far more important than the reality of it – a gap that often has huge implications for terrorist groups. States often make great efforts to appear supportive, but behind the scenes often do not follow this up with tangible aid. For example, some states trumpeted their support for the Palestinians even as they sealed their borders to prevent them from using their country as a base or moved to crush the PLO's independence. States will take additional measures to control the terrorist cause because of this influence, even at the price of the opposition movement's effectiveness. Syria, for example, sought to dominate the Palestinian movement both to ensure that it could manipulate it for domestic and strategic reasons and, even more important, so that the Palestinian leadership could not influence the regime's domestic standing.

Military or operational aid

At times, the rewards of supporting a terrorist movement go beyond politics. Just as states can help a terrorist group become more lethal, terrorists at times can make states stronger and more deadly. Terrorists, particularly if they are affiliated with a broader insurgency, can become an adjunct of a regime's military power and reach, fighting as soldiers in a civil war or striking at dissidents wherever they may be found. In four of the relationships in Table 2.0, such support was an important factor in the regimes' relationship with a terrorist group, though in only one was it a primary motivation.

Perhaps the most notorious, and certainly the most ambitious, use of a terrorist group to target domestic opponents was the Sudan's, and later the Taliban's, cooperation with al-Qa'ida against their domestic opponents. Sudanese leaders hoped Bin Ladin would subsidize several development projects in the country and put up money for twenty-three training camps that they wanted to build – wishes that Bin Ladin fulfilled. Some of those trained included militia members of the NIF. Bin Ladin also trained his own fighters to use against Christian rebels in southern Sudan.[46] The Taliban was even more ambitious. As will be discussed in Chapter 7, al-Qa'ida provided the Taliban with money and thousands of shock troops, who proved vital in the Taliban's efforts to subdue the Northern Alliance and other groups it was fighting as part of

[46] Burke, *Al-Qaeda*, p. 132 and Anonymous, *Through Our Enemies' Eyes*, p. 126.

the Afghan civil war. Iraq also used the MEK to augment government efforts to suppress Shi'a and Kurdish rebellions in 1991.[47]

Terrorists are often used against critics of a regime. Bin Ladin helped Turabi and the NIF, and later the Taliban, assassinate opposition leaders.[48] Iran regularly used the Lebanese Hizballah and other groups it sponsored to target enemies of the Iranian regime. For example, Hizballah members participated in the 1992 assassination of four Iranian Kurdish dissident leaders in Germany. Iranian proxies in Iraq also targeted groups such as the Mujahedin-e Khalq.

Despite these instances of material aid, it should be remembered that terrorists, in general, are weak allies when compared with the forces of most states. Most terrorist groups have few men under arms. Even the biggest almost always lack armor, artillery, air power, or other essentials of modern military power. When Syrian opponents of Hafez al-Asad tried to use the Palestinian group al-Sa'iqa to counter his control of the Syrian army, Asad easily brushed them aside.

Sources of restraint

Because of the tremendous impact that states can have on a group's capabilities and on a government's counterterrorism response, it is tempting to view state support for terrorism as entirely negative. And this is largely the case. However, at times a state's influence may lead a terrorist group to moderate its activities or to become more pragmatic. At first blush, such restraint appears puzzling. What motivates a state to rein in the very terrorist groups they are helping to become more lethal?

Probably the most important source of restraint is that the sponsor fears a reprisal or even escalation from the terrorists' target state. The decision to support terrorism is often taken precisely because the state fears a conventional conflict or otherwise wants to limit its involvement. Too violent a provocation may compel the militarily superior state to act and create domestic and international support for its government when it does so. Iran stopped supporting attacks by Gulf Shi'a on US forces in the Persian Gulf after the 1996 Khobar Towers bombing – despite a continued desire to expel Americans from the region – in part because it

---

[47] US Department of State, *Patterns of Global Terrorism 2003*, p. 128.
[48] Anonymous, *Through Our Enemies' Eyes*, p. 125.

feared an increase in political, economic, and perhaps even military pressure.[49] Tehran feared that it might have inadvertently crossed the line it had long walked between confrontation and provocation. Arab states often drew the line when the PLO threatened to drag them into a war with Israel or threatened their ties to the West.[50] Iran did not let the SCIRI make an all-out push to topple Saddam's regime when it was reeling after the 1991 Gulf War – despite the massacres of Iraqi Shi'a from which SCIRI drew its support and Tehran claimed to champion – because Tehran feared a confrontation with the victorious United States and other coalition forces.[51] As will be noted in Chapter 10, this concern over escalation can be exploited to reduce a state's overall support for terrorism.

States may rein in their proxies if they feel terrorism would lead to a direct military clash, even if the terrorists do not escalate. Syria often unleashed or cracked down on Hizballah or Palestinian groups depending on progress in peace negotiations with Israel.

Another important reason that states limit their support is because their proxies are not trustworthy. Saddam Husayn, for example, worked closely only with terrorist groups that he felt he could control completely. Thus, he often worked against groups like Fatah and did not cooperate with others like Hizballah that had a high degree of autonomy or held loyalties to other states. His regime avoided working with such groups even though they were far more popular and capable than the proxies Iraq eventually used. Iran turned against several Palestinian groups it sponsored and instead worked with Hizballah to indirectly influence the conflict, in part because it found that its local contacts were siphoning off the money to line their own pockets.[52]

States may also limit the activities of their proxies in an attempt to limit damage to their reputation. The more open and extensive the support – and the more active the group in question – the more obvious the involvement of a sponsor and the more scrutiny these links have. Syria, for example, since 1986 has tried to distance itself from direct involvement in terrorism, even as it has maintained ties (some close) to

---

[49] Author's interview with Kenneth Pollack.
[50] Rubin, *The Transformation of Palestinian Politics*, p. 140.
[51] Ehteshami, *After Khomeini*, p. 152.
[52] Levitt, "Hezbollah's West Bank Terror Network."

numerous terrorist groups. Damascus has tried to limit its proxies' activities on Syrian soil, often using Lebanon as a base instead.

State support may make the terrorist group less likely to use chemical, biological, radiological, or nuclear weapons.[53] Because these weapons can be devastating – or, at the very least, psychologically terrifying even when the number harmed is low – they are far more likely to provoke escalation. In addition, these weapons are widely seen as horrible, potentially delegitimating for both the group and its state sponsor. Perhaps not surprisingly, Iran, Iraq, Syria, Libya, North Korea, and other states that have supported terrorist groups have not transferred chemical weapons to their proxies, despite their capability to do so.

Finally, states may see the terrorists as potential threats to their own interests should they become strong enough. Pakistan limited its support for the JKLF, which sought independence from India but not union with Pakistan, in part because it feared that it would be strong enough to dominate the Kashmiri movement and work against Pakistan's own interests. Similarly, the various sponsors of the PLO wanted a tame organization that would work in the interests of Arab states, not one that would jeopardize those states' interests if they conflicted with Palestinian nationalism.

States often exercise considerable influence over terrorist groups, not only through the arms and money they provide but also because they offer essential support and protection on which the group depends for its very survival. Assessments of the impact of state sponsorship, however, usually focus only on how it makes the group more capable but ignore the way in which the state's motivations shape the group itself and its operations. Particularly important is recognizing what terrorist groups do not do. A state's influence is often best observed by considering attacks not conducted or particular targets not struck. The weak intervention of SCIRI in Iraq during the Shi'a uprising against Saddam, and Hizballah's restraint in using long-range artillery against Israel are a few examples that illustrate how states may limit their proxies. Such non-events, though difficult to discern, are a critical piece of the puzzle of state sponsorship.

[53] Parachini, "Putting WMD Terrorism into Perspective," p. 42.

3

The nature and impact of state support

Victims of terrorism are quick to blame any government that gives terrorists sanctuary, provides them with money, or takes any step that falls short of sustained attempts to crush the movement. This focus is understandable. State support for a terrorist group not only is morally wrong but also makes the group far more capable and hinders efforts to counter it. Not surprisingly, state-supported groups are widely depicted as one of the greatest problems for counterterrorism.

This depiction, however, needs refinement. Although states can boost a terrorist group's overall capabilities, many state-supported groups remain weak or ineffective. Still others have collapsed despite state backing because of their own incompetence or lack of appeal. Most important, the effect of state support is not uniform. States can shape a wide range of group capabilities, but the impact varies from state to state and from group to group. States also place limits on their proxies and can even set back the group's cause.

This chapter reviews the type of support that states have given to terrorist groups in recent years and discusses its effects on the groups and the governments they oppose.

An overview of support
Although most of the attention given to state sponsors focuses on their links to a group's actual operations, this focus obscures the much broader role

states often play.[1] States can assist terrorist groups in a wide range of ways, not all of which are directly linked to the group's attacks on non-combatants.

When assessing state sponsorship, both the type of support provided and its extent must be weighed. Some categories of support are more important than others: a haven is often the most important form of assistance a state can provide, while it is comparably easy for a group to acquire weapons openly or by smuggling. Even within these categories, the range can be considerable as support occurs along a spectrum. A haven may involve allowing one or two operatives to find shelter from a hostile state after an attack or it may include allowing a group to run dozens of training camps and a massive recruitment center. Thus, judgments on the scope and importance of state support must weigh both the type and degree of support given.

Table 3.0 provides an overview of the types of support states have provided to terrorist groups since the end of the Cold War. As the table suggests, training and operations are one of the most common forms of support provided, with thirty instances – a tie with the supply of arms, money, or logistical aid. Offering a headquarters or other forms of sanctuary is also common, occurring twenty-seven times. Diplomatic backing is a less common but still regular occurrence, with sixteen instances. Ideological direction is relatively infrequent, occurring eleven times. Least common is organizational assistance, which takes place only six times.

Some of these forms of support cluster together. Not surprisingly, training and operations often (though not always) go together with money, arms, and logistics. Both of these forms provide immediate capabilities for terrorist groups to act – a state that wants to build a group's capabilities in the short term thus may do both. Sanctuary also correlates with training and operations and money and logistics. Perhaps not surprisingly, states willing to provide such a visible and important form of support do not balk at providing other, more discreet, forms of aid.

---

[1] This section draws in part on work I did with the RAND Corporation on outside support for insurgent movements. See Byman *et al.*, *Trends in Outside Support for Insurgent Movements*, pp. 83–102 in particular. My findings here are somewhat different, both because they are enriched by additional research and because the RAND work focused on insurgencies, while this section focuses on terrorist groups.

Table 3.0 *Types of state support to terrorist groups since the end of the Cold War*

State Sponsor	Terrorist Group	Training and Operations	Money, Arms, and Logistics	Diplomatic Backing	Help with Organizing	Ideological Direction	Sanctuary (HQs, major training facilities)
Afghanistan (Taliban only)	al-Qa'ida[a]						X
	Chechen groups	X	X				X
	Eastern Turkistan Islamic Movement (ETIM) (China)	X	X				
	Islamic Movement of Uzbekistan (IMU)	X					
	Kashmiri groups	X		X		X	X
Greece	PKK	X	X	X			
Iran	Hizballah	X	X	X	X	X	X
	SCIRI	X	X	X	X	X	X
	Palestinian Islamists (HAMAS, PIJ)	X	X	X	X (PIJ only)		
	Palestinian leftists (PFLP-GC)	X	X	X			X
	PKK	X	X				X

Table 3.0 (cont.)

State Sponsor	Terrorist Group	Training and Operations	Money, Arms, and Logistics	Diplomatic Backing	Help with Organizing	Ideological Direction	Sanctuary (HQs, major training facilities)
	Tehrik-eJafariya-e Pakistan	X	X	X		X	
	Bahraini Islamists		X		X	X	X
	Saudi Hizballah	X	X		X	X	X
Iraq	PKK						X
	ANO, PLF and other leftist Palestinian groups		X	X			X
	MEK	X	X				X
Liberia	RUF	X	X	X	X		X
Libya	Leftist Palestinian groups (e.g., ANO, PFLP-GC, etc.)	X	X	X			X
	PIJ		X				
	New People's Army (Communist Party of the Philippines)		X				
	IRA	X	X				

Country	Group						
Pakistan	Kashmiri secular (JKLF)	X		X		X	X
	Kashmiri Islamist (e.g., Harakat ul-Mujahedeen, Jaish-e-Muhammad, Lashkar-e-Taiba)			X	X	X	X
	Punjabi Groups (e.g. Khalistan-Kashmir International)	X		X	X	X	X
Sudan	al-Qa'ida	X			X	X	X
	AIAI	X			X	X	X
	Various Algerian Groups	X	X		X	X	X
	Al-Nahd (Tunisia)	X	X		X	X	X
	Palestinian Islamist groups (HAMAS, PIJ)	X	X	X	X	X	X
	Egyptian Groups (IG, EIJ)	X	X	X	X	X	X
	Hizballah					X	
	Allied Democratic Forces (ADF)				X	X	

Table 3.0 (cont.)

State Sponsor	Terrorist Group	Training and Operations	Money, Arms, and Logistics	Diplomatic Backing	Help with Organizing	Ideological Direction	Sanctuary (HQs, major training facilities)
Syria	Leftist secular Palestinians (e.g., PFLP-GC, DFLP, PFLP, PLF, PSF)	X	X	X			X
	Islamist Palestinians (HAMAS, PIJ)						X
	PKK	X	X	X			X
	Hizballah	X	X				X
Total							
	Instances	30	30	16	8	11	27

[a] As discussed in Chapter 7, al-Qa'ida may have exerted more influence on the Taliban than the other way around. Thus, it is hard to disentangle what support was being given in Afghanistan by the Taliban versus what was being given by al-Qa'ida and sanctioned by the Taliban. Most of the groups that received support appear to have ideologies more similar to that of al-Qa'ida than that of the Taliban, with the exception of several Kashmiri groups that openly touted the Taliban as an ideal model.

Table 3.0 also suggests a decline in the number of active state sponsors since the end of the Cold War. In the mid-1990s, major state sponsors included Afghanistan, Iran, Libya, Pakistan, Sudan, and Syria. However, both Sudan and Libya had largely ended their support for terrorist groups by the end of the decade. The US invasion of Afghanistan in 2001 toppled the Taliban one of the leading sponsors of terrorism in recent years. Iran, Syria, Pakistan, and others remain active, but no comparable sponsors have emerged to take the place of those who have abandoned support for terrorism.

Types of support

States offer six categories of support to terrorists: training and operations; money, arms, and logistics; diplomatic backing; organizational assistance; ideological direction; and (perhaps most importantly) sanctuary.

TRAINING AND OPERATIONS

Training is the most common form of state assistance. Many terrorist recruits are impoverished peasants, frustrated students, alienated workers, or others who have never learned to fire a gun, conceal themselves, or otherwise carry out the functions needed for successful terrorism. Basic training may involve teaching a group how to use explosives or small arms. More advanced training may include surveillance and countersurveillance techniques or the design of explosives. Indirect training is also common. For example, Iran has used its favorite proxy, the Lebanese Hizballah, to train a range of Palestinian groups and at times other radicals.

States often offer other forms of operational aid in addition to training, enabling groups to better attack particular targets. One extreme might be joint operations, where a state's intelligence services work directly with a terrorist group. Iranian intelligence, for example, worked directly with Hizballah operatives to assassinate Iranian dissidents in Europe. At times, a state may offer a terrorist group intelligence to assist in its attacks. Both Iran and Syria reportedly provided Hizballah with information to assist in its attacks on US forces in Lebanon in 1983. Intelligence assistance, of course, is a two-way street. States receive intelligence from their proxies, which provide them with information on local politics and the military dispositions of their adversaries.

MONEY, ARMS, AND LOGISTICAL AID

For many years, providing a group with small arms or other weapons was an important form of aid. Libya gave the Provisional IRA literally tons of small arms in the 1980s, enabling the movement – which for many years had relied on the smuggling of a dozen or so machine guns from the United States as one of its few means of gaining advanced weapons – to pose a far greater threat to British forces and the Provisional IRA's rivals in Northern Ireland.[2] With the burgeoning international arms market, however, weapons are often (though not always) readily available.[3] As terrorist groups, as opposed to insurgents, often need few weapons, their needs can usually be satisfied without state support. Some areas, usually because they are well policed, may be exceptions. The West Bank and Gaza Strip for many years contained few weapons, and outsiders' ability to provide weapons was a major source of their influence.

Although arms receive the most attention, money remains a more vital form of assistance. As is frequently noted, terrorist acts are cheap. Paul Pillar points out that the truck bomb used in the 1993 World Trade Center attack cost only $400.[4] A machine gun, plane tickets, and other essentials for a terrorist attack are usually inexpensive. Moreover, many experts have criticized a focus on money by noting that terrorists are highly motivated and are far less influenced by greed than typical humans.[5] Money, however, remains invaluable for terrorists, helping them recruit, ensure a supply of passports and the maintenance of safe houses, and otherwise develop their organization. A state's willingness to provide it often is enough for a terrorist group to seek its assistance. Money, of course, allows a group to buy weapons and explosives. Libya, for example, sent $3.5 million to the PIRA in the 1970s, a vital contribution for the IRA at a time when it was in an all-out struggle with British authorities.[6] Money also helps in creating and sustaining a logistics network. Even more important, money allows a group to buy time. Operatives who are not scrounging for a living are able

---

[2] Moloney, *A Secret History of the IRA*, pp. 17–20.
[3] For a review, see *Small Arms Survey 2003*.
[4] Pillar, *Terrorism and US Foreign Policy*, p. 94.
[5] This criticism has been frequently made in relation to efforts to track the financing of al-Qa'ida. See Anonymous, *Through Our Enemies' Eyes*, p. 282.
[6] Moloney, *A Secret History of the IRA*, p. 10. Libya in the 1980s later gave the IRA even more money.

to devote themselves to training and planning operations. Money can also help a terrorist's family benefit rather than suffer if a member joins the organization and thus cannot pursue other forms of income.

Most important, money helps in recruitment. Although from the outside terrorist groups seem stable, most of them – particularly the larger ones – are engaged in a fierce competition for popularity and recruits with rival groups.[7] Better funded groups are able to issue more propaganda, to pay their fighters more, and to engage in a range of social welfare activities that make them more attractive than their rivals. Both the Lebanese Hizballah and the Kashmiri group Hizb-ul Mujahedin took advantage of Iran's and Pakistan's financial support respectively to care for the families of their fighters and build networks that enabled them to outpace their rivals and emerge as dominant groups.

States can also help a group conduct operations indirectly through logistical assistance. States can offer individual terrorists passports – their own or ones stolen or forged from other countries – to enable them to travel more freely. A state's diplomats or intelligence officers may act as recruiters or talent spotters, identifying potential new members on the group's behalf. The state may fund front companies or non-government organizations that offer jobs and legitimate documentation for terrorists masquerading as employees. States can also give terrorists permission, tacit or explicit, to travel through their territory on the way to and from conducting attacks.

DIPLOMATIC BACKING

Diplomatic support involves using a state's influence and prestige to officially endorse or otherwise advance a terrorist group or its cause. Terrorists crave recognition. The support of a state can legitimize a group's cause and methods and help it attract more recruits and money.

The Palestinian experience demonstrates the value of diplomatic support. In the late 1960s and 1970s, various Arab states worked together to ensure that the world recognized the Palestinian cause, even though it was championed by the Palestine Liberation Organization (PLO), a terrorist group. This effort succeeded so well that by the end of the 1970s the PLO had diplomatic relations with more states than Israel.[8] Such support

---

[7] McCormick, "Terrorist Decision Making," pp. 486–490.

[8] Hoffman, *Inside Terrorism*, p. 75. Indeed, Peter Rodman notes that the Europeans embraced the PLO well before the PLO accepted UN resolutions

is particularly important for groups that espouse an ethno-nationalist agenda. For these groups, the ultimate goal – gaining a state – depends heavily on international support and recognition.[9]

Diplomatic support often takes more subtle forms. Often, it consists of supporting the political wing of a terrorist group or otherwise backing certain aspects of its cause. This assistance legitimates the terrorist cause if not always its means. A related form of support is criticism of a target government's counterterrorism efforts. Widespread criticism of brutality in Russia's attempt to crush the rebellion in Chechnya, for example, legitimates the claims of radicals about the barbarity of the regime they oppose and enhances the legitimacy of their quest for independence.

ORGANIZATIONAL ASSISTANCE

Helping a terrorist group organize is often a vital but underappreciated role that states can play in assisting terrorists. Particularly in the early days of a struggle, individuals might want to join a terrorist group but not know where to turn, or there might be many small groups or factions that are largely ineffectual because they are so divided. Moreover, the group's members may be highly inexperienced and not know the best way to structure their organization to avoid their adversary's military and intelligence services. States may provide skilled professionals to help bring these individuals and small groups together. By giving groups advice on their organization, it can reduce the chances of an immediate collapse.

Particularly as a terrorist group is establishing itself, states can help it recruit new members. Money can play a big role, but states can also provide the expertise that enables a terrorist group to develop its own recruitment network. In addition, states can publicize a terrorist group's cause and achievements (and downplay those of its rivals) as a way of advancing their favored movement or its rivals.

Organizational assistance overlaps with logistical and diplomatic support, but it is more intrusive and often more important in its effects. In essence, the state is helping to create and structure a terrorist movement, not merely lending its weight to an existing organization or helping it conduct a few additional attacks.

---

linked to the peace process or rejected terrorism. Rodman, *More Precious than Peace*, p. 500.

[9] Hoffman, "The Modern Terrorist Mindset," p. 78.

State expertise can be vital in helping the terrorist group overcome the response of its adversary. Over 90 percent of terrorist groups do not survive their first year.[10] Those few that survive often do so because they have an adaptable and discrete cell structure and because they have learned operational security. This may result from inspired leaders or hard experience, but a state can quickly transmit these skills, enabling a group to avoid what might otherwise be disastrous beginners' mistakes.

States can also force unity among otherwise fractious groups. Because of the highly ideological nature of many terrorist struggles, divisions are common as groups are committed to different objectives. Personality disputes are particularly common, and the travails of life underground further make cooperation difficult, as clandestine groups are often unable to communicate with one another.[11] As J. Bowyer Bell contends, "Undergrounds are inefficient. The need for cover means that secrecy erodes efficiency."[12] A state, however, can help groups overcome many of these problems, either through coercion or persuasion, forcing recalcitrant leaders to work together or simply rewarding cooperation.

Iran, for example, helped unite eight small Afghan Shi'a groups to form the guerrilla group Hezb-i Wahdat (the Unity Party) in 1988, and played a similar role in bringing together like-minded Lebanese Shi'a factions to form Hizballah. Iran's ideological credentials and identity as a champion of the Shiites helped it unite like-minded groups under one banner, as did Tehran's willingness to increase support for those groups that joined together.

IDEOLOGICAL DIRECTION

States shape not only a terrorist group's operations and organization, but also its objectives and, ultimately, its ideals. Some states directly guide a group, offering it an ideological blueprint from which to operate. Iran, for example, sought to create groups throughout the Muslim world that shared its interpretation of Islam, particularly the concept of *velayat-e faqih* (the Guardianship of the Jurist), which upended Shi'a Muslims' traditional political quiescence and called for the most learned religious figure to exercise political power. Indeed, Iran sought to have various groups around

[10] Ibid., p. 84.
[11] See McCormick and Owen, "Security and Coordination in a Clandestine Organization."
[12] Bell, "The Armed Struggle and Underground Intelligence," p. 117.

the Muslim world follow its own Supreme Leader as the ultimate source of political and religious power rather than look to their own leaders or other non-Iranians. Similarly, Pakistan sought to guide Kashmiri groups away from pure Kashmiri nationalism (which was in opposition to Islamabad's own claim to Kashmiri territory) and more toward Islamic radicalism, which emphasized Kashmir's Muslim nature, and hence Pakistan's rightful sovereignty over the disputed land. In these cases, Iran and Pakistan not only helped the organizations build themselves with logistical and operational aid, but also tried to influence the ideas and leadership to ensure that the movement's goals were in harmony with the desires of the state sponsor.

States may often inspire political movements to take up arms through their example – an inspiration that indirectly leads to the creation of a terrorist group. (Such indirect backing, with no deliberate effort by the government, would not count as state support by my definition, though it remains an important related phenomenon.) The Cuban revolution led to the formation of over 200 "foco" insurrections throughout Latin America, which unsuccessfully tried to apply what they saw as the Cuban model to their own political struggle.[13] Similarly, the Iranian revolution inspired Islamist groups around the Middle East. Saudi Arabia's traditionally quiescent and oppressed Shi'a population, for example, took heart after the Iranian revolution, demonstrating, and even rioting against the Saudi regime.[14] Other Islamist groups saw the revolution as dramatic proof that religiously orientated political action would succeed. This occurred in many cases where the groups themselves sought a highly different type of state than that championed by Iran. Several Sunni groups, many of which considered Shi'a Muslims to be heretics, believed that the Iranian revolution was a model for their own actions.

Inspiration can also be indirect by creating a climate where terrorists can operate more effectively. A state can proselytize or sponsor other activities that provide a terrorist group with recruits or other supporters. For example, Saudi Arabia funded preachers, constructed mosques, and issued textbooks that endorsed a radical interpretation of Islam. This was not intended to directly aid violent *salafi* groups like al-Qa'ida, but it nevertheless did make it far easier for them to gain recruits or otherwise draw on a sympathetic audience.

---

[13] Ibid., p. 115.   [14] Ramazani, *Revolutionary Iran*, p. 40.

SANCTUARY

One of the most important forms of assistance a state can offer a terrorist group is a safe haven. Just as guerrilla groups become far more potent if they have a sanctuary in which to organize, plan, and train, so too do terrorist organizations (whether they are guerrilla ones or not). Sanctuary facilitates all other forms of assistance. In a sanctuary, a group can plot, recruit, proselytize, contact supporters around the world, raise money and – perhaps most important – enjoy a respite from the enemy regime's counterterrorism effort that enables operatives to escape from the constant stress that characterizes life underground.[15]

Safe havens are particularly important for larger terrorist groups that also operate as insurgencies. Iraqi Shiites, for example, were able to organize themselves and receive essential military training in Iran – activities that would have been impossible in Iraq given Saddam Husayn's tightly controlled regime. Pakistan helped establish a network of camps in Pakistani and Afghan territory for Kashmiri separatists on a scale that would have been impossible on Indian-controlled territory.

Safe havens also allow militants to dictate the pace of operations and retain the initiative. Kashmiri militants, for instance, often reside in Pakistan until the weather, local political conditions, and other factors turn in their favor or are conducive to launching cross-border initiatives and attacks.

At times, neighboring states provide insurgents or terrorists with a haven simply because they are unable or incapable of ousting the rebels themselves. Thus, the Islamic Movement of Uzbekistan (IMU) enjoyed a *de facto* haven in the Ferghana Valley where the borders of Uzbekistan, Tajikistan, and Kyrgyzstan meet, because none of these regimes can police this area well. Similarly, in the early 1970s, Lebanon hosted a variety of Palestinian groups because the central government in Beirut was too weak to defeat them militarily. Indeed, the government had tried and failed to defeat the Palestinians militarily, and in the end was forced to acquiesce to what became known as "Fatahland."[16] In such circumstances, providing such a sanctuary is not "sponsorship" because there

---

[15] For an argument on the importance of such stress, see Hoffman, "The Modern Terrorist Mindset," p. 88.
[16] Hiro, *Lebanon*, pp. 81–110.

is not the intention of support, but the benefit to the terrorist group is often similar.

Some insurgencies may also be able to create a safe haven within the boundaries of the state in which they are fighting. Groups that enjoy strong support in particular regions, such as the Liberation Tigers of Tamil Eelam which draws support in the Tamil-populated parts of northern Sri Lanka, are often able to enjoy tremendous freedom of action and even create alternative government institutions in the region under their influence. Geography also plays a role. The Shining Path took advantage of Peru's mountains and jungles, creating liberated zones in parts of Peru. After the Taliban lost power in 2001, they regrouped as a guerrilla movement in the mountainous terrain along the Afghan and Pakistan borders, which historically has proven difficult for any government to control.

Refugee camps can also function as a form of safe haven – one that usually requires the support, or at least acquiescence, of the host state. The Taliban emerged from the squalid refugee camps in Pakistan; the PLO drew its fighters from Palestinian refugee camps in Jordan, Lebanon, and elsewhere in the Arab world; and HAMAS today draws heavily on refugee camps in the Gaza Strip for recruits. Terrorist movements use these camps to organize, train, recruit, acquire arms, and otherwise advance their struggle. This is most likely to occur when the host government favors the refugee cause or is otherwise too weak to control the activities of the displaced populations on its territory. Refugee camps may also prove a safe haven when international organizations help create the camp, making it politically difficult for government forces to attack there. In such cases, refugee camps are liable to become a safe place for the combatants' dependents, a base for organizing, and a source of food and shelter for the fighters.

The right to transit is related to the possession of a safe haven. When rebels can pass through neighboring states (either through the connivance of an allied government or due to its weakness) it becomes far harder for their adversaries to defeat them. In a few instances, states may also permit insurgents to transit a country or to receive support from another backer indirectly. Syria has allowed Iran to funnel weapons to Hizballah through its territory. Such support is often a low-cost form of assistance, allowing the transit state to control the aid flow and at times even divert it, while still maintaining some distance from the terrorist cause.

Impact on state counterterrorism efforts

The above description of how states can assist terrorist groups suggests the broad range of state activities and its impact on a terrorist group's strength, organization, and operations. Such a description, however, fails to capture the full impact of state support. Indeed, often the biggest impact state support has is observed best by looking at how it hinders a target government's counterterrorism campaign against the group. State aid can help a terrorist group endure, which is one of the group's keys to success. As Bruce Hoffman remarked, terrorists win by not losing.[17] No particular operation, even a highly bloody one, is likely to gain victory for terrorists and may even lead the government they oppose to gain support and become stronger. Over time, however, terrorism can discredit the government and make a population more amenable to giving in, if only to end the seemingly interminable violence.

Another way that states can help terrorist groups is by making it harder for their targets to strike back at them. States strike at terrorist groups in a variety of ways. These include using military force to kill terrorists and destroy their operating bases; arresting or detaining terrorists and trying them in a criminal justice system; tracking and disrupting their finances; and convincing would-be supporters that the terrorists are illegitimate and have little hope of success.[18] State support complicates all these techniques. The discussion below looks at several problems governments face when confronting a state-sponsored group: obstacles to delivering a knockout blow; difficulties in going after terrorists' logistics; intelligence barriers; an inability to use judicial means; and problems in delegitimating the group.

KNOCKOUT DIFFICULTIES

Many terrorist groups are small, particularly those that are not insurgencies. The Abu Nidal Organization (ANO), the Democratic Front for the Liberation of Palestine (DFLP), November 17, and the Red Army Faction at their peaks had active membership in the low hundreds or much lower. The arrest of a key figure can doom a small group. Rapid interrogation may enable police and security forces to quickly locate other cell members, and at times arrest much of the organization. Several

---

[17] Hoffman, "Rethinking Terrorism and Counterterrorism Since 9/11," p. 311.
[18] For a review, see Pillar, *Terrorism and US Foreign Policy*, pp. 73–129.

arrests in short succession can devastate a group, leaving it unable to communicate internally and constantly on the run.

In 1987, the French government effectively destroyed the group Accion Directe by arresting its leaders.[19] In July 2002, the Greek government quickly crushed November 17 with the capture of one operative after a bungled attack. Even larger groups are vulnerable to successive blows. After several years of bitter civil strife in the early and mid-1990s, the Egyptian government finally scored a series of intelligence successes against the Egyptian Islamic Jihad (EIJ) and the Islamic Group (IG), greatly reducing the threat they posed (though the risk of terrorism continues to some degree).[20]

When a group enjoys sanctuary and organizational assistance from a foreign country, however, such a knockout blow is far more difficult. Often the leader resides in a foreign country; the arrest of operatives in the targeted country, by itself, will not lead to the successful arrest of the leader. Turkish army and security forces regularly devastated the PKK's cadres in Turkey and scored numerous operational successes. However, as long as the PKK's leader, Abdullah Ocalan, lived in Syria he could serve as a rallying point and direct operations despite these counterterrorism successes. Other PKK leaders also lived abroad, enabling the PKK's core to stay intact.

A base in another country also limits one controversial tool: assassination. Both the morality and efficacy of assassination are regularly debated.[21] Assassination has many downsides – it can lead to retaliation, enrage a broader population, and discredit the government's overall counterterrorism campaign, among other problems. However, assassination can at times reduce the possibility of additional casualties from military action, avoid legal complications, and – when a leader is unusual or irreplaceable – fundamentally alter or cripple a group.[22] The Israeli assassination of Fathi Shiqaqi of the Palestine Islamic Jihad

---

[19] Crenshaw, "How Terrorism Ends," p. 83.

[20] Kepel, *Jihad*, pp. 291–295. For the contribution made by the US government to devastating the EIJ's support network, see Higgins and Cooper, "CIA-Backed Team Used Brutal Means to Break Up Terrorist Cell in Albania."

[21] For a discussion, see David, "Israel's Policy of Targeted Killing," and Stein "By Any Name Illegal and Immoral: Response to Israel's Policy of Targeted Killing." See also Lotrionte, "When to Target Leaders."

[22] Lotrionte, "When to Target Leaders," pp. 79–82.

is often cited as an instance when the killing of a terrorist group's leader proved crippling.[23]

As with other potential knockout blows, assassination risks involving a government in a direct clash with another state. Such escalation may be acceptable, at times even welcomed. Israel, for example, did not hesitate to assassinate numerous leaders of Palestinian groups and Hizballah in Lebanon, as it did not fear escalation from the enfeebled regime in Beirut or its masters in Damascus. In general, however, the diplomatic complications (as well as the additional difficulty of conducting a successful strike in a foreign country) often deter a country from acting. Israel failed to assassinate HAMAS leader Khaled Mishal in Jordan, a failure that led to a diplomatic humiliation and the rupturing of relations with Amman, leading Israel to release HAMAS' spiritual leader, Sheik Ahmed Yassin, to soothe tensions.

UNIMPEDED LOGISTICS

A successful terrorist act is often the culmination of months, at times even years, of planning and preparation. For understandable reasons, the world focuses on the man who seizes a hostage or the woman who plants a bomb. These people, however, are often only part of a larger organization. Such operatives are often supported by a vast apparatus of people who procure false documents, run safe houses, offer training on explosives and surveillance, and take care of the terrorist's family should they die or go to prison. Indeed, the actual attacker may be far more replaceable than the other specialized cogs in the terrorist group's machine. As Colonel Yves Godard, one of the architects of France's crushing of the FLN in the "Battle of Algiers," contended, "the man who places the bomb is but an arm that tomorrow will be replaced by another arm."[24]

Shattering this logistics organization is often vital to successful counterterrorism. Organizational collapse is a common reason for the defeat of a terrorist movement.[25] Bruce Hoffman and Kim Cragin, in their summary of successful counterterrorism practices, emphasized the importance of

---

[23] The Palestine Islamic Jihad, of course, continued its murderous activities after Shiqaqi's death. Nevertheless, for several years the group was hindered by a lack of leadership, greatly reducing its ability to conduct terrorism.

[24] As quoted in Horne, *A Savage War of Peace*, p. 194.

[25] Crenshaw, "How Terrorism Ends," p. 3.

stopping logistics. French officials found that only by going after logistics networks were they able to go from hit-or-miss disruption of ongoing plots to the successful prevention of attacks in the long term.[26] Simply put, it is far harder for the terrorist group to replace logisticians than operatives.

The United States faced this problem in its unsuccessful effort to defeat al-Qa'ida before the 2001 invasion of Afghanistan. US and allied intelligence services disrupted numerous plots around the world before the September 11 attacks. However, al-Qa'ida's haven in Afghanistan enabled it to train and equip a small army with little interference. One intelligence community officer described his chagrin at being unable to go after the source of the terrorists as "trying to chop down a tree by picking the fruit."[27]

LIMITS ON INTELLIGENCE GATHERING

It is a truism that successful counterterrorism depends heavily on intelligence. The vast majority of terrorists are outgunned and outmanned. Their primary, perhaps only, form of protection is secrecy.[28] If terrorists' names and locations are revealed, regimes' security forces are often able to quickly arrest or kill them.

State support places limits on both the ability to collect intelligence and the ability to act on it. In general, it is far easier to place spies and informants in areas where the government controls territory. After the 1967 war, Israel's domestic intelligence service, Shabak, established a network of literally thousands of informers throughout the West Bank and Gaza Strip. This network enabled Israel to disrupt many terrorist attacks and prevent anti-Israeli groups from forming in the first place. For two decades, Palestinians in the occupied territories were quiescent, and even after they exploded in the first and second *intifadas*, Israel continues to gain excellent intelligence on Palestinian activities through its thousands of informers.

---

[26] Hoffman and Cragin, "Four Lessons from Five Countries" and Shapiro and Suzan, "The French Experience of Counter-terrorism," pp. 79–82.

[27] As quoted in Joint Inquiry Staff Statement, "Hearings on the Intelligence Community's Response to Past Terrorist Attacks against the United States from February 1993 to September 2001."

[28] McCormick and Owen, "Security and Coordination in a Clandestine Organization," p. 175.

When Israel began to encounter unexpected resistance from Lebanese Shi'a after its 1982 invasion of Lebanon, it took the unusual step of deploying Shabak to Lebanon in large numbers. In Lebanon, Shabak officers worked with the Israeli Defense Forces (IDF), to try to recreate the set of informers, safe houses, and other intelligence infrastructure that exists in Palestinian territories. Shabak tried to recruit informers among the Shi'a and used harsh interrogations to dissuade potential supporters from backing Hizballah and affiliated groups.[29]

Israel's efforts met with far less success in Lebanon than they did in Palestinian territories after the 1967 war. A major Israeli problem was that it did not control Lebanese territory the way it controlled the West Bank and Gaza. As a result, Hizballah had far better local intelligence than the Israelis, both due to the familiarity of its operatives with local conditions and because it had a vast network of sympathizers. In addition, Hizballah was effectively able to coerce or intimidate those Shi'a who might otherwise not support its efforts, while Israeli threats were less credible because their presence on the ground was not permanent. Over time, Hizballah also developed its own counterintelligence capabilities, enabling it to weed out informers and to plant its own operatives in communities that cooperated with the Israelis.

Coercion, of course, is not the only means of gathering intelligence. As Martha Crenshaw notes, "Reforms that decrease the utility of terrorism or positive inducements that encourage individual defections can be as important as the deployment of coercive resources."[30] The Italian government scored a decisive victory over the Red Brigades, which in the 1970s had proven a major threat to civil order, by giving "repentant" members of the group a reduced jail sentence and better treatment – as long as they informed on their fellows.[31] Such intelligence is less valuable if much of a group's activities are based outside the country.

Even if a government learns where the terrorists are, its attempts to act are often frustrated. Israel could reach out in Lebanon to arrest or kill Hizballah operatives. Its ability to strike Hizballah operatives or other leaders living in Iran, however, is extremely limited. Action against

---

[29] Black and Morris, *Israel's Secret Wars*, pp. 395–396.
[30] Crenshaw, "How Terrorism Declines," p. 81.   [31] Ibid., p. 82.

terrorists in these countries often amounts to an act of war against the government that hosts them, a far more momentous decision.

LIMITS TO A CRIMINAL JUSTICE APPROACH

One means of fighting terrorism is to use courts, trials, and a country's legal system to arrest and try suspected terrorists. Although criminal justice approaches are often derided as soft on terrorism, they offer several advantages. They enjoy widespread legitimacy, in contrast to indefinite detention, let alone assassination. If successful, they remove terrorists from the streets and put them in jail, where (usually) they are no longer able to continue their violent activities. Such a process often generates considerable intelligence, leading to additional information that can disrupt a terrorist group.[32]

When a group enjoys a state as a patron, however, this approach is often limited at best and absurd at worst. Most obviously, many members of the group live outside the government's control, limiting the utility of the justice system. This problem is particularly acute for more senior group members. A government's attempt to have the suspect extradited will almost certainly fail if the state hosting him supports the group's activities. Going above the law and "forcibly rendering" a suspect (i.e., kidnapping him), however, discredits the legitimacy that is one of the main attractions of a criminal justice approach.

This problem proved acute for US attempts to target al-Qa'ida when it enjoyed the sponsorship of the Taliban. In much of the world, the United States worked with other intelligence and law enforcement agencies successfully to disrupt or harass al-Qa'ida, but, in Afghanistan, the Taliban refused to cooperate. One FBI agent mocked the idea of using law enforcement in response to al-Qa'ida's activities in Afghanistan: "[it] is like telling the FBI after Pearl Harbor, 'go to Tokyo and arrest the Emperor'."[33] Abraham Sofaer, a senior Reagan administration official who worked on terrorism issues, also ridiculed the emphasis on law enforcement in the struggle against al-Qa'ida after the 1998 Embassy bombings, which killed 224 people in Kenya and Tanzania: "When it

---

[32] Pillar, *Terrorism and US Foreign Policy*, pp. 80–81.

[33] Joint Inquiry Staff Statement, "Hearings on the Intelligence Community's Response to Past Terrorist Attacks against the United States from February 1993 to September 2001."

came to legal action, though, we pulled out the stops. We eventually indicted bin Laden on 224 counts of murder. Characteristically, he failed to show up for his trial."[34]

LEGITIMATION

Ultimate success against terrorism (as opposed to the defeat of a particular terrorist group) often depends on delegitimating the cause the group fights for and the tactics the group uses.[35] Much of what a terrorist group seeks is legitimacy and the recognition that comes with it. When it has the support of its target community, it is often able to advance its cause by claiming to be a true voice of the people. This sense of legitimacy allows the group to advance ahead of its rivals, to gain additional funding, and to attract new recruits. When states support the cause, the group can present its case internationally and even make a bid for the recognition of it as a *de facto* government.

Although it is difficult to completely delegitimate a cause with every potential supporter, at times government efforts can attain considerable success. Many Americans saw the Ku Klux Klan's use of violence against African-Americans and their white sympathizers as legitimate in the 1920s. Despite its use of terrorism, the Klan enjoyed widespread respectability and played a major role in electoral politics. Today, the Klan still has supporters, but its cause and its violence are widely abhorred, making it far less effective. The Peruvian government similarly delegitimated Sendero Luminoso after it captured its leader, Abimael Guzman. The government broadcast pictures of the humiliated leader and his pleas to his followers to end violence, puncturing a movement held up in part through a cult of personality.

State support legitimates a terrorist group and makes government delegitimation efforts almost impossible. As noted above, the PLO was widely recognized as a *de facto* government in the 1970s, despite the at best limited success of its operations against Israel. Even those governments that did not support the PLO feared that a rejection of the cause or too close an embrace would anger the organization's Arab state supporters, a cost few

---

[34] Sofaer, "Statement to the National Commission on Terrorist Attacks Upon the United States."
[35] Hoffman and Cragin, "Four Lessons from Five Countries."

Table 3.1 *The impact of state support on government counterterrorism efforts*

Types of support from sponsoring state	Government counterterrorism strategies				
	Knockout Blow	Attacking Logistics	Intelligence Gathering	Criminal Justice	Delegitimation of Group
Training and Operations	3		2	3	
Money, Arms, and Logistics	1	1	3	3	
Diplomatic Backing				2	1
Help with Organizing	3	3			
Ideological Direction					2
Providing Sanctuary	1	1	1	1	

Note: A "1" represents a high impact; a "2" represents a modest impact; and a "3" represents a limited impact. No entry indicates the type of support does not affect the particular counterterrorism strategy.

were willing to pay.[36] Support need not be as widespread as that enjoyed by the PLO. Often, a group's potential followers care more about the opinion of a few supporting states than the more ineffable "world community." Lebanese Shi'a, for example, cared more about the opinion of the revolutionary Shi'a government in Iran than they did about that of the world's major Western powers.

The interplay between the types of support states provide and its impact on government counterterrorism efforts is presented in Table 3.1. As the table indicates, the impact of sponsorship varies considerably according to the form provided. Different forms of state sponsorship pose highly different challenges for states seeking to counter the group.

Such a coding, of course, is highly subjective. Nevertheless, it suggests how different types of support can greatly complicate government counterterrorism efforts – in different ways, of course. Providing sanctuary, in general, is the most frustrating form of support, complicating almost every type of government counterterrorism measure. Logistical support is also often vital, making it far harder for a government to deliver a knockout blow or reduce a group's ability to conduct operations. Diplomatic backing, while not vital for day-to-day counterterrorism operations, can be essential for countering a government campaign to delegitimate a group and its cause. In general, the provision of training, organizational assistance, and ideological direction can have a tremendous impact on a group's lethality, its relationship with other radicals, and the types of activities it conducts, but have far less of an immediate impact on state counterterrorism efforts.

The drawbacks of state support

State support is not an unalloyed good for terrorist groups. Even the most supportive and ideologically sympathetic regimes have their own, distinct national interests and domestic politics, making them unlikely to completely embrace the terrorists' agenda. And many states see the terrorists as proxies who can be discarded according to the needs of the moment.

One of the biggest costs to a terrorist group when it gains state support is a decline in its freedom of action. A state may impose limits on the type of targets a terrorist group may strike, the timing of operations, or the

---

[36] Rubin, *Revolution Until Victory?*, p. 128.

methods used. Terrorist groups would have to respond at the time and place of the state's choosing, not their own.

Often the restraints states impose are best observed in what terrorist groups do not do. As Iran sought to improve its reputation in Europe and the Middle East, the Lebanese Hizballah cut back its attacks on targets in Europe and on Israeli targets worldwide, focusing instead on expelling Israel from the security zone along the Lebanon–Israel border: a struggle widely seen as legitimate by many Europeans, and almost all Arabs.

A deeper problem involves a group's legitimacy. Many terrorist groups fight in the name of liberation, whether national or religious. If a group is perceived as being controlled by a foreign power, however, its credibility as a liberation force diminishes. The prestige of the cause of Kashmiri independence, which once enjoyed wide support among Kashmiris, has declined as Kashmiris became convinced that the fighters were proxies for Pakistan's interests, not their own. The Mujahedin-e Khalq (MEK), a terrorist group that opposes the clerical regime in Tehran, lost any legitimacy it had when it began to conduct operations out of Iraq during the Iran–Iraq war. As Wilfried Buchta contends, "The large majority of Iranians inside and outside the country reject the MEK because of its support for Baghdad during the Iran–Iraq War and its continuing alliance with Saddam. As a result, it has only a small, dwindling power base in Iran."[37]

States will often turn terrorist groups against each other in an attempt to control the overall cause. Pakistan supported the Jammu and Kashmir Liberation Front's (JKLF) Islamic rivals, even though the JKLF was initially stronger, because Islamabad did not support the JKLF's agenda. Syria backed numerous Palestinian challengers to Yasir Arafat's leadership of the PLO, preferring weak proxies under Damascus' thumb to a stronger, but more independent, movement. Jordan, which for years had an uneasy relationship with various Palestinian terrorist groups, in 1970 turned on them ferociously after several of the more radical ones tried to foment a civil war. After months of combat, Jordanian military forces prevailed. The result was the destruction of the Palestinian militant presence in Jordan, with literally thousands of PLO, PFLP, and other Palestinian group members forced to flee the country, along with many of their families (as well as many uninvolved Palestinians).

[37] Buchta, *Who Rules Iran?*, p. 116.

Pakistan and Syria exemplify a typical problem of state support from the point of view of the terrorist group: the trade-off between stronger groups and a stronger overall movement. These countries' support for individual groups made them far more deadly and capable. However, by dividing the overall opposition and encouraging rivalries within it, they made the overall cause far weaker.

At times, a state may even crack down on the terrorist group it once supported, effectively turning a haven into a prison. Until being expelled from Libya in 1999, the Abu Nidal Organization enjoyed a "haven" there. Yet in the previous few years, Qaddafi had clamped down on the group, preventing it from conducting operations that might damage his attempts at a rapprochement with the United States. Such fickle support can be bloody. A PLO intelligence chief estimated that the Arab states – not Israel – inflicted three quarters of the casualties the organization suffered in its history.[38]

State support can at times even weaken a terrorist group's operations and appeal. State support interrupts the evolutionary process that successful terrorists go through as they learn how to evade or weather a state's counterterrorism responses. Such interruption aids survival, but often the group members do not learn the operational skills necessary to prosper on their own. Perhaps most important, a state patron can lead a terrorist group to lose touch with its most important constituency: the very people it seeks to lead.[39] The terrorist group thus may develop a political and military strategy that alienates the people, making them less likely to support the organization in the long term.

Because of these limits and drawbacks, many of the most capable groups walk a careful line between accepting the myriad benefits of state support and maintaining their own independence. Yasir Arafat's Fatah, one of the most successful terrorist groups in history, managed to cooperate with almost every state in the Arab world at one point or another – and to be in open conflict with almost every state at another point. Al-Qa'ida worked hand-in-glove with the Taliban, but if anything the terrorist group maintained the upper hand over the state. The Lebanese Hizballah, which enjoys exceptionally close ties to Tehran

---

[38] Rubin, *Revolution Until Victory?*, p. 124.
[39] Chaliand, *Terrorism*, p. 58.

and works carefully with Damascus, remains its own organization and has not become entirely a proxy of either one of its sponsors.

Walking such a line is often impossible, however. Pakistan destroyed the JKLF when it tried to balance Islamabad's interests with the desires of its Kashmiri constituents. Iraq's Saddam Husayn only supported terrorist groups that he could control, refusing to work with more independent groups in a sustained manner.

These risks can make state support a devil's bargain. The benefits for terrorist groups are considerable, and often mean the difference between life and death and success or failure. Yet terrorist groups can find their cause swallowed up in a larger game of interstate politics, a process that can lead to irrelevance and failure.

4

Iran and the Lebanese Hizballah

Since the Islamic Revolution in 1979, Iran has been one of the world's most active sponsors of terrorism. Tehran has armed, trained, inspired, organized, and otherwise supported dozens of violent groups over the years. Iran has backed not only groups in its Persian Gulf neighborhood, but also terrorists in Lebanon, Israel, Bosnia, the Philippines, and elsewhere.[1] This support remains strong even today. Almost twenty-five years after the revolution, the US State Department still labels Iran "the most active state sponsor of terrorism."[2]

Of the many terrorist groups that Iran has sponsored, none is more important to Tehran than the Lebanese Hizballah.[3] Their close

---

[1] Shaul Bakhash, for example, claims that in the 1980s Iran directly aided Muslim radicals in Malaysia and the Philippines, and that its example inspired Shiites in North Yemen, Saudi Arabia, Turkey, and Pakistan. Bakhash, *Reign of the Ayatollahs*, pp. 235–236. Michael Eisenstadt notes that Iran has worked with Sunni Islamist terrorists such as HAMAS, the Palestine Islamic Jihad, the Turkish Islamic Action, the Islamic Group in Egypt, al-Nahda in Tunisia, and the Islamic Salvation Front in Algeria, as well as radical secular groups like the PFLP-GC and the Kurdish Workers' Party. Eisenstadt, *Iranian Military Power*, p. 72.

[2] US Department of State, *Patterns of Global Terrorism 2002*, p. 77.

[3] Iranian-linked groups frequently use the label "Hizballah," leading to much confusion. In Iran, "Hizballahis" are associated with pro-regime militants, many of whom fought street battles against rival leftist or other organizations in the early days of the revolution. Over time, this term became a label used to signify loyalty to the Islamic regime. Hizballah movements have reportedly

relationship is perhaps the strongest and most effective relationship between a state sponsor and a terrorist group in history. Iran helped found, organize, and train Hizballah, eventually creating a strong and relatively independent terrorist group. In exchange, Hizballah has served Iran loyally, striking Iran's various foreign enemies, helping assassinate Iranian dissidents, and otherwise advancing the interests of the Islamic Republic.

Iran initially supported Hizballah to spread its Islamic revolution but, over time, strategic reasons have also come to the fore. These changes have occurred largely due to a decline in revolutionary fervor in Iran, Hizballah's gradual accommodation to Lebanon's political and strategic realities, and Tehran's realization that a failure to use Hizballah discreetly can be quite costly. The impact of Iranian support was profound. Hizballah over time became the strongest militia in Lebanon and one of the world's premier terrorist organizations. As Hizballah's skill grew, so too did its political sophistication. The movement's leaders tempered their revolutionary zeal with a heavy dose of pragmatism and recognized many limits to their activities.

This chapter reviews Iran's support for the Lebanese Hizballah, examining Tehran's motivations and the impact of its support.[4]

Iran and the Lebanese Hizballah

The ties that bind Iran and Lebanon, particularly those that tie the two countries' religious communities, are deep and predate the Islamic revolution by centuries. In the sixteenth century, Iran's Safavid rulers embraced Shi'ism, a minority sect within Islam but now the dominant

appeared in Kuwait, Bahrain, and Saudi Arabia, among other countries. These movements often have links to Iran, but have few close ties to the Lebanese Hizballah. At times, groups adopting the name "Hizballah" are not linked closely to Tehran, such as the Turkish Hizballah.

[4] This chapter does not examine the direct use of violence, often unattributed, by agents of the Iranian state, such as intelligence officers or members of the Islamic Revolutionary Guards Corps. For example, in the 1990s Iranian intelligence agents stalked US official personnel in the Balkans, the Persian Gulf, and Tajikistan in order to gather information for possible attacks. Eisenstadt, "The Military Dimension," p. 87; Mann, "Iranian Links to International Terrorism." However, as this book focuses on terrorism by state-supported groups, not state actors themselves, these actions are not discussed.

sect in Iran. Iran, however, lacked clerics who could guide the flock in their new faith, so the Safavids turned to Lebanon and other countries with established Shi'a communities to help spread the faith. Lebanon, Iran, and various Shi'a-dominated cities in southern Iraq formed an important triangle of Shi'a religious and cultural discourse.[5] For centuries, these personal and religious networks remained robust, even though Iran's various monarchs generally did not meddle extensively in Lebanon.

The 1979 Islamic revolution, however, dramatically changed Iran's foreign policy orientation. The clerical regime in Tehran began to emphasize Iran's religious mission and its desire to uplift the downtrodden over a narrow interpretation of national interest focused on power and security. Lebanon had one of the Middle East's largest Shi'a communities, and this community was poor and dispossessed. Thus, Lebanon was a natural place for Iran to turn as an outlet for its revolutionary passion. In addition, Lebanon was embroiled in a civil war, further complicated by a border war with Israel – a complication that attracted the attention of Iran's clerical leadership, who considered themselves Israel's mortal enemies.

Lebanon was already in ferment even before the Iranian revolution. In 1975, disputes over the division of power among Lebanon's eighteen different religious confessions and ethnic groups, and concerns about the growing influence of Palestinian militias in the country, boiled over into civil war. Several of Lebanon's neighbors backed various militias, exacerbating the conflict and leading Syria to intervene in force in 1976. The conflict continued to simmer, with Lebanon's various sects and communities regularly turning to violence rather than the political system to express their grievances. Further complicating this fractious scene, the Palestine Liberation Organization and other Palestinian groups used the country as a base for their anti-Israel operations, leading Israel to respond with cross-border attacks, assassinations, and other forms of pressure.[6]

---

[5] As the Ottoman Empire, which ruled Lebanon, and Safavid Iran clashed, it viewed this relationship with suspicion, leading many Lebanese Shiites to seek sanctuary in Iran. Fuller, *The "Center of the Universe,"* p. 120.

[6] For reviews of Lebanon's civil war, see Hiro, *Lebanon* and Hudson, "The Breakdown of Democracy in Lebanon." See Pollack, *Arabs at War*, pp. 514–522 for a description of Syria's military intervention and

Even before the civil war began in 1975, Lebanon's Shiite Muslim community – the largest of all of Lebanon's communal groups – had begun to assert itself. Traditionally underrepresented in politics and economically disadvantaged, the Shi'a began to mobilize under the leadership of Imam Musa al-Sadr, a charismatic Iran-born cleric who was educated in Iraq. Sadr sought to shake off the traditional quiescence of the Shi'a and end the dominance of conservative, traditional families who had led the community for generations. Sadr had come from Iran to give spiritual leadership to the Lebanese Shi'a in 1959 at the invitation of the Mufti of Tyre, forming the Lebanese Shiite Islamic Higher Council in 1967 and the Movement for the Deprived, along with the associated militia Amal in 1974.[7] Amal helped train several future Iranian revolutionaries.

The ferment caused by Lebanon's civil strife and the Shi'a resurgence offered an almost ideal situation for Iran to export its revolutionary model. In 1982, when Israel invaded Lebanon to oust the Palestinians and became engaged in a conflict with Syrian forces, Damascus sought support. Iran's alliance with Syria in the Iran–Iraq war made Iran a natural partner. Damascus quickly found itself overwhelmed by Israel and threatened with a loss of its painfully gained position in Lebanon. Tehran seized the opportunity and deployed 1,000 Islamic Revolutionary Guard Corp (IRGC) personnel – the revolutionary vanguard of Iran's military that often engages in covert revolutionary activity – to Lebanon's Bekaa valley. This number quickly peaked at 1,500, and then leveled out at between 300 and 500.[8]

Iran's active intervention initially was directed as much against the leading Shi'a movement as it was against Israel. Amal, although heavily influenced by Islam, was in essence a secular movement, seeking to unite Lebanon's Shi'a along communal rather than ideological lines. Moreover, when al-Sadr mysteriously disappeared on a visit to Libya

Rabinovich, *The War for Lebanon, 1970–1985* for an overview of Israel's concerns and actions.

[7] Amal is an acronym of the *Afwaj al-Muqwama al-Lubnaniya*, or Lebanese Resistance Detachments, the acronym of which means "hope." The classic work on Lebanon's Shi'a and its politicization is Norton, *Amal and the Shi'a*.

[8] Norton, "Hizballah," and Shapira, "The Origins of Hizballah," p. 123. See Katzmann, *The Warriors of Islam* for more on the IRGC role. See Pollack, *Arabs at War*, pp. 540–550 for a review of the Syrian military performance against Israel in 1982.

in 1978, his less charismatic, and religiously unqualified, deputy Nabih Berri assumed the helm. Berri reduced the Islamic character of the movement.[9] Amal's decision to work with the Israeli-backed National Salvation Authority in 1982 – and to refuse Iran's "guidance" that it sever ties with the Authority – led Tehran to work actively to undermine the movement.[10] The National Salvation Authority was an attempt by Israel to impose a government favorable to its interests in Lebanon. As Shimon Shapira contends, "For Tehran, this body symbolized the Western takeover of Lebanon and the perpetuation of the 'Zionist occupation' of the country."[11]

The creation of Hizballah was meant to counter Amal's perceived collaboration and to spread Iran's revolution to Lebanon. The IRGC worked with Iranian intelligence and Iranian diplomats as well as Syrian officials to create Hizballah from a motley assortment of small Shiite organizations. These included the Islamic Amal movement (a splinter of the overall Amal organization), the Association of Muslim Ulema in Lebanon, the Lebanese Da'wa, and the Association of Muslim Students, among others. Iranian clerics and paramilitary forces also reached out to the younger generation of religious leaders in Lebanon, as well as several of the leading Shi'a clans in the Bekaa Valley. Iran helped the fledgling movement train and indoctrinate new members in the Bekaa Valley and developed a social services and fundraising network there. Over time, the movement spread to Beirut, where it incorporated the many followers of Shaykh Mohammad Husayn Fadlallah, a leading Lebanese religious scholar who at the time endorsed many of the ideas of the Iranian revolution. From there, the movement spread to the Amal stronghold of southern Lebanon, where it incorporated many local fighters who were battling the Israelis largely on their own.[12]

---

[9] For background on al-Sadr, see Ajami, *The Vanished Imam*; Shapira, "The *Imam* Musa al-Sadr"; and Hamzeh, "Islamism in Lebanon." Amal had received support from Iran before the revolution, as part of the Shah's attempt to expand Iran's influence. See Wege, "Hizbollah Organization," p. 152.

[10] Ranstorp, *Hizb'allah in Lebanon*, p. 31.

[11] Shapira, "The Origins of Hizballah," pp. 121–122.

[12] See Kramer, "Hizbullah: The Calculus of Jihad"; Shapira, "The Origins of Hizballah," p. 124; Wege, "Hizbollah Organization," p. 154; Hajjar, "Hizballah," pp. 6–9; and Ranstorp, *Hizb 'allah in Lebanon*, pp. 25–33.

Hizballah, of course, also exploited Lebanon's civil strife and numerous Israeli blunders. Many Lebanese Shi'a, particularly those in areas where Palestinian militias operated, initially welcomed the Israelis and supported their efforts to oust the militias. Israel quickly overstayed its welcome, and at times its actions, such as an attempt in October 1983 to drive a military convoy through a religious procession, demonstrated a profound disrespect for the Shi'a. Israel's subsequent counterinsurgency campaign, which involved targeted assassinations and reprisals for attacks, only exacerbated tension, leading to a constant series of low-level attacks that led Israel in June 1985 to withdraw to a "security zone" – a buffer in southern Lebanon manned by Israel's allies, the South Lebanese Army.[13]

In the 1980s, Hizballah had perhaps 5,000 fighters under arms, several hundred of whom belonged to the various front organizations such as the Revolutionary Justice Organization, the Oppressed of the Earth Organization, and Islamic Jihad that Hizballah used for its terrorist operations.[14] As the years went by Hizballah's cadre of fighters shrank slightly but grew far more skilled and professional. By the time of the Israeli withdrawal from Lebanon in May 2000, Hizballah had approximately 500 full-time fighters and another 1,000 part-time cadres.[15]

Hizballah's grim track record

Hizballah quickly became the tip of the spear in the effort to expel the Americans, other Western peacekeepers, and the Israelis from Lebanon. Hizballah literally exploded into America's consciousness with devastating suicide attacks (new at the time) on the US Embassy in Beirut in April 1983, where 63 people died, including 17 Americans, and on the

---

[13] Jaber, *Hezbollah*, pp. 16–27.

[14] Hizballah has admitted that these organizations are not separate entities. Ranstorp, *Hizb 'allah in Lebanon*, p. 53. See also Hamzeh, "Islamism in Lebanon." Other experts report that Hizballah had 5,000 fighters and 5,000 more reservists by the end of the 1980s, while still others put the figure lower, at 4,000 members of the militia. Wege, "Hizbollah Organization," p. 155; Kramer, "The Moral Logic of Jihad."

[15] Norton, "Hizballah and the Israeli Withdrawal from Southern Lebanon." Other sources put the number of full-time fighters even lower, at around 300 full-time fighters. See Blanford, "Hizballah Attacks Force Israel to Take a Hard Look."

US Marine Barracks in October 1983, killing 241 US Marines (another attack at the same time killed 58 French peacekeepers).[16] These attacks, and the sense that the peacekeepers had little peace to keep, led to a rapid US departure in February 1984. Hizballah also shut down pro-Iraq groups in Lebanon at Iran's behest.[17]

Hizballah's use of terrorism continued after the US departure. During the course of the 1980s, Hizballah took 17 Americans, 15 Frenchmen, 14 Britons, 7 Swiss, and 7 West Germans hostage, as well as 27 others of various nationalities. Ten hostages died in captivity.[18] Hostages were taken to secure the release of Iran's and Hizballah's prisoners, to force concessions from Western governments, to drive out foreigners from Lebanon, or more simply to demonstrate the powerlessness of the United States or other major powers.[19] Hizballah was also heavily involved in the hijacking of TWA 847, in which one American hostage was killed.[20] In the 1980s and 1990s, Hizballah also worked with Iran to kill dissident Iranians, such as members of Kurdish and other opposition groups residing in Europe. In March 1992, Hizballah and Iran worked together to bomb the Israeli Embassy in Argentina, killing twenty-nine and in July 1994 it attacked the Jewish Community Center in Buenos Aires, killing eighty-six. Hizballah also aided other groups that shared its agenda. A Lebanese Hizballah member was indicted for helping design the truck bomb that destroyed the US military facility of Khobar Towers in Saudi Arabia in 1996, killing seventeen American troops.[21]

---

[16] Many of Hizballah's most notorious attacks on US, Israeli, and other Western targets would *not* constitute terrorism under my definition, as they involve attacks on military forces rather than non-combatants. However, Hizballah's hostage taking, attacks on Embassies, strikes on dissidents, and many other activities would clearly qualify as terrorism under my definition.

[17] Kramer, "The Oracle of Hizbullah."

[18] Jaber, *Hezbollah*, p. 113.

[19] Kramer, "The Moral Logic of Hizballah."

[20] For a review of the impact of this hijacking on the United States, see Schultz, *Turmoil and Triumph*, pp. 655–664.

[21] Iran sponsored Saudi Hizballah, which carried out the bombing, and also trained cell members. One suspect detained by the FBI and later deported to Saudi Arabia noted that the IRGC recruited him and that an IRGC leader directed several operations in the Kingdom. The suspects also worked with the Iranian Embassy in Damascus for logistical support. For a review, see Walsh, "Louis Freeh's Last Case."

Israel also suffered repeated truck bombings and other attacks against its facilities. In November 1983, Hizballah destroyed the headquarters of the Israeli Defense Force in Tyre, killing 141. Hizballah also began a long, bitter guerrilla war against Israel. Initially carried out by local, relatively autonomous fighters in the south, over time they became more and more organized and effective. Many of the tactics Hizballah initially used, such as driving truck bombs into Israeli convoys and facilities, represented a mixture of terrorism and guerrilla tactics.

As grim as this track record is, it is also important to note that the nature of Hizballah's involvement in terrorism has changed. In the 1980s, Hizballah was perhaps the world's most active terrorist organization, assassinating anti-Iranian figures, bombing a range of targets around the world as well as in Lebanon, holding hostages, and otherwise targeting non-combatants. In the 1990s, however, the movement reduced its direct involvement in terrorism, focusing more on its guerrilla struggle against Israel.

However, with Iranian encouragement, over time Hizballah has become a sponsor of terrorism in its own right, often seeking to build other radical groups in place of conducting its own activities. Hizballah's direct attacks on Israel fell after Israel withdrew from Lebanon in May 2000. But after the second *intifada* broke out in September 2000, Hizballah began to export what journalist James Kitfield has dubbed "the Hizballah Model" to Palestine. Hizballah has trained HAMAS and Palestine Islamic Jihad (PIJ) members and worked with officials of the Palestinian Authority to establish cells, as well as trying to develop its own network and contacts inside Israel. In January 2002, Iran and Hizballah worked together to send a boatload of arms aboard the *Karine-A* to the Palestinian Authority to help it in its struggle against Israel. In May 2003 Israel's navy stopped a boat that had missile ignition switches and a Hizballah expert, which Israel claims was intended to help Palestinian militants increase the accuracy of their Qassam rockets.[22]

Hizballah also developed a truly global network. Hizballah cells have been found in Europe, Africa, South America, North America, and Asia. Operatives in these cells provide logistical support for global attacks,

---

[22] International Crisis Group, "Hizballah," p. 10; Schweitzer, "Hizballah"; Kitfield, "The Iranian Connection," p. 1469.

raise money, recruit local operatives, and collect intelligence, among other duties.[23] In 1997, US investigators even uncovered a Hizballah cell in Charlotte, North Carolina, that was raising money for Hizballah through the arbitrage of tobacco and using the profits to buy a range of sophisticated equipment for the movement, such as night vision devices, global positioning satellite systems, and aircraft analysis and design software.[24]

Type of support

To achieve its myriad ambitions in Lebanon and in other countries where Hizballah operates, Iran provided the organization with a wide range of support. This included direct military support, training, financial backing, organizational aid, and numerous other forms of assistance.

Iran provided limited direct military assistance to help Hizballah establish itself. The 500 or so IRGC members stationed in Lebanon formed the core of the Iranian presence, helping create an ever-stronger cadre of well-trained Hizballah guerrillas and terrorists. Perhaps because of this direct assistance, Iranian influence was felt most deeply in the Bekaa Valley and less so in south Lebanon.[25]

Other Iranian officials helped guide Hizballah, providing it with both tactical and strategic direction. Ambassador Ali Akbar Mohtashamipour, Iran's Ambassador to Syria after the revolution, helped supervise attacks such as the bombing of the US and French multinational forces contingents, the bombing of the US Embassy in Beirut, and Embassy annex, and otherwise exerted strong influence. In the 1980s, Iran's representatives in Syria and Lebanon, as well as the IRGC forces working directly with Hizballah, helped oversee Hizballah as it took Western hostages and provided it with intelligence.[26] In the 1990s, Iranian intelligence officials helped coordinate and direct many Hizballah operations, particularly those that occurred outside Lebanon. The Iranian Embassy

---

[23] See Naval Postgraduate School, "Terrorist Group Profiles" and Schweitzer, "Hizballah."

[24] See "United States of America *v.* Mohamad Youssef Hammoud *et al.*"

[25] Wege, "Hizbollah Organization," p. 155.

[26] Ranstorp, *Hizb 'allah in Lebanon*, p. 70; Jaber, *Hezbollah*, pp. 82, 117. Jaber claims that Syria and Iran helped with logistics and planning, but did not specify the target of the attack.

in Argentina reportedly assisted in the 1992 bombing of the Israeli Embassy and the 1994 car bombing of the Jewish welfare center in Buenos Aires.[27]

Iran also proselytized and increased the movement's revolutionary ardor. The IRGC, for example, preached the virtues of revolutionary Islam as well as providing military tactics. It also stressed the value of martyrdom, even as it provided more standard military training.[28]

Iran also offered considerable financial support to Hizballah – frequently more than a $100 million a year. This money enabled Hizballah to sustain a large organization and to expand its social welfare network – another way of gaining popular backing. Hizballah runs schools, clinics, agricultural cooperatives, television and radio stations, and hospitals, as well as mosques. A. Nizar Hamzeh estimates that in the mid-1980s, Iran was financing 90 percent of Hizballah's social programs.[29] In 2003, Hizballah's funding from Iran probably stood at between $50 million and $100 million.

At times, Iran was also a refuge for Hizballah members. After Israel's May 1994 kidnapping of senior Hizballah commander Mustafa al-Dirani, several Hizballah officials involved in terrorism and hostage-taking fled to Tehran. Hizballah also has sent members to Iran for training.[30]

---

[27] In 2003, Judge Juan Jose Galeano issued an arrest warrant for Iran's former ambassador to Argentina. *The Economist*, "The Explosive Arrest of An Ambassador," p. 25.

[28] Kramer, "Hizbullah."

[29] Hamzeh, "Lebanon's Hizbullah." See also Shapira, "The Origins of Hizballah"; Blanford, "Hizballah Attacks Force Israel to Take a Hard Look"; Hamzeh, "Islamism in Lebanon." Ranstorp estimates that Iran's funding averaged $60 million a year to Hizballah. Ranstorp, *Hizb 'allah in Lebanon*, pp. 82–83. Jaber contends that Iran gives between $5 million and $10 million a month, and at times more. Jaber, *Hezbollah*, p. 150. Rajaee contends that Iranian assistance reached as high as $300 million and that much of it came from various quasi-government foundations as well as more official sources. Rajaee, "Unraveling the Iranian Connection," unpublished paper. Much of the money for social services comes from Iranian foundations, such as the Martyrs' Foundation, which aided the families of those wounded in the fighting against Israel.

[30] Ranstorp, *Hizb 'allah in Lebanon*, p. 86. For examples of how Hizballah and Iran work together to recruit and train, see Levitt, "The Hizballah Threat in Africa."

Hizballah also turns to Iran for assistance in organizing itself and operating in Lebanon as a political movement. Mohtashamipour and other Iranian leaders were instrumental in helping structure Hizballah, which was set up along lines similar to those of anti-Shah resistance movements in Iran. Iranian officials initially sat on Hizballah's governing council.

THE SCOPE OF IRANIAN INFLUENCE

Iran exercises tremendous influence over Hizballah through its financial and military support. Many recruits, moreover, joined the movement due to the stipend they received – $150–200 a month, along with free education and medical care. Iranian officials' presence on Hizballah's governing bodies further increased Iran's influence. Yet these formal ties if anything understate Iran's influence. In both Iran and Lebanon, many important relationships are defined by personal networks, not bureaucratic organization. The religious ties between Hizballah's and Iran's leadership, many of whom studied together in Iraq, ensure regular communication between the two.[31]

Iran's organizational assistance furthers Iran's direct influence.[32] Particularly in the 1980s, Hizballah looked to Iran for guidance. When senior Hizballah leaders are deadlocked, Iran's Supreme Leader is asked to make the final decision. Major decisions, such as Hizballah's move to participate in the 1992 parliamentary elections after years of rejecting Lebanon's sectarian political system, are vetted with Tehran.[33] As Sami

---

[31] Ranstorp, *Hizb 'allah in Lebanon*, pp. 36, 61 and Norton, "Hizballah," p. 151. The classic work on personal politics and Iran is Zonis, *The Political Elite of Iran*.

[32] Hizballah also enjoys direct access to Iran's senior leadership. Initially, the IRGC controlled Iran's relationship with Hizballah through the Office of Liberation Movements, but in 1986 the Ministry of Foreign Affairs assumed nominal control. In addition, the IRGC head reports directly to the Supreme Leader, offering another link. Even more important, many clerics affiliated with Hizballah have ties to the Iranian clerical establishment, providing a host of informal linkages. Ranstorp, *Hizb 'allah in Lebanon*, pp. 33, 81 and Wege, "Hizballah Organization," p. 157.

[33] Ranstorp, *Hizb 'allah in Lebanon*, p. 70; Hamzeh, "Lebanon's Hizbullah"; International Crisis Group, "Hizballah," p. 3.

Hajjar notes, "The link to Iran is, therefore, more than tactical or cursory."[34]

Iran's ties are particularly strong to Hizballah's terrorist wing, which is organizationally distinct from the movement's political, social, and guerrilla functions. Hizballah expert Hala Jaber contends that certain Lebanese clans that are prominent in Hizballah's terrorist operations, such as the Musawis and the Hamiyehs, work directly with the Iranians as well as affiliating with Hizballah. Similarly, she claims Imad Mugniyah, Hizballah's terrorist mastermind, reports directly to the Iranians. Such individuals are thus both members of Hizballah and terrorists who report directly to the Iranians. Unlike many senior Hizballah members, some of Iran's favored Hizballah terrorists hold Iranian diplomatic passports.[35]

Hizballah, in turn, proved a loyal proxy for Tehran. In Hizballah's February 16, 1985 declaration of its ideological program and strategy – its first public declaration – the movement pledged its absolute loyalty to Iran's Supreme Leader, Ayatollah Khomeini. Hizballah also strongly condemned America and Israel as well as noting that Lebanese Christians must be "pummeled into submission." Like Iran, Hizballah portrayed itself as a movement seeking the liberation of Muslims, not as a limited actor focused on sectarian Lebanon's power balance. One leading Hizballah figure declared in 1985 that "Our relationship with the Islamic revolution [in Iran] is one of a junior to a senior ... of a soldier to his commander."[36] Although the organization's autonomy from Iran grew, it remained an important instrument of Iranian foreign policy. Hizballah subsequently endorsed Khomeini's successor, Ayatollah Khamenei, even though he lacked Khomeini's political stature and religious credentials.[37] Hizballah operatives have worked closely with Iranian officials to carry out Iran's aims worldwide, even when they do not suit Hizballah's direct interests.

Hizballah, however, retained some autonomy from Tehran. Hizballah operatives organized several terrorist actions for personal reasons. Mugniyah, for example, kidnapped four Americans to press the

---

[34] Hajjar, "Hizballah," p. 9.   [35] Jaber, *Hezbollah*, pp. 105–117.
[36] As quoted in Kramer, "The Moral Logic of Hizballah."
[37] For a review of this shift in credentials, see Brumberg, "Khomeini's Legacy," pp. 67–71.

government of Kuwait to release his brother-in-law, who was held for committing terrorist acts in Kuwait. Similarly, another Hizballah cell organized around the Hamadi family took two hostages to press the German government to release Muhammad Hamadi, a terrorist convicted of murdering an American in the 1985 TWA Flight 847 hijacking.[38]

Motivations

Iran's motivations for supporting Hizballah have varied in strength over time. The ideology of the revolution inspired Iran in its initial intervention and has played an important role in shaping Iran's backing of Hizballah to this day. Prestige also drove Iran, as the regime sought to demonstrate its revolutionary *bona fides* at home and abroad. As the relationship matured, more strategic considerations came into play – concerns that led Iran to limit Hizballah's activities even as Tehran tried to maintain a strong relationship.

MOTIVATION ONE: SPREADING THE REVOLUTION

In the heady days after the Islamic revolution, Tehran tried to export its revolutionary ideology throughout the Muslim world. During this time, Iran's favored proxies were fellow Shiite Muslims, particularly in areas where Iran had historic ties. Tehran aided Shi'a revolutionary movements in Iraq, Bahrain, Saudi Arabia, and elsewhere. Lebanon, with its large Shiite population and longstanding ties to Iran's religious leadership, became a cornerstone of this effort.[39]

---

[38] Schbley, "Torn between God, Family, and Money," p. 187.

[39] The nature of Iran's revolution hindered its export. As Graham Fuller noted in 1991, "The face of the Islamic revolution in Iran has not been an attractive one to the rest of the world" – a face that has only grown grimmer in the years that followed. Fuller, *The "Center of the Universe,"* p. 93. The Arab–Persian divide also posed a problem. Many Arab Sunnis admired the example of a revolution in the name of Islam, but as Fuller contends, "most Arabs just don't like Persians" (see Fuller, *The "Center of the Universe,"* p. 93). Iran's identification with Shiism in effect gave Arab Shi'a a link to it, increasing their pride and support for Iran's activities. However, by focusing primarily on foreign Shiites, Iran diminished its appeal to other Muslims. As Olivier Roy notes, Iran "boxed itself into the Shiite ghetto without actually controlling this ghetto." Roy, *The Failure of Political Islam,* p. 184. See also Ajami, *The Vanished Imam,* p. 191.

The clerical regime in Tehran viewed supporting revolution overseas as part of its revolutionary duty. The theological justifications of the Iranian revolution emphasized the spread of Islam regardless of state boundaries.[40] Ayatollah Khomeini, shortly after taking power, declared, "We should try hard to export our revolution to the world ... we [shall] confront the world with our ideology."[41] Indeed, Iran's constitution calls on its military forces to "extend the sovereignty of God's law throughout the world."[42]

For Iran's new leaders, supporting Islam meant supporting revolution. Typifying a view common to revolutionary regimes, Iran's leaders saw themselves on the defensive yet believed that aggressively promoting their revolution was the best means of ensuring its survival.[43] Ayatollah Khomeini declared that "[A]ll the superpowers and the [great] powers have risen to destroy us. If we remain in an enclosed environment we shall definitely face defeat."[44]

Iran's backing for Hizballah went far beyond military training or arms supplies, as is typical when a country backs a terrorist or insurgent movement for strategic reasons, and reflected its ideological and revolutionary slant. Iran sent senior clerics as well as military officers to Lebanon, and the IRGC also engaged in recruitment and indoctrination as well as military training.[45] Iran tried to foster a revolutionary spirit among the Shi'a that mirrored the ethos of the Islamic revolution in Iran. In particular, Tehran sought a replacement for Amal, as that organization did not endorse the Iranian revolution and tolerated the presence of Israeli forces, which were anathema to Tehran.[46] When the IRGC initially arrived in Lebanon, its base in the Baalbeck area of the Bekaa Valley became a microcosm of revolutionary Iran.[47] Women wore veils, pictures of Ayatollah Khomeini were ubiquitous, and the debates in Iran were mirrored in Lebanon.

---

[40] For an excellent review of the ideological origins of Iran's revolution, see Dabashi, *Theology of Discontent*.
[41] As quoted in Ehteshami, *After Khomeini*, p. 131.
[42] As quoted in Bakhash, *Reign of the Ayatollahs*, p. 233.
[43] For a review of the war-prone tendencies of revolutionary states, see Walt, *Revolution and War*.
[44] As quoted in Ramazani, *Revolutionary Iran*, p. 24.
[45] Ranstorp, *Hizb 'allah in Lebanon*, pp. 34–35.
[46] Jaber, *Hezbollah*, pp. 47–55. [47] Ibid., p. 108.

But Tehran sought more than the replacement of Amal with a more ideologically sympathetic proxy. Even within revolutionary Islamist currents, Iran sought to shape its proxies. For example, Iran encouraged clergy with whom it had ties to abandon Lebanon's Da'wa Party, which opposed mass recruitment (Iran's preferred strategy) in favor of a secret, underground struggle. This encouragement occurred even though the Da'wa Party had longstanding links to Iran's clerical leadership and had similar long-term ideological objectives. Similarly, Iran has tried to influence the choice of leadership in Hizballah, seeking more obedient officials.[48]

Not surprisingly given this emphasis, Hizballah's ideology followed the Iranian line. In a break with the traditional views of Lebanese Shi'a religious leaders, the movement declared that it sought an Islamic state in Lebanon modeled after Iran. Hizballah even accepted the doctrine of the *velayet-e faqih,* the controversial philosophy put forth by Ayatollah Khomieni that called for the merging of political and religious authority under the most learned cleric.[49] Hizballah also subscribed to other Iranian views, such as the division of the world into oppressors and the oppressed, enmity to Israel and the United States, and the rejection of national boundaries in favor of religious identity. Indeed, Ayatollah Fadlallah, the spiritual guide for many Hizballah members (who after 1989 hewed a more independent line from Tehran), initially called for defending the Islamic revolution before achieving the movement's aims in Lebanon.[50]

---

[48] Ranstorp, *Hizb 'allah in Lebanon*, pp. 30, 75.

[49] See Kramer, "Hizbullah" and Kramer, "The Moral Logic of Hizballah." Khomeini's doctrine represented numerous breaks with traditional Islamic teachings. In general, Khomeini favored revolutionary concerns over traditional Islamic law, at times dismissing traditional interpretations in favor of his political agenda. See Brumberg, *Reinventing Khomeini*, pp. 80–97; Mohsen Milani, *The Making of Iran's Islamic Revolution*; and Roy, *The Failure of Political Islam*, pp. 175–176.

[50] Ranstorp, *Hizb 'allah in Lebanon*, pp. 46–49; Saad-Ghoreyeb, *Hizbu'llah*, p. 16. The relationship between Shaykh Fadlallah and Hizballah is a complex and shifting one. Fadlallah clearly endorsed many of the organization's activities, and indeed Hizballah used his mosque as a center for its activities. Most important, many Lebanese Shi'a and much of the rank-and-file of Hizballah look to him for spiritual and political guidance. Fadlallah originally opposed Iran's move to create Hizballah, fearing divisions in the Shi'a

This ideological influence was also manifest in Hizballah's organizational structure. Hizballah's leadership is dominated by clerics. The highest decision-making bodies are composed almost entirely of senior clerics, and Hizballah's local councils draw on regional religious leaders. Clerics, in turn, exploit their mosque as a political base. This structure mirrors that of Iran after the revolution.[51]

PRESTIGE AND INTERNAL DISSENT

Iran also gained prestige from supporting Hizballah. The movement's increasingly successful resistance to Israel raised its stature in the Muslim and Arab world, which in turn reflected well on Tehran. Theology and power politics went hand in hand for Tehran: without being involved against Israel, it was far harder for Iran to portray itself as the revolutionary vanguard of the Muslim world.[52]

Iran also used Hizballah operatives to attack its own dissidents. Hizballah operatives were involved in several attacks in Europe against opponents of the Iranian regime. As noted below, Hizballah helped attack a former senior member of the Shah's regime in France in the 1980s. Hizballah members participated in the September 1992 assassination of several Iranian Kurdish opposition leaders in Germany. In essence, Hizballah agents acted as part of Iran's intelligence and security forces.

STRATEGIC RATIONALES

Strategy also shaped Iran's decision-making. Hizballah fought Iran's enemies and served as a tool of Iranian influence. Iran supported Hizballah's goals of removing Israeli and Western influence from Lebanon, as Iran saw Israel and the West as its own enemies. Hizballah's expulsion of the United States and other Western powers from Lebanon was celebrated as a victory in Tehran, as were the movement's myriad successes against Israel. Hizballah's capabilities also served as a coercive tool for Iran, enabling it to threaten the United States if it felt Washington's pressure was too strong.

community. He then, however, allowed his own followers to join once it became clear the movement would go ahead. Since then, Fadlallah repeatedly stressed his distance from the organization and at times issued rulings critical of the organization's activities, particularly with regard to hostage taking. See Kramer, "The Oracle of Hizbullah," for a review.

[51] Jaber, *Hezbollah*, pp. 55–70.   [52] Ranstorp, *Hizb 'allah in Lebanon*, p. 50.

These ambitions, while having a strategic guise, also reflected Iran's ideological concerns. Iran's enmity with Israel, the United States, and many other powers reflect the clerical regime's revolutionary ideology, not strategic necessity. Israel had been a historic ally of Iran until the new revolutionary regime vociferously rejected these ties. Similarly, many Western states sought an accommodation with Iran, while Tehran rejected their cultural and political influence on principle.

Supporting Hizballah also gave Iran another weapon to use against Iraq and its supporters. In 1985 and 1986, Hizballah carried out several attacks in France and kidnapped French citizens, in part due to French support for Iraq and because the French had imprisoned Anis Naccache, who headed an assassination team that tried to kill Iran's former Prime Minister, Shahpour Bakhtiar in Paris. Wahid Gorji, an Iranian intelligence official, coordinated the attacks, using a cell of Lebanese Hizballah members and another of Tunisians and Moroccans from France to carry out the attack. The Hizballah members involved worked closely with the IRGC and the Iranian Embassy in Paris.[53]

Much of the purpose of the attack was to end France's considerable military backing of Baghdad. France continued to support Baghdad, but terrorism did contribute to France's decision to expel Masud Rajavi, the head of the Mujahedin-e Khalq, a terrorist group engaged in a bitter struggle with the clerical regime. In addition, the threat of continued terrorism led France to release Wahid Gorji, despite his links to terrorism.[54]

Hizballah also helped Iran achieve a number of its narrow objectives. Kidnappings of Western officials helped to reduce Western influence in Lebanon, a goal of both Iran and Hizballah, and to advance Iran's interests in Lebanon. For example, the first American taken hostage by Hizballah – David Dodge, the President of the American University of Beirut – was kidnapped as leverage in gaining the release of four senior Iranian officials kidnapped by Phalangist Christian militants.[55]

---

[53] Ranstorp, *Hizb'allah in Lebanon*, pp. 94–97; Kramer, "Hizbullah."

[54] Eisenstadt, *Iranian Military Power*, p. 73; Shapiro and Suzan, "The French Experience of Counterterrorism," p. 74.

[55] The American University of Beirut was a particular target, in part because it epitomized US cultural presence in the country. Ranstorp, *Hizb 'allah in Lebanon*, pp. 88–91.

In addition to combating Iran's new enemies, Hizballah also allowed Iran to project power well beyond its borders. Augustus Richard Norton contends that Hizballah acts as a geopolitical toehold for Tehran in the Levant.[56] After the revolution, Iran's military forces quickly became embroiled in the grueling eight-year war with Iraq. Following the war, Iran's weapons gradually became obsolete, further reducing the country's conventional military power.[57] Nevertheless, Iran became a player in the struggle against Israel despite the weakness of its conventional military forces.

Support for Hizballah allowed Iran to send a message to the United States as well. Despite a high level of hostility to Iran in senior US circles, concern over the fate of US hostages in Lebanon led the United States in 1985 and 1986 to send Iran much-needed spare parts and ammunition for US-made weapons systems in the hopes of gaining the release of hostages held by Hizballah.[58] This use of Hizballah against US interests continued after the hostages were released. Given the close US–Israeli relationship, Iran's support for Hizballah (and other groups that disrupted the Middle East Peace Process) was a means of countering the US isolation of Tehran and forcing Washington to take Tehran's interests into account.[59]

Hizballah's current efforts to export its own model to the Palestinian arena also serve Iran's strategic interests. Tehran has long tried to disrupt the Israeli–Arab peace talks, supporting several Palestinian groups that use terrorism and call for the annihilation of Israel. Iran fears that a peace would legitimate Israel, whose existence Iran rejects, and further marginalize Tehran in the Middle East. By backing the Palestinians indirectly, Tehran's role is ostensibly deniable while it is still able to secure its objectives.

---

[56] Norton, "Hizballah," p. 147.

[57] For a review of Iran's conventional military power, see Cordesman, *Iran's Military Forces in Transition*, pp. 405–416 and Byman and Wise, *The Persian Gulf in the Coming Decade*, pp. 19–25.

[58] Hizballah did release three hostages, but it subsequently took additional Western hostages. Ranstorp, *Hizb 'allah in Lebanon*, pp. 164–168.

[59] Author's interview with Ambassador Martin Indyk.

The impact of Iranian sponsorship

Despite ups and downs in their relationship, Hizballah and Iran remain close. Funding and military support remain intact, as does cooperation in overseas operations. The struggle against Israel remains a particularly important point of cooperation, as the movement offers Tehran its greatest source of influence over one of the dominant issues in Middle East politics.

Under Iran's tutelage, Hizballah quickly grew from a rag-tag assortment of guerrillas fighting with little coordination to a disciplined, skilled, and dedicated movement. Hizballah steadily displaced the once-dominant Amal as the leading movement representing Lebanon's Shiites. Hizballah conducted the lion's share of the attacks that forced Israel to withdraw to the "security zone" along the Israel–Lebanon border in 1985.[60] After that withdrawal, the movement waged an increasingly sophisticated guerrilla campaign, exploiting careful intelligence and ideal terrain for guerrilla combat to drive one of the world's best militaries out of Lebanon.[61] Today, Hizballah may be the most skilled terrorist group in the world. Then Director of Central Intelligence George Tenet testified in 2003 that Hizballah was "a notch above" al-Qa'ida in many ways. Similarly, then Deputy Secretary of State Armitage labeled Hizballah the "A Team" of terrorism.

Iran deserves credit for much of this transformation. As Amal Saad-Ghorayeb notes, "[W]ithout Iran's political, financial, and logistical support, [Hizballah's] military capability and organisational development would have been greatly retarded. Even by Hizbu'llah's reckoning, it would have taken an additional 50 years for the movement to score the same achievements in the absence of Iranian backing."[62]

Iran's sponsorship greatly hindered the efforts of Israel and other governments to fight Hizballah. The support of revolutionary Iran legitimated the movement to many Lebanese Shi'a, bolstering its credibility. On an operational level, Iran's support for Hizballah helped it

[60] Hamzeh, "Lebanon's Hizbullah."
[61] The "security zone" in which Hizballah battled Israel for fifteen years has numerous wadis, many of which are covered with shrubs, that allow concealment and ambushes. See Eshel, "Counterguerrilla Warfare in South Lebanon," pp. 40–41.
[62] Saad-Ghoreyeb, "Hizbu'llah," p. 14.

generate new, trained cadre to replace its many fallen members, enabling it to weather conflict with Amal and the Israelis. In addition, Israel was not able to stop the flow of money, arms, and other forms of support to Hizballah, enabling the movement to withstand repeated Israeli counterattacks.

Iran also shaped the nature of Hizballah's operations. In Lebanon after the Israeli invasion, Iran helped the fledgling movement strike at US and French peacekeepers and drive the Israelis out of much of the country. With the exception of the attacks in Argentina, Hizballah's overseas attacks have largely served Iran's narrow interests, not the group's objectives in Lebanon.

Iran also helped Hizballah shift away from dramatic suicide operations toward more effective guerrilla tactics. Israel's redeployment to the security zone, and the withdrawal of Western forces, made suicide attacks far less effective, as the targets were much better defended. Iranian forces, however, helped the organization improve its conventional capabilities, enabling it to strike Israel and its Lebanese allies more effectively.[63]

Iran's influence, however, was felt far beyond Hizballah's terrorist and guerrilla operations. Iran reshaped the political identity of Lebanon's Shiite community. Hizballah steadily overtook the more secular, less revolutionary Amal as the voice of Lebanon's Shiite population. Amal's middle-class base deserted it, and it became increasingly dependent on Damascus for its power and influence.[64]

Iran also deserves considerable credit for Hizballah's political successes and large social network. Iranian subsidies help Hizballah reach out to far more Lebanese than it would be able to do on its own. Moreover, Iran's assistance with organization allowed Hizballah to mobilize many Lebanese more effectively.

Iranian financial and military support allowed the movement to steadily outpace its rivals. Drawing on Iranian funding, Hizballah was able to make a tremendous effort to provide support for the Lebanese suffering from Israeli attacks. For example, in response to "Operation Accountability," Israel's bombing campaign in 1993, Hizballah provided financial support and humanitarian assistance to those left homeless after the raids.[65] Such

---

[63] Kramer, "The Moral Logic of Hizballah."   [64] Norton, "Hizballah," p. 151.
[65] Shapira, "The Origins of Hizballah," p. 128; Jones, "Israeli Counter-Insurgency Strategy and War in South Lebanon," p. 96.

humanitarian efforts bolstered the movement's prestige and enabled it to appeal to a wider audience.

Much of the credit for this transformation, however, must go to Hizballah itself. The movement consistently generated inspiring and competent leaders. Hizballah officials managed to rally and unite their community even as they balanced the demands of Iran and Syria. Increasingly, they displayed a deft political touch that led their stature in Lebanon itself to grow. Although it received training from Iran, the movement over time trained itself, with its experienced guerrillas steadily increasing their ability to inflict casualties on the Israelis. The ratio of Hizballah casualties to Israeli Defense Force (IDF) casualties fell from five to one in the 1980s and early 1990s to two to one in the mid-1990s. By the mid-1990s, the Israeli casualty rate in Lebanon was almost 10 percent, an extremely high rate for a military highly averse to casualties.[66] Indeed, one Israeli officer noted that "Hizb'Allah are a mini-Israeli army. They can do everything as well as we can."[67]

Sources of conflict and change

Iran's intimate relationship with Hizballah became more distant over time, though by the standards of most state-sponsored terrorist groups the two remain extremely close. Iran's support for Hizballah changed for several reasons: a decline in Iran's revolutionary ardor; Hizballah's increased awareness of, and responsiveness to, Lebanon's political and geostrategic realities; and growing costs from outside pressure.

DECLINING REVOLUTIONARY ARDOR

As long as Ayatollah Khomeini lived, Iran prided itself on its status as the world's leading revolutionary state. During this time, Hizballah was both a poster child for Iran's commitment to export its revolution and, increasingly, part of its arsenal for intimidating states in the Persian Gulf and the West that supported Iran's nemesis, Iraq.

Following the end of the war in 1988 and the death of Ayatollah Khomeini in 1989, a period that Iran scholar Anoushiravan Ehteshami

[66] Norton, "Hizballah," p. 153; Jones, "Israeli Counter-Insurgency Strategy and War in South Lebanon," p. 89. On Israeli casualty sensitivity, see Cohen *et al.*, *Knives, Tanks, and Missiles*, p. 55.

[67] As quoted in Jones, "Israeli Counter-Insurgency Strategy and War in South Lebanon," p. 92.

has labeled "The Iranian Second Republic," the focus of terrorism again shifted, with significant consequences for the Iran–Hizballah relationship.[68] Exporting the revolution itself became less of a priority. Tehran instead used terrorists to assassinate dissidents, disrupt the Arab–Israeli peace process, and counter the US military presence in the Persian Gulf. Hizballah could play a role in all these concerns, but the wholesale commitment to Hizballah's quest to make Lebanon the next Islamic republic waned.

By the end of the decade, the revolution had lost its momentum, and Iran's population and many leaders were increasingly disenchanted with the pan-Islamic vision put forth by Khomeini.[69] Iran's leaders remained committed to revolution at home and abroad, but other factors – notably economics, but also a desire to improve relations with states in the Persian Gulf – made Tehran eager for the good opinion of capital-rich states in the West and more cautious in general in its foreign policy. This shift was felt immediately in the Gulf, where Tehran cut (but did not end) ties to groups seeking to overthrow area regimes. Iran also focused the majority of the attacks it backed on targeting anti-regime dissidents.

Iran distanced itself slightly from Hizballah during the Second Republic, seeing it as an important and useful protégé, but no longer offering it exceptional levels of access and support. Tehran played an important role in helping end the hostage-taking in Lebanon, as the Bush administration had emphasized that Tehran would remain a pariah as long as the hostages were not freed. Iran's leaders believed that by facilitating the hostages' release they could move toward political and economic reintegration – concerns that, at the outset of Iran's revolution, would have been minor at best. As concessions, the United States also resolved several outstanding financial settlements between the two governments and agreed to refrain from retributions against Hizballah after the release of the last hostages.[70]

---

[68] See Ehteshami, *After Khomeini*, for a review.

[69] Iran at times had trouble managing Hizballah as it was not always able to present a united front. For example, in the late 1980s Iran's senior leadership sought to broker an end to the murderous Hizballah–Amal conflict, in order to improve Iran's relationship with Syria. The IRGC contingent in Lebanon, however, continued to provide support to Hizballah at this time, despite pressure from Tehran. Ranstorp, *Hizb'allah in Lebanon*, p. 84.

[70] Ranstorp, *Hizb 'allah in Lebanon*, p. 167.

As Ali Akbar Hashemi Rafsanjani and other pragmatists took power in Iran, they engineered changes in Hizballah's leadership that led to the replacement of the more radical Subhi al-Tufayli with the more pragmatic Abbas Musawi as the movement's Secretary General.[71] In 1997, Hizballah suffered a leadership crisis as Subhi al-Tufayli sought to rally poor Shi'a in opposition to both the government and the movement's more mainstream movement. Several Iranian hardliners, most of whom had lost influence in Iran since the 1980s, supported Tufayli. His defeat, and the Iranian regime's support for relative moderates such as Hassan Nasrallah, reflected the ascendancy of pragmatists in Iran and in Lebanon.

The election of the reformist President Mohammad Khatami in 1997 marked a third stage in Iran's support for radical groups that saw a decline in anti-dissident operations and strikes against the Gulf states but an increase in support for Palestinian violence against Israel. The Khatami government sought to cut or reduce ties to many terrorist organizations. However, the Khatami leadership was relatively weak. It did manage to purge the intelligence service of many radicals, but it did not exercise control over the IRGC and other elements involved in supporting radical activity.[72]

Under Khatami, Iranian terrorism focused far more on Israel and far less on other causes. Many members of Iran's clerical elite still strongly back Palestinian and Lebanese Islamists, both for their emotional (and thus political) appeal and because they are part of the mythology of revolution that Iran shares.[73] Iran reduced support for various non-Iranian Shiite groups, particularly in the Persian Gulf. Tehran also cut ties to Sunni Muslim radicals in Egypt, Jordan, Sudan, and elsewhere. Even where ties remained close – as in Lebanon and Iraq – Iran was

---

[71] Rajaee, "Unraveling the Iranian Connection."

[72] Sick, "Iran," pp. 83, 93 and Buchta, *Who Rules Iran*, pp. 22–45. The neat divisions of Iran's policies into three eras, of course, does not completely match the shifts in Iran's support for terrorism or, necessarily, broader changes in Iranian politics. Nevertheless, these periods represent three very different eras with regard to the sponsorship of terrorism. In 2004, the political situation in Iran appears to have shifted yet again, with more hard-line supporters of the revolution consolidating their power against would-be reformers.

[73] Gasiorowski, "Iran: Can the Islamic Republic Survive?" p. 134.

less active in using the groups aggressively. In many of these cases, the network remained intact but relatively inactive, giving Iran a potential lever that it could employ if necessary.[74]

As Iran's foreign policy mellowed, so too did Hizballah. Survey work of Hizballah members done in the 1990s suggests that the palpable animosity toward the United States and the West in general had declined since a previous survey taken in 1986.[75] The death of Khomeini also led many Lebanese Shi'a, including several long affiliated with Hizballah, to assert more ideological independence from Tehran.[76] For example, Shaykh Fadlallah in 1989 urged the movement to be more "Lebanonized," as he himself did not follow Iran's spiritual leadership after the death of Ayatollah Khomeini. The movement itself has declared that Iran's Supreme Leader, Ayatollah Ali Khamenei, is its guide – Fadlallah appears to be more a "source of inspiration" than a hands on leader. However, it is Fadlallah who enjoys the respect of most of Lebanon's Shiite community, not Khamenei. Iran reportedly became angry at Fadlallah's theological and political independence.[77]

The Lebanonization of Hizballah

Hizballah increasingly became influenced by Lebanese political realities as well as by Tehran's opinions. The movement had always struggled to reconcile its self-image as a non-national Islamic movement and the realities of Lebanon. As Martin Kramer notes, "Hizbullah was Islamic by day, Lebanese by night."[78] In 1988, Hizballah and Amal engaged in a brutal war that led to thousands of Shi'a deaths. Hizballah often prevailed in the clashes, but Syria intervened to prevent an outright victory.[79] In 1991, Syria consolidated its control over Lebanon, effectively ending the civil war that had plagued the country for over fifteen years.

---

[74] Byman *et al.*, *Iran's Security Policy in the Post-Revolutionary Era*, pp. 92–93.

[75] Schbley, "Torn Between God, Family, and Money," p. 185.

[76] It is a measure of the movement's relative and growing independence, however, that as Iran demoted Hizballah supporters in its Ministry of Foreign Affairs in 1989, Hizballah in turn downgraded the roles of Iran's ambassadors to Syria and Lebanon on its senior bodies. Ranstorp, *Hizb 'allah in Lebanon*, p. 82.

[77] Miller, "Faces of Fundamentalism," p. 131; Hamzeh, "Lebanon's Hizbullah"; Jaber, *Hezbollah*, p. 179; Saad-Ghorayeb, *Hizbu'llah*, p. 6.

[78] Kramer, "Hizbullah."   [79] Ibid.

As a result, the Lebanese Shi'a were no longer threatened by the ravages of war and all political movements had to accommodate themselves to Damascus. As Syria exercised its influence through the traditional Lebanese political structure, Hizballah had to accept this as the price of continued survival. Under the Ta'if agreement that structured the postwar peace in Lebanon, Hizballah was allowed to remain armed but promised to restrict its military activities to southern Lebanon and the Bekaa valley, while acting as a political party elsewhere in the country.[80] By the mid-1990s, the movement had clearly abandoned its policy of establishing by force an Islamic state in Lebanon, a key tenet of Iran's revolutionary credo. Its decision to participate in Lebanon's sectarian political system – one that rewarded power explicitly on a confessional system – signified its acceptance of the country's religious divisions. The movement that in 1985 had called for the "pummeling" of Lebanon's Christians now subordinated its zeal to convert military into political success.

Syria controlled Lebanon through the "elected" government: if Hizballah was to have influence in Lebanon, it needed to join the parliamentary process. Over time, Hizballah developed an extremely effective electoral machine, exploiting both its resistance to Israel and its social network for political gain. Hizballah drew on this military resistance, its charitable work, and its lack of corruption to gain political support.[81] Hizballah election posters called for votes on behalf of the movement of martyrs. Its parliamentary bloc – which it called the "Loyalty to the Resistance" faction – was the largest single bloc in parliament. In 1992, it won eight seats and its allies won four, representing the largest bloc in parliament. In 1996, this fell to nine, as Syria clipped Hizballah's wings to make sure the movement knew its limits. In 2000, it again won twelve seats. Military success was vital to this prominence. A Hizballah electoral slogan pictured Hizballah fighters and declared, "They resist with their blood. Resist with your vote."[82] The movement also exploits its social service network.[83] As one Christian who voted for Hizballah explained to a would-be rival, "Where were you when we needed emergency snow removal and fuel?

---

[80] Cowell, "Syria and Iran Agree Militias Can Remain in Parts of Lebanon," p. 6.
[81] Simon and Stevenson, "Declawing the 'Party of God,'" p. 32.
[82] Norton, "Hizballah," p. 152.   [83] Hamzeh, "Lebanon's Hizbullah."

In this village, everyone is going to vote for Hizballah."[84] By 1998, Hizballah even supported Christian candidates in an effort to demonstrate its move away from radicalism.[85]

This political participation also led to increased moderation, as many of Hizballah's constituents sought peace and stability, not unending conflict with Israel and the United States. Hizballah rejected the forcible implementation of an Islamic state, recognizing both Lebanon's demographic realities and the fact that few Shiites supported an Islamic Republic in Lebanon. In 1992 and 1996, it bowed to Syrian pressure and worked with its former archrival, Amal, in forming its electoral lists. Hizballah's Secretary General Shaykh Hassan Nasrallah even indicated that the movement would not actively resist any Lebanese government decision to make peace with Israel. Hizballah's political activities have constrained its military operations. Strikes on Israel that would provoke retaliation must be carefully considered, as this would anger key constituents who seek tourism, development, investment, and other benefits of stability.[86]

In Hizballah's fight against Israel, it even accepted "rules" for its warfare – a distinct shift for a movement that had openly attacked Israeli civilian targets around the world. On April 26, 1996, US Secretary of State Warren Christopher negotiated an understanding between Hizballah and Israel, whereby neither side would attack civilians. As part of these constraints, Hizballah increasingly respected "red lines" and focused only on Israel's military presence in south Lebanon. It did launch rocket attacks on Israel, but many of these were in response to Israeli assassinations of Hizballah leaders or Israeli bombings of Lebanese villages. Hizballah has also exercised restraint in its attacks on Israel. For example, it has long-range (270 mm) rockets that could strike deeper into Israeli territory, hitting major cities such as Haifa, but has not used them.[87]

---

[84] As quoted in Harik, "Between Islam and the System," p. 51.

[85] The decision to participate in parliament led to splits and divisions within the movement.

[86] Saad-Ghoreyeb, *Hizbu'llah*, pp. 23–36, 115; Jaber, *Hezbollah*, pp. 56–77; Harik, "Between Islam and the System," p. 58; "Interview with Sheikh Hassan Nasrallah: Peace Requires Departure of Palestinians," p. 32; Simon and Stevenson, "Declawing the 'Party of God,'" p. 39; and International Crisis Group, "Hizbollah," p. 7.

[87] Jones, "Israeli Counter-Insurgency Strategy and War in South Lebanon," pp. 90–92; Hajjar, "Hizballah," pp. 27–33.

Hizballah's increasing role in Lebanese politics has led it to move away from its fierce loyalty to Iran. Hizballah's activities increasingly reflect the movement's needs and aspirations in Lebanon, not just the interests of its Iranian backers. The movement abandoned Fadlallah's enthusiastic declaration that Hizballah should defend the Iranian revolution at all costs. In the 1990s, Secretary General Nasrallah had indicated that if Iran's interests and Lebanon's interests came into conflict, Hizballah would favor those of Lebanon.[88]

Growing costs of supporting Hizballah

The costs to Iran for its support of terrorism were considerable. The United States attempted to punish Iran in a variety of ways, most of which were economic. Israel did not attack Iran directly, but tried to coerce Hizballah through direct strikes and by putting pressure on the government and people of Lebanon. Iran also suffered some fallout in its relationship with Syria and with its neighbors because of its ties to terrorist groups such as Hizballah.

US EFFORTS TO COMPEL AN END TO SPONSORSHIP

US efforts to isolate the clerical regime and punish it economically proved problematic. Although Iran and the United States differed over Iran's regional ambitions and pursuit of weapons of mass destruction, two of the primary US concerns that led to US pressure – Iran's disruption of the Middle East Peace Process and its support for terrorist groups – were linked to Tehran's support for radicalism in general and Hizballah in particular.[89]

Arguably, the United States pressured Iran more than almost any other country in the world during the 1980s and 1990s. After the hostage crisis, the United States cut diplomatic ties with Tehran. During Iran's war with Iraq, the United States provided intelligence, financial

---

[88] Saad-Ghoreyeb, *Hizbu'llah*, p. 82.

[89] For a list of US grievances, see US Department of State, "Background Note: Iran"; US Congress, "Testimony of Paula A. DeSutter, Assistant Secretary for Verification and Compliance, Before the US–Israeli Joint Parliamentary Committee"; and US Congress, "Testimony of Richard L. Armitage, Deputy Secretary of State, Testimony before the Senate Foreign Relations Committee."

assistance, and other forms of aid to help Baghdad triumph.[90] In 1983, the United States initiated "Operation Staunch" to prevent Iran from receiving arms. In addition, Iraq received $2 billion as a trade credit.[91] These measures greatly hindered the war effort against Iraq, making it far harder to buy arms, particularly from America, formerly Iran's major supplier. Washington also provided limited support to Iranian exiles in an attempt to weaken the regime.[92]

At times, tension escalated into outright conflict. In response to Iranian attacks on US-reflagged oil tankers in 1988, the United States sank several ships of the Iranian navy and also destroyed several Iranian oil platforms. These attacks ended Iran's attempts to intimidate Iraq's allies among the conservative Gulf sheikhdoms into ending their support for Baghdad.

The United States also maintained a large military presence in the Gulf after the 1991 war with Iraq. The US troop presence in the Gulf varied between 8,000 and 25,000. The United States also established a series of basing agreements and prepositioning arrangements with all the Gulf monarchies. This presence was in large part intended to deter Iraqi aggression and contain the regime in Baghdad. However, implicitly – and at times openly – the United States sought to use this presence to deter any Iranian adventurism and weaken Iran's regional influence.

The United States also took several covert measures to counter Iran. In 1995, the United States Congress proposed $20 million to overthrow Iran's government. This attempt at rather overt covert action, however, does not appear to have made any significant progress. In 1997, in contrast, the United States launched Operation Sapphire, which led to the identification and expulsion of Iranian intelligence officers around the world.[93]

Sanctions have proven the cornerstone of US policy toward Iran since the 1979 Islamic revolution but have not persuaded Tehran to abandon its support for terrorism.[94] Immediately after the revolution, Iranian

---

[90] For a description of recent US policy, see US Congress, "Testimony of Richard L. Armitage"; and Eisenstadt, *Iranian Military Power*, p. 76.

[91] Ranstorp, *Hizb 'allah in Lebanon*, p. 117.

[92] Hiro claims this support was extensive. Hiro, *Iran under the Ayatollahs*, p. 327. However, subsequent works on CIA covert efforts indicate that no serious effort was mounted to destabilize the regime.

[93] Slavin, "Officials: US 'Outed' Iran's Spies in 1997."

[94] For a review, see Alikhani, *Sanctioning Iran*.

students and other activists seized the US Embassy, holding sixty-six (eventually fifty-two) American hostages.[95] In response to this and other provocations, the United States froze $12 billion in Iranian assets, suspended hundreds of millions of dollars worth of arms purchases, and banned imports from Iran. Although the UN failed to join in and require all member states to punish Iran, Western European states and Japan also banned the export of arms, prevented new contracts from being signed, and limited investment in the revolutionary state. Because the sanctions were multilateral, the United States enjoyed additional leverage. Iran freed the hostages in 1981, and in return most of its assets were unfrozen and many states resumed trade with it.[96]

US sanctions continued even after the hostage crisis ended. Washington remained hostile to the Iranian regime as it began an ambitious effort to export its revolution, backing radical groups, including many that used terrorism, throughout the Middle East. In addition to punishing Iran for its support of terrorism, Washington imposed these sanctions due to other grievances: to curtail Iran's weapons of mass destruction programs, to limit Iran's rebuilding of its conventional military arsenal, and to dissuade Iran from opposing the Middle East Peace Process.[97]

As the years wore on, the number and types of US sanctions kept expanding. In 1984, Iran was added to the state sponsor list, which brought a host of mandatory economic restrictions. In particular, the United States denied Iran arms – a serious loss, as the prerevolutionary regime relied almost entirely on US weapons systems and was engaged in a life-or-death struggle with the Iraqi regime from 1980 to 1988. In 1987, the United States stopped imports from Iran because of terrorism. This pressure did not end with the end of the Cold War. In 1995 President Clinton prohibited investment in Iran's oil industry.[98]

---

[95] The number fell over time to fifty-two, and they were released on January 20, 1981.

[96] O'Sullivan, *Shrewd Sanctions*, pp. 48–49. The European sanctions, however, had several loopholes that made them far stronger on paper than in reality. Although they banned new contracts with the Islamic republic, they allowed existing contracts to be "expanded," in essence allowing new sales. The rather weak nature of these sanctions contributed to the Carter administration's decision to opt for a rescue mission, as they believed international support would not be forthcoming.

[97] Ibid., pp. 47–49.   [98] Ibid., pp. 49–51.

The United States also opposed an oil pipeline that would cross Iranian territory and blocked international bank loans.

The United States also went beyond direct sanctions on Iran, and used economic punishment against other countries that assisted or invested in Iran. In 1996, the Anti-Terrorism and Effective Death Penalty Act outlawed any financial relations with Iran and also prohibited assistance to countries that provided military aid to Iran. Later in the year, Congress passed the Iran and Libya Sanctions Act (ILSA), which imposed penalties on foreign companies that invested more than $20 million in Iran's oil industry.[99]

Even as US pressure increased in the mid-1990s, several European states tried to foster moderation in Iran through the so-called "critical dialogue." European states, even though they had suffered from Iranian terrorism more recently than had the United States, did not see Iran as a major threat. Moreover, some European leaders believed that dialogue would reduce Iran's hostility.[100]

Even though the Europeans preferred dialogue, Iran risked multilateral sanctions because of its continued use of terrorism in the early and mid-1990s. The killing of dissidents in Europe and the religious decree calling for the murder of British author Salman Rushdie both strained relations with European capitals. US diplomatic pressure on Europe to act against Iran further increased the pressure. The Khobar Towers bombing also increased the risk of a strong US response and gave Washington additional leverage to use with its allies when it pressed them on terrorism.

Over time, however, the cumulative effect of sanctions and isolation – and, more importantly, the risk that additional attacks would lead to increased pressure – led Iran to reduce its direct involvement in terrorism.[101] Fearing that this growing pressure would jeopardize his government's economic program and isolate his regime, Rafsanjani drew back. He ended the assassination of dissidents in Europe and mended fences with the Gulf monarchies. Rafsanjani and other Iranian leaders proved particularly sensitive to the risk of a joint US–European front.[102]

---

[99] Iran and Libya Sanctions Act.   [100] O'Sullivan, *Shrewd Sanctions*, p. 90.
[101] Sick, "Iran: Confronting Terrorism," p. 93.
[102] This concern continues to this day. Gasiorowski, "Iran," 136.

The intense US pressure eased in the late 1990s, as the United States hoped that the new, reformist government of President Khatami, elected in 1997, would lead to a rapprochement with Iran. In 1997, the Clinton administration removed Iran from the list of states involved in narcotics trafficking and placed the Mujahedin-e Khalq, a murderous terrorist group that had enjoyed some sympathy in Washington because it was opposed to the clerical regime, on the terrorism list. In 1998, the Clinton administration issued a waiver to ILSA for the French oil company, Total, to invest in Iran's oil industry. Secretary Albright also gave a speech that welcomed Khatami's election and called for an improved relationship.[103] One year later, permission was given to export food and medicine to Iran. In 2000, the Secretary of State lifted restrictions on the import of Iranian carpets, caviar, and pistachios.[104] For the most part, these gestures had little impact on Iran's economy but were meant to symbolize US openness to a rapprochement.

Though unsuccessful in stopping terrorism, the range of US sanctions did hurt Iran considerably. Financial pressure, in particular Washington's successful efforts to block IMF and World Bank funding to Iran, made Iran's response to its debt crisis more wrenching. Until the 1998 waiver for Total, ILSA also discouraged foreign investment, which along with other sanctions delayed the development of Iran's dilapidated oil infrastructure. Meghan O'Sullivan, however, contends that sanctions are only a small part of the explanation for Iran's economic morass. She notes that the plunge in the price of oil, the war with Iraq, and political mismanagement would have led to a crisis in any event.[105]

Although the economic impact on Iran was real, it did not affect the political orientation of the regime, particularly with regard to terrorism. Iran did shift its terrorist activity away from Europe and the Gulf and toward Israel, but this shift did not advance, and arguably set back, overall US objectives. Moreover, the sanctions increased Iran's hostility toward the United States, "proving" that Washington sought to crush the Islamic revolution.[106]

Iran was able to resist sanctions for several reasons. Most important, the costs were manageable, as Iran also offset much of the potential

---

[103] Albright, *Madame Secretary*, p. 320.
[104] O'Sullivan, *Shrewd Sanctions*, pp. 50–57.   [105] Ibid., pp. 61, 67–72.
[106] Ibid., p. 86.

damage. Although the United States was a major market for Iranian products, Tehran diversified its trade partners and worked through third countries to reach the United States. Moreover, Iran's major export – oil – is in essence a global commodity, and the cutoff of one market to one supplier has no significant impact on a country's ability to gain the maximum price for its exports.

Because Iran's regime depended heavily on Islamic radicalism and Persian nationalism, both of which opposed any perceived kowtowing to Washington, the political costs of complying with US pressure were considerable. Iranian leaders risked being branded as puppets of the United States if they gave in to US pressure, a particularly heavy charge as the regime came to power in part on a wave of anti-Americanism.

The cost to the United States was also considerable. Sanctions, of course, meant that US companies lost trade and investment opportunities. Indirect sanctions proved particularly costly. ILSA led to vociferous protests from European and other governments.[107]

FAILED ISRAELI ATTEMPTS TO STOP HIZBALLAH

While the United States pressed Tehran directly, Israel went after its proxy. Between 1983 and 2000, Israeli forces conducted a range of military operations to stop Hizballah activity in southern Lebanon. Israel regularly ambushed guerrillas, raided their training camps, and engaged in air strikes. For many years, these operations enjoyed considerable success on a tactical level, leading to casualty ratios of ten to one or often higher in Israel's favor. In the 1980s, Hizballah took many losses when attacking the Israelis, and Israeli reprisals angered many local Shiites, leading Hizballah to curtail, but not end, its operations.[108]

In 1991, however, Hizballah restructured its command, giving its guerrilla forces more local autonomy and reducing the size of the movement so that it could be more professional and less vulnerable to Israeli attacks and intelligence penetrations. The fighters also increasingly specialized and improved their security and logistics capabilities. The movement learned how to make better use of Lebanon's broken terrain, how to plan sophisticated roadside explosives, and how to coordinate small units against Israeli forces, increasing the number of casualties it inflicted. Hizballah also attacked Israeli positions with heavier and more sophisticated

---

[107] Ibid., p. 55.   [108] Jaber, *Hezbollah*, pp. 29–31.

weapons.[109] As a result of these changes, Hizballah became a formidable guerrilla force that increasingly began to exact a cost on the Israelis.

By 1993, Hizballah's improved military effectiveness was taking its toll, and one strike in that year led to the deaths of seven Israeli soldiers – a political disaster for the government. For seven days in July 1993, Israel conducted Operation Accountability, which involved numerous air and artillery strikes on Hizballah's positions in Lebanon. The operation was intended to destroy Hizballah facilities in southern Lebanon and put pressure on the government. Perhaps 120 Lebanese civilians died in the operation, and Hizballah's retaliation with Katyusha rocket attacks on Israeli settlements killed two Israeli civilians. The operation displaced over 300,000 Lebanese and Palestinians.[110]

Part of the operation was designed to undermine Hizballah's popular support. Israel targeted villages in Hizballah areas of operations, even though many civilians remained. Israel hoped that the local Lebanese population would turn against Hizballah if Israel destroyed water, electricity, schools, and other parts of the infrastructure.[111] Israeli officials also hoped that the refugee flows would force the government of Lebanon to act. Prime Minister Yitzhak Rabin noted, "The goal of the operation is to get the southern Lebanese population to move northward, hoping that this will tell the Lebanese Government something about the refugees who may get as far north as Beirut."[112]

In April 1996, Israel launched Operation Grapes of Wrath, which lasted sixteen days. This operation was similar to Operation Accountability, as it again tried to put pressure on Hizballah and the Lebanese government by creating refugee flows and destroying Lebanon's infrastructure. This operation involved 600 air raids and massive artillery barrages. Again, Hizballah responded by firing hundreds of Katyusha rockets into Israel. Human Rights Watch reports that 154 Lebanese civilians died in the operation.

Again, Israel targeted Lebanese civilians in villages in the Hizballah theater of operations after warning them that a failure to flee would be

---

[109] Ibid., pp. 37–42; Eshel, "Counterguerrilla Warfare in South Lebanon," pp. 40–45.

[110] See Human Rights Watch, *Civilian Pawns*, pp. 8–16 for an overview of problems during Operation Accountability.

[111] Ibid., p. 12.   [112] As quoted in ibid., p. 10, n. 16.

considered proof that they were tied to Hizballah. Israel also targeted hospitals linked to Hizballah. In its public statements and those of the South Lebanese Army, Israel emphasized that it would respond to Hizballah rocket attacks by striking at Lebanese villages and emphasized that responsibility for this lay with the Lebanese government.

Israel also targeted Lebanon's infrastructure, such as Beirut's electricity supply. As then Deputy Defense Minister Ori Orr noted, "The Lebanese government can do more. It must understand that Lebanon's gross domestic product will not grow." Similarly, Uri Lubrani, who coordinated Israel's activities in Lebanon, noted, "We have said that we are going to hit Lebanese government infrastructure just to drive the point home ... They should be responsible."[113]

Even after these large-scale operations ended, military pressure has remained an important part of Israel's strategy for countering Hizballah. The threat of additional military strikes was always implicit. Israel also uses military overflights in an attempt to intimidate the Lebanese government.[114]

Despite the damage inflicted, these attempts at coercion failed, and even backfired, for several reasons. The attacks outraged many Lebanese, and they bolstered the prestige of Hizballah. Attacks on Hizballah's humanitarian infrastructure, for example, were viewed as illegitimate, even though Hizballah's humanitarian institutions contribute to the movement's overall resistance activities. As a result, much of the population rallied behind Hizballah, including many Lebanese Christians. Hizballah exploited this anger, distributing food and medicine to the civilian victims and otherwise portraying itself as a humanitarian organization.[115] Hizballah's sponsors like Iran reportedly increased financial assistance to the movement after the operations.[116]

---

[113] Orr is quoted in Human Rights Watch, "Israel/Lebanon: 'Operation Grapes of Wrath,'" p. 15 and Lubrani is quoted on p. 17. See also pp. 5–6 and 14–15 for an overview of Israeli objectives.

[114] Hizballah has faced pressure to respond to these overflights, as they challenge Hizballah's self-proclaimed role as the defender of Lebanon. Blanford, "Diplomats Say Israel Set to Continue Overflights Over Lebanon."

[115] Jones, "Israeli Counter-Insurgency Strategy and War in South Lebanon," p. 96; Jaber, *Hezbollah*, p. 199; Gambill, "The Balance of Terror," p. 63.

[116] Eisenstadt, *Iranian Military Power*, p. 74.

Second, the attacks did little to dent Hizballah's rather rudimentary military infrastructure. Hizballah fighters easily hid among the local population. Israel lacked the detailed intelligence necessary to separate the guerrillas from the rest of the population. The weapons Israel used – air strikes and artillery – are of little use for such fine-grained tasks. Perhaps only thirteen Hizballah fighters died in Operation Grapes of Wrath, and Israel failed to capture any Katyusha rockets.[117]

Third, the attacks increased international support for Hizballah because of the civilian death toll. On April 18, 1996 Israel shelled the United Nations (UN) base at Qana, killing over 100 men, women, and children who had sheltered in the UN facility. Despite Israeli claims that Hizballah was using the civilians and the UN as a shield for its activities, the Israeli attacks were widely criticized as deliberately striking non-combatants.[118] Israel's mistakes bolstered Hizballah's claim that it was fighting a war of liberation, not engaging in terrorism.

Most importantly, the Lebanese government was an exceptionally difficult government to coerce. Lebanon has been a satrapy of Syria since 1990. Syria had deployed perhaps 30,000 troops in the country, and it dominated the political system. The Lebanese government's own forces are weak, poorly trained, and unable to rein in Hizballah. With Lebanon unable to act, only Syria could truly crack down on Hizballah. And Damascus was more than content to see Israel suffer politically even at the cost of the devastation of Lebanon.

LIMITED TENSION WITH SYRIA'S AND IRAN'S NEIGHBORS
Hizballah's position in Lebanon also led to friction with Syria, an important ally for the clerical regime and an important sponsor for Hizballah. Iran and Syria always had an uneasy alliance in Lebanon. As discussed in Chapter 5, Syria sought hegemony in Lebanon, not revolution. Damascus also had increasingly close ties to Amal, Hizballah's main rival, as well as at times to every militant group in Lebanon. Iran's attempts to mobilize Lebanon's Shi'a, press the war against Israel, and create an Islamic state at times threatened Syria's

---

[117] Jaber, *Hezbollah*, p. 178.
[118] For a review, see United Nations, "Report of the Secretary General's Military Advisor Concerning the Shelling of the UN Compound at Qana on 18 April 1996."

hegemonic position. Because Syria was Iran's only Arab ally in its war with Iraq – and because Syria had a dominant position in Lebanon and was a transit point for Iranian arms and personnel – Tehran at times bowed to Syria's wishes. Indeed, in 1987 Syrian troops killed twenty Hizballah militiamen in Beirut in order to exert their control.[119] Damascus also threatened to improve ties to Baghdad if Iran did not limit its activities. In addition, while Syria supported Hizballah's attacks on Israel, it sought to control them in order to ensure that any escalation occurred on Damascus's schedule.

Placating Syria was vital for both Hizballah and Iran. Syria controlled Iran's access to Lebanon, regulating it as necessary if a confrontation occurred. Syria also exercised tremendous indirect influence over Lebanon through its various Lebanese proxies in the 1980s, and in the 1990s had tens of thousands of troops and intelligence personnel in the country. Neither Hizballah nor Iran could operate freely without at least tacit Syrian approval.[120]

Iran's support for terrorism also led neighboring states to band together against it. After Iran supported Shi'a radicals who attempted to overthrow the Al Khalifa government in Bahrain, Manama signed a security cooperation agreement with the United States. Saudi Arabia also increased its military cooperation with the United States. In addition, in 1981 the Gulf States banded together, forming the Gulf Cooperation Council (GCC) and increasing the unity of their policies *vis-à-vis* Iran. A primary purpose of the GCC was to guard against destabilization from Tehran. Similarly, Turkey began working closely on cooperation with Israel, in part because both shared a threat from Iranian-backed subversion.[121]

---

[119] Jaber, *Hezbollah*, p. 32.

[120] Ibid., p. 35; Ehteshami, *After Khomeini*, p. 134; Ranstorp, *Hizb 'allah in Lebanon*, pp. 110–115.

[121] On the GCC formation and Iran, see Hiro, *Iran under the Ayatollahs*, pp. 338–340. Israel and Turkey shared numerous other goals in their military cooperation, many of which were more important than concern over Iranian-backed terrorism. These included a mutual enmity toward Syria (and Syrian-backed radicalism), shared security ties to the United States, and Israel's expertise in helping Turkey upgrade its military forces.

Final words

Supporting Hizballah's use of terrorism served several of Iran's objectives. Terrorist attacks and hostage-taking humiliated the United States, forcing it out of Lebanon and leading Washington to make clandestine deals that provided Iran with spare parts for US weapons systems. Similarly, Hizballah gave Iran a weapon against Israel and a means of pressing backers of its archenemy, Iraq.

Terrorism also offered Iran a degree of deniability. By working through proxies, Iran was able to achieve its own interests of intimidation against states supporting Iraq without paying the consequences that more direct involvement might entail. The United States believed Iran was culpable for the bombing of Khobar Towers, for example, but did not retaliate. Indeed, Middle East expert Michael Eisenstadt argues that Iran's primary reason for supporting terrorism is that it advances Iran's agenda without provoking military retaliation.[122]

Terrorism, however, imposed considerable costs that greatly hurt Iran's interests. Iran suffered diplomatically, as the US sought to make it a global pariah. This isolation hurt Tehran directly, both economically, and in its long and bitter war against Iraq. Not only did the United States press Iran directly, but Iran's neighbors banded together against it as well. Moreover, even in Lebanon Iran met with at most limited success. The Lebanese Hizballah has moved away from its most ambitious objectives even though in essence it remains a revolutionary movement.

Iran's relationship with Hizballah demonstrates both the impressive gains a state can make by sponsoring a terrorist group and the considerable costs it may pay. Hizballah served Tehran and served it well. The movement retained a degree of independence from Tehran, however. More important from Iran's point of view, support for Hizballah and other terrorist groups hurt Iran's efforts to end its isolation and furthered the clerical regime's image as aggressive and dangerous.

---

[122] Eisenstadt, *Iranian Military Power*, p. 68.

5

Syria and Palestinian radical groups

Syria has long been described as one of the world's most active state sponsors of terrorism and, indeed, support for radical groups has long been an integral part of Syrian foreign policy. However, this support is nuanced and complex, reflecting Damascus's desire to both exploit terrorist groups and limit them. Damascus has bolstered the Palestinian cause and constrained it, encouraged radicals in Lebanon and crushed them, and otherwise demonstrated considerable care and variance in how it uses terrorist groups. In many ways, Syria represents an "antagonistic" sponsor of terrorism, helping many particular groups become stronger but also working to control them and subordinate their overall cause to Syrian domestic and geopolitical goals.

Such a cloudy picture is striking, as the list of Syrian links to terrorist organizations is long. Over the years, Damascus has assisted a range of secular left-wing Palestinian groups, such as Fatah, the Democratic Front for the Liberation of Palestine, the Abu Musa group, al-Saiqa, the Abu Nidal Organization (ANO), Popular Front for the Liberation of Palestine (PFLP), the Popular Front for the Liberation of Palestine–General Command (PFLP-GC), and various defectors from Fatah. Syria also has provided sanctuary and other forms of assistance to Palestinian Islamist groups such as the Palestine Islamic Jihad (PIJ) and HAMAS. In addition to supporting Palestinian groups active against Israel, Damascus gave sanctuary to the Kurdistan Workers' Party (PKK), which sought a Kurdistan independent from Turkey, until 1998. In the 1980s, Syria also provided facilities and allowed training of the Japanese

Red Army Faction (JRA), the Armenian Secret Army for the Liberation of Armenia (ASALA), and the Pakistani al Zulfikar.[1] Syria allows Iran to arm and train Hizballah as both a terrorist group and a guerrilla movement, and gives Hizballah sanctuary in Lebanon, which Syria dominates, for its guerrilla campaign. Hizballah, in addition to attacking Israel directly, also trains and supports several Palestinian groups, as discussed in Chapter 4.[2]

The list of Syria's enemies is also long. Israeli targets received considerable attention, and in the 1970s and 1980s American targets were also prominent. But Syria also used terrorism to attack its domestic opponents, to intimidate moderate Arab states such as Jordan, to weaken regional rivals like Iraq, and to exert control over the Palestinian cause by undermining or killing Palestinian leaders who refused to knuckle under to Damascus.

Syria has supported these various groups for a variety of reasons. Many of the initial reasons for Syria's involvement with radical groups were ideological. The various Arab nationalist regimes that came to power in the 1960s saw themselves as revolutionaries, and forming alliances with like-minded Palestinians was a natural step. Moreover, almost every major Arab government at this time backed violent domestic rivals of regimes it opposed. If ideology was not enough, terrorist groups offered Damascus additional leverage in its struggle against Israel, Turkey, and other foes – leverage that it lacks due to the inferiority of its conventional military forces. In recent years, much of Syria's use of terrorism has been to improve its strategic position *vis-à-vis* Israel with regard to peace negotiations. This strategic explanation, however, is incomplete, particularly with regard to the various Palestinian groups. Syria has sought to control and direct the Palestinian cause, even at the price of the movement's overall political and operational effectiveness. The Palestinian cause is bound up in the regime's self-proclaimed role as

---

[1] US House of Representatives, "Statement by Philip Wilcox before the House Committee on International Relations"; Rubin, *The Transformation of Palestinian Politics*, p. 146; US Department of State, "Syrian Support for International Terrorism: 1983–1986," p. 2.

[2] The US government maintains that Syria currently has 20,000 troops deployed in Lebanon, a figure that has diminished since Syria consolidated its control in 1991 but nevertheless is quite high. US Department of State, "Background Note: Syria," electronic version.

the champion of Arab steadfastness, an image that in turn is essential to its domestic legitimacy.

Because Syria is linked to radical groups for so many reasons, halting Syrian support has proven difficult. Israel has repeatedly threatened a strong military response, and the United States has imposed numerous economic penalties. The United States also engaged Damascus, particularly with regard to the Middle East Peace Process. In response to this pressure, Damascus ended the use of its own operatives for clandestine attacks on civilians in 1986. In addition, it has often placed severe limits on its proxies. Nevertheless, Syria's leadership has not shut off the tap completely.

The effect on various groups is not uniform. Some groups at times have become stronger, but most have paid a heavy price. In particular, Syria often sought to weaken major groups like Fatah and placed limits on its activities.

This chapter reviews the history of Syrian support for terrorist groups, focusing primarily on the various Palestinian factions that Damascus has aided over the last three decades though by necessity it at times discusses Syrian involvement with other important groups.[3] It also provides a brief overview of the successful Turkish effort to end Damascus' support for the PKK, as it offers a valuable contrast to the less successful US and Israeli efforts.

Syria's relationship with Palestinian militants

Syria's relationship with the Palestinian cause was troubled from its inception. Damascus has long staunchly supported various Palestinian movements – and, for just as long, sought to control, limit, manipulate, and thwart them when they threatened the regime's security and political interests. This ambivalence has led Damascus to champion the Palestinian cause, to provide various violent movements with a massive array of support, and to crush elements of the movement, dealing bloody and decisive blows against it. Today, Syria remains an important supporter of many Palestinian rejectionist movements but does not control the cause as a whole.

Syria, like other neighbors of the Palestine Mandate, claimed part of the territory as its own. In the first Arab–Israeli war in 1947–49, Syria

---

[3] The Lebanese Hizballah as an organization and its ties to Iran are discussed in considerable detail in Chapter 4.

sent its own troops to help destroy the nascent Jewish state and provided headquarters, arms, volunteers, and supplies for the irregular Arab Army of Liberation – a move motivated both by opposition to Zionism and by a wish to thwart the ambitions of Jordan's King Abdallah. Hostility to Israel and support for the Palestinian cause grew dramatically after the Arab defeat.[4]

After the war with Israel, the Syrian leadership became embroiled in internal feuding and the constant recurrence of military coups. After a brief, failed, union with Egypt that lasted from 1958 to 1961, Syrian elites within Arab nationalist circles engaged in a constant competition for power. In a game of rhetorical one-upmanship, all the rival movements – Baathists, Nasserists, communists, and factions within these groups – competed to demonstrate their hostility toward Israel and their support for Arab nationalism. Even after the Baath took power in 1963, this competition continued as various movements sought to regain their dominance and as factions within the Baath competed for power.

Arab nationalism, the Palestinian cause, and the Baath regime became inexorably intertwined. Baathism declared its mission to be unifying Arab states, a goal that idealistic Syrian leaders honored in the 1958 union with Egypt but quickly shed in practice when the union proved a pretext for Egyptian dominance. When this focus of pan-Arabism failed, Syria focused its unification energies on the Palestinian struggle. Moreover, Baathism saw itself as a revolutionary movement. As such, it naturally sought out partners that shared its agenda. Palestinian groups with a leftist, pan-Arab agenda were natural partners.

As Syrian leaders competed to demonstrate their commitment to the Palestinian cause, Arab leaders created the Palestine Liberation Organization (PLO). Arab regimes, particularly Nasser's Egypt, moved to create the PLO in 1963 to deflect and control Palestinian nationalism. In particular, Nasser and other Arab leaders sought to ensure that the Palestinian cause did not drag Egypt into war with Israel that would otherwise serve the ends of other Arab states, not the Palestinian people.[5]

---

[4] Landis, "Syria and the Palestine War." See also Morris, *Israel's Border Wars 1949–1956*, for a review of the tensions that led to the 1956 war. Morris argues that Syria in general exercised tight control over Palestinian infiltrators (pp. 96–98).
[5] Seale, *Asad*, p. 121.

The PLO's leadership was chosen for its loyalty to Nasser and other Arab leaders, not to the Palestinian people. The movement was in essence a talk shop, making no independent contributions to Palestinian independence.

For the various Syrian leaders, support for aggression against Israel was a way to rally popular support around the regime. This support helped legitimate regimes that took power in a *coup d'état* and thus lacked popular legitimacy. In addition, it served as a diversion from Syria's myriad economic and other domestic woes.

It is important to recognize that at this time almost every Arab leader had transnational claims and believed he could legitimately interfere in the internal affairs of another Arab country. Syria was not alone in working with Palestinians or other radical groups. Nasser, King Hussein of Jordan, and other leaders regularly meddled in Syrian politics, and support for various revolutionary movements, many of which used terrorism, was simply one tool of many.

Not surprisingly, many Palestinian nationalists rejected their subordination to Arab regimes and pushed for direct action against Israel. In 1964, George Habash founded the Popular Front for the Liberation of Palestine, and in 1965, Yasir Arafat's Fatah became active.[6] These and other groups began to engage in a guerrilla struggle against Israel. Syria's radical leaders, in contrast to the leaders of Jordan and Lebanon, supported these groups for ideological reasons, to demonstrate their revolutionary credentials at home, and because they opposed Egypt's dominance of the PLO.

Damascus' support for Palestinian guerrillas played a major role in causing the 1967 war. Damascus was the only Arab state actively supporting Fatah's attacks before the war.[7] Syrian leaders sought to "kindle the spark" in their words, promoting dozens of Palestinian cross-border attacks as a means of sparking a broader war.[8] Syria also used Palestinian guerrillas to respond to Israeli attacks in the prelude to the 1967 war. Syria sponsored numerous Palestinian guerrilla attacks by Fatah and

---

[6] Fatah was founded in 1959. Other groups active before 1967 were Ahmed Jibril's Palestine Liberation Front and Nayif Hawatmeh's Vengeance Youth. Tessler, *A History of the Israeli-Palestinian Conflict*, p. 376. See also Central Intelligence Agency, *Palestinian Organizations*.

[7] Tessler, *A History of the Israeli-Palestinian Conflict*, p. 377.

[8] Ma'oz, *Syria and Israel*, pp. 84 and 89.

other groups, characterizing its support with rhetoric such as "Our army and our people will give our backing to every Arab fighter acting for the return of Palestine."[9]

Syrian leaders failed to recognize that they were playing with fire, as Israel proved willing to escalate in response to the guerrilla attacks.[10] These attacks led to Israeli responses, which in turn led to quiet Egyptian efforts to persuade Damascus not to support Fatah attacks. Syria, however, refused to crack down – a decision that legitimated an Israeli attack in the eyes of the Israeli public and the US government. Ironically, Syrian leaders saw their own actions as restrained. Damascus believed that support for the guerrillas enabled it to avoid a humiliating passivity while also avoiding a war that it would lose.[11] Israel, however, saw Syria as preparing for a full-scale guerrilla war and sought to stop cross-border attacks.[12]

Syrian actions helped foster a cycle of hostility that escalated into war. Because the Palestinian cause was felt keenly in many Arab countries, the actions of Syria affected other regimes. The Egyptian-backed PLO, in order to counter the competition from Syrian-backed radicals and others demanding action, stepped up its rhetoric against Israel – a decision that in turn inflamed Arab popular opinion and moved it in support of war. Each step moved all parties closer to the brink.

THE 1967 TRANSFORMATION

The 1967 war indirectly paved a path for Hafez al-Asad to assume power, which he did formally in 1970. The disastrous Arab performance in the war discredited the leadership of several Arab countries. It also gave pragmatists in the Baath Party, like Asad, who favored cooperation with other, non-revolutionary Arab states against Israel, stronger arguments than the ideologues who sought social change at home and abroad, even if it meant temporary weakness against Israel.[13] For Asad, the Palestinians had proven a particular concern. Because the cause was a symbol of Arab nationalism (and thus tied to the regime's legitimacy), Asad feared their actions could again spiral out of control.

---

[9] Oren, *Six Days of War*, p. 45.   [10] Seale, *Asad*, pp. 124–125 and 132.
[11] Oren, *Six Days of War*, pp. 46–49.
[12] Tessler, *A History of the Israeli-Palestinian Conflict*, pp. 378–385.
[13] Van Dam, *The Struggle for Power in Syria*, p. 63.

In addition, anti-Asad radicals tried to use al-Saiqa, a Palestinian commando group sponsored by the Syrian Baath party, to counter the Syrian military that Asad dominated.[14]

The 1967 war also transformed the Palestinian movement. Before the 1967 war, the PLO was at best a minor player in Arab politics and contributed little to the struggle against Israel.[15] However, the Arab regimes' calls for the Palestinians to trust Arab states to restore their homes rang hollow after the overwhelming Israeli victory. With the 1967 defeat, the traditional leadership of the PLO and their call for reliance on Arab states became discredited, and a new generation led by Yasir Arafat assumed control of the movement, with his Fatah organization as the chief component.[16] The cross-border attacks of a few Palestinian guerrillas, however limited and unsuccessful in tactical terms, came to be seen as a symbol of continued Arab resistance. In February 1969, Arafat assumed control over the PLO.

The PLO under Arafat became an umbrella organization that came to include numerous component groups, the most important and largest of which is Yasir Arafat's Fatah. All the groups share a commitment to a Palestinian state, but they often disagree – at times violently – with one another on how to achieve this state and what it will look like in the end. Some groups, such as the PFLP, have left and rejoined the PLO. Other important groups, like the PFLP-GC, PIJ, and HAMAS, are not part of the PLO. These movements rejected Arafat's leadership, criticizing him for his willingness to cooperate with various conservative Arab states and (as time went on) his acceptance of Israel's right to exist.[17] HAMAS and PIJ, of course, also rejected Arafat's secular view of the Palestinian cause.

Terrorism, for the Palestinians, was used in conjunction with guerrilla war, and at times as an alternative. Guerrilla efforts largely failed after the 1967 war, and Israel successfully ousted Palestinian militants from the West Bank and Gaza strip. Similarly, the ousting of the PLO from Jordan in 1970 led the movement to embrace terrorism against Jordan in

---

[14] Hinnebusch, *Syria*, pp. 58–60; Seale, *Asad*, pp. 156–157.
[15] Tessler, *A History of the Israeli-Palestinian Conflict*, p. 375.
[16] Kimmerling and Migdal, *Palestinians*, pp. 222–223.
[17] Central Intelligence Agency, *Palestinian Organizations*.

revenge and because it had few other options given its weak capabilities as a guerrilla movement.[18]

For the Palestinians, the question of how much to ally with, and rely on, Arab regimes was highly contentious. Arafat's Fatah and other core Palestinian organizations initially championed a doctrine of social revolution as well as opposition to Israel. Before 1967, this led Fatah to reject the leadership of the PLO because it was subordinate to Arab regimes. When Arafat took over the PLO, however, he began to work with various Arab governments. Yet the nature and extent of ties to foreign governments often split the nationalist movement. Splinters called for more aggressive terrorist and guerrilla operations, a refusal to compromise on the return of all of historic Palestine, and a commitment to social revolution. Particularly after the early 1970s, they were often behind the more spectacular terrorist attacks on Israel or other targets.[19]

For both the Syrian leadership and the Palestinians, the struggle in Jordan that culminated in "Black September" in 1970 was a defining moment. Syria backed various Palestinian groups that sought to topple the Jordanian monarchy. Syrian leaders were motivated as much by their hostility to King Hussein as by their love for the Palestinians. When the Jordanian military appeared to triumph, Damascus intervened with its own forces. This intervention, however, was stillborn as Israeli threats to intervene, combined with disagreements among the Syrian leadership, led Syria to pull back its forces. The Palestinians were soundly defeated and forced to relocate to Lebanon. Hundreds of thousands of Palestinians entered Lebanon, bringing with them their arms and their political loyalties.

A TROUBLED PARTNERSHIP

Under Hafez al-Asad, Syria and the Palestinian cause had an ambivalent relationship. As Patrick Seale contends, "in theory he [Asad] was with it heart and soul, in practice it was a constant source of trouble."[20] Asad held a genuine ideological commitment to the Palestinian cause, but he also sought to continue to use the PLO and other Palestinian factions as a weapon against Israel. He sought to regain the Golan Heights, which was lost in the 1967 war, and more generally to demonstrate Syria's

---

[18] Tessler, *A History of the Israeli-Palestinian Conflict*, p. 463.
[19] Kimmerling and Migdal, *Palestinians*, pp. 224–225.   [20] Seale, *Asad*, p. 282.

continued opposition to Israel. Given Syria's conventional military inferiority, Asad had few other strategic levers against Israel.

In addition to using Palestinians against Israel, Syria also used Palestinian factions as part of its rivalry with its Arab neighbors.[21] Syria, of course, supported the Palestinians in their struggle against King Hussein in 1970. As the Syria–Jordan rivalry continued in the 1980s, Hafez al-Asad employed the Abu Nidal Organization from 1983 to 1985 to intimidate Jordan's King Hussein by attacking Jordanian officials in Europe. Jordan and the PLO were working together to negotiate with Israel, excluding Damascus from the process – an attempt that reached its zenith in February 1985. The Syrian intimidation campaign contributed to Jordan's decision to back away from initial efforts to work with Israel and the PLO to cut a deal on the West Bank.[22] These attacks on Jordan and on Israel sent a strong message that Israel and other concerned powers had to take Damascus' concerns into account if the region were ever to be stable.

Despite its utility in the struggle against Israel and for regional leadership, the Palestinian cause was a two-edged sword. As Syria learned, Palestinian guerrilla attacks could escalate into an all-out war that Syria would lose. In addition, enthusiasm for the Palestinian struggle could inflame the passions of the Arab world, leading to pressure on Arab regimes to act and even to revolts against the existing leaders. Given that these options would be disastrous for Syria, it had to control as well as to exploit the Palestinian cause. Control was particularly important after Asad consolidated power and Syria gave an impressive showing in the 1973 war with Israel. At this point, Syria became far more of a status quo power. In part, Asad wanted the backing of the oil-rich Arab Gulf states for his economic reform attempts.[23] As a result, Syria both worked with the PLO at times and actively backed many of its rivals.

The Syrian regime also depended heavily on the Palestinian cause for legitimacy.[24] Under Hafez al-Asad, the minority Alawis, a sect of Islam

---

[21] Ma'oz, *Syria and Israel*, p. 162.

[22] Seale, *Asad*, pp. 464–466; Quandt, *Peace Process*, pp. 354–356.; US Department of State, "Syrian Support for International Terrorism: 1983–1986," p. 2.

[23] Rabinovich, *The War for Lebanon*, p. 51.

[24] For a review of how the regime tries to control and manipulate various political symbols and its impact on political discourse, see Wedeen, *Ambiguities of Domination*.

representing approximately 11 percent of Syria's population, came to dominate the country.[25] The Alawis are considered to be heretics by many devout Sunni Muslims (who make up over half of Syria's population), weakening their legitimacy.[26] When the Syrian Muslim Brotherhood challenged the government from 1976 until 1982, it was opposing what it declared to be an apostate "Alawi regime."[27] Although the regime brutally crushed the uprising, its sectarian nature remains a problem. As Raymond Hinnebusch notes, "Resentment of Alawi dominance remains the main source of the regime's legitimacy deficit."[28]

This legitimacy deficit is accentuated by the realpolitik of the Baath regime, which has long sought – successfully – to play a major regional role.[29] In 1976, Syria backed right-wing Christian groups in Lebanon against the Palestinians and leftist rivals, fearing that a Christian defeat would provoke either anarchy or a radical regime that would drag Syria into a disastrous conflict with Israel, which would then intervene to rescue the Christians. This support, however, damaged Syria's reputation among Arab nationalists, increasing sympathy for regime critics such as the Muslim Brotherhood.[30]

To counter the perception that it is an illegitimate minority regime, the leadership played up Arab unity, which runs across confessional lines. To this end, it sought to portray itself as the most steadfast of the Arab states in the struggle against Israel. Part and parcel of this image was

---

[25] Hinnebusch, *Syria*, p. 69. The reasons for Alawi dominance are complex. Like other minority groups, the Alawis were favored by the French colonial government. They were particularly prevalent in the military and the Baath party. This position enabled them to triumph over rival communities, such as the Druze and Arab Christians, which also were favored by the French colonial regime. Van Dam, *The Struggle for Power in Syria*, pp. 4, 7–8, 17, 26–27.

[26] Zisser, "Appearance and Reality." Even within the Alawis, Asad relied heavily on his Qalbiyya tribe for key positions.

[27] Hinnebusch, *Syria*, p. 70; International Crisis Group, "*Syria under Bashar (II),*" p. 18. Hinnebusch points out, however, that there were many Sunnis among the elite and that Alawis had multiple identities that went beyond their religious sect (pp. 70–72). For a comprehensive review, see Van Dam, *The Struggle for Power in Syria*, pp. 89–117.

[28] Hinnebusch, *Syria*, p. 72.   [29] For a review, see Zisser, *Assad's Legacy*.

[30] Hinnebusch, *Syria*, pp. 97 and 155–156; Hiro, *Lebanon*, p. 202; Rabinovich, *The War for Lebanon*, pp. 48–54.

championing the rights of the Palestinians. Such support was particularly important, as the Muslim Brotherhood and other critics also claimed to be staunch supporters of the Palestinian cause.[31]

For Syrian leaders the Palestinian cause became more important because of its implications for Syrian politics and security than because of its inherent legitimacy. As Hinnebusch notes, "Syrian leaders began to claim that the Arab national interest coincided with Syria's particular military-security needs."[32] This, in turn, gave them rights to other Arab states' oil wealth and the right to control the Palestinian cause.

From the PLO's point of view, Syria's attempts to dominate the movement and control its actions were a grave threat. The Palestinians were concerned about Damascus' desire to dominate Lebanon, the PLO's main base from 1970 until 1982, and its opposition to the PLO's claim to be "the sole legitimate representative of the Palestinian people."[33] Palestinian leaders tried to resist Syrian control, which in turn led to violent clashes. Most devastatingly, Syria intervened militarily against the Palestinians in Lebanon in 1976, using its military forces to prevent the victory of Palestinians and their allies over Christian forces in the civil war.

Syria's relationship with the PLO leader Arafat mirrored this overall sense of bitterness and ambivalence. As early as 1966, Syria jailed Arafat after he began to act too independently.[34] Syria also consistently supported Arafat's rivals as a counter to his influence. In 1970, for example, Syria backed the Popular Democratic Front for the Liberation of Palestine (PDFLP), al-Saiqa, and the PFLP-GC. Thus Asad supported literally thousands of armed Palestinians who did not support Arafat.[35] When the Arafat–Asad dispute was in high gear in the mid-1980s, Syria supported the umbrella National Alliance as an alternative to the PLO

---

[31] Cooptation was also central to Asad's rule. Asad also granted senior positions to the Sunnis, allowing them – on paper – to play a leading role. He also expanded parliament and other institutions to represent various social actors not represented in Baath party ranks. As part of this cooptation, Asad also sought to ensure that leading Sunni causes, such as Arab nationalism, were championed by his regime. Perthes, *Syria under Bashar al-Asad*, p. 15; Zisser, "Appearance and Reality."

[32] Hinnebusch, *Syria*, p. 140.

[33] Rabinovich, *The War for Lebanon*, pp. 52 and 86; Hiro, *Lebanon*, p. 37.

[34] Seale, *Asad*, p. 125.

[35] Tessler, *A History of the Israeli-Palestinian Conflict*, pp. 430–431.

confederation, attracting such key components as the PFLP.[36] Syria also encouraged Abu Musa, a Fatah leader, to rebel against Arafat in May 1983. This rebellion failed to topple Arafat, but it did force Fatah to abandon Lebanon as its main operating base and leadership sanctuary – more so, in fact, than Israel's 1982 invasion.[37] Dennis Ross, reflecting on his role as the senior US negotiator with Asad in the 1990s, noted: "He passionately disliked Arafat ... He spoke with pride about having put Arafat in jail and was wistful in explaining that he came under pressure to release him and had done so."[38] Strategic and political necessity, however, at times compelled Arafat and Asad to work together. Despite bitter armed clashes in Lebanon in 1976, the two started to coordinate their positions closely after Egypt began to negotiate a separate peace with Israel.[39]

Syria was willing to crack down on the Palestinians even at the risk of jeopardizing relations with Moscow. The Soviet Union had ties to various leftist groups in Lebanon and the Palestinian militants living there. Syria's decision to attack these groups led Moscow to criticize Asad, to postpone arms deliveries (at a time when Syria was still weak after losses in the 1973 war with Israel) and otherwise distance itself (though not cut ties) from Damascus.[40] Rivals such as Iraq were quick to seize on the intervention to criticize Asad and were joined by the leaders of Libya and Algeria.[41]

Until 1986, Syria was also quite active in using its own agents for operations often labeled as terrorism. Syrian agents attacked Syrian dissidents, Palestinians who sided with Yasir Arafat, Iraqi officials, and moderate Arab state officials as well as Israeli and Jewish targets.[42]

---

[36] Central Intelligence Agency, *Palestinian Organizations*.

[37] Van Dam, *The Struggle for Power in Syria*, p. 67; Kimmerling and Migdal, *Palestinians*, pp. 235–236; Mishal and Sela, *The Palestinian HAMAS*, p. 39; Seale, *Asad*, p. 411; Tessler, *A History of the Israeli-Palestinian Conflict*, pp. 633–636. In Lebanon in the 1980s, Syria encouraged the Amal movement to subjugate the Palestinian refugee camps in order to prevent Fatah from returning. Agha, "The Syrian-Iranian Axis in Lebanon," p. 26.

[38] Ross, *The Missing Peace*, p. 144.

[39] Rabinovich, *The War for Lebanon*, p. 102; Seale, *Asad*, p. 257.

[40] Seale, *Asad*, p. 287.   [41] Hiro, *Lebanon*, p. 41.

[42] See US Department of State. "Syrian Support for International Terrorism." As noted in Chapter 1, because these actions are not carried out by a non-state actor, but rather as part of a covert state campaign, I do not consider them "terrorism" but more akin to an act of war.

After 1986, Syria refrained from using its own operatives to mount clandestine attacks and, in general, tried to minimize its direct hand in any violence. Damascus began to rely more on terrorist groups such as ANO than on its own personnel for these attacks. It also continued to support various Palestinian terrorist groups as well as factions in Lebanon; in return for which these groups did Syria's bidding, but often left particular operational details up to the groups themselves to preserve deniability.

As his effort to distance Syria from direct involvement in terrorism-like activities after 1986 suggests, Hafez al-Asad learned over time how to modulate support for terrorism in response to outside pressure. Syria could achieve many of its aims by working through proxies and by using Lebanon as a base for the most overt activities, both of which increased Damascus's ability to deny responsibility.

SHAPING THE PEACE WITH ISRAEL

After the Cold War ended, Damascus continued to support a wide range of Palestinian groups that remain active against Israel. These links proved important as the PLO engaged in negotiations with Israel, paving the way for what at the time it was hoped would be a final settlement between Palestinians and Israelis – one that did not necessarily meet Syria's interests.

To disrupt this settlement and keep the Palestinian movement weak, Syria supported an array of anti-Israel movements that rejected the peace process. When the PLO leadership became the leaders of the Palestinian National Authority (PA) in 1994, and thus the heads of a *de facto* state, Syria tried to destroy any support in Lebanon for the PA among the exile community.[43] As Barry Rubin notes, Syria "claimed to champion the Palestinian cause but used that boast to justify criticizing and subverting the PA."[44]

Most importantly, Syria backed various rejectionist movements that opposed peace and the PA's authority. In 1991, after the Madrid peace conference that brought Israel, Palestinian leaders, and various Arab states together, HAMAS and other militant Palestinians (mostly secular and Marxist) established the Ten Front in Syria to oppose negotiations.[45]

---

[43] Rubin, *The Transformation of Palestinian Politics*, p. 152.
[44] Ibid., p. 151. [45] Mishal and Sela, *The Palestinian HAMAS*, p. 87.

The PFLP, the DFLP, PIJ, HAMAS, and Hizballah all conducted attacks on Israel, the latter three being particularly active before as well as after the second *intifada* broke out in September 2000.[46] Some of these groups used terrorism, while others, particularly Hizballah, concentrated primarily on guerrilla war.

Syrian leaders supported and strengthened these groups, though they seldom shared the specifics of their agendas. Syria, of course, rejected the Islamist groups' visions of proper governance. Even more important, Damascus was often seriously engaged in peace negotiations with Israel (with a heavy US role to boot), and thus used its backing of terrorism to extract concessions on Israel with regard to the particulars of the border or to ensure that Syria itself was not excluded from any settlement. Thus, ironically, Damascus viewed terrorism as vital to its peace negotiation strategy. However, having built its legitimacy on being the most stead-fast Arab regime, it was hard to back away from the more militant Palestinian groups. Domestic critics of Asad's regime were often quick to seize on any perceived softening toward Israel.[47]

Syria increased the violence of the second *intifada*, though Damascus did not precipitate it.[48] The Palestinian leadership Damascus backs has pressed Palestinians inside the West Bank and Gaza to be more militant. The various leaders of HAMAS and PIJ, for example, in August 2002 urged various Palestinian factions to reject a ceasefire with Israel.[49] Damascus' provision of a sanctuary and other more limited forms of support has also made the groups more resilient, enabling them to endure Israeli counterattacks.

The impact of the attacks by groups with ties to Syria was considerable, going far beyond the death toll they inflicted. The attacks demonstrated that the Palestinian Authority was not able to stop the violence completely, though its cooperation with Israel did reduce terrorism for many years.[50] This, in turn, fed Israeli suspicions of Arafat and made the Israeli public doubt that concessions would lead to peace.

---

[46] Levitt, "Prepared Statement of Matthew Levitt."
[47] Rabinovich, *Waging Peace*, pp. 135–136.
[48] For a review of the causes of the second uprising, see Pressman, "The Second Intifada."
[49] Levitt, "Prepared Statement of Matthew Levitt."
[50] For a review of the value of intelligence cooperation, particularly as facilitated by the United States, see Klovens, "The CIA Role in the Peace Process."

Syria exercises some control over the rejectionist groups it backs, though this is far from absolute. Syria has urged groups that it influenced not to attack the United States. In the bland words of the Philip Wilcox, the Special Coordinator for Counterterrorism in 1996, "Syria has had a restraining effect in that respect."[51]

FEW CHANGES UNDER BASHAR

Despite initial hopes that he would prove a reformer, after his father died in 2000, Bashar al-Asad has made at best cosmetic changes to open up Syria's political system or change its basic foreign policy orientation.[52] Like his father, Bashar al-Asad openly ties his regime to the Palestinian cause.[53] The State Department reports that Syria still provides political and material support to numerous Palestinian rejectionist movements and names HAMAS, the PIJ, the PFLP-GC, and the PFLP.[54] Syria claims these groups and other Palestinian movements are legitimate armed resistance groups, not terrorists.

If anything, Bashar appears to be in a weaker domestic position regarding support for rejectionist groups. His father steadily consolidated power, ruling for thirty years in the face of numerous domestic and foreign challenges. As such, he had a strong power base within his regime and considerable credibility as an opponent against Israel. Bashar, in contrast, was rushed into senior positions by his father and has not built up the same authority and credibility. He holds power in part by not challenging any of the country's main factions.[55]

Bashar, like his father, has used the struggle against Israel to ward off domestic challenges. For example, his regime tried to legitimize a crackdown on reformist elements in 2003 by stressing that Israel was posing a direct threat at the time.[56] As a result, he has avoided having a foreign

---

[51] US House of Representatives, "Statement by Philip Wilcox before the House Committee on International Relations," p. 9.

[52] US Senate, William J. Burns, "Statement before the Senate Foreign Relations Committee" (October 30, 2003).

[53] Bashar al-Asad has also openly declared that Syria supports Lebanese "resistance" movements such as Hizballah.

[54] US Department of State, *Patterns of Global Terrorism 2003*, p. 93.

[55] Perthes, *Syria under Bashar al-Asad*, pp. 4–6. International Crisis Group, *Syria under Bashar (II)*, p. 5.

[56] Perthes, *Syria under Bashar al-Asad*, p. 14.

policy that would lead to conflict with the Palestinian cause or otherwise threaten his credibility among nationalists.

Bashar tries to balance strategic interest with domestic politics. Syria maintains an interest in an eventual land-for-peace swap with Israel, and Damascus has tried to send messages to Jerusalem that it does not want a confrontation with Israel. At the same time, however, Bashar's rhetoric is at times vitriolic, and he maintains support for Hizballah, HAMAS, and other leading anti-Israel groups. Syria specialist Volker Perthes describes Bashar's rhetoric "as a kind of calculated populism: a conscious attempt to enhance his popularity among the young generation in Syria and other Arab countries, and thereby enhance his assets at home."[57]

Types of support

Syria has provided a wide range of support to numerous Palestinian terrorist groups over the years. In the 1970s and 1980s, it worked extremely closely with several Palestinian groups, directing their operations and offering them funding and training. Organizational aid was particularly important. Damascus encouraged several groups to separate themselves from the Palestinian mainstream in order to undermine Arafat.

Since the end of the Cold War, providing a safe haven is the most important form of support Syria provides. The Department of State notes that members of HAMAS, PIJ, PFLP, and the PFLP-GC all reside in Syria, and several groups maintain headquarters there. The sanctuary in Syria allows groups to coordinate their activities, organize, and otherwise operate with little interference, even though Damascus itself is often not directly involved in these activities.[58] Given Israel's highly skilled military and impressive counterterrorism capabilities, Palestinian groups have benefited considerably by being able to conduct these activities with at most limited Israeli interference.

Damascus claims the various groups only conduct political activities from Syrian soil – a hotly disputed claim.[59] Ambassador Cofer Black, the State Department Special Coordinator for Counterterrorism, testified

---

[57] Ibid., p. 42.

[58] US House of Representatives, "Statement by Philip Wilcox before the House Committee on International Relations," p. 10.

[59] US Department of State, *Patterns of Global Terrorism 2003*, pp. 120, 130–132.

that the United States has "seen evidence that some of these offices are, in fact, used for operational purposes."[60] The State Department reports that the PIJ receives "limited logistic support assistance from Syria," as does the PFLP and PFLP-GC.[61] Syria also gives military support to the PFLP-GC and provides Hizballah with diplomatic, political, and logistical support.[62] The United States contends that HAMAS and PIJ do not receive funding or arms directly from Syria but that Syria probably allows them to fundraise and buy or receive arms from others with little interference.[63] In addition, Palestinian groups often smuggle weapons from Syria to their operatives.[64] These claims suggest that Syria helps these groups sustain themselves and organize, though several of these – particularly HAMAS – would remain potent organizations even without a major Syria role.[65]

Syria also uses its dominance of Lebanon as a means of indirectly hosting and training terrorist and guerrilla groups. Palestinian groups use Lebanon as a headquarters, a recruiting base, an operations center, and a place for training. With Syrian permission, Iran trains Hizballah and various Palestinian groups in the Bekaa valley in the use of rockets and surface-to-air missiles.[66]

---

[60] Black, "Syria and Terrorism."

[61] US Department of State, *Patterns of Global Terrorism 2003*, p. 130.

[62] Ibid., p. 122.

[63] US House of Representatives, "Statement by Philip Wilcox before the House Committee on International Relations," pp. 8–11. Most of HAMAS's money initially came from Palestinian sources. HAMAS also receives money from individuals donating to charitable activities and supporters in the Persian Gulf, North America, and Europe. Mishal and Sela, *The Palestinian HAMAS*, p. 87.

[64] Levitt, "Confronting Syrian Support for Terrorist Groups."

[65] Israel also claims that terrorist training camps are active in Syria. For example, camps in Syria run by the PLFP-GC are used to train PIJ and al-Aqsa Martyrs' Brigade members. HAMAS has recruited operatives in various Arab countries and sent them to Syria for training in weapons, intelligence, and suicide operations. Israel also claims that the PIJ leadership in Damascus has close ties to PIJ operatives in the West Bank and at times orders specific attacks. The PIJ leadership in Damascus also directs money to operatives in the West Bank. "Prepared Statement of Matthew Levitt" and Levitt, "Confronting Syrian Support for Terrorist Groups."

[66] Levitt, "Prepared Statement of Matthew Levitt."

Syria has long offered the Palestinian cause diplomatic support. For much of the early 1970s, Asad championed the PLO and trumpeted Palestinian ambitions even as he worked behind the scenes to undermine them. Syria also helped lead the effort to have the PLO be proclaimed the "sole representative" of the Palestinian people.[67] When it suited Syria's interests, the PLO was treated as a *de facto* state, joining various anti-Israel "fronts" and otherwise being treated superficially as a partner.[68] Similarly, Syrian leaders – along with leaders of pro-Western states such as Saudi Arabia and Kuwait – met with HAMAS spiritual leader Sheikh Yassin in 1998 after his release from prison, signifying their support for his cause and their rejection of attempts to isolate Palestinian rejectionists.[69] Syrian officials also repeatedly lauded the Islamic resistance movement.[70]

Motivations

Syria's backing of various Palestinian factions stems from a mix of ideological, domestic, and strategic concerns. Together, these explain not only Damascus' decision to support the Palestinian cause, but also its preference for working against Arafat and dominating the movement, even to the point of attacking it directly and greatly weakening it.

Strategic concerns

By supporting various Palestinian groups against Israel, Syria was able to continue its struggle against the Jewish state. After 1967, the grandiose vision of annihilating Israel was replaced by the more pragmatic goals of increasing Syria's influence (and limiting that of Israel) and recapturing the Golan Heights. Israel's rout of Syria in 1967, and its lesser but still decisive victory in 1973, demonstrated that Damascus had no path to

---

[67] Ma'oz, *Syria and Israel*, p. 162.

[68] For example, after Egyptian President Anwar Sadat visited Israel in 1977, the PLO joined Syria, Libya, Algeria, and South Yemen to form the "Steadfastness Front." Seale, *Asad*, p. 346.

[69] Hroub, *HAMAS*, p. 154.

[70] For example, on the first anniversary of the second *intifada*, Syria hosted the leadership of Hizballah, HAMAS, PIJ, PFLP-GC, and the PFLP as part of a conference of liberation movements. The Middle East Media Research Institute, "Terror in America (14): Syria's Position: Define Terrorism Not Fight It."

conventional military superiority. In 1982, Israel's victory over Syrian forces in Lebanon was overwhelming. Egypt's decision to seek peace with Israel, which began after the 1973 war and was formalized in the 1978 Camp David Treaty, made a directly military conflict unthinkable from a Syrian point of view.

In addition to the country's military weakness, Syria also had few political levers against Israel. Asad enjoyed at best lukewarm support from many of his supposed allies in the Arab world, and some – such as the late King Hussein of Jordan, and Saddam Husayn of Iraq – were often bitter enemies. Since the loss of Soviet support after the end of the Cold War, Syria also lost access to a diplomatic counterweight to Washington and a source of free or subsidized weaponry. In any event, Damascus had never had a relationship with Moscow close to that of Israel's with the United States.

For Hafez al-Asad to achieve any of his strategic goals, he needed a means of inflicting pain on Israel. Only then, in his eyes, would the Jewish state be forced to make concessions on the Golan Heights or otherwise accommodate Syria. Palestinian terrorism served Syria's interests, forcing Israel to recognize that it could not enjoy true peace without Damascus' blessing. Syria's support for Hizballah served a similar role of giving a weak Damascus another potent weapon against Israel. Similarly, backing the PKK also helped Damascus maintain some leverage against Turkey, which also enjoys conventional military superiority.

By keeping rejectionist factions strong, Damascus augmented its influence over the peace process from the Palestinian side as well as the Israeli side. Backing rejectionist groups helped Syria ensure its strategic goal of not being excluded from any peace that the Palestinian leadership forged with Israel. The PLO, and later the PA, was too weak to control all the movements that opposed its position. Thus, it found it difficult to negotiate with Israel or others unless it enjoyed at least the tacit acceptance of some rejectionist factions – a weakness Damascus tried to leverage.

Palestinian terrorism also was useful to force Syria's neighbors and other Arab states to follow Damascus' lead. Jordan's King Hussein, for example, did not go his own way on negotiations with Israel in the 1980s in part because of Syrian-backed Palestinian terrorism. Again, Syria did not control these neighbors through terrorism, but the threat of terrorism gave Damascus influence over their decisions. Syria also uses its support to demonstrate its superiority to its Arab rivals in the competition for Arab leadership. In particular, it has contrasted Syria's steadfastness as demonstrated by its support for rejectionist Palestinians with Egypt's and Jordan's willingness to negotiate unilaterally with Israel.[71]

Asad also used Palestinian factions to augment its own armed forces. Before intervening in Lebanon with Syrian troops in 1976, Asad in December 1975 had sent units of the Palestine Liberation Army (a Syrian-controlled Palestinian proxy) and al-Saiqa as a way of putting pressure on local forces.[72] Palestinians also fought with Syrians against Israel in 1982 in Lebanon.

As a state that refused to enter peace negotiations with Israel, Syria also gained financially from its backing of the Palestinian cause. After tying Syrian negotiations to the Palestinian cause after the 1973 war, Asad received increased financial backing from wealthy Gulf states that, like Syria, sought to demonstrate their commitment to Arab nationalism by backing opponents of Israel.[73]

Damascus' decision after 1986 to use terrorist groups instead of its own agents allowed it deniability. As the US State Department report noted at the time, "Damascus utilizes these groups to attack or intimidate enemies and opponents and to exert its influence in the region. Yet at the same time, it can disavow knowledge of their operations."[74] This deniability served a useful purpose, enabling Syria to distance itself when necessary from the actions of its proxies.

DOMESTIC CONCERNS

Strategic concerns, however, only explain part of the picture. If the Palestinians were to be forged into a Syrian sword to wield against Israel, this would effectively be done by having a strong, united Palestinian movement rather than a fractured one. Syria, however, preferred a movement it could control to a strong movement. Thus, it deliberately divided and weakened the Palestinian cause.

---

[71] Murphy, "Syria-US Policy Directions."
[72] Seale, *Asad*, p. 280; Rabinovich, *The War for Lebanon*, p. 49.
[73] Seale, *Asad*, pp. 255–257.
[74] US Department of State. "Syrian Support for International Terrorism: 1983–1986," p. 1.

Domestic politics played a central role in Syria's support for Palestinian radical groups and for the Palestinian cause more broadly. The Baath regime, like several others before it, saw itself as a revolutionary movement and thus formed ties to other revolutionary groups, particularly among the Palestinians. Arab nationalist sentiment is keenly felt in Syria – every regime since the end of colonialism has sought to capitalize on this.[75] Because the Palestinian movement became equated with Arab unity and Arab nationalism, supporting it was a means of getting the Syrian people to support the regime.[76] Once this relationship was born, backing away from it would prove difficult.

Being seen as steadfast against Israel and behind the Palestinian cause was particularly vital for both Asads because their regimes' legitimacy was often called into question. The elder Asad took power in a military coup that had little popular support. The Syrian regime was not institutionalized, despite repeated regime attempts to use the Baath party to achieve this. Syria lacked strong political parties, an efficient bureaucracy, respected courts, or other basic institutions. In essence, Asad ruled through the military, the security services, the Alawi community, economic cooptation, and family ties, all of which undermined efforts to build strong institutions. His regime also initially engaged in a land reform that was unpopular among many segments of Syrian society.

The minority character of the regime proved a particular challenge. Many Syrian Sunnis believed that the Alawis were not true Muslims, and thus questioned the Asad family's right to rule. The regime's massive crackdown on the Muslim Brotherhood ended the overt rebellion in 1982, but Alawi–Sunni sectarian tensions may have even grown since then. Foreign rivals of Asad's regime, such as the Baathist regime in Iraq and at times King Hussein's regime in Jordan, played on this theme of illegitimate Alawi domination in their criticism of the government.[77]

Syria offsets this criticism by demonstrating its Arab nationalist credentials. Damascus basks in the praise given to it by various Palestinian movements. HAMAS, for example, enjoys strong support from Arab publics and Islamist movements, and Syria's support for the movement

---

[75] Jouejati, "With Syria, Use Carrots." For a historic overview of the development of Syrian nationalism, see Khoury, *Syria and the French Mandate.*
[76] Rubin, *The Transformation of Palestinian Politics*, p. 257, note 69.
[77] Van Dam, *The Struggle for Power in Syria*, pp. 96, 106, and 116–117.

generates some goodwill among these audiences.[78] During a crisis related to Israel's deportation of 400 Islamist leaders to south Lebanon from December 1992 to December 1993, HAMAS leaders wrote a letter to Hafez al-Asad, praising his support and declaring "Damascus is our pre-eminent leader."[79] Moreover, in exchange for this support, Palestinian groups have refrained from working with domestic movements opposed to Syrian leadership. HAMAS does not cooperate with Syrian Islamists against the Baath regime despite sharing their general goals.[80]

The importance of domestic factors in Syria's support for the Palestinian groups is reflected in the bureaucratic structure of the regime itself. Many Palestinian groups are handled through the Directorate of Internal Security rather than through Syria's external intelligence services.[81]

Contrasting Syria's relationship with various Palestinian groups and the Lebanese Hizballah is instructive. The Lebanese Hizballah's identity as a Shi'a organization and its association with Lebanon make it less of a threat to the regime's domestic credibility. Thus, Syria has not actively worked to divide the movement and create numerous rivals as it has done with Palestinian militants.[82]

The limited role of ideology

Ideology contributed to Damascus' initial decision to back Palestinian militants, but Syria's disastrous defeat in the 1967 war led it to shed ideology as a main motivation. In the early 1960s, Syrian leaders vied with one another to demonstrate their commitment to Arab nationalism, both as part of a contest for power and because of a heartfelt commitment. They saw the Palestinians as Arab brothers who were victims of Israeli oppression and imperialism. After 1967, radicals among the leadership who supported unconditional backing of Palestinian guerrillas lost in a power struggle to pragmatists, led by Hafiz al-Asad. Asad did

---

[78] Hroub, *HAMAS*, p. 257.   [79] As quoted in ibid., p. 159, footnote 24.
[80] Ibid., p. 257.
[81] I would like to thank Emile El-Hokayem for bringing this to my attention.
[82] I would like to thank Tamara Wittes for drawing my attention to this distinction. Syria, of course, has backed Amal, a longtime rival to Hizballah, in Lebanon.

have a strong personal belief in the Palestinian cause and in his last years saw himself as the only remaining leader true to Arab nationalist ideals.[83] His personal belief, however, was always secondary to his strategic ambitions for Syria and his concern about preserving his regime.

Nor does ideology shape who receives Syria's aid. Damascus has worked with almost every Palestinian faction as well as the Lebanese Hizballah, the PKK, and other groups that embrace a wide range of beliefs and agendas. Ideology, in fact, would normally compel Damascus to oppose the Islamist organizations. The Baath regime is avowedly secular and has crushed the Muslim Brotherhood (whose Gazan counterpart produced HAMAS) inside Syria itself. Nevertheless, both the Islamists and secular groups have received aid.

Today, ideology plays at best a limited role in Syria's overall foreign policy. Bashar, like his father, opposes the idea of Israel, seeing it as a modern, hostile, form of colonialism. Bashar has also made anti-Semitic statements.[84] Yet, in general, ideology was largely a mask for strategic and domestic concerns. As the International Crisis Group notes about Bashar, "His approach is ideological in the sense that ideological fidelity is an important ingredient in a pragmatic strategy of regime survival. This has meant avoiding any radical departure from his father's approach, which would have exposed him to strong domestic criticism."[85]

The identity and nature of the groups that have received Syria's support reflect the effort to balance strategic and domestic concerns as well as the relatively minor role that ideology plays. Syria opposes a negotiated settlement for the Palestinians and thus seeks to keep the Palestinian rejectionist cause strong, a stance that also demonstrates the regime's nationalist *bona fides*. But the groups themselves cannot be too strong, as they could then escalate independently against Israel and force Damascus into a damaging confrontation with its stronger neighbor. In general, Syria has far closer ties to small groups that are easy to control than it does to more popular movements, such as Fatah. More popular large movements are too independent of the Syrian regime, enabling them to pose a threat to the regime's strategic and political position.

---

[83] Ross, *The Missing Peace*, p. 142.

[84] Simon and Stevenson, "Declaring the 'Party of God'," p. 33.

[85] International Crisis Group, *Syria under Bashar (II)*, p. 6.

The impact of Syrian support

Syrian support for Palestinian groups has had a tremendous effect on the Palestinian cause, on Syria, and on the region.

IMPACT ON PALESTINIAN GROUPS

Syrian support made several individual Palestinian groups more lethal and stronger in some ways, but it often detracted from their strength in more subtle ways and hurt the Palestinian cause as a whole.

Because groups like the PFLP enjoy sanctuary and other support from Syria, it was far harder for Israel to target their leadership, end their logistics and fundraising networks, and otherwise take decisive action against the groups.[86] Support was particularly important for many of the small groups that Syria aided, such as the PFLP-GC. Many of these groups lacked broad support among Palestinians in the diaspora or in the West Bank and Gaza. Without outside support, they would have been hard pressed to build and sustain their organizations. Indeed, groups such as al-Saiqa and the Abu Musa faction depended almost entirely on Damascus for their organizations' survival.

The sanctuary Syria provided also gave groups a reprieve from the bloody rivalries within the Palestinian movement. The PA could crack down on PIJ or rival secular groups in the West Bank and Gaza, but it was powerless to go after their leadership in Damascus or other foreign states. Such a sanctuary was particularly important in the mid-1990s, when PA pressure greatly hindered HAMAS and other groups in Palestinian territories.

Legitimacy was another benefit that Palestinian groups gained from their ties to Syria. Damascus, for example, did not criticize the series of HAMAS bombings after Israel's January 1996 assassination of HAMAS bombmaker Yahya Ayyash, even as other Arab countries roundly criticized HAMAS. As a result, the more violent Palestinian groups were better able to legitimate their continued resistance despite their tactics and despite the promise of negotiations that more moderate groups held out.

Syria's operational assistance was limited after the end of the Cold War. Damascus typically provided a haven for a group and capitalized on its existing capabilities. At times, it allowed the group to develop its

---

[86] Although several members of HAMAS' "political" branch resided in Damascus, almost all its operational leaders were in Gaza.

capabilities further through training in Lebanon – training that Syria disingenuously claimed was out of its control. In general, however, Syria did not do what Iran did with its proxies and use its military to transform them from rag-tag fighters to premier guerrillas or terrorists.

Syrian support, moreover, came with a heavy price. Individual groups were at times augmented, but the overall cause was set back. Damascus' support widened fissures in the Palestinian nationalist movement and helped prevent a cohesive leadership from taking control. Syria repeatedly undermined the movement whenever it threatened the regime's domestic position and strategic interests.

Indeed, Syria's efforts to counter Arafat and close his bases in Lebanon after the 1982 Israel invasion indirectly paved the way for HAMAS and other groups to challenge Arafat's leadership. Syria's decision forced the momentum of the movement away from Lebanon and other neighbors of Israel to Palestinians in the occupied territories themselves. The PLO gradually became discredited as a source of change, leading Palestinians in the territories to act on their own behalf during the first *intifada*.[87] The numerous Palestinian factions also enabled Israel and other opponents to exploit the actions of one movement to use against others. Israel, for example, used the ANO attack on its ambassador in Britain in 1982 as a pretext to drive the PLO out of Lebanon, even though the ANO and the PLO were bitter rivals.[88] Similarly, Israeli politicians critical of peace efforts in the 1990s cited HAMAS and PIJ attacks as examples of Palestinian perfidy, despite the rivalry between the PA and these Islamist groups.

This lack of unity proved perhaps the Palestinians' biggest weakness over the years. Palestinian organizations often spent far more time competing with one another than in their struggle against Israel. In war, the Palestinians were not able to marshal their resources effectively. In peace, they were not able to present a united front and convince Israel or other states that they could deliver on what they promised. Syria, of course, did not create this lack of unity, but it did foster it and make it far worse.

---

[87] Mishal and Sela, *The Palestinian HAMAS*, p. 39; Kepel, *Jihad*, pp. 152–153. For a review of some of the organizational problems, see Sahliyeh, *The PLO after the War in Lebanon*.

[88] Tessler, *A History of the Israeli–Palestinian Conflict*, pp. 572–573.

Terrorism abetted by Syria and other state sponsors helped undermine the peace process between Israel and its Arab neighbors, particularly the Palestinians. Syria supported groups that rejected any compromise with Israel. As a result, Arafat was less able to persuade, or coerce, his rivals into becoming a peaceful opposition. Arafat, for example, was unable to stop HAMAS and PIJ violence in 1996, a failure that directly led to the election of the hard-line Benjamin Netanyahu, who was far less willing to make concessions to the PA. Arafat also came to look impotent, undemocratic, and like an Israeli quisling, as the Israeli government demanded he act to stop terrorism.[89] Terrorism also led to Israeli crackdowns and suspicion in Israel, both about Arafat's motives and about his capacity to end violence. As a result, one of the main benefits Israelis hoped to gain in exchange for Palestinian concessions – to end terrorist violence – was diminished.[90] As such, keeping the rejectionists strong discredited moderates in Israel, who argued that peace negotiations would lead to a decline in violence. Of course, primary responsibility for the failure of the peace process should not be laid at Damascus' door. Nevertheless, Syria helped topple what was always a fragile house of cards.

The PLO and other Palestinian organizations also suffered tremendous casualties in their confrontations with Syria. Damascus' crackdown in Lebanon was particularly bloody. A former PLO intelligence chief estimated that three quarters of Palestinian casualties came at the hands of Arab states, with Syria being a leading perpetrator.[91] Perhaps not surprisingly, Syria may be the regime that Palestinians hate more than any other, including Jordan. Few Palestinians privately praise Syria, despite Damascus' efforts.

Damascus also placed limits on its proxies' freedom. Since 1970, for example, Syria has not allowed Palestinian groups to attack Israel from Syrian soil.[92] Nor has Syria transferred the more advanced conventional weapons in its arsenal (to say nothing of having refrained from transferring part of its massive chemical weapons arsenal) despite the tactical

---

[89] I would like to thank Tamara Wittes for her thoughts on this point.
[90] Rubin, *The Transformation of Palestinian Politics*, p. 146; Kepel, *Jihad*, p. 331.
[91] Rubin, *The Transformation of Palestinian Politics*, p. 140.
[92] Jouejati, "With Syria, Use Carrots."

benefits this might bring to a Palestinian group.[93] In part, this reflects Syria's conventional military weakness. Damascus feared that too bloody or outrageous an attack would lead to an all-out confrontation with Israel. Domestic concerns played in as well. Syria was particularly concerned that allowing Islamist movements full freedom of action would strengthen its own Islamic opposition.[94]

Indeed, it is plausible that several groups would have been far bloodier if they had not received support from Damascus. Since the end of the Cold War, the leftist Palestinian groups closest to Syria were limited in their use of violence. HAMAS, PIJ, and others were far bloodier, but they have far more freedom of action than other groups that Damascus sponsors. The Lebanese Hizballah, too, has often obeyed red lines partly out of deference to Syria's concerns, and Syria has at times clamped down on Hizballah if it felt it would help Syria's other interests.[95]

Syrian support also allowed some groups to avoid building a strong base among Palestinians themselves to survive – at best a mixed blessing. Al-Saiqa and the Abu Musa faction never had to gain broad support among Palestinians, and as a result found their strength limited. In part because it enjoyed strong support from Iran, the PIJ did not build social institutions or a large group of supporters, in contrast to the substantial social service network established by HAMAS. This, in turn, made it easier politically for the PA to crack down on the PIJ.[96]

Major Palestinian groups were able to retain their independence despite Damascus' constant and often ruthless attempts to control the movement. Arafat's PLO suffered splits, repression, and assassinations but still preserved its autonomy from Syria. Even when Syria and the PLO were not actively fighting each other, the PLO took important decisions independently of Damascus and was often highly critical of Asad.[97] In part, the PLO managed this by playing Syria off against other

---

[93] Syria, for example, possesses long-range artillery and Scud missiles but has not transferred these to terrorist groups. For a review of Syria's arsenal, Jaffee Center for Strategic Studies, "Syria," pp. 1–18.

[94] Hroub, *HAMAS*, p. 148.

[95] See Ross, *The Missing Peace*, p. 233 for a description of one instance where Asad offered to restrain Hizballah in order to improve the chances of successful peace negotiations.

[96] Rubin, *The Transformation of Palestinian Politics*, p. 119.

[97] Ma'oz, *Syria and Israel*, p. 238.

Arab rivals, but it also built a strong base of support among Palestinians. HAMAS, like the PLO, worked hard to avoid becoming entangled in the rivalries of Arab states. HAMAS often went against Syria's wishes when they conflicted with the movement's needs. For example, in 1993 it implicitly recognized Arafat's leadership by holding talks with Arafat as the PA was being established, despite Syria's opposition. HAMAS leaders recognized that the movement inside the Palestinian territories needed an accommodation with Arafat, both for practical reasons and because Palestinian sentiment at the time favored national unity.[98] As Khaled Hroub contends, "It did not want to become the protégé of one or another alliance or to become a partisan of one or another regime."[99]

IMPACT ON SYRIA

Support for Palestinian terrorism did offer Syria many benefits. Through terrorism, Syria has helped undermine a comprehensive Arab–Israeli peace. In particular, terrorism helped prevent a separate Israeli–Palestinian peace, which would have left Syria isolated and with few levers to use in pursuit of regaining the Golan Heights.

Syria was at times also able to use terrorism to intimidate its neighbors. The campaign against Jordan from 1983 to 1985 through the Abu Nidal Organization and others did make Amman less willing to cut a deal with Israel and the Palestinians that Damascus opposed. This campaign also demonstrated to Washington that any regional deal had to include Syria.[100]

Syria's tough stand against Israel and support for the Palestinian cause also paid off for the regime politically. Over time, the regime gained considerable credibility as a steadfast opponent of Israel. Even many opponents of Hafez al-Asad supported his approach to Israel.[101] Syria also gained protection from outside challengers to its legitimacy. HAMAS has never challenged the Baath party's legitimacy, despite its shared heritage with the party's Islamist opposition.[102]

---

[98] Mishal and Sela, *The Palestinian HAMAS*, p. 99.
[99] Hroub, *HAMAS*, p. 165.
[100] Brand, *Jordan's Inter-Arab Relations*, p. 177; Rabinovich, *The War for Lebanon, 1970–1985*, p. 188.
[101] Perthes, *Syria under Bashar al-Asad*, p. 33.
[102] Hroub, *HAMAS*, p. 166.

Support for terror, however, had severe costs for Syria. Backing Palestinian rejectionists led Syria into clashes with Israel, some of which were disastrous. In 1967 and 1982, Syria's military forces were routed, and the regime's credibility was hurt. Syria's backing for the latest round of violence that began in September 2000 also has met with a limited military response. In April 2001, Israel killed four Syrian soldiers in Lebanon when it bombed a Syrian radar station there after a Hizballah attack. Under similar circumstances, it struck another Syrian radar station in July 2001. In October 2003, Israeli warplanes bombed a training camp for Palestinians in response to a suicide attack by PIJ.[103] The US response to Israel's strikes was supportive, with President Bush declaring "We would be doing the same thing."[104]

Syria was able to limit the risk to its security by controlling the Palestinians. In contrast to conflicts in 1967 and 1970 (in Jordan), the Palestinian cause did not lead Syria into a war it would lose with Israel. Damascus' ruthless intervention in Lebanon in 1975–76, and again in the 1980s, greatly hindered the Palestinians' freedom of movement, enabling Syria to control its actions and avoid a destabilizing conflict with Israel. This strategy was not a complete success, as the Israeli–Syrian confrontation in Lebanon in 1982 indicates, but in general the Palestinian cause did not drag Syria into all-out wars as it did in the first decades after Israel's creation.

In Syria's negotiations with Israel over the Golan Heights, terrorism was both a benefit and a curse. Terrorism, of course, helped lead Israel to the negotiating table. Without the pain of terrorism, Israel had few incentives to surrender territory. On the other hand, because of terrorism, the Israeli public did not trust Syria. After a series of suicide bombings in 1996, the Israeli public became skeptical of the possibility of peace. Syria's refusal to shut down the headquarters of groups such as PIJ or even to publicly express sorrow made both the Israeli people and the government doubtful that Asad truly wanted peace. Damascus' unwillingness to move away from terrorists made it far harder for the Israeli government to forge a peace that it could sell to its own people. By the

---

[103] Luft, "All Quiet on the Eastern Front?" p. 19. The camp struck in October 2003 was probably abandoned. Many believe the attack was meant as a warning to Syria rather than an attempt to directly inflict punishment.

[104] As quoted in International Crisis Group, *Syria under Bashar (I)*, p. 5.

late 1990s, negotiations had reached the point where only minor material issues separated the two parties. However, Israeli leaders were often hesitant to make concessions, in part because mistrust of Damascus was so widespread.[105]

Syria was also tarred with the brush of its proxies, even in cases where it may not have ordered the attacks. Patrick Seale, for example, contends that Asad did not order Abu Nidal's attacks on Israeli targets at the Rome and Vienna airports in December 1985, or 1986 attacks in Karachi and Istanbul even though Abu Nidal's gunmen had continued to use Syrian camps and lodging.[106] Nevertheless, Syria was widely blamed and felt compelled to respond in 1987 by expelling Abu Nidal's organization from its territory.[107]

Support for terrorism damaged the Syrian regime's reputation with the United States in particular. Syrian-backed Palestinian terrorism often had little direct impact on US citizens, but it did affect the security of Israel – an important US concern. (Syrian support for Hizballah, in contrast, did contribute to the deaths of hundreds of Americans in the 1980s, but Damascus has not been implicated in a Hizballah attack that has killed Americans since then.) More broadly, various US administrations have considered support for terrorism inherently objectionable and have limited their contacts with Damascus as a result. For various administrations opposed to terrorism in general and committed to helping Israel seek peace, Damascus' backing of various rejectionist groups soured any hopes of a broader reconciliation.[108] Because of Syria's ties to terrorism, many of the financial inducements that led Jordan and Egypt

---

[105] Ross, *The Missing Peace*, p. 244. See also Slater, "Lost Opportunities for Peace in the Arab–Israeli Conflict," pp. 96–97 and Rabinovich, *Waging Peace*, pp. 130–131. Rabinovich notes that Asad's health problems were severe by 2000 and that he was preparing for the smooth succession of his son Bashar at this point. Thus, he was unwilling by 2000 to make concessions that might have led to criticism at home, making it hard for any proposal to have worked. See also Ross, *The Missing Peace*, pp. 583–587.

[106] The State Department reported that Abu Nidal received travel documents and the right of transit, as well as a base for its facilities in Syria and in Lebanon. US Department of State, "Syrian Support for International Terrorism: 1983–1986," pp. 1–3. However, the report also notes that Libya in fact sponsored these attacks but that some of the team received training and transit in Damascus.

[107] Seale, *Asad*, p. 467.

[108] Ibid., p. 367.

to the peace table were not available to Syria. Moreover, as noted below, the United States has imposed sanctions and otherwise worked against Syria, in part because of its support for terrorism.

Continued support in the face of pressure

The United States and Israel have both tried to halt Syrian supported terrorism with little success. It is not surprising that Israel's limited measures have failed to end Syrian support. As noted above, Israel invaded Lebanon to expel the PLO and conducted military reprisals against Syria as late as 2003. These measures, however, have done little to sway Damascus and may have even affirmed its determination to support Palestinian groups.

Backing down in the face of limited Israeli pressure would be both a strategic and domestic political disaster for the Baath regime. Strategically, support for terrorism is one of the few assets the Syrian regime enjoys in its struggle against Israel. If Israel could neutralize this with its conventional military power, Damascus would have no way of compelling Israel to make concessions on the Golan Heights or other issues. The domestic political impact would be even greater. The regime's legitimacy hangs heavily on its Arab nationalist credentials, which in turn depend on its opposition to Israel. Backing down in a public manner with nothing in return would eliminate what little appeal the Baath regime enjoys among the Syrian public.

Syria, however, does carefully modulate its pressure in order to avoid provoking an Israeli response that it cannot withstand. As such, it tries to preserve deniability and use Lebanon as a base for many of the groups, both of which maintain the fiction that Syria itself has at best limited involvement in anti-Israel violence. Moreover, it restricts the operations and arms provided, ensuring that the bloodshed does not rise to the point where Israel is forced to respond due to domestic pressure. Modulating the violence and preserving deniability also keep regional states behind Syria, making it harder for Israel to gain the diplomatic support it needs to act. Given Israel's many other pressing security problems, only some of which are linked to Damascus, stopping Syrian backing for rejectionist groups often is not a priority.[109]

---

[109] For example, in the late 1980s Israel avoided a confrontation with Syria over its support for terrorism as it had to focus on the first *intifada*. Ma'oz, *Syria and Israel*, p. 195.

The United States, too, has failed to persuade or coerce Syria into ending its support for terrorism despite many years of pressure. Syria was a charter member of the 1979 list of state sponsors of terrorism and has long suffered a range of US diplomatic and economic pressure to end support for terrorism. Following the 1979 legislation, the United States cut off all economic aid. The United States has restricted arms sales, economic assistance, and access to dual use items and also opposed funding for Syria through multilateral economic institutions.[110]

In part, US coercion is undercut by the inconsistent US response to Syrian-backed violence. Washington has kept diplomatic ties to Syria, in contrast to other countries officially identified as state sponsors of terrorism. Despite being designated a state sponsor of terrorism since the list's creation in 1979, the United States has allowed trade and investment in Syria.[111] In addition, the United States did not respond directly against Syria for such acts as the 1983 bombing of the US and French forces in Lebanon, despite boasting by Syrian officials years later that they had approved the operation.[112] The United States also worked with Syria in Lebanon in the late 1980s and afterward, effectively accepting a Syrian satrapy there.

What explains this caution? Asad, both father and son, have tried to preserve their reputations as pragmatic and realistic negotiating partners, avoiding the ideological blindness that at times characterized Iran, the Taliban's Afghanistan, and Sudan. Moreover, in the 1990s it was clear that terrorism was linked to plausible concessions on Israel's part, particularly with regard to the Golan.

The prospect of an Israel–Syria peace also proved a major source of US caution. For much of the 1990s, US efforts to end Syrian support for terrorism were bound up in the Middle East Peace Process. As former Clinton and Bush administration official Flynt Leverett testified, "[O]ur outstanding bilateral differences were to be resolved as part of a peace settlement between Israel and Syria. For example, it was generally understood that, as part of such a settlement, Syria would have no need for and

---

[110] US House of Representatives, "Statement by Philip Wilcox before the House Committee on International Relations," p. 6.

[111] Hufbauer *et al.*, "Using Sanctions to Fight Terrorism."

[112] Karmon, "Syrian Support to Hizballah."

would sever its ties to Palestinian rejectionists and disarm Hizballah fighters in southern Lebanon."[113]

When the peace process collapsed at the outset of the second *intifada* in September 2000, pressure on Syria was initially limited as US officials sought to restart it. After the September 11 attacks, however, Damascus' ties to terrorist groups became far more important to US officials than what was seen as an increasingly frail hope of restarting the peace process. As a result, the United States also stepped up the rhetorical heat on Damascus. In June 2002, President Bush demanded that Bashar al-Asad "choose the right side in the war on terror."[114] He later demanded that Damascus close terrorist training camps. Other senior US officials echoed the President's line.[115] Congress also passed the Syrian Accountability and Lebanon Sovereignty Restoration Act (SALSRA), which increased economic restrictions on Syria.[116]

Damascus has responded to pressure by limiting its proxies and providing some cooperation on terrorism in general, but not by clamping down completely. For example, in 2003 Syria closed "media offices" of several Palestinian groups in Damascus. It also urged HAMAS and PIJ to sign a ceasefire agreement with Israel. At the same time, however, senior Palestinian rejectionist leaders remained in Syria and continued to use cell phones and their computers to direct operations.[117] During the run-up to the 2003 US–Iraq war, Syria also was able to convince Hizballah to limit its guerrilla attacks and to temporarily halt Iranian arms supplies to the group.[118] Damascus has provided information on al-Qa'ida that has saved the lives of US citizens and helped in the investigation of the September 11 attacks.

[113] Leverett, "Syria–US Policy Directions."
[114] "President Bush Calls for New Palestinian Leadership."
[115] "Powell Urges End to Hezbollah Border Presence," *Ha'aretz*, May 5, 2003.
[116] SALSRA bans the sale of arms or dual-use items and demands other forms of sanctions on top of these restrictions. It also prohibits the export of items on the United States Munitions List or Commerce Control List, and prohibits US assistance in various forms, such as money from the Overseas Private Investment Corporation. "US Policy toward Syria and the Syria Accountability Act," p. 2; As quoted in International Crisis Group, *Syria under Bashar (I)*, p. 4.
[117] International Crisis Group, *Syria under Bashar (I)*, p. 9. See also footnote 62.
[118] Ibid., p. 13.

Syria's use of token concessions, select cooperation, and limits on its proxies has worked to head off more decisive measures against it. In general, Syria has demonstrated a remarkable ability to support terrorists while minimizing the penalties for doing so. Gary Gambill, a harsh critic of the Asad regime and US policy toward Syria, contends "Assad – arguably the most skilled statesman of the twentieth century – had a knack for recognizing where American 'red lines' were drawn. He was keenly aware of the boundary between actions that would be reluctantly tolerated by the US and those that would provoke retaliation or reappraisal of policy."[119]

Turkey, Syria, and the PKK

In 1998, Turkey used the threat of massive force to compel Syria to expel Abdullah Ocalan, the leader of the separatist terrorist group, the Kurdish Workers' Party (PKK). Ocalan's expulsion from Syria led to his subsequent capture, which in turn contributed to the PKK's collapse.[120] This experience stands in marked contrast to the failed efforts to convince Damascus to end its support for Palestinian groups.

The PKK, which was formed in 1973, began a bloody rebellion in the mid-1980s that has claimed over 35,000 lives. The PKK blended Marxism and Kurdish nationalism, and sought an independent state for Turkey's Kurds. Most of the PKK's attacks focused on Turkish army and security targets, but it has also attacked local politicians, tourists and tourist sites, Turkish diplomatic and commercial facilities, and suspected collaborators, among others.

Ocalan had enjoyed a haven in Syria since 1980, when he fled there to avoid a Turkish crackdown on Kurdish activists. From Syria, he exercised tight control over the PKK, helping to coordinate the PKK's military operations and direct its political activities. Many of the PKK's senior lieutenants also found refuge in Syria as well as in Lebanon, which had been under Syrian control since 1990.[121]

---

[119] Gambill, "The American–Syrian Crisis and the End of Constructive Engagement," electronic version.

[120] The Turkish government managed to convince or coerce Ocalan to appeal to his followers to stop the violence, a dramatic move given the cult of personality he enjoyed. Improved Turkish counterinsurgency measures also played a major role in the PKK's defeat.

[121] Barkey, "Turkey and the PKK." See also Olson, "Turkey–Syria Relations, 1997 to 2000," pp. 101–117.

Syria's motivations for backing the PKK were unclear. Henri Barkey and Dogu Ergil note that support for the PKK may have been a tool for Syria to use in pressing Turkey over the sharing of water from the Euphrates River.[122] In a more general sense, Syria saw Turkey as a threat because of its close ties to the West and its burgeoning strategic relationship with Israel. In addition, Syria had long borne a grudge against Turkey because of its annexation of the area around Alexandretta (Hatay). Domestic politics may also have played a role in Syria's support for the PKK. Many Baath Party members, particularly among the Alawi core of the party, were refugees from Alexandretta, which France ceded to Turkey in 1939.[123]

Turkey initially tried to use diplomacy to end state support. For over a decade, it pressed Damascus to cut its backing of the PKK, along with Iran and Iraq.[124] In general, diplomacy alone did little to sway its neighbors.

Turkey took a much tougher stance in September 1998. Atilla Ates, the commander of Turkey's ground forces, threatened Syria with military action if it did not expel Ocalan – a threat later repeated by various senior civilian and military leaders, including Turkey's Chief of Staff and then President. It is not clear if Turkey actually mobilized its forces specifically to press Syria, but in any event the threat was deemed credible because Turkey had just concluded its participation in NATO exercises.[125] The Turkish army also regularly crossed into Iraq to attack PKK facilities and forces that had taken refuge there, demonstrating the regime's determination to crush the rebellion and willingness to use force to that end. Turkey's military alliance with Israel, which had expanded throughout the 1990s, also gave Turkey additional leverage.

Fearing a confrontation, Damascus backed down. Syria expelled Ocalan and signed the "Adana Agreement," which required that Syria end support for Turkey's Kurdish insurgency. The Adana Agreement

---

[122] Barkey, "Turkey and the PKK"; Ergil, "Aspects of the Kurdish Problem in Turkey," p. 171.

[123] Hinnebusch, *Syria*, p. 31.

[124] Karmon, "Syrian Support to Hizballah." In March 2002, Iran labeled the PKK a terrorist group and Turkey agreed to consider the Mujahedin-e Khalq a terrorist group in exchange.

[125] See in particular Olson, "Turkey–Syria Relations, 1997 to 2000," pp. 104–111. See also Barkey, "Turkey and the PKK."

involved important and humiliating concessions for Damascus, including the recognition of the PKK as a terrorist organization, closing all PKK camps and arresting its members, stopping its activities in Lebanon, and otherwise going from a supporter of the PKK to an opponent.[126] The State Department reported in 1999 that in general Syria upheld its agreement with Turkey.[127]

The expulsion of Ocalan was a major blow to the PKK and eventually led to his capture in Kenya, as he fled from country to country without finding sanctuary before being captured by Turkish forces. The PKK had lost its leader, and the cult of personality he had fostered made this a devastating blow. Moreover, in prison Turkish officials convinced Ocalan to publicly renounce violence and even called his movement a mistake, further straining the movement.[128] By 2000, the movement had fizzled out.

The Syrian abandonment of the PKK stands in sharp contrast to Damascus' continued support for Palestinian rejectionists and for Hizballah. What explains this difference? The Baath regime's support for the PKK had far less strategic value and at best limited domestic political reward. The strategic and symbolic value Syria's leaders placed on the Euphrates water paled before that of the Golan Heights. Moreover, there was no strong pro-Kurd movement in Turkey comparable to the widespread support that the Palestinian movement enjoyed. Indeed, Pan-Kurdish sentiment posed a threat to Syria by energizing the country's own Kurdish population. Expelling Ocalan and ending support thus carried far fewer costs to the regime, even though it still meant a humiliating concession in the face of open Turkish pressure. Moreover, unlike Israel, the Turkish threat to attack was more credible because the governments were not involved in high-profile peace talks and because Ankara, in contrast to Israel, did not suffer international opprobrium. Indeed, Syrian leaders may have feared that Turkey would occupy parts of Syria, creating yet another problem like the Golan Heights that might linger for decades.[129]

---

[126] Karmon, "Syrian Support to Hizballah"; Perthes, *Syria under Bashar al-Asad*, p. 36.
[127] US Department of State, *Patterns of Global Terrorism 1999*, p. 37.
[128] Pillar, *Terrorism and US Foreign Policy*, p. 136.
[129] Olson, "Turkey–Syria Relations, 1997 to 2000," pp. 113–115.

Nevertheless, backing down on the PKK does suggest that Syria is sensitive to the costs that terrorism can impose. The danger of a Turkish attack clearly outweighed the marginal benefits of backing the PKK. Similarly, Damascus' decision not to directly use its own operatives for attacks on civilians and to limit the activities conducted on Syrian soil also suggest the Baath regime carefully tailors its support for terrorism to minimize the penalties it suffers.

Conclusions

Syria's favored proxies have changed over the years, but Damascus' purpose has remained consistent: to gain additional strategic leverage against its foes and to shore up the regime's limited legitimacy at home. Syria has achieved these objectives, though this success proved costly. The Baath regime hurt its reputation with the United States and diminished its ability to make peace with Israel. The impact was even more profound, and more painful, on its Palestinian proxies. Syria's support for rivals to Arafat's leadership divided the movement (and at times decimated it), making it weaker and less able to challenge Israel on the battlefield or to placate it at the negotiating table. Given the benefits of Palestinian terrorism, and the risks to regime legitimacy by abandoning these groups, it is no surprise that neither Israel nor the United States was able to convince the Syrian leadership to abandon terrorism.

6

Pakistan and Kashmir

Pakistan is not on the US list of state sponsors of terrorism, and indeed is often praised as a vital ally in the war on terrorism. Since September 11, 2001, the Pakistani government has detained hundreds of al-Qa'ida members, including several of its most senior officials, and Pakistani and US forces work together to hunt down al-Qa'ida members who fled from Afghanistan. Yet even as Pakistan cooperates on al-Qa'ida, it sponsors several terrorist groups, particularly those active in the disputed state of Kashmir. Since 1989, Pakistan has funded, armed, trained, and otherwise supported a host of Kashmiri organizations in their struggle against Indian rule. Although US pressure after the September 11 attacks led this support to diminish at times, Islamabad's ties to, and backing of, various groups in Kashmir remains significant. Indeed, with the possible exception of Iran, Pakistan is probably today's most active sponsor of terrorism.[1]

Pakistan's support for radicals in Kashmir is part of its overall effort to back various insurgent movements in Kashmir. In general, Pakistan is not interested in the Kashmiri militants exclusively because of their involvement in terrorism. Islamabad's emphasis is on guerrilla war. Kashmiri groups, however, use attacks on civilians to gain tactical

---

[1] This chapter uses terms such as "Kashmiri militants," "Kashmiri groups," and "groups in Kashmir," interchangeably to signify political movements using violence in Kashmir. However, several of the active groups, particularly Jaish-e-Mohammad and Lashkar-e-Tayyeba may have relatively few Kashmiris among their ranks, being composed primarily of non-Kashmiri Muslims.

advantages in their guerrilla war as well as for more traditional terrorist purposes such as undermining New Delhi's rule and defeating rivals within the opposition movement. It is widely believed that Pakistani intelligence at times helps groups select targets, including civilian ones, and knows about major attacks such as the December 2001 attack on the Indian Parliament in advance.

To understand Pakistan's support for terrorism, it is essential to recognize why Pakistan backs insurgent movements. This link between support for insurgencies and support for terrorism often explains why states support terrorist groups. As noted Chapter 2, many of the terrorist groups active today are also insurgencies. Like Pakistan, the states that support them often are more interested in their activities as insurgent groups than as terrorist groups.

Pakistan's support for Kashmiri radicals has borne considerable fruit, particularly in its all-consuming struggle versus India. Despite New Delhi's wishes, Kashmir has not been incorporated into India as a "normal" state. The ongoing strife has forced India to deploy hundreds of thousands of troops to Kashmir at great human and financial cost. Various governments in Islamabad have also exploited the Kashmir dispute to increase their fraying legitimacy and mobilize domestic sentiment – particularly from Pakistan's increasingly active religious parties – behind their rule.

Pakistan has paid a heavy price for such victories. Support for Kashmiri groups has tarnished Pakistan's image internationally and led to costly and dangerous clashes with India. Even more ominously, this support has had ramifications in Pakistan itself, increasing extremism and creating a threat to the government's continued rule.

This chapter first reviews Kashmir's contentious modern history. It then examines the causes and course of the violence that began in 1989 and has led to tens of thousands of deaths so far. With this context in mind, the chapter reviews the type of support Pakistan provides and its motivations for backing Kashmiri groups. It then assesses the impact of Pakistani support, both on the groups and on Pakistan itself. The final section examines attempts to stop Pakistani support and notes why they have met with at best limited success.

Background

Before India's and Pakistan's independence from Britain in 1947, the territory of Jammu and Kashmir (hereinafter referred to only as

Kashmir) was one of 562 "princely states": entities that enjoyed a high degree of autonomy but swore fealty to the British Raj. The territory has three provinces: the Kashmir Valley, the most populated area, Jammu, and Ladakh. The Kashmir Valley is approximately 95 percent Sunni Muslim, while Jammu is split between Hindus and Muslims, and Ladakh is largely divided between Shi'a Muslims and Buddhists. In 1981, 3 million people lived in the Valley of Kashmir, 2.7 million lived in Jammu, and 134,000 million in Ladakh. Security problems hindered subsequent attempts to conduct a census.[2]

In 1947, Maharaja Hari Singh was the monarch, a Hindu ruling over a Muslim majority. Sheikh Mohammed Abdullah, a Kashmiri Muslim who worked actively with Kashmiri Hindus, led the main political opposition party, the Jammu and Kashmir National Conference. Both Pakistan and India saw the incorporation of Kashmir into their territory as necessary to fulfill their visions of their new countries. Pakistan's rulers believed its Muslim majority made it rightfully theirs – after all, Pakistan was founded in part because its leaders feared that Muslims would suffer under Hindu rule – and that India's desire to control Kashmir reflected a broader goal of undermining Pakistan's independent status. India, in contrast, saw the accession of a Muslim-majority state as vital to its notion that it was a secular, not a Hindu, nation that was hospitable to all religions.[3] In contrast to many other mixed Hindu–Muslim regions, Kashmir was on the border of the two new countries, making it difficult for either side to argue that territorial contiguity required its accession. Over time, India also came to fear a demonstration effect in Kashmir. Should Kashmir successfully secede, it feared that Assam, Tamil Nadu, Punjab, and other states in the Indian union with movements seeking independence would separate as well.

The Maharaja, however, initially sought to have Kashmir be independent from both countries and dodged offers from both Pakistani and Indian leaders. Many subsequent activists, including opponents of the Maharaja, also supported Kashmiri independence. They cited *Kashmiriyat* – in essence a separate Kashmiri identity derived from a common language and shared cultural and historical traits – to justify

---

[2] International Crisis Group, "Kashmir: The View from Srinagar," p. 2.
[3] Ganguly, *The Crisis in Kashmir*, pp. 8–9.

independence. In their eyes, *Kashmiriyat* transcended religious identity and unified Kashmir's Hindu, Muslim, and Buddhist communities.

While the Maharaja vacillated, mass killings of Muslims in the Punjab heightened already high communal tensions throughout India. In Kashmir, Muslims near the cities of Poonch and Muzaffarabad – many of whom spoke Punjabi – rebelled, and their leaders called for union with Pakistan. This sparked popular support in Pakistan itself, as tribal members from Muslim Pashtun areas in Pakistan's North West Frontier Province sought to aid their Muslim brethren against the Maharaja's forces. Soon the new government in Islamabad joined in and, in October 1947, provided the tribesmen with supplies and granted them free passage so they could join the fighting. Pakistan also used its own troops in disguise to invade Kashmir. Muslim soldiers from Kashmir itself joined this force, which massacred and raped its way toward Kashmir's capital, Srinagar.

Confronted with this motley mix of mutineers, foreign tribesmen, angry locals, and Pakistani soldiers, the panicked Maharaja appealed to New Delhi. Thus, Pakistan's effort backfired and led the Maharaja to choose sides. Kashmir's Foreign Minister Mahajan noted that "No raids could take place if the Pakistani authorities wished to stop them."[4] Indian leaders seized the opportunity afforded by the invasion and demanded accession to India as the price of Indian support. Indian forces quickly deployed, and full-scale fighting between India and Pakistan began in November 1947. Pakistani forces retained control of approximately one third of Kashmir (known as Azad Kashmir to Pakistan and as Pakistan Occupied Kashmir to India), but Indian troops had successfully cleared Pakistani forces out of the Kashmir Valley, the most populated part of the area. The two countries separated their forces along the ceasefire line, the so-called "Line of Control," on January 1, 1949. The fighting and communal strife in general led hundreds of thousands of Kashmiri Muslims to flee to Pakistan.[5]

---

[4] As quoted in Schofield, *Kashmir in Conflict*, p. 47.

[5] Ganguly, *The Crisis in Kashmir*, pp. 10–11; Wirsing, *India, Pakistan, and the Kashmir Dispute*, pp. 39–54; Jones, *Pakistan*, pp. 63, p. 64; International Crisis Group, "Kashmir: Learning from the Past," pp. 5–6. Accession was supposed to be ratified by the people of Kashmir, but this was deemed impossible during the initial crisis. This lack of ratification, however, became a major sticking point for those opposing New Delhi's rule. Pakistan contends that

Under the 1952 Delhi Agreement, India promised Kashmir a unique status in its federal system that ensured a high level of autonomy, the retention of certain titles and tax rights, and other forms of privilege. New Delhi also pledged to hold a plebiscite that would ratify Kashmir's political status.[6] This agreement, however, was honored largely in the breach as Kashmir stagnated politically after independence. Sheikh Abdullah, the new state's Prime Minister, kept power highly personalized, as did his successors after Abdullah was imprisoned by India in 1953. Abdullah was subsequently released again – and then jailed again – as New Delhi vacillated between conciliating Kashmiris and quashing them. Elections were rigged, and free discussion limited. As Sumit Ganguly notes, "No honest political opposition was ever allowed to develop in the state."[7]

Pakistan never fully accepted Indian control over Kashmir, and this contributed to a second war in September 1965. Islamabad believed, correctly, that New Delhi was moving to fully integrate Kashmir into India both by ending its special status and by withdrawing the promised plebiscite. Pakistani leaders also feared that US and British arms being provided to India to bolster it against China would make it far stronger militarily, creating a window in which Pakistan would have to act if it hoped for any chance of success. In 1964, Pakistan sent irregular forces and army troops across the ceasefire line, but this did not spark a popular revolt. Nevertheless, the Pakistani effort led to skirmishes, and then a brief all-out war in September 1965.

The war was inconclusive, and a subsequent war in 1971 (which resulted in the creation of independent Bangladesh out of East Pakistan) also failed to dislodge India from Kashmir. India's decisive victory in 1971 led to the signing of the Simla Agreement in 1972, which transformed the ceasefire line in Kashmir into a more formal "line of control." Pakistan also ceded several forward positions on the border, which India had seized during the 1971 war.[8]

India's acceptance of UN Security Council Resolutions 47 and 80 that endorse a plebiscite indicate that India is bound to hold such a vote. Ganguly cites the work of former Pakistani Major General Akbar Khan, *Raiders in Kashmir*, to support his contention of the extensive Pakistani role in the initial fighting in Kashmir.

[6] International Crisis Group, "Kashmir: Learning from the Past," pp. 8–9.

[7] Ganguly, *The Crisis in Kashmir*, p. 29.

[8] International Crisis Group, "Kashmir: The View from Islamabad," pp. 4–5.

Indian social reform efforts and political mismanagement succeeded in loosening India's grasp on Kashmir where Pakistani military force had failed. The increase in education, greater physical and social mobility, and exposure to the media made Kashmiris aware of how much less democratic Kashmir was than the rest of India and made them resentful of their inferior status.[9] Moreover, many Kashmiri leaders remained jailed or in exile – including several such as Sheikh Abdullah who had accepted Kashmir's status as a state of India – further discrediting the state government.

These reforms failed when the Indian government tried to curtail the greater autonomy that Kashmir had won by the 1970s and essentially forced Kashmiris to accept the dominance of the Congress Party. In the 1980s, the government in New Delhi tried to increase central control over Kashmir and increase the influence of the ruling Congress Party, further eroding the legitimacy of Kashmir's already weak institutions. New Delhi sought to have the line of control become the international border and to make Kashmir a state of the Indian union similar to other states. The government used limited social unrest as a pretext for draconian measures to ensure civil order. Increasingly, those governing in Kashmir, including Farooq Abdullah, who inherited the leadership of the Kashmiri nationalist cause when his father died in 1982, were seen as puppets of the Indian state, not as leaders of their people. This perception became far stronger in 1986 when Farooq Abdullah joined his National Conference Party in an electoral alliance with the ruling Congress Party, despite the fact that the Congress Party had earlier arranged for him to be dismissed from power.[10]

The 1987 elections, however, catalyzed this general discontent and focused it on the illegitimacy of the political system. In 1986, several Kashmiri religious parties had joined together and formed the Muslim United Front (MUF) to contest the elections. Drawing on the religious network of schools and mosques, the MUF stressed a nationalist platform and rejected Farooq Abdullah's perceived collaboration with New Delhi. Indeed, Abdullah's alliance with the Congress Party meant that the only

---

[9] Ganguly, *The Crisis in Kashmir,* pp. 30–39.

[10] Ibid., pp. 88–100; International Crisis Group, "Kashmir: Learning from the Past," p. 20. The Indian government in general was not pleased with Abdullah or the kleptocracy he installed but was not able to find an alternative to him with similar stature.

opposition parties were those of the MUF. In the election, however, the MUF won only 4 of the 76 seats, with the Congress–National Conference alliance winning 60. Vote-rigging was massive, voters were intimidated, and MUF workers arrested. Independent observers estimated that the MUF would have won one third of the seats had the vote been fair.[11] Many future militants had once opposed the government peacefully, trying to work against the encroachment of New Delhi through political means. After the 1987 elections, however, they believed they had no avenues for peaceful political change. Voices that rejected the system outright became far more credible to the general population.

Not surprisingly, the leaders tainted by their participation in the anemic electoral process lost their legitimacy. Moreover, Farooq Abdullah did not command the same respect as his father and lacked his political deftness, leading to divisions in the nationalist movement. The rise in India of the Bharatiya Janata Party (BJP), which stressed Hindu nationalism, also contributed to Kashmiri Muslims' sense that India had no place for them.[12]

As traditional political movements failed or became coopted, protest increasingly took an ethnoreligious form. In 1966, the National Liberation Front – a forerunner of the Jammu and Kashmir Liberation Front (JKLF), which was formed in 1977 and initially dominated the struggle for independence after 1989 – formed and began operations based on the Pakistani side of the line of control. The JKLF pushed for Kashmir's independence and advocated a secular state. It was largely ineffective until the electoral process became discredited. Moreover, the worldwide Islamic political revival in the 1970s, the Afghan struggle against the Soviets in the 1980s, and the concurrent growth of Muslim schools in Kashmir led to the increased salience of religious identity. The traditional opposition leadership advocating *Kashmiriyat* became discredited through their constant interactions with New Delhi that produced little gain.[13]

---

[11] Schofield, *Kashmir in Conflict*, pp. 136–137; International Crisis Group, "Kashmir: The View from Srinagar," p. 8.

[12] Schofield, *Kashmir in Conflict*, pp. 137–138 and 146. International Crisis Group, "Kashmir: The View from Srinagar," p. 11.

[13] Ganguly argues that geographic isolation, a failure of secular political movements, and Kashmir's internal political boundaries all contributed to this. Ganguly, *The Crisis in Kashmir*, p. 41. The various areas that make up the

A renewed crisis

The above social changes and political grievances contributed to the explosion of violence in 1989, a conflict that so far has cost approximately 60,000 lives, led to the disappearance of 6,000 more Kashmiris, and displaced 350,000 Kashmiri Hindus from the Valley of Kashmir.[14] The *Tahrik* ("the movement") is often dated as beginning on December 8, 1989, when the JKLF kidnapped the daughter of a prominent politician. Violence had simmered, however, since the discredited election of 1987. Active militant groups included not only the JKLF, but also various Islamist groups such as the Hizb-ul-Mujahedin, Al Baraq, Al Omar, and Al Fateh.

Once the violence had broken out, the initial Indian response greatly bolstered the militants' cause. In 1990, India dismissed Abdullah's government and put Kashmir under its direct control. Kashmir's governor, Jagmohan Malhotra, tried to end the insurgency through harsh repression. The government fired on mass demonstrations, abolished the legislative assembly, arbitrarily arrested Kashmiri males, and otherwise tried to solve the problem with brute force.

The militants exploited the harsh government measures. Terror was used to convince many Hindus to flee their homes, even though relatively few Kashmiri Muslims were supportive of anti-Hindu violence. The militants also kidnapped and murdered local officials, businessmen, media officials, educators, and other prominent persons, particularly those who were seen as willing to collaborate with New Delhi.[15] The unpopularity of Indian rule legitimated the violence in the eyes of many Kashmiris, transforming broad disgruntlement into increased support for the militants.

Jammu and Kashmir areas have highly different religious compositions. For many years, Kashmiri Muslims had seen themselves both as a distinct people and as a distinct religious group. See also Hewitt, "An Area of Darkness, Still?," and Ganguly, *The Crisis in Kashmir*, pp. 41–42.

[14] The Indian government puts the figure at 30,000, while Kashmiri groups claim that 80,000 died. The International Crisis Group puts the figure at 60,000, most of whom were civilian. International Crisis Group, "Kashmir: Learning from the Past," p. 1. See International Crisis Group, "Kashmir: The View from New Delhi," p. 2 for information on disappearances and pp. 11–12 for information on the displaced. Most of the uprising is concentrated in the Kashmir Valley, but the Doda District of Jammu also regularly sees violence.

[15] Schofield, *Kashmir in Conflict*, pp. 151–154.

One Kashmiri government official noted, "What Jagmohan did in five months they (the militants) could not have achieved in five years."[16]

Pakistan played little part in instigating the uprising. Ganguly, who in general argues that Pakistan played an important role in sustaining and directing the crisis, notes that Islamabad was surprised by the uprising and did not create the 1989 unrest.[17] Indeed, when India and Pakistan came close to war in 1986–87, Kashmir was a peripheral issue.[18]

Ferment in Kashmir began to decline (albeit fitfully) in the mid-1990s, as many indigenous Kashmiris became exhausted by the war and as Indian policies became more effective. The militants' own brutality also worked against them. Over time, many insurgents became as focused on criminal activities as on politics. Murder of Hindus, shakedowns of middle-class Kashmiris, repeated rape, and the forceful conscription of young men to serve in the militias all led to a decline in support. The Indian government's improved ability to gather intelligence and effective use of pro-government militias also hindered the militants' efforts. Over time, the Indian government tried to bolster local autonomy, develop the legitimacy of local government, increase development spending, and otherwise try to win over Kashmiris. Although New Delhi's political strategy was often fitful and subordinate to military concerns, there were few mass demonstrations after 1993.[19] In 1995, India held elections to restore a more legitimate government. Elections were met with more violence and the results were often portrayed as illegitimate. At times, violence spiked. By 2002, however, election turnout was quite high despite militant attempts to disrupt the polls.[20]

[16] As quoted in ibid., p. 154.

[17] Ganguly, *Conflict Unending*, p. 88.

[18] Schofield, *Kashmir in Conflict*, p. 149; International Crisis Group, "Kashmir: The View from Islamabad," p. 6.

[19] Schofield, *Kashmir in Conflict,* p. 173; Ganguly, *The Crisis in Kashmir,* p. 139; Wirsing, *India, Pakistan, and the Kashmir Dispute,* p. 137; Ganguly, *Conflict Unending*, p. 122. For a review of many Indian measures to try to win over Kashmiris, see Government of India, *Annual Report, 2002–2003*, pp. 20–30; see also International Crisis Group, "Kashmir: Learning from the Past," p. 15; International Crisis Group, "Kashmir: The View from Srinagar," p. 9.

[20] International Crisis Group, "Kashmir: Learning from the Past," p. 16. Alexander Evans describes how the violence peaked again in 2001. See Evans, "The Kashmir Insurgency," pp. 73–75.

The crisis took on a new, and in many ways even more destabilizing, aspect in 1999, when Pakistani military forces occupied over 100 Indian posts in the Kargil Mountains, which had been vacated during the winter. (The Pakistani government used a paramilitary force, the Northern Light Infantry, for the operation but claimed it was carried out by a united front of Kashmiri militants.[21]) Pakistani leaders became concerned that the insurgency in Kashmir was losing steam and felt that bold action was necessary to revive it. However, when Pakistan infiltrated its own regular army units into the mountaintops that shadowed the Kargil highway, it threatened India's control over part of the province. This led to a direct clash between Indian and Pakistani military forces, leading to over 1,000 deaths and international pressure on Pakistan to withdraw.[22]

WHO ARE THE MILITANTS?

Pakistan has backed a bewildering array of militant groups in Kashmir. These include the Jammu and Kashmir Liberation Front, Al-Badr, Hizb-ul-Mujahedin, Harkat-ul-Mujahedin (formerly Harkat-al-Ansar), Jaish-e-Mohammad, and Lashkar-e-Tayyeba, among others. As the number of organizations suggests, the resistance is fragmented. Robert Wirsing estimated that two dozen groups operated in Kashmir in the early 1990s, and that six of those "really count."[23] The proliferation of groups is in part a deliberate move on the part of Pakistan, which has tried to "segment" the militant market to attract different types of support for the movements and to ensure its control.[24]

Until 1990, the JKLF was the leading Kashmiri resistance group, but as the decade wore on Islamist-oriented radicals came to the fore.[25] The JKLF sought independence for Kashmir, not union with Pakistan. Moreover, the JKLF leadership resisted Pakistan's efforts to impose its will on the movement. The JKLF was also more amenable to compromise

---

[21] See Fair, *Militants in the Kargil Conflict.*

[22] Jones, *Pakistan,* p. 93; Schofield, *Kashmir in Conflict,* pp. 208–211; Reidel, "American Diplomacy and the 1999 Kargil Summit at Blair House."

[23] Wirsing, *India, Pakistan, and the Kashmir Dispute,* p. 132. For an excellent overview of the many militant organizations, their links to various parties and factions in Pakistan, and the personalities involved, see Rana, *Gateway to Terrorism.*

[24] I would like to thank Chris Fair for drawing this to my attention.

[25] Evans, "The Kashmir Insurgency," p. 69.

with New Delhi and was concerned about losing popular support by attacking civilians. Because of these perceived defects, Islamabad began to back Islamist horses.

As the JKLF fell out of favor, the Hizb-ul-Mujahedin, which supported union with Pakistan and had a far more uncompromising attitude in general, assumed the leading role in the resistance, a move reinforced by the 1994 decision of some JKLF leaders to renounce violence, a decision that split the movement. The JKLF faction that remained committed to violence was in effect destroyed by Indian forces in 1996. The Hizb-ul-Mujahedin was formed in October 1989 and seeks the union of Jammu and Kashmir with Pakistan. The Hizb-ul-Mujahedin is tied to Pakistan's Jamiat-e-Islami party, a leading Islamist movement. Unlike many of the other Kashmiri Islamist groups, it draws primarily on local Kashmiris for support.[26]

Hizb-ul-Mujahedin received considerable funding from Pakistani intelligence initially. As with the JKLF, Islamabad proved a fickle patron. Over time – as the Jamiat-e-Islami party fell out of favor in Pakistan and as more radical groups emerged – Pakistani intelligence shifted its support in favor of Jaish-e-Mohammad, Harkat-ul-Mujahedin, and Lashkar-e-Tayyeba, which together have several thousand members.[27] These groups are far more ambitious than the JKLF or even Hizb-ul-Mujahedin. They seek not only to join Kashmir with Pakistan, but also to Islamicize Kashmir and spread their ideology throughout the region.[28]

---

[26] International Crisis Group, "Kashmir: The View from Srinagar," p. 17. A group of militants seeking a lesser role for the Jamiat-e-Islami split from the Hizb-ul-Mujahedin to form Al Badr. The Hizb-ul-Mujahedin may have broken up in January 2003. See Jamal, "The Hizbul Mujahedin Once Again Breaks Up."

[27] Pro-Pakistan groups that draw heavily on Kashmiris on the Pakistan side of the border and on foreign fighters include Lashkhar-e-Tayyeba, the Jaish-e-Mohammad, and Harkat-ul-Mujahedin. Lashkhar-e-Tayyeba appears to draw primarily on Punjabis, not on Kashmiris. See *Patterns of Global Terrorism 2003*, pp. 123, 126–127. Many Kashmiris believe the foreign fighters are braver and more skilled than the Kashmiris. International Crisis Group, "Kashmir: The View from Srinagar," p. 17. The Harkat-ul Mujahedin changed its name after the United States formally declared it to be a foreign terrorist organization.

[28] Evans, "The Kashmir Insurgency," p. 71.

There is considerable intermixing of the personnel from radical groups, as the fortunes of individual groups and their leaders ebb and flow. For example, many members of the Harkat-ul-Mujahedin joined the Jaish-e-Mohammad, which was formed by Maulana Masood Azhar, a leading ideologue of the Harkat-ul-Mujahedin.

The overall number of militants is not clear. In 1991, one British reporter estimated 45,000 armed and trained fighters, but the Indian government claimed this figure was extremely high. Over time, this number declined due to Indian counterinsurgency successes, disillusionment with the militants' violence, and infighting among their ranks.[29] After the initial uprising, the Indian government estimated the number of active militants fell to 6,000.

The militants are far from united. The United Jihad Council is in theory a unified command, but in practice each group pursues its own strategy.[30] Militants among the separatists have attacked other opponents of New Delhi whom they see as insufficiently committed. Islamabad has also engineered the split of various militant groups. After the JKLF began to call for negotiations, Pakistan worked with other Kashmiri groups to wipe it out. In 2002, militants killed Abdul Ghani Lone, a moderate champion of the Kashmiri cause who supported negotiations with the government of India. The militants also target journalists to ensure biased reporting.[31]

At times, different militant groups accepted ceasefires or negotiated with the government, but pressure from other radicals made a sustained peace difficult. As noted above, the JKLF called for a ceasefire in 1994. In 2000, Hizb-ul-Mujahedin accepted a ceasefire, which was rejected by other Islamist groups that continued to commit atrocities and killed Hindus to prevent the peace process from succeeding.[32]

TERRORISM OR GUERRILLA WAR?

Many of the 60,000 or so deaths in the recent conflict were part and parcel of guerrilla conflict: attacks on soldiers, government officials, and supposed collaborators. Even many of the civilian casualties can be seen

---

[29] Schofield, *Kashmir in Conflict*, pp. 157 and 172.
[30] Evans, "The Kashmir Insurgency," p. 70.
[31] International Crisis Group, "Kashmir: The View from New Delhi," p. 17.
[32] Schofield, *Kashmir in Conflict*, p. 230.

as the inevitable accidents that occur in a guerrilla war. However, many of the civilian deaths can also be considered terrorism, even by narrow definitions of that term.[33] Pakistan-backed groups have engaged in kidnapping, attacks on politicians of almost all persuasions, and other measures against civilians. Human Rights Watch reports that Pakistani-backed militants murdered hundreds of Muslims and Hindus because they supported the government or otherwise opposed the militant groups. In February 2000, Islamic radicals – perhaps from Lashkar-e-Tayyeba or the Hizb-ul-Mujahedin – massacred thirty-four Sikhs in Kashmir. The government of India claims that over 10,000 civilians have died from militant attacks and that the militants engaged in over 5,000 incidents of destruction of property. The conflict has also devastated regional government and infrastructure. Public education, tax collection, power supplies, and other government services operate fitfully, if at all.[34]

Human Rights Watch also reports that militants used violence to drive Hindus out of the state of Kashmir. They massacred Hindu villagers, assassinated Hindu leaders, destroyed Hindu temples, and otherwise threatened Hindus with violence. Thousands of Hindus fled the Valley or were displaced within Kashmir.[35] This terrorism has also spilled outside of Kashmir: in 1999, Harkat-ul-Mujahedin hijacked an Indian Airlines plane, successfully forcing the release of several militant leaders.[36]

An overview of Pakistan's support for Kashmiri militants

Pakistan's role in creating the violence that escalated after 1989 was limited, but it quickly exploited the strife and made it far harder for the Indian government to defeat the insurgents. Before the 1989 uprising,

---

[33] The South Asia Terrorism Portal, which is often viewed as a mouthpiece for the government of India, describes dozens of events each year involving deliberate attacks on civilians, family members of political and military targets, members of non-Muslim communities, and other non-combatants. See South Asia Terrorism Portal, "Major Incidents of Terrorist Violence in Jammu and Kashmir, 1990–2003."

[34] Schofield, *Kashmir in Conflict*, p. 228; Human Rights Watch, "Behind the Kashmir Conflict"; Government of India, *Annual Report, 2002–2003*, pp. 12–13; Wirsing, *India, Pakistan, and the Kashmir Dispute*, p. 142.

[35] Human Rights Watch, "Behind the Kashmir Conflict"; US Committee for Refugees, "Displacement from Kashmir."

[36] Schofield, *Kashmir in Conflict*, p. 227.

policymakers in Pakistan believed that India's conventional military superiority enabled it to defend its claim to Kashmir indefinitely. The uprising – and the concurrent collapse of the Soviet Union that occurred in part due to Moscow's disaster at the hands of Islamist fighters in Afghanistan – fostered the belief that India would not be able to manage the restive Muslim population in Kashmir. Pakistan's nuclear program also was a vital part of Islamabad's calculus, leading it to conclude that it could foster an intense insurgency with little fear of Indian military escalation.[37]

To encourage the uprising, Islamabad provided a vast range of assistance to the insurgents, including diplomatic and political support as well as sanctuary, arms, and training. Pakistan exploited the apparatus it had set up in the 1980s to channel support to the anti-Soviet *mujahedin* in Afghanistan, instead directing it toward Kashmir.[38] Pakistan sought to help the insurgents wage a guerrilla war on India, but Islamabad's direct role in particular attacks on non-combatants is often not clear. However, Islamabad clearly knew of plans for many major attacks and had accepted that terrorism would occur as part of its efforts to assist the overall insurgency.

All the leading Kashmiri militant groups fighting New Delhi had bases in Pakistan. The JKLF originally made its home on the Pakistani side of the border, and a succession of religious groups followed suit over time. Hizb-ul-Mujahedin was based in Pakistan's North West Frontier Province; Lashkar-e-Tayyeba was headquartered in Muridke, which is near the city of Lahore in Pakistan; and Harkat-ul-Mujahedin and Jaysh-e Mohammad were based in Muzaffarabad on Pakistan's side of the Kashmir border.[39] This haven allowed these groups to recruit, train, plan, proselytize, and enjoy a respite from Indian counterinsurgency efforts. Despite numerous Indian successes, New Delhi was not able to follow up on successful cell disruptions and crush its opponents.

Pakistani officials also helped train the Kashmiri militants directly. Retired Pakistani army officers and non-commissioned officers who were supposedly "moonlighting" from their regular duties instructed

---

[37] Wirsing, *India, Pakistan, and the Kashmir Dispute*, p. 121. See also Tellis et al., *Limited Conflicts Under the Nuclear Umbrella*.

[38] Kux, *The United States and Pakistan, 1947–2000*, p. 305.

[39] Schofield, *Kashmir in Conflict*, p. 155.

recruits in guerrilla warfare, evasion techniques, and the use of light arms.[40] By 2001, Pakistan had over 90 training camps in Pakistan-occupied Kashmir. Much of the training occurred in Afghanistan, under the eyes of the Pakistan-backed Taliban and al-Qa'ida. In Afghanistan, various militant groups forged ties to each other as well as to international *jihadists* linked to al-Qa'ida.[41] As discussed in Chapter 7, the training was often sophisticated.

Assistance in planning was another vital contribution. The ISI helped militants cross the fortified and patrolled line of control from base camps in Pakistan.[42] India also claims that Pakistan still serves as a command and control hub, with militants in Kashmir calling back to Pakistan to gain tactical guidance, acquire supplies, and execute plans.[43] Planning also extended to political coordination. To increase the militants' coordination, Pakistan organized the United Jihad Council.

Pakistan also finances the guerrillas. Although precise figures are not available (in part due to differences over what constitutes direct support), common estimates range from $40 million to as high as $250 million (a figure claimed by the Indian government) annually. This money, in turn, helped the militants recruit many poor Pakistanis who had few other opportunities.[44]

Pakistan also bolsters the militants' manpower. Islamabad facilitates the recruitment and transit of Pakistani and foreign volunteers seeking to fight in Kashmir. India claimed in 2002 that over 60 percent of the militants fighting in Kashmir came from outside the state – a number that has varied between 1,000 and 2,500 in recent years.[45] The Pakistani

---

[40] India claims that literally tens of thousands of Kashmiris have received arms training in Pakistan. Wirsing, *India, Pakistan, and the Kashmir Dispute*, pp. 120 and 136; Chalk, "Pakistan's Role in the Kashmir Insurgency."

[41] Rana, *Gateway to Terrorism*, pp. 100–101.

[42] Wirsing, *India, Pakistan, and the Kashmir Dispute*, p. 120.

[43] Government of India, *Annual Report, 2002–2003*, p. 15.

[44] Intelligence officials estimated in 2000 that Pakistan was providing $57 million worth of support. Peter Chalk cites Indian intelligence in giving an estimate of between $125 million and $250 million. See "The Islamists' Drug Connection"; Chalk, "Pakistan's Role in the Kashmir Insurgency"; and "United Jihad Groups." Jaysh-e Mohammad was almost totally dependent on Pakistan for financing, while other Kashmiri groups drew on religious charities as well.

[45] International Crisis Group, "Kashmir: The View from New Delhi," p. 1.

government worked with the Taliban and with international *jihadist* organizations such as al-Qa'ida to send foreign fighters to Kashmir.[46]

Pakistan also provided indirect military support with its own forces. In Pakistan, the military acts as a facilitator, helping supply militants *en route* to Kashmir. At times, the Pakistani military would provide covering fire to distract Indian troops, helping the militants cross the border.[47]

Pakistan openly encourages the Kashmiris to fight New Delhi and champions their cause internationally. Islamabad issues constant slogans exhorting Kashmiris to resist New Delhi. In Pakistan itself, it schedules rallies in support of Kashmiri fighters and calls upon Pakistanis to donate to their causes. To gain international support, Pakistan highlights Indian human rights abuses in Kashmir, which are numerous.[48]

WHO SUPPORTS THE MILITANTS?

All parts of Pakistan's government back the Kashmir cause, though with different degrees of enthusiasm. Many Pakistanis, particularly in Punjabi areas, see Kashmir as a vital part of the country's national identity and believe it was unjustly excluded from Pakistan at partition. Other leaders are less enthusiastic but see Kashmir as a unifying issue for a country torn by internal divisions. Despite occasional Pakistani denials, the vast range of support it offers to the militants would not be possible without the participation of many parts of the Pakistani government and society. The support occurs despite constant changes in government, which have different mixes of traditional elites, religious parties, and military officials. As Robert Wirsing notes after reviewing various Pakistani denials of assistance, "When all is said and done, however, there is very little likelihood that many infiltrators have made their way across the LOC [line of control] into Indian Kashmir without the knowledge and active cooperation of the Pakistan army, of the

---

[46] Rashid, *Taliban*, p. 137. The Indian government claims that almost 3,000 foreign militants died in Kashmir between 1989 and 2003. Government of India, *Annual Report, 2002–2003*, p. 13.

[47] Wirsing, *India, Pakistan, and the Kashmir Dispute*, p. 120.

[48] "Kashmiri Terrorism on the Rise"; Wirsing, *India, Pakistan, and the Kashmir Dispute*, p. 122; International Crisis Group, "Kashmir: The View from Islamabad," p. 3; International Crisis Group, "Kashmir: The View from New Delhi," p. 2.

Afghanistan-seasoned ISI, and, indeed, of key elements in the civil bureaucracies of Pakistan and Azad Kashmir."[49]

Much of Pakistan's support is encouraged, and at times implemented, by Islamist groups in Pakistan itself.[50] These groups often act autonomously, though their actions were usually blessed by the government and the military. The Jamiat-e-Islami party, which unlike many other religious parties seeks to transcend narrow sectarian movements, operated training camps for Kashmiri militants, particularly the Hizb-ul-Mujahedin. The Jamiat-ul-Ulema-e-Islami (JUI), which makes the JI look progressive, is a Deobandi organization that began to work closely with the army and intelligence services in Kashmir after 1993, when it formed an alliance with Prime Minister Bhutto, who had resumed power after being removed in 1990.[51] The JUI worked with the Harkat-ul-Mujahedin, a radical group that relied heavily on foreign fighters. Lashkar-e-Tayyeba, another brutal organization, sprang from the militant wing of Ahl-e-Hadith, a puritanical reform movement that drew considerable support from Saudi Arabia but that is hostile to Deobandi groups.[52] The support provided is also indirect. The JUI and other religious groups run many of the 40,000 or so religious schools, which, as Jessica Stern contends, "supply the labor for 'jihad.'"[53] According to some observers, the Musharraf governments appeared to have designed a division of labor for the major actors. Domestic militant organizations recruited, trained, and outfitted members. Pakistani intelligence then provided weapons, more sophisticated equipment, and at times training. The Pakistani Army offered them food and a place to rest as they infiltrated Kashmir, among many other forms of assistance.[54]

Perhaps because there is broad bureaucratic and political support for the Kashmir cause, no government in Islamabad can calibrate its support

[49] Wirsing, *India, Pakistan, and the Kashmir Dispute*, p. 120.
[50] Support for militants in Kashmir is a logical step for most Pakistani parties and factions, as the vast majority also support domestic organizations in Pakistan itself that use terror. Establishing "street power" and intimidating potential opponents is a time-honored tactic for Pakistani leaders.
[51] Wirsing, *India, Pakistan, and the Kashmir Dispute*, p. 120 and Rashid, *Taliban*, p. 90.
[52] Cohen, *The Idea of Pakistan*.
[53] Stern, "Pakistan's Jihad Culture," p. 120.
[54] Khan, "Business as Usual," p. 38.

solely according to strategic objectives. Too many vested interests have developed, making it hard to curtail support. Over time, Pakistani intelligence and the military came to dominate Kashmir policy and at times undermined the negotiations of civilian governments that sought to negotiate over Pakistan.[55] Similarly, many Islamist groups are highly committed to Kashmir and oppose various government attempts to play down support or rein in militants in the face of international pressure or Indian threats.

LIMITS TO PAKISTAN'S SUPPORT

Although the range of Pakistani support is vast, at times Islamabad has limited its contributions. Limits on Pakistan's support are best observed by what is not given to the militants. They do not receive the best arms from Pakistan's arsenal, and Islamabad prefers to keep much of its support deniable, if not exactly hidden. Many recruits receive only a few weeks training and have little equipment.[56] Direct military support is given grudgingly and infrequently.

One reason for Pakistan's limited support is that it fears the militants even as its exploits them. Islamabad has moved strongly to quash any move toward Kashmiri independence, which would presumably include Azad Kashmir as well as the parts now controlled by India. To this end, it aided various Islamist forces that called for union with Pakistan over groups like the JKLF, which initially enjoyed more support from Kashmiris and might be more effective in resisting New Delhi, as it can tap into a broader range of Kashmiri support.[57]

Pakistan was also limited by fear of another war with India. For example, it halted a march organized by the JKLF from Pakistani

---

[55] In contrast to many assertions that the ISID operates independently of the central government, it clearly operates under its control, with senior ISID officials reporting to President Musharraf and, in the case of former ISID chief General Mahmood Ahmed, being replaced when he failed to follow Musharraf's lead. ISID officials are in the regular military chain of command, making them further responsive to the military regime's directive. International Crisis Group, "Kashmir: The View from Islamabad," pp. 10 and 18. At times, the military increased support for insurgents, and it even overthrew several elected governments that were engaged in negotiations over Kashmir.

[56] Wirsing, *India, Pakistan, and the Kashmir Dispute*, p. 122.

[57] Ibid., pp. 122–123.

territory across the border, fearing this would provoke an incident with India that would ignite a broader conflagration.[58] Islamabad recognizes India's conventional military superiority and knows that an all-out confrontation could prove disastrous. Pakistan's nuclear arsenal has offset its concern over Indian escalation considerably, however.

Pakistani motivations

Pakistan aids the Kashmiri cause due to a mix of domestic politics and strategic objectives. As noted above, most of the support focuses on the Kashmiris' guerrilla activities, but this quickly spills over into more blatant terrorism.

STRATEGIC OBJECTIVES

Pakistan always harbored irredentist ambitions for Kashmir, though over time these became increasingly distant. Islamabad has long seen Kashmir as rightfully belonging to Pakistan due to its Muslim majority. For many years after independence, Pakistani leaders also believed Kashmir would give Pakistan additional "strategic depth" in its conflict with India and provide access to major rivers in the region. Such depth is seen as particularly important, as Punjab, Pakistan's most-populated province, borders Kashmir, leaving Pakistan highly vulnerable if there is a conflict with India.[59]

Over time, however, the prospects of outright military victory over India became remote. India's military is approximately twice the size of Pakistan's, and India's GDP is almost ten times larger.[60] As a result, India has a larger, more skilled, and better military. It soundly defeated Pakistan in the last major war in 1971, and the gap has grown since then in India's favor.

Today, Pakistan has a host of other objectives that fall short of the successful absorption of Kashmir but involve its strategic rivalry with India. One of these is "bleeding" India. Many Pakistani military leaders believed that by bogging India down in the Kashmiri quagmire, they could balance a strategic equation that would otherwise favor

---

[58] Ibid., p. 124.
[59] International Crisis Group, "Kashmir: The View from Islamabad," p. 11.
[60] In 2002, India's GDP was $2.6 trillion, while Pakistan's was just less than $300 billion. *CIA World Factbook 2003*.

New Delhi. As Ganguly notes, in 1989 Pakistani leaders "saw an excellent opportunity to impose significant material and other costs on India at little cost to themselves."[61] Supporting Kashmiri guerrillas was a cheap way to force India to devote much of its military force to counterinsurgency.[62]

Backing militants also ensures that India cannot achieve its primary objective: absorbing Kashmir into India proper as a "normal" state. By backing the militants, Pakistan keeps Kashmir apart from the Indian union.[63] Moreover, the constant crises at times force the engagement of the United States and other powers that would prefer not to be involved in regional disputes.

Pakistan also backs militants in retaliation for India's meddling in Pakistan's own ethnic problems.[64] Islamabad blames India for backing East Pakistan, now Bangladesh, in its successful secessionist war in 1971.[65] Similarly, Islamabad claims that India backed a host of Pakistani groups to foster civil violence in Pakistan in the mid-1990s.

Part of why Pakistan sought nuclear weapons was to gain immunity from India's conventional military force superiority. General Aslam Beg, the Army Chief of Staff, noted in 2002 that Pakistan's nuclear capability is a "critical equalizer" and acts as a "restraining influence" on India.[66] As such, Pakistanis feel confident in making limited challenges to India despite their conventional military inferiority.

---

[61] Ganguly, *Conflict Unending*, p. 92.

[62] Stern, "Pakistan's Jihad Culture," p. 116 and International Crisis Group, "Kashmir: The View from Islamabad," p. 12.

[63] Ganguly notes that "Pakistan, sensing an opportunity to weaken India's hold on Kashmir, funded, trained, and organized a loose, unstructured movement into a coherent, organized enterprise directed toward challenging the writ of the Indian state in Kashmir." Ganguly, *The Crisis in Kashmir*, p. 41.

[64] Wirsing, *India, Pakistan, and the Kashmir Dispute*, p. 121.

[65] Stern, "Pakistan's Jihad Culture," p. 115.

[66] As quoted in International Crisis Group, "Kashmir: The View from Islamabad," p. 7. See also Ganguly, *Conflict Unending*, p. 88. The risk of increased guerrilla and conventional conflict because of the "security" provided by nuclear weapons is a classic instance of what Glenn Snyder described as the "security/instability" paradox. See Snyder, *Deterrence and Defense* for more on this concept.

DOMESTIC POLITICS

Over time, domestic politics have become almost as important as strategic concerns. Pakistan's military was the most consistent and important group backing the insurgency. Repeated losses to India humiliated Pakistani officers, and they felt a genuine sense of nationalism that embraced Kashmir. Moreover, by playing up the threat from India the Pakistani military could justify its involvement in domestic politics and demand a large share of Pakistan's strained budget.[67]

For any regime, appeasing the military's commitment to Kashmir was necessary, as the military is a key power broker in Pakistan, having overthrown several civilian governments. Even under civilian rule, the military dominated national security affairs and derailed attempts by various civilian governments to improve relations with India.[68]

Successive Pakistani governments also sought to use their support for militants in Kashmir to court favor with religious groups in Pakistan itself. In the 1980s, General Zia-ul Haq instructed Pakistani intelligence to organize, fund, and train Kashmiris, using Islam to motivate them. This effort was part of Zia's overall campaign of "Islamicization," where he tried to enhance his domestic legitimacy at the price of his secular rivals. From 1977 until his death in 1988, Zia's government tried to co-opt the Islamists through concessions in order to prevent them from challenging the regime and existing elites. Domestically, this involved such measures as using regime-collected religious taxes to support extremist religious schools, bringing the Jamiat-e-Islami into government, expanding the role of religious law as part of the penal code, and other measures.[69] Different regimes also used Islamist radicals to intimidate their domestic political opponents.[70]

---

[67] For example, General Beg declared in 2002 that Pakistan needed both strong military forces and nuclear weapons because of India's belligerence in Kashmir. International Crisis Group, "Kashmir: The View from Islamabad," p. 7.

[68] Ibid., pp. ii and 1.

[69] Ganguly, *The Crisis in Kashmir*, p. 77 and Kepel, *Jihad*, pp. 98–103. For an overview of the JI, see Nasr, *The Vanguard of the Islamic Revolution*. Zia's predecessor, the civilian Zulfi Bhutto, also catered to the Islamists in a variety of ways as a means to unite the country.

[70] Cohen, *The Idea of Pakistan*.

Support continued even after Zia died in 1988 and civilian government returned under Benazir Bhutto. The Kashmiri cause enjoyed considerable popularity in Pakistan, and when violence broke out in 1989 it was politically difficult for Islamabad not to support it. The problem was made worse because Bhutto's domestic position was weak, leading her to abandon an earlier attempt at a rapprochement with India and openly back the Kashmiri revolt. Other opposition parties jumped in, with all politicians competing to declare their support for the Kashmiris and opposition to New Delhi.[71]

Different leaders favored different domestic groups, but they all had ties to Kashmiri militants. Zia in particular had worked with the Jamiat-e-Islami, which helped form Hizb-ul-Mujahedin. In 1993, Bhutto took power and sought to weaken the power structure Zia had created. She worked with the ultramilitant Jamiat-ul-Ulema-e-Islami, which in turned bolstered the Harkat-ul-Mujahedin over the Hizb-ul-Mujahedin.

Over time, as Pakistani civilian governments became weaker and as the military government of Musharraf that replaced them grasped at legitimacy, the religious parties gained in influence.[72] This growth in the Islamists' strength has if anything accelerated in recent years, bolstered by the collapse of other political parties and causes. Various secular leaders who stressed nationalism or reform became discredited by rampant corruption and economic stagnation. In the October 2002 elections, the Islamists made their strongest showing ever, gaining 60 seats in parliament (out of 342) and taking control over the Northwest Frontier Province and Baluchistan.[73] Beginning in the 1990s, part of the motivation for Pakistani support comes from an unwillingness to confront

---

[71] Ganguly, *Conflict Unending*, p. 92.

[72] For a review of this growth and an assessment of the influence of religious parties today, see Nasr, "Military Rule, Islamism, and Democracy in Pakistan."

[73] Much of this success involved the Islamists joining forces and ending their traditional squabbling and the Musharraf government's desire to weaken the traditional, more secular, parties. Pooling Islamists' votes magnified their electoral power under Pakistan's procedures. The Islamist parties also were able to campaign unofficially in mosques before the official campaigning season began, giving them an advantage over secular parties. In addition, the Musharraf government made many types of political gatherings illegal while letting Islamists continue to spread their message at mosques.

powerful domestic groups, particularly religious ones that provide much of the support for the militants.

Pakistan became increasingly tied to the insurgency regardless of the preferences of individual leaders. Different Pakistani political parties, military and civilian leaders, and bureaucratic actors all had their favored proxies, but the weakness of the Pakistani state made it hard for anyone to exert complete control. Moreover, the militant groups active in Kashmir are widely viewed as legitimate freedom fighters, in contrast to several sectarian groups in Pakistan that many Pakistanis are more willing to characterize as terrorist organizations. As a result, it became increasingly impossible for any leader to make significant concessions regarding Kashmir, regardless of the diplomatic and strategic cost to Islamabad. As General Musharraf declared, "Kashmir runs in our blood. No Pakistani can afford to sever links with Kashmir."[74]

The impact of Pakistani support

Pakistan fundamentally changed the nature of the struggle in Kashmir. The vast range of Pakistani backing enabled the Kashmiris to sustain and expand what might otherwise have been a limited and short-lived struggle. Islamabad's support strengthened more radical Islamist militants over forces seeking independence. It also introduced a new dimension to the conflict by helping organize and insert large numbers of foreign militants into the struggle. As a result of this backing, India was not able to consolidate its control and was forced to devote considerable resources to crushing the rebellion. These successes, however, came at a high price. Pakistan became increasingly embroiled in the conflict, bringing it almost over the brink to a conventional war with India. In addition, Islamabad's international reputation was tarnished. Most important, instability in Pakistan itself grew, and the leadership in Islamabad has found it difficult to move away from the radicals.

Strategically, Pakistan has met with many successes. It succeeded in preventing New Delhi from consolidating its control over Kashmir. Despite being controlled by India for over fifty years, Kashmir is in no way a "normal" state in the Indian union, and its name is synonymous internationally with violence. Given the weakness and disarray of

---

[74] As quoted in, International Crisis Group, "Kashmir: The View from Islamabad," p. 12.

the overall resistance, Pakistan's support often means the difference between defeat, survival, and even leadership of the movement. As Wirsing notes, Pakistan's "patronage has no doubt exerted a powerful influence on the rise and fall in fortunes of practically every militant group active there."[75]

Efforts to "bleed" India have also paid off. By the early 1990s, India was forced to deploy hundreds of thousands of security forces to Kashmir. As of 2000, India still had 250,000 security personnel in Kashmir. India had to take these forces away from the standard duties against Pakistan and focus them more on policing infiltration routes and otherwise fighting the insurgency – tasks that are both frustrating and demoralizing for conventional military forces.[76] Moreover, when the Kargil crisis occurred, Indian leaders found their troops were not fully prepared for conventional war.

Pakistani support posed severe limits to India's counterinsurgency campaign. The leadership of most of the movements was effectively out of reach for India, hindering the delivery of a crushing below. Nor was India able to stop the insurgents' logistics network, as they were always able to find a source of arms, funding, and other supplies from Pakistan. Islamabad's support also helped legitimate the insurgents' cause, both in Kashmir and in the broader world.

Pakistan played a major role in transforming the nature of the rebellion, strengthening Islamist forces that favored union with Pakistan over secular ones like the JKLF that sought Kashmir's independence. Politically active Kashmiris who did not embrace Islamabad's agenda were sidelined or killed. Over time, Pakistani money, training, and other forms of support made groups like the Hizb-ul-Mujahedin and later the Harkat-ul-Mujahedin more lethal and more attractive to potential recruits. As Victoria Schofield notes, "Inevitably those groups who derived support from Pakistan were more vocal in expressing their desire ultimately to join Pakistan."[77]

[75] Wirsing, *India, Pakistan, and the Kashmir Dispute*, p. 134.
[76] International Crisis Group, "Kashmir: Learning from the Past," p. 15; Wirsing, *India, Pakistan, and the Kashmir Dispute*, p. 150; and, Evans, "The Kashmir Insurgency," p. 78.
[77] Schofield, *Kashmir in Conflict*, p. 201.

AT WHAT COST SUCCESS?

Despite the above accomplishments, many of which are considerable, Pakistan suffered heavily because of its support for the Kashmiri cause. Several Pakistani strategic objectives were not met or even were set back. The biggest impact, however, has been at home, heightening the fragility of a highly unstable state.

Pakistan, of course, did not achieve its maximal strategic objectives. Although Kashmir is not successfully integrated into India, it remains far from being united with Pakistan. While the Kashmir conflict has bled India heavily, this has not led to disaster. The Indian economy has grown remarkably in the last fifteen years, while Pakistan's has stagnated.

Pakistan's support for the militants has also hurt its overall image. The United States, for example, saw India as the primary barrier to the settlement of the Kashmir dispute in the years after independence and partition. By the 1990s, however, Islamabad's support for terrorism linked to Kashmir contributed to a souring of the US–Pakistan relationship.[78]

Indeed, Pakistani support for militants at times drove Kashmiris closer to New Delhi. Pakistan's 1947 support for Muslim Kashmiris pushed the *maharaja* into New Delhi's arms. Almost fifty years later, the Arab fighters sent to Kashmir by Pakistan hurt the legitimacy of the guerrillas, diminishing their claim to act on behalf of the people of Kashmir.[79] The brutality of many Pakistan-backed groups further alienated Kashmiris, turning them against Islamabad. A 2002 A.C. Nielson survey indicates that few Kashmiris seek union with Pakistan, though many still favor independence from India.[80]

A particular problem in recent years is that many of the militant groups involved in Pakistani follow Deobandi, Wahhabi, Ahl-e Hadith, or other puritanical streams of Sunni Islam that are hostile to the Sufi Islam practiced by many Kashmiris. As such, they have destroyed traditional Sufi shrines as idolatrous, attacked Kashmiri women who work or go to school with acid, or otherwise tried to impose a restrictive form of Islam on the Kashmiri Muslims they are supposedly trying to save from oppression.[81]

---

[78] Kux, *The United States and Pakistan, 1947–2000*, pp. 31 and 316.
[79] Rashid, *Taliban*, p. 137.
[80] Cited in "Kashmiris Don't Want to Join Pak: Survey."
[81] Fair, *Militants in the Kargil Conflict.*

The dispute over Kashmir contributes to the overall India–Pakistan tension, increasing the risk of a military confrontation that would almost certainly lead to disaster for Pakistan. Two of India and Pakistan's three major wars were over Kashmir. In addition to the struggle upon independence in 1947, Pakistan and India also fought a war linked to Kashmir in 1965. Kashmir also led India and Pakistan into conflicts that almost spiraled into a broader war in 1999 following the Kargil conflict and in December 2001 after the Parliament attack. The 1999 Kargil crisis illustrates the risk of escalation. Both India and Pakistan appeared to be mobilizing for a large conflict, and US intelligence believed an all-out war was possible.[82]

The economic costs are also high. Even without the risks of all-out war, the conflict is costly for Pakistan. In 1993, Pakistan spent 35 percent of its GDP on defense, in large part because of its continuing conflict with India.[83] The International Crisis Group notes that the spiraling military costs in Pakistan have led to the neglect of education and health, while foreign debt has skyrocketed. As the violence increased, this hindered foreign investment in Pakistan, further exacerbating the country's economic woes.[84]

The depredations of Kashmiri guerrillas also hurt Pakistan's international reputation and ties to Washington – moves that weakened its overall position *vis-à-vis* India. During the Cold War, Islamabad was an important ally of the United States, and the two governments worked closely together to support the anti-Soviet Islamic resistance in Afghanistan in the 1980s. In 1999, the United States firmly moved away from its traditional support for Pakistan over India by pressing Pakistan to withdraw from Kargil as a precondition for asking India to stop its attacks. This firm stance in turn helped India and the United States end decades of mutual suspicion. As former Clinton administration official Bruce Reidel wrote, "Doors opened in New Delhi to Americans that had been shut for years. The Indian elite – including

---

[82] Jones, *Pakistan: Eye of the Storm*, pp. 80–81; International Crisis Group, "Kashmir: The View from Islamabad," p. i; and Reidel, "American Diplomacy and the 1999 Kargil Summit at Blair House."

[83] Griffin, *Reaping the Whirlwind*, p. 66.

[84] International Crisis Group, "Kashmir: The View from Islamabad," pp. 8–11; Stern, "Pakistan's Jihad Culture," p. 116.

the military – and the Indian public began to shed long held negative perceptions of the US."[85]

The sheer number of actors involved in supporting the Kashmiri groups – and the turbulent Pakistani political scene – weakens the Kashmiri opposition to New Delhi. Pakistan helped numerous groups become strong, but no group was able to assume a dominant position. At times, the groups even worked with India to destroy their rivals. The Hizb-ul-Mujahedin killed JKLF members and assisted Indian security in finding JKLF hideouts.[86] Pakistan's support for myriad groups made them more docile, but also weaker.

By supporting the guerrilla cause in Kashmir, Pakistan has also worsened its own stability. Several Kashmiri groups shared the same religious schools, training camps, and even operatives as radical groups within Pakistan.[87] Many Islamists, including those not linked to violence, do not separate domestic Pakistani politics from their actions in Afghanistan and Kashmir.[88] It is now impossible to disentangle Pakistani groups with radical agendas in Kashmir from those with radical agendas in Pakistan itself. Groups such as Lashkar-e-Jhangvi (an anti-Shi'a sectarian group), Jaish-e-Mohammad (a militant group focused on Kashmir), and Jamiat-ul-Ulema-e-Islami (a domestic religious group) increasingly have overlapping memberships. Thus, Jaish-e-Mohammad members have conducted sectarian attacks in Pakistan itself, in contrast to the group's supposed focus on Kashmir.

Many of the Islamist activists in Kashmir also want a new regime in Islamabad. As one member of Lashkar-e-Tayyeba commented, "We won't stop – even if India gave us Kashmir ... We want to see a Taliban-style regime here."[89] And several groups are as good as their word. Even before the post-September 11 crackdown, one Sunni group, Lashkar-e-Jhangvi, tried to assassinate Prime Minister Muhammad Nawaz Sharif in 1999. Musharraf also suffered assassination attempts in 2003, probably from individuals tied to the organizations he has tried

---

[85] Reidel, "American Diplomacy and the 1999 Kargil Summit at Blair House."

[86] Schofield, *Kashmir in Conflict*, p. 157.

[87] Stern, "Pakistan's Jihad Culture," p. 125. However, Lashkar-e-Tayyeba reportedly avoided using Taliban facilities because of the organization's scorn for the Taliban's Deobandi practices.

[88] Cohen, *The Idea of Pakistan.*

[89] As quoted in Stern, "Pakistan's Jihad Culture," p. 121.

to restrain and to the Taliban and al-Qa'ida, which he has turned against. This instability also further hurts Pakistan's economy, as the country is considered a high-risk investment area.[90]

Sectarian conflict in Pakistan also increased as a result of the Kashmir conflict. Many of the groups Pakistan supports in Kashmir endorse an extreme version of Sunni Islam, rejecting other Muslim sects, such as the Shi'a, as apostates. Their religious schools preach an intolerance of other sects. These groups carry out murders and pogroms against Shi'a in Pakistan itself, fraying communal relations. Hundreds of Pakistanis have died as Shi'a–Sunni tension has increased.[91]

The costs to the Kashmiris, of course, are far greater. The once-serene state is now a byword for violence. In addition to the vast number of casualties and displacements, the violence and India's response have also set back economic progress. Moreover, Kashmir's never-strong political institutions suffered grievous harm, leaving the area with a poorer government than the rest of India.

Two steps forward, two steps back?

Indian efforts to coerce Pakistan into halting its support for terrorist groups had little impact before the September 11, 2001 terrorist attacks in the United States. After Pakistan exploited the violence that began in 1989, Indian leaders criticized Pakistan harshly and at times made vague threats of military retaliation. India has also cut trade and tried to isolate Pakistan. However, both economic ties and travel were already limited, and further restrictions had little impact.

The September 11, 2001 terrorist attacks led Musharraf to cut ties to the Taliban, and by association al-Qa'ida. Musharraf also began curtailing the activities of Kashmiri groups, and announced he would work against the steady Islamicization of society. In January (and later in May) 2002, Musharraf promised to stop cross-border infiltration, banned Lashkar-e-Tayyeba, Jaish-e-Mohammad, and several other groups, and arrested over 2,000 radicals. Before a visit to Washington in June 2003, Musharraf criticized the religious parties and warned against Pakistan's "Talibanization." The profile of the radical groups is lower,

---

[90] Cohen, *The Idea of Pakistan.*
[91] International Crisis Group, "Unfulfilled Promises," pp. 10–11.

and some observers note that it is harder for militant groups to raise money, to recruit, and to train openly.[92]

US pressure was a major source of the change. Washington had long criticized Pakistan for its support of Kashmiri groups and the Taliban. The United States was particularly concerned that the Kashmir dispute would spiral out of control and spark a nuclear conflict, not just a bloody conventional war.[93] For much of the 1990s, the threat to declare Pakistan a state sponsor of terrorism loomed over the relationship. In addition, in 1992 the United States had ended hundreds of millions of dollars in annual aid and refused to deliver military aircraft – decisions justified in part because of Islamabad's links to various radical groups. US officials also repeatedly pressed Pakistan to end its links to terrorist groups.[94] On balance, however, these threats were negligible given the strategic and domestic stakes for Islamabad.

The September 11 attacks changed the rules. Angering Washington after September 11 risked moving the United States permanently into India's camp and risked destroying Pakistan's wobbly economy. Siding with the United States halted the tilt toward India and provided a sorely needed financial infusion. Pakistan's military in particular benefited. The United States pledged $3 billion to Musharraf's government in security and development aid and waived many sanctions.[95] Congress also allowed the Bush administration to waive the restriction on foreign assistance to governments that attained power in a military coup.

Although in general Musharraf has helped crack down on al-Qa'ida, his government's record on Kashmiri groups is uneven at best. Musharraf's promise to hold back militants in 2002 only lasted for two months.[96] Many of the radicals arrested were released, and several of the banned organizations simply reformed under different names – though a year later several were again banned. Some leaders openly

---

[92] Fair, *Militants in the Kargil Conflict.*

[93] This concern was present almost immediately after the 1989 uprising began and reached its height during the Kargil conflict. Kux, *The United States and Pakistan, 1947–2000*, p. 306.

[94] Griffin, *Reaping the Whirlwind*, pp. 63 and 107; Kux, *The United States and Pakistan, 1947–2000*, pp. 316 and 322.

[95] International Crisis Group, "Kashmir: The View from Islamabad," p. 13. See Cohen, *The Idea of Pakistan.*

[96] Khan, "The Waiting Game," p. 37.

collect money and preach *jihad*. Musharraf had pledged after the September 11 attacks to register religious seminaries that were hotbeds of support for radical movements and to revise their curriculum. As of January 2004, however, the religious schools have not been registered, and curriculum reform has not occurred. In addition, the public school curriculum remains heavily Islamicized, with public institutions also providing considerable support for various *jihadists*. The Musharraf government also has not passed laws that would regulate radical fundraising.[97] The infrastructure that supports violence in Kashmir is still in place. As Richard Haass, then the State Department's director for policy planning, noted, "I'll be honest: We have not succeeded, and we are at times, shall we say, disappointed and frustrated with that reality."[98]

The government of India claims that Pakistani-supported terrorism actually increased in 2002. Notable attacks included the March 30, 2002 attack on Raghunath Mandir, the May 14 attack in Kaluchak, where thirty died, the July 13 attack in Rajiv Nagar, where twenty-eight died, and the Nunwan attack where nine died.[99] In February of 2003, Central Intelligence Agency (CIA) Director George Tenet testified that Pakistani support to Kashmiri separatist groups was continuing.[100]

Several reasons explain the limits to Pakistan's cooperation. Pakistan's enmity toward India remains intense, and many members of the armed forces see Pakistan's turn away from the militants as a betrayal. The problem is particularly profound at the lower levels of the armed forces and intelligence services, though increasing numbers of senior officials are also linked to religious groups.[101] The central government's control over much of the country, including several major cities such as Karachi and Peshawar, is also weak. In addition, the Musharraf government, like its many predecessors in the 1980s and 1990s, seeks to legitimate its rule and gain the support of Pakistan's religious parties against its secular opponents. The religious parties both support various

[97] Jones, *Pakistan*, p. 284; International Crisis Group, "Kashmir: Learning from the Past," p. 18 and International Crisis Group, "Unfulfilled Promises," pp. 4–6; Watson and Zaidi, "Militant Flourishes in Plain Sight."
[98] As quoted in Kessler, "Pakistan Fails to Rein in Guerrillas," p. 14.
[99] Government of India, *Annual Report, 2002–2003*, pp. 12–19.
[100] Tenet, "The Worldwide Threat in 2003."
[101] McGirk and Calabresi, "Is Pakistan a Friend or Foe?" and Cohen, *The Idea of Pakistan*.

jihadist groups in Kashmir and are intensely hostile to any government attempt to control fundraising or religious education, even though the schools provide recruits for Kashmiri groups. They are more than ready to criticize any government that betrays their Kashmiri proxies.[102] Pakistan's cooperation on al-Qa'ida limits US leverage on Kashmir. The United States now needs Pakistan, limiting Washington's freedom to use its influence.

Conclusion

Pakistan is one of the world's top sponsors of terrorism, but this terrorism has focused heavily on one issue: Kashmir. Islamabad did not create the violence in Kashmir, but its efforts to exploit it made the conflict far more deadly and allowed Kashmiri groups to survive far longer than they otherwise would have. The Kashmiri militants' operations have benefited Pakistan in its struggle against India, and the cause is used to bolster the regime's domestic position. These strategic and domestic interests limit the impact of outside pressure, even though Pakistan's support for violence hurts the country economically, creates the risk of domestic instability, and has contributed to a draining confrontation with India. Musharraf (and most other conceivable leaders) are willing to make short-term, tactical concessions but drag their feet when asked to abandon the cause.

[102] In December 2003 religious parties cooperated to give Musharraf the votes he needed to extend his presidency until 2007. International Crisis Group, "Unfulfilled Promises," pp. 2 and 9–10.

7

Afghanistan under the Taliban

Al-Qa'ida (Arabic for "the foundation" or "the base") is the most lethal terrorist group in modern history. The attacks it conducted on September 11, 2001 killed almost 3,000 people, far and away the bloodiest single terrorist attack ever.[1] The movement has also conducted or supported dozens of other terrorist attacks, backed a range of ferocious Islamist insurgencies that have killed tens of thousands, and promulgated a violent ideology that glorifies violence in the name of God.

Al-Qa'ida is often portrayed as an organization that lacks a state sponsor. Terms like "postmodern" and "networked" are regularly used to characterize the movement and to suggest that it does not depend on any state for its survival. However, from May 1996 until the end of the 2001, al-Qa'ida was based in Afghanistan and enjoyed tremendous support from the ruling Taliban regime there. Mullah Omar and other Taliban leaders provided al-Qa'ida with a haven from which it could launch attacks, train recruits for a variety of *jihads*, and otherwise conduct its struggle against the United States, moderate Arab regimes, and other governments it opposed. Al-Qa'ida did not depend on the Taliban for its survival, but the Taliban's support proved vital for many of the organization's achievements.

---

[1] Before September 11, fewer than 1,000 Americans had died from international terrorism. Hoffman, "Rethinking Terrorism and Counterterrorism Since 9/11," p. 303.

By any sensible definition of state sponsorship, the Taliban's Afghanistan qualifies as a highly energetic and enthusiastic sponser. The Taliban controlled 90 percent of the country by September 11, 2001 and during much of its rule in Afghanistan exercised firmer control than had any other Afghan government in modern times, including several that predated the 1979 Soviet invasion. Although only three countries had extended official diplomatic recognition to the Taliban (and one, Saudi Arabia, soon rescinded it), the movement was almost universally recognized as the dominant political authority in Afghanistan. The United States chose not to recognize it in part because it did not want to legitimate the hostile and brutal regime and in part because an officially recognized government would immediately have been placed on the state sponsorship of terrorism and narcotics trafficking lists, which would have tied the hands of the executive branch in relations with the Taliban.

From its base in Afghanistan, al-Qa'ida enjoyed many remarkable successes. The group was largely unknown outside extremist circles when it relocated from the Sudan to Afghanistan in 1996. This quickly changed. Even before killing almost 3,000 people on September 11, 2001, its fame had spread due to such devastating and spectacular attacks as the August 7, 1998 simultaneous bombings of two US embassies in Africa and the October 12, 2000 strike on USS *Cole*. Although attention has understandably focused on the movement's use of terrorism, al-Qa'ida also acted as the "quartermaster of *jihad*," to use Daniel Benjamin and Steven Simon's arresting phrase.[2] In this capacity, al-Qa'ida in essence waged war against regimes in Egypt, Algeria, Uzbekistan, Indonesia, the Philippines, India, Russia, and elsewhere in the world – a colossal undertaking.

Examining the relationship between the Taliban and al-Qa'ida is essential for understanding the problem of state sponsorship. As the most lethal terrorist group of modern times, it is important to understand where and how al-Qa'ida has gained support. In addition, the relationship between the two was unequal, perhaps even favoring al-Qa'ida. As such, al-Qa'ida may have had more influence on its state sponsor than the other way around, shaping the Taliban's ideology and contributing to its retention of power in Afghanistan. Such a relationship is perhaps unique in the annals of terrorism, where almost invariably

[2] Benjamin and Simon, *The Age of Sacred Terror*, p. 113.

states are far more powerful than terrorist groups. Another important point is that the Taliban did not act to restrict al-Qa'ida, in contrast to the apparent limits that Syria, Iran, Pakistan, and other longstanding sponsors all put on their proxies. Finally, the story of the Taliban's support for al-Qa'ida is a triangular one: it includes Pakistan, its Taliban ally, and the Taliban's partner al-Qa'ida.

This chapter discusses the rise of the Taliban, including the role that Pakistan played in the movement's initial spread. It also examines the interaction between al-Qa'ida and the Taliban and assesses the various unsuccessful efforts to break this relationship.

The Taliban emerge

The Soviet invasion of Afghanistan in 1979 plunged the country into a bloody period of strife and resistance. For a decade, Afghan fighters acting in the name of God fought the foreign invaders. In a defeat that surprised the world, the Soviets withdrew in 1989.[3]

After the withdrawal of Soviet forces and the subsequent collapse of the Soviet-backed regime in 1992, Afghanistan entered a disastrous period of civil strife and warlordism. Different military commanders took control of different regions, drawing primarily on ethnic and tribal loyalists to ensure their rule. Afghanistan was split into several autonomous mini-states, and in several of these, particularly in the south where Afghanistan's once-dominant Pashtun community lived, rival warlords battled for control. Pakistan, Iran, Saudi Arabia, Russia, and other states poured weapons and money into the country to support their proxies. In a Hobbesian struggle, commanders fought one another constantly, while the traditional leadership of Afghanistan – religious leaders, tribal chiefs, and others – declined in importance.[4]

The war with the Soviets and the subsequent civil war shattered Afghanistan and profoundly changed its politics. Over 1 million Afghans died in the struggle, and as much as one third of the population fled, with almost 2 million settling in Iran and perhaps 3 million living in

[3] For a history, see Kakar, *Afghanistan*. For a description of the military campaign, see Yousaf and Adkin, *Afghanistan, the Bear Trap*.

[4] Rashid, *Taliban*, p. 97 and Griffin, *Reaping the Whirlwind*, pp. 30–32. For an overview of Afghanistan after the Soviet withdrawal but before the Taliban's emergence, see Rubin, *The Search for Peace in Afghanistan*.

Pakistan. For many years, there were more refugees from the Afghan struggle than from any other conflict in the world. Afghanistan's rudimentary infrastructure and weak political institutions quickly collapsed, leaving the country devastated. Afghans were always pious, but their traditional form of Islam was tolerant and allowed Hindus, Sikhs, and Jews to play a role in the community – roles that ended in the 1990s as the war increased the country's zealotry. The war also shifted the communal balance of power, giving Tajiks, Uzbeks, the Shi'a Hazaras, and others their own weapons and power, ending the dominant position of Afghanistan's Pashtun community. Tribalism and banditry increased, while the always-weak central government in Kabul became completely powerless.[5]

The Taliban was born among the Afghan refugee population in Pakistan. The Jamiat-e Ulema Islam (JUI), which had close links to the government of Benazir Bhutto which took power in Pakistan in 1993, ran hundreds of religious schools in Pashtun areas in Pakistan. The Taliban emerged as a student movement from these schools. These students represented the new generation of Afghans rather than the leaders who had emerged as the established resistance to the Soviet Union. The schools, and later the Taliban, emphasized an extreme version of Islam along with elements of *pashtunwali*, the ancient tribal credo of Pashtun tribes that glorifies hospitality as a key component of honor.[6]

Led by Mullah Mohammed Omar, the Taliban began as a small group of fighters who achieved a reputation for decency by supposedly hanging from a tank barrel a local commander whose forces had abducted and raped two teenage girls, a move that led to appeals for help from neighboring communities afflicted by former *mujahedin* turned bandits.[7] After a brief period of inactivity, the Taliban began to act as guards for local merchants, particularly those trading in Pakistan. It then

---

[5] Rashid, *Taliban*, pp. 82–83.

[6] Ibid., pp. 26 and 90–97; Goodson, *Afghanistan's Endless War*, p. 99. Pakistan's Jamaat-e Islami (JI) worked with Pakistani intelligence to send over 30,000 Muslim radicals to Afghanistan between 1982 and 1992.

[7] Omar himself had been a mid-level commander during the anti-Soviet struggle. He was not from a distinguished clan and had not received a comprehensive religious education. US Department of State, "Finally a Talkative Talib: Origins and Membership of the Religious Students' Movement." Journalists

moved to Qandahar and quickly captured the city.[8] Qandahar was Afghanistan's second largest city and the heart of the Pashtun area. By establishing control over Qandahar, the Taliban had emerged as the champion of the Pashtun community.

The movement had a reputation both for its faith and for its honesty, the latter being a particularly rare quality in Afghanistan in the 1990s. Moreover, the Taliban imposed order and disarmed warlords wherever they went, a welcome relief from the years of strife under the Soviets and then under the rampaging warlords.[9] The Taliban also had a financial advantage, gaining money from Saudi Arabia, from donors linked to Bin Ladin and his network, and from its support from smugglers, who appreciated the Taliban's efforts to end banditry, which facilitated organized smuggling, in the south. Finally, the movement could draw on Pakistan's substantial military assistance (described below). This reputation and these resources, combined with its solid support in Pashtun areas, gave the movement appeal to many Afghans battered by two decades of war.[10] As Ahmed Rashid noted, Afghans accepted the Taliban due to "a mixture of fear, acceptance, total exhaustion, and devastation."[11]

The Taliban quickly spread across Afghanistan, particularly in the south, where many of the 40 percent of Afghanistan's population who are Pashtuns live. The movement drew on its already strong ties to Pakistan, gaining money, weapons, and at times direct military aid. The Taliban bribed many local commanders to gain their support, while others bowed to its large forces, clear commitment, and growing

---

have not been able to locate a witness to the tank barrel hanging, and it may be apocryphal. Coll, *Ghost Wars*, p. 283.

[8] Griffin, *Reaping the Whirlwind*, p. 32.

[9] Julie Sirrs contends that much of the countryside was not in disorder and that schools and many government offices continued to function in parts of the country. She also notes that while the Taliban brought order to some parts of the country, they also brought war to much of the country that had been relatively peaceful. Sirrs, "Lifting the Veil on Afghanistan."

[10] Griffin, *Reaping the Whirlwind*, pp. 34–35 and Goodson, *Afghanistan's Endless War*, pp. 108–111. Coll notes that the Saudis continued sending money to various radical Islamists after the Soviet withdrawal, in part due to their geopolitical competition with Iran and in part to appease radicals at home. Coll, *Ghost Wars*, pp. 216–217.

[11] Rashid, *Taliban*, p. 4.

popularity. The movement's lightening successes transformed it from a band of 30 men in the spring of 1994 to an army of 25,000 a year later.[12] The size of the Taliban army subsequently hovered between 25,000 and 30,000 men, roughly one third of whom were students from Pakistani religious seminars.[13]

The Taliban found resistance far stiffer when it left Pashtun-dominated areas. Tajiks, Uzbeks, and other Afghan communities feared that the Taliban represented the Pashtun community only, despite its protestations to speak for all Muslims. When the Taliban conquered these non-Pashtun areas, it often ruled as an occupier, not as a liberator.[14] It also distrusted the more sophisticated citizens of Kabul and ran the country from Qandahar. Most ominously, the movement saw Shiites, the sect of 15 percent of Afghanistan's Muslims, as heretics. At times, Taliban fighters massacred them by the thousands.[15] Even in areas where its supporters lived, the Taliban ruled brutally, imposing a harsh form of Islamic law, denying women the most basic rights, and engaging in numerous human rights abuses. Afghanistan's infant mortality rate remained high, while life expectancy was short.[16]

The Taliban was a highly ideological movement, even before it came into contact with Bin Ladin. Its leader, Mullah Omar, appeared to genuinely believe that Afghanistan's foreign and domestic policies should follow his interpretation of Islam, not realpolitik or domestic politics. Thus he refused to conciliate his enemies at home and did not hesitate to anger foreign governments. He declared that the Taliban seeks "to establish the laws of God on Earth and prepared to sacrifice everything in pursuit of that goal." As a leading scholar of the region, Olivier Roy, noted in 1997, "Of course, the problem with the Taliban is that they mean what they say."[17]

---

[12] Burke, *Al-Qaeda*, p. 113 and Griffin, *Reaping the Whirlwind*, p. 36.

[13] Rashid, *Taliban*, p. 100; Goodson, *Afghanistan's Endless War*, p. 77; and Bergen, *Holy War, Inc.*, p. 148.

[14] This hostility was anticipated in 1997. See US Department of State, "Scenesetter for Your Visit to Islamabad: Afghan Angle."

[15] Vollman, "Across the Divide," p. 61.

[16] Ibid., pp. 63–64. For a review of the Taliban's dismal human rights record, see Drumbl, "The Taliban's 'Other' Crimes."

[17] As quoted in Coll, *Ghost Wars*, p. 289 and footnote 21, p. 611.

The movement appeared to grow more extreme as it consolidated power. The Taliban was not initially hostile to the United States. Writing in 1998 (and drawing on evidence collected before that), Peter Marsden notes that the Taliban sought "purification of Afghanistan alone" and did not want to export their system.[18] Visitors to Qandahar in the mid-1990s noted that people were not required to pray and that some women did not wear burqas – a tolerance that ended as the decade wore on.[19]

In parallel with its growing intolerance, the Taliban's cooperation with, and reliance on, Arab and other foreign fighters linked to al-Qa'ida grew. Before the capture of Kabul in September 1996, the Taliban had few contacts with Arab Afghans. After Bin Ladin relocated to Afghanistan from Sudan in May 1996, however, his group and the Taliban began to cooperate with increasingly frequency. The Taliban also opened Afghanistan's doors to hosts of militants, not just those who were part of al-Qa'ida.[20] Among the many groups hosted by the Taliban were fighters from the Islamic Movement of Uzbekistan, Pakistanis fighting in Kashmir, radical Sunni Pakistanis bent on killing Pakistani Shi'a, Chechen fighters battling Russia, and Sunni Muslims opposed to Iran's Shi'a government.

Not surprisingly, the Taliban came to have many enemies. The fractious warlords of Afghanistan coalesced into the anti-Taliban National Islamic United Front for the Salvation of Afghanistan, usually referred to as the Northern Alliance. The alliance at times drew backing from Iran, India, Russia, Uzbekistan, Kyrgyzstan, Turkey, Kazakhstan, and Tajikistan, all of which opposed the Taliban's efforts to back radicals in their own countries, sought to support their favored communal groups against the Pashtun-dominated Taliban, and counter what they saw as undue Pakistani influence in Afghanistan.[21]

Despite this wide-ranging opposition, the Taliban steadily conquered much of Afghanistan. One by one, non-Pashtun areas fell to the Taliban.

[18] Marsden, *The Taliban*, p. 61.
[19] US Department of State, "Scenesetter for Your Visit to Islamabad: Afghan Angle."
[20] Al-Zayyat, *The Road to Al-Qaeda*, p. 59.
[21] Rashid, *Taliban*, p. 5. See also Council on Foreign Relations, "The Northern Alliance."

By September 11, 2001, the movement controlled approximately 90 percent of the country and appeared poised to unify the country under its dominance.

The Taliban's fall from power came suddenly. The September 11 carnage was quickly tied to al-Qa'ida, and the United States moved almost immediately to destroy the regime. The United States began a military campaign that relied on precision bombing combined with the use of special operations forces and the anti-Taliban Northern Alliance resistance. The bombing commenced on October 7 and, by November 9, the northern city of Mazar-e Sharif had fallen to the Northern Alliance. Four days later, the capital of Kabul fell, and on December 6 the Taliban lost their hold on their stronghold, Qandahar.[22]

Despite being driven from Afghanistan's cities, the Taliban survived as a fierce guerrilla group. They regularly attack foreign aid workers, US and other Western troops, the security forces of the new regime of Hamid Karzai, and other Afghans perceived as collaborators. They continue to receive financial support from Pakistan's Jamiat-e-Ulema Islam (JUI) Party, which is part of the governing coalition that runs the Pakistani state of Baluchistan. The country as a whole remains at risk of sliding back into all-out civil war.[23]

Pakistan and the Taliban

The story of the Taliban's rise cannot be told without recognizing the central role played by its foreign patron, Pakistan. After the withdrawal of the Soviets in 1989, Pakistan backed various *mujahedin* leaders, such as Gulbuddin Hekmatyar, with whom it had worked during the anti-Soviet struggle. By 1994, Islamabad's proxies had shown themselves to be dismal failures: brutal, riven by infighting and – most important, from Pakistan's perspective – incompetent. Moreover, Pakistan's Prime Minister Benazir Bhutto, who took power in 1993, correctly saw several

---

[22] For an excellent review of the military campaign, see Biddle, *Afghanistan and the Future of Warfare.*

[23] Rashid, "The Mess in Afghanistan," pp. 24–27. For an interesting overview of pro-Taliban parts of Pakistan, see Griswald, "Where the Taliban Roam," For a broader critique of US policy toward Afghanistan, see the Council on Foreign Relations report "Afghanistan: Are We Losing the Peace?" and Anomymous, *Imperial Hubris.*

of Pakistan's then proxies as tied to political movements and bureau-cratic elements in Pakistan that opposed her rule.[24]

The extent of Pakistan's role in the Taliban's creation and initial successes remains unclear, but as the movement gained strength it increasingly became Islamabad's favored proxy. Pakistan's military and intelligence service provided arms, ammunition, supplies for com-bat, financial aid, and training. Pakistan also helped recruit fighters for the Taliban, often working with domestic religious associations. The Pakistani government at times even tried to represent the Taliban's interests overseas.[25]

The range of Pakistani support was massive. Pakistani military advisers trained the Taliban, making it more tactically skilled and better able to run the logistics effort for a massive war effort. In 1997, the year after the Taliban captured Kabul, Pakistan gave the movement $30 million in aid, including weapons, food, fuel, and other necessities. Pakistan provided $10 million to the Taliban to pay for the salaries of government officials. Pakistani soldiers at times may have fought alongside the Taliban, aiding it in key battles.[26] Pakistani diplomats defended the Taliban at the United Nations and other international fora, and fought against sanctions and other forms of punishment.[27]

Support for the Taliban went far beyond official government circles and included major political parties, religious networks, and many ordinary Pakistanis. When the Taliban first emerged, hundreds of

---

[24] Maley, *The Afghanistan Wars*, p. 219.

[25] Griffin, *Reaping the Whirlwind*, pp. 33–34; Goodson, *Afghanistan's Endless War*, p. 111; Human Rights Watch, *Afghanistan – Crisis of Impunity: The Role of Pakistan, Russia and Iran in Fuelling the Civil War*, pp. 23–26. Taliban officials claim that Pakistan only aided them after they had estab-lished themselves, but several sources claim that the Taliban were largely the creation of senior Pakistani officials. US Department of State, "Finally a Talkative Talib."

[26] Burke, *Al-Qaeda*, p. 116; Maley, *The Afghanistan Wars*, p. 235; and Rashid, *Taliban*, p. 183. Sirrs notes that the anti-Taliban Northern Alliance claimed that as much as 50 percent of the Taliban corpses they saw had Pakistani civilian identity cards. Sirrs, "The Taliban's International Ambitions," pp. 61–63. Given that many Afghan refugees lived in Pakistan for more than twenty years, however, it is difficult to discern how many are of Afghan origin.

[27] Coll, *Ghost Wars*, p. 548.

Pakistani volunteers joined the Afghan refugee fighters who comprised much of the Taliban's fighting force – Larry Goodson estimates that Pakistanis comprised one quarter of the Taliban's forces, and several other estimates are even higher.[28] Pakistani political parties and religious movements outside the government also aided the Taliban. The JUI, of course, established the religious schools that gave birth to and nurtured the Taliban and shaped its ideology. Parties like the JUI did not distinguish between Kashmir, Pakistan, and Afghanistan when pursuing their ambitions.

Over time, these parties and privately run schools provided much of the manpower for the Taliban. One Taliban official noted that the *"madrasa* network" – the network of religious seminaries – in Pakistani areas near the border sent "thousands" of recruits to join the Taliban. At decisive points, such as the July 1999 offensive in northern Afghanistan, up to 8,000 Pakistani volunteers participated.[29]

As the Taliban swept through Afghanistan, the movement gained the support of much of Pakistan's political establishment. Even though Pakistan's political groups fought bitterly against one another – and the military, the true power, distrusted politicians of all stripes – they all supported the Taliban when they were in power. For Islamabad, the Taliban represented a force that could unify Afghanistan while keeping it close to Pakistan. Pakistani leaders valued Afghanistan for the perceived strategic depth it offered in a war with India (Pakistani forces would presumably regroup in Afghanistan if pushed back by Indian forces) and as a bridge to Central Asia. Moreover, the Pashtun-dominated movement sat well with the Pakistani officer corps and intelligence services, which also held many Pashtuns.[30]

---

[28] Goodson, *Afghanistan's Endless War*, p. 118 and Bergen, *Holy War, Inc.*, p. 148.

[29] US Department of State, "Finally a Talkative Talib" and Goodson, *Afghanistan's Endless War*, pp. 82–83.

[30] Rashid, *Taliban*, pp. 27–28, and 98; Burke, *Al-Qaeda*, p. 114; Kepel, *Jihad*, pp. 227–228; and Sirrs, "The Taliban's International Ambitions," pp. 64–65. The Taliban drew particularly heavily from the Pashtun tribes in southern Afghanistan near Qandahar. Other Pashtuns were better represented within the movement than were non-Pashtuns, but those from Qandahar dominated. The Taliban's leaders were primarily from the Durrani tribal association, which had dominated Afghanistan before the Soviet invasion but had lost out

Kashmir also played an increasingly important role in Pakistan's calculations toward Afghanistan. Islamabad sent many Kashmiri fighters to Afghanistan to train and to gain combat experience. As foreign fighters increased their role in Kashmir, Afghanistan became important as a place to house, train, and recruit them. Just as Syria used Lebanon as the location for its proxies to arm and train, Afghanistan became a preferred location for Pakistan to conduct such training, as it enabled Islamabad to claim that it was not a state sponsor of terrorism in its own right.[31]

Despite all this support, the Taliban was not Pakistan's puppet. Even before the movement consolidated power, Taliban officials were noting privately that "Afghans are proud people who do not like the Pakistanis always trying to run things and place the Afghans on a lower level."[32] Similarly, a senior al-Qa'ida official warned other Arabs that Pakistan would eventually try to find a substitute for the Taliban that would subordinate itself to Islamabad.[33] Over time, as the Taliban established itself, it used its ties to Pakistan's government, opposition parties, Islamic societies, and drug networks to ensure its autonomy in the face of any pressure. The Taliban even refused to drop Afghanistan's long-standing claim to parts of Pakistan's Northwest Frontier Province, a remarkable statement of independence given the Taliban's reliance on Pakistan for support.[34]

The Taliban also weakened the Pakistani state, contributing to economic problems and social unrest. The Taliban encouraged both Pashtun nationalism and Islamic extremism in Pakistan itself, further fraying an already weak social fabric. Pakistan also lost revenue from tolls and tariffs, as smuggling from Afghanistan replaced legitimate commerce. In 1998, the Taliban provided sanctuary for the Sipah-e-Sahaba Pakistan (SSP), a murderous anti-Shiite group that had split from the JUI and was hounded from Pakistan after it killed hundreds of Shiites there. Thousands of SSP members joined the Taliban's

to Ghilzai Pashtuns as well as to other ethnic groups. Goodson, *Afghanistan's Endless War*, p. 107. The Taliban's effort to dominate the community involved assassinations of other Pashtun leaders and other brutal measures, which in turn alienated many Pashtun notables. Coll, *Ghost Wars*, p. 459.

[31] Rashid, *Taliban*, p. 186.
[32] US Department of State, "Finally a Talkative Talib."
[33] United States of America *v.* Usama bin Ladin, Exhibit 300B-T.
[34] Rashid, *Taliban*, pp. 185–188.

ranks.[35] Because the Taliban's activities risked radicalizing its patron, some commentators began to talk of the "Talibanization" of Pakistan.[36]

Enter Al-Qa'ida

Like the Taliban, the Afghan *jihad* led to al-Qa'ida's creation. After the Soviet invasion of Afghanistan in 1979, Muslim volunteers, particularly from the Arab world and Pakistan, flocked to join the Afghan resistance. Tens of thousands of foreign Muslims participated, and the experience forged deep bonds among Muslims of many different nations.

Although the contribution these volunteers made in the defeat of the Soviet Union was negligible, their participation had a lasting effect on the Muslim world's consciousness. A small band of dedicated fighters, acting in the name of God, had defeated a seemingly invincible superpower. These *jihadists* were toasted around the Muslim world, emerging as popular heroes and publicly lauded by governments that in private would have rejoiced in their deaths.

Al-Qa'ida sprang up in Afghanistan around 1988. Founded by the Palestinian religious leader Abdullah Azzam in cooperation with Usama bin Ladin, it sought to unify the many Muslim fighters who had come to Afghanistan. The movement drew on the "Maktab al-Khidmat" (MAK) or Bureau of Services, that operated a recruiting and logistics network for *jihadists* fighting the Soviet Union in Afghanistan. One of al-Qa'ida's own histories of the movement noted that it initially sought to keep "alive the Jihadist spirit among Muslims in general, and Arabs in particular, by opening bases for their Jihad along with maintaining contact lines with them" after the Afghan struggle against the Soviets ended.[37] It initially sought to raise money, facilitate travel for *jihad*, provide training, and offer logistics.

When Bin Ladin took over the movement after Azzam was murdered in 1989, however, his aims were broader. The movement took on an operational role as well as backing associated causes. Bin Ladin sought to bring *jihad* to other parts of the Muslim world he saw as oppressed and to overthrow corrupt Muslim regimes. One of its most unusual

[35] Rashid, *Taliban*, pp. 92 and 185–188.
[36] Vollman, "Across the Divide," p. 60.
[37] United States of America *v.* Enaam M. Arnaout, p. 34.

goals, however, was to strike at the United States, which Bin Ladin blamed for stationing troops on the holy soil of the Arabian peninsula, for backing Israel, for starving the people of Iraq through sanctions, and for a host of other grievances linked to the perceived denigration of the Muslim world.[38]

Al-Qa'ida was small initially, but it gradually grew in Afghanistan until 1992, and then in the Sudan, where it was based from 1992 through 1996. During this time, al-Qa'ida forged ties to a host of like-minded (and not so like-minded) Sunni insurgent and terrorist groups. It sought to support their efforts against various regimes in the Muslim world and spread a call for anti-American *jihad*, as well as to conduct its own operations.

Bin Ladin relocated to Afghanistan in May or June of 1996, bringing with him the leadership core of al-Qa'ida. Al-Qa'ida already had training camps in Afghanistan, from where it supported insurgencies in Chechnya, Kashmir, and Tajikistan. The Afghan *jihad* was a *cause célèbre* in the Muslim world during the 1980s, bringing together Muslims from around the world. Moreover, Bin Ladin and other al-Qa'ida members appeared to have a genuine admiration for the Taliban's efforts to bring the rule of Islamic law to Afghanistan and for Mullah Omar himself. After several years, Bin Ladin may have even sworn loyalty to Omar.[39]

Bin Ladin initially located himself in Jalalabad, which was not under the Taliban's control – a sign, perhaps, that he and the Taliban initially were not intimate allies. However, the Taliban initially welcomed Bin Ladin, despite his links to terrorism. Bin Ladin was widely admired for his participation in the anti-Soviet struggle during the 1980s. Moreover, the Taliban saw his support for various jihads as laudable. In addition, Bin Ladin brought considerable financial resources with him. A senior al-Qa'ida leader informed other *jihadists* that the Taliban was exceptionally welcoming to Arabs who had fought the Russians in Afghanistan.[40]

---

[38] Anonymous, *Through Our Enemies' Eyes*, pp. 50–53 and Bergen, *Holy War, Inc.*, pp. 21–22, 98–101, 208.

[39] Anonymous, *Imperial Hubris*, p. 141; National Commission on Terrorist Attacks Upon the United States, "Overview of the Enemy," p. 7.

[40] United States of America *v.* Usama bin Ladin, Exhibit 300B-T. See also United States of America *v.* Usama Bin Ladin, *et al.*, section 5325.

The two movements converge

The Taliban and al-Qa'ida share ideological similarities, but the two did not overlap perfectly, especially at first. The Taliban's reality was formed by the miserable refugee camps along the Pakistan–Afghan border where many members had lived.[41] Reflecting these parochial origins, the Taliban initially focused their *jihad* on their own society, trying to remake Afghanistan to reflect conservative Deobandi teachings. Politically, the Taliban used Islam to articulate a range of grievances. Their ideal was, in Jason Burke's words, a "mystic vision of rural Pashtun village life,"[42] and they focused their governance on what they saw as ensuring the moral well-being of the community.

The Deobandi school was initially created in India in the middle of the century as a way of ensuring that Islamic law and teachings would continue after British colonizers had displaced Muslim rulers and thus ended the guarantee that the state would enforce *shari'a* and that Muslims would dominate Hindus. Over time, Deobandi schools began to emphasize separation from, rather than accommodation with, non-Muslim society. The movement grew dramatically. Jason Burke notes that in 1879 there were only 12 Deobandi schools, while in 1967 there were almost 10,000 – a growth made possible in part by support from wealthy Arabs from the Persian Gulf, who saw Deobandi teachings as similar to Wahhabist that they favored. During the 1980s, the JUI, which was set up by the Deobandis, had no ties to the ISID and thus its *mujahedin* received little support from Pakistan. Over time, Deobandi political and social movements became involved in sectarian strife in Pakistan and began to receive Saudi funding after their rivals embraced Iraq in the first Gulf War in 1991. This made the movement more extreme and supportive of violence against those that they did not consider doctrinally sound.[43]

Al-Qa'ida, in contrast, represents a school of thought that can be described as "*salafi-jihadist.*"[44] *Salafis* seek to restore what they believe to be the true nature of Islam, harking back to the religion's earliest days when the Prophet and his companions held power and served as a model

---

[41] Maley, *The Afghanistan Wars*, p. 223.   [42] Burke, *Al-Qaeda*, p. 110.

[43] Rashid, *Taliban*, p. 89; Kepel, *Jihad*, pp. 223–226; and, Burke, *Al-Qaeda*, pp. 85–87.

[44] Kepel, "The Origins and Development of the Jihadist Movement," p. 97.

community for all Muslims. More generally, the *salafist* movement is a modernizing one, attempting to remove many of the accretions that adherents believe has corrupted Islam. Many of their members are well educated and sophisticated, in sharp contrast to the more backward and provincial Taliban. Many *salafis*, however, are peaceful apolitical, or both. Al-Qa'ida combined the *salafi* puritanical streak with an emphasis on the necessity of *jihad*. Bin Ladin and other leaders constantly stress the duty of all Muslims to participate in the struggle, arguing that the Islamic world is under attack from the West and secularists within Muslim lands.

Islamists attracted to al-Qa'ida see themselves as on the defensive and use this argument to justify their strikes on the United States. This distinction between the offensive and the defensive is more than semantics. Many Muslim scholars argue that the defense of Islam is a duty that all individuals must fulfill, in contrast to efforts to extend the faith, which some members of the Muslim community can discharge on behalf of all the faithful. In the *jihadists'* eyes, the United States has long attacked the Muslim world, subjugating its lands and dishonoring its people.[45]

As these different backgrounds suggest, the two movements at first were not in harmony. Saudi officials claim that the Taliban initially offered to hand over Bin Ladin to the Kingdom, which preferred not to take custody of him.[46] Many Al-Qa'ida members saw the Taliban's Afghanistan as a backward wasteland lacking phones, computers, and other essentials. One al-Qa'ida lieutenant complained that the locals were religiously ignorant and "would do anything for money." Another member declared, "This place is worse than a tomb."[47] The Taliban, in turn, saw Bin Ladin as arrogant and disrespectful. Some Taliban officials cared little about the global *jihad*, seeking instead stability in Afghanistan and the region. Others resented Bin Ladin's issuance of *fatwas* for which he lacked religious authority, and felt that his media events were dangerous for the country.[48]

[45] Anonymous, *Through Our Enemies' Eyes*, p. 53 and Benjamin and Simon, *Age of Sacred Terror*, pp. 49–50.
[46] Coll, *Ghost Wars*, p. 341.
[47] As quoted in Cullison and Higgins, "Strained Alliance: Al Qaeda's Sour Days in Afghanistan."
[48] See also Cullison and Higgins, "A Computer in Kabul Yields a Chilling Array of al Qaeda Memos," electronic version. Mullah Omar believed that only

Relations appeared to fray by August 1998, before the Embassy bombings, though information on the two movements' ties at this time is contradictory. Bin Ladin and Mullah Omar reportedly quarreled bitterly, and al-Qa'ida leaders feared they might lose their training camps in Afghanistan. Mullah Omar also refused to allow further attacks on the United States at this point. Indeed, Mullah Omar reportedly had closed one camp and was considering closing the others. Omar and other Taliban leaders were even discussing expelling Bin Ladin with Saudi officials. Mullah Omar was not reportedly concerned about US retaliation, but rather about regular Pakistani pressure. The August 7, 1998 strikes on US Embassies in Kenya and Tanzania furthered threatened this relationship.[49]

The US cruise missile strikes on terrorist training camps in Afghanistan on August 20, 1998 – Operation Infinite Reach – appeared to mark a turning point.[50] The strikes were intended to kill Bin Ladin and affiliated terrorist leaders and to demonstrate American will.[51] Rather than intimidating the Taliban, the attacks demonstrated to its leaders the West's hostility and placed the movement in a politically difficult position of being asked to make concessions under threat. The Taliban's anger at Bin Ladin for conducting the attacks was more than outweighed by its outrage at the United States for its response. Although in the months before the bombing the Taliban had indicated that it might be willing to surrender Bin Ladin or curtail his activities, the day after the bombing, Mullah Omar declared, "Even if all the countries in the world unite, we would defend Osama by our blood."[52] The head of Saudi

Deobandi *ulema* have the authority to issue *fatwas*. For al-Qa'ida and many other political Islamists in the Arab world, however, much of the *ulema* is viewed as compromised, making the laity more credible to interpret religion. Burke, *Al-Qaeda*, p. 165.

[49] National Commission on Terrorist Attacks Upon the United States, "Outline of the 9/11 Plot," p. 19. Burke, *Al-Qaeda*, p. 165 and Coll, *Ghost Wars*, pp. 400–401. Several sources support the view of tension between the Taliban and al-Qa'ida. However, by this time Omar and Bin Ladin had already developed a strong personal bond, and al-Qa'ida was playing an increasing role in helping the Taliban throughout Afghanistan. Coll, *Ghost Wars*, p. 380.

[50] Rashid, *Taliban*, p. 182.

[51] Albright, *Madame Secretary*, pp. 368, 376.

[52] As quoted in Griffin, *Reaping the Whirlwind*, p. 174.

Intelligence, Prince Turki al Faysal, met with Mullah Omar after the bombing and found that previous promises that the Taliban would send Bin Ladin back to Saudi Arabia or at least expel him were no longer binding.

The US cruise missile strikes on Afghanistan thus solidified a shaky bond, leading Mullah Omar to at first protect and, over time, embrace al-Qa'ida. Bin Ladin played on Omar's sense of pride, lionizing him as the true Caliph and issuing screeds denouncing the United Nations (UN) and other potential sources of restraint on the Taliban. The Taliban soon turned on several moderate Pashtun leaders, such as Abdul Ahad Karzai, and assassinated them or curtailed their active political role. As Bin Ladin and other Arab Afghans worked closely with the Taliban, the two movements cross-fertilized, and the *salafist* ideas took root under the Taliban. Over time, al-Qa'ida began to exert a tremendous influence over the Taliban.[53]

Criticism from the UN, from non-governmental organizations (NGOs), and Western powers, which often manifested in the form of cuts in aid or a refusal to treat the Taliban as Afghanistan's legitimate government, also soured the movement on ties with the West.[54] In 2001, the Taliban demonstrated its increasingly extreme beliefs by expelling foreign relief workers who were playing an important role in providing food and medical care to Afghanistan's many poor and dispossessed. The movement also destroyed two ancient statues of the Buddha at Bamiyan – a move criticized by other Islamist movements, to say nothing of Western audiences and other religions – and Pakistan, which received considerable aid from several countries with large Buddhist populations. Mullah Omar reportedly dismissed this pressure by referring to the Day of Judgment: "Allah will ask me, 'Omar, you have brought a superpower called the Soviet Union to its knees. You could not break two statues?' And what would Mullah Omar reply? On the Day of Judgment all of

---

[53] Cullison and Higgins, "Strained Alliance"; Maley, *The Afghanistan Wars*, p. 256; Kepel, *Jihad*, pp. 233–234; and McGeary, "The Taliban Troubles," *Time Europe*, pp. 46–50. The convergence between al-Qa'ida and the Taliban also occurred as Mullah Omar came to dominate Taliban decision-making. Omar initially worked closely with other religious leaders, but over time he consulted them less and less. Maley, *The Afghanistan Wars*, p. 224.

[54] US Department of State, "Scenesetter for Your Visit to Islamabad: Afghan Angle."

these mountains will turn into sand and fly into the air. And what if these statues in this shape go before Allah? What face, then, will Mullah Omar show to God."[55]

The Taliban also came to share al-Qa'ida's enthusiasm for exporting *jihad*. The Taliban renamed their country "The Islamic Emirate of Afghanistan." In addition to al-Qa'ida, the Taliban also hosted a range of Islamist insurgent groups active against neighboring countries. By September 2001, the Taliban was supporting revolutionary groups fighting the neighboring governments of Iran, Uzbekistan, China, and Tajikistan, as well as al-Qa'ida and its affiliates.

Thus, by September 2001, a common ideology bonded al-Qa'ida and the Taliban. The Taliban, like al-Qa'ida, rejected any accommodation with Muslim moderates, let alone the infidel West.[56] As Julie Sirrs argued before the overthrow of the Taliban, "Indeed, the Taliban are sheltering bin Ladin first and foremost because of a shared worldview."[57]

The importance of ideology in explaining the Taliban's behavior is further suggested by the Taliban's policies in Afghanistan itself. Promoting conservative social values – such as forcing women to wear the *burqa*, requiring men to have long beards, and forbidding television, radio, and music – took precedence over more standard tasks of governing such as providing water or power. Perhaps the only government agency that worked efficiently was the Office for the Propagation of Virtue and the Prevention of Vice, which enforced morality as the Taliban saw it. Indeed, the Taliban eviscerated state institutions, limiting the role of their government to enforcing morality, taxing smuggling and commerce, and fighting their war with the opposition Northern Alliance and other groups. Mullah Omar and other Taliban leaders disdained Kabul, despite its political importance, seeing the "purer" Qandahar as a more suitable base. The movement saw its primary role as building a true Islamic community, not as running a modern state.[58] As Larry Goodson noted, "The Taliban are a social movement and a tribal militia running a country."[59]

When the September 11 attacks came, the two movements and their leaders had become exceptionally close. The distant admiration of 1996,

---

[55] Coll, *Ghost Wars*, p. 549.
[56] Rashid, *Taliban*, p. 93.   [57] Sirrs, "Lifting the Veil on Afghanistan," p. 47.
[58] Kepel, *Jihad*, pp. 228–231.
[59] Goodson, *Afghanistan's Endless War*, p. 115.

and the reported tension of early 1998, were long gone. In their place, was a tight alliance between al-Qa'ida and the Taliban, bound by a shared ideology and mutual respect. The Taliban would go to any lengths for al-Qa'ida. Mullah Omar declared to Western reporters in 2001, "Half my country was destroyed by 23 years of war. If the remaining half of Afghanistan is destroyed in trying to save bin Ladin, I am ready."[60]

Scope of support

Al-Qa'ida found the Taliban's Afghanistan a useful (though hardly ideal) sanctuary for several reasons. The primary benefit of Afghanistan for al-Qa'ida was that the Taliban appear to have imposed few if any restrictions on al-Qa'ida, a freedom rare in the annals of state–terrorist group relations. Al-Qa'ida fighters could enter or exit Afghanistan without visas and travel freely within the country's borders.[61] From its base in Afghanistan, al-Qa'ida was exceptionally active. It planned operations, trained operatives for its own organization and others, seeded new insurgencies and terrorist groups throughout the world, propagated its *jihadist* ideology, and otherwise pursued its ambitious agenda. Some of its actions include:

- Conducting a series of lethal and highly skilled terrorist attacks, including (but by no means limited to) the August 7, 1998 bombings of US embassies in Kenya and Tanzania, killing over 224 (among them 12 Americans) and wounding over 5,000, many of whom were permanently blinded; the October 12, 2000 attack on the USS *Cole* that killed 17 American seamen; and overseeing the September 11, 2001 attacks that killed almost 3,000 people.
- Training Arabs, Uzbeks, Chechens, and other Muslims to fight in Central Asia. This included guerrilla and terrorist training for

---

[60] Zabriskie, "Mullah Omar," p. 94. The interview occurred before the September 11 attacks. There are many reports that Omar and Bin Ladin became linked through marriage, but Omar's driver claims this never occurred. See Johnson *et al.*, "Mullah Omar off the Record," pp. 26–28 and Maley, *The Afghanistan Wars*, p. 255.

[61] National Commission on Terrorist Attacks Upon the United States. "Overview of the Enemy," p. 7.

    groups fighting in Chechnya and Uzbekistan, which have waged long-running insurgencies and conducted numerous terrorist attacks.

- Backing Kashmiri and other radicals fighting against India. These groups have conducted a long-running insurgency in Kashmir and also made numerous attacks on civilian targets in India itself.
- Sponsoring a host of small terrorist groups throughout the Arab and Muslim world, such as the Islamic Aden-Abyan Army in Yemen, Ansar al-Islam in Iraq, and Asbat al-Ansar in Lebanon.
- Supporting Islamist insurgencies in Southeast Asia, including the Abu Sayyaf Group in the Philippines and the Jamaat Islamiyya in Indonesia.
- Developing a global network of radicals that is active in dozens of countries in Africa, Asia, and Europe as well as the Middle East.[62]

As the above list suggests, from his Afghan safe haven, Bin Ladin trained a small army to wage insurgencies around the world. Al-Qa'ida had dozens of training camps in Afghanistan. US officials believe that between 10,000 and 20,000 foreign volunteers trained in Afghanistan after Bin Ladin relocated there in 1996.[63]

    Much of the training consisted of teaching guerrilla tactics in preparation for helping the Taliban defeat the Northern Alliance. Al-Qa'ida veterans gave classes on small unit tactics, the use of plastic explosives such as C-3 and C-4, the calculation of artillery fire ranges, first aid, mining roads, and other necessities for guerrilla war. Al-Qa'ida also amassed knowledge on a range of topics useful to *jihadists* such as small unit tactics, explosives, and the manufacture of chemical and biological weapons, in part by acquiring and translating US military training manuals. By 2001, the training was very sophisticated: Pakistani groups, for example, would learn how to use M-16s, because these are used in Kashmir, while other groups would learn on AK-47s, which are more common elsewhere.[64]

---

[62] For a broader list, see Anonymous, *Through Our Enemies' Eyes*, pp. 179, 198–204.

[63] National Commission on Terrorist Attacks Upon the United States, *The 9/11 Commission Report*, p. 67.

[64] Chivers and Rohde, "The Jihad Files: Training the Troops," p. A1; Rohde and Chivers, "The Jihad Files: Life in bin Laden's Army"; Judah, "The Center of the World," p. 10.

Al-Qa'ida members in Afghanistan pursued chemical and biological weapons, though the effort appears to have made little overall progress. Al-Qa'ida leaders had a start-up program and were corresponding with scientists in Egypt and elsewhere. In Afghanistan, al-Qa'ida members, at times working in conjunction with Pakistani scientists, plotted how to acquire, weaponize, and use anthrax, cyanide, and other chemical and biological agents. Disturbingly, al-Qa'ida's number two figure, Ayman Zawahiri, lamented that the organization only became aware of the lethal power of these weapons after Americans repeatedly noted that they could be easily produced.[65]

The sanctuary also was a place for a much smaller group of select recruits to learn specialized skills that would make them more formidable terrorists as well as guerrilla fighters. An FBI official estimates that "hundreds" of terrorists were trained, as opposed to "thousands" of guerrillas.[66] Small groups of fighters trained in Afghanistan were taken aside where they learned how to observe foreign embassies, assassinate guarded officials, recruit agents, make explosives, and other tricks of the terrorist trade.[67] Some camps taught bomb-making, surveillance, and sabotage.[68] These camps churned out skilled terrorists in large numbers, and they conducted operations around the world. As Michael Sheehan, the State Department's former coordinator for counterterrorism noted, "Afghanistan was the swamp these mosquitoes kept coming out of."[69]

From Afghanistan, al-Qa'ida began to realize one of its chief objectives: knitting together different Islamist militant groups and focusing them on the United States and other Western powers. Although *jihadists* had trained in Afghanistan long before Bin Ladin relocated there, none of the training focused on the United States until Bin Ladin's arrival.[70] Much of the training al-Qa'ida provided consisted of videos, pamphlets, and talks intended to inspire and indoctrinate new recruits with the same

---

[65] Cullison and Higgins, "A Computer in Kabul Yields a Chilling Array of al Qaeda Memos," electronic version.

[66] Wilshire, "Testimony before the Senate Committee on Foreign Relations, Subcommittee on International Operations and Terrorism," p. 9.

[67] Rohde and Chivers, "The Jihad Files: Life in bin Laden's Army"; Anonymous, *Imperial Hubris*, p. 217.

[68] Bartholet *et al.*, "Al Qaeda Runs for the Hills," pp. 20–26.

[69] Chivers and Rohde, "The Jihad Files: Training the Troops," p. A1.

[70] Burke, *Al-Qaeda*, p. 152.

worldview, not just to give them a better skill set. The instruction emphasized the illegitimate nature of many Arab regimes and the evil of Israel
and the United States. The Afghan sanctuary also gave activists a location
to forge new ties, increasing the importance of the indoctrination effort.
Recruits from over twenty countries came to Afghanistan in the 1990s.
Al-Qa'ida helped activists network within their countries and more
globally.[71]

Afghanistan also served as a logistics center for planning various
operations. Two of the most significant al-Qa'ida attacks before
September 11 – the August 7, 1998 strikes on US Embassies in Kenya
and Tanzania, and the October 12, 2000 attack on USS *Cole* – were
planned and coordinated by operatives from Afghanistan, many of
whom returned there after the attacks. Al-Qa'ida members also were
given Afghan passports.[72]

As the scope of al-Qa'ida's attacks and organizational efforts indicates, the haven in Afghanistan was a tremendous boon for the organization. Al-Qa'ida successfully organized and trained a small army of
insurgents, propagated its worldview, and conducted a series of increasingly impressive terrorist attacks. The al-Qa'ida that relocated to
Afghanistan from Sudan in 1996 was a pale shadow of the organization
that attacked the United States on September 11, 2001.

By the time the United States invaded Afghanistan in 2001, al-Qa'ida
was a well-trained force. In contrast to the Taliban, al-Qa'ida fighters
held their ground when attacked by US forces and their local allies, used
terrain well to conceal themselves, and were able to coordinate their
firepower. US military officials considered them comparable to the
world's most skilled guerrillas. This represents a marked departure

---

[71] A *New York Times* investigation of documents left by al-Qa'ida in
Afghanistan indicates that the countries included Algeria, Bangladesh,
Bosnia, Britain, Canada, China, Egypt, Iraq, Jordan, Kuwait, Libya,
Morocco, Pakistan, the Philippines, Russia, Saudi Arabia, Somalia, Syria,
Tajikistan, Turkey, Turkmenistan, Uzbekistan, the United States, and
Yemen. Rohde and Chivers, "The Jihad Files: Life in bin Laden's Army."
See also National Commission on Terrorist Attacks Upon the United States.
"Overview of the Enemy," p. 9.
[72] Bergen, *Holy War, Inc.*, p. 190. Bartholet *et al.*, "Al Qaeda Runs for the
Hills," pp. 20–26.

from the 1980s, when the Arab forces were viewed as weak, unskilled, and inferior to their Afghan allies.[73]

A TWO-WAY RELATIONSHIP

Al-Qa'ida's relationship with the Taliban was reciprocal in a way that was unprecedented for a terrorist group and a state sponsor. The Taliban offered al-Qa'ida a sanctuary, but in other forms of support, such as training, logistics, and ideological guidance, al-Qa'ida was more advanced than its sponsor. Bin Ladin channeled tens of millions of dollars a year to the Taliban, which comprised much of the Taliban's official budget.[74] Much of this money came through Islamic charities and other private donations that Bin Ladin was able to influence. When offering money, Bin Ladin had an excellent sense of timing. For example, he provided $3 million to help the Taliban seize Kabul in 1996.[75]

Equally important, al-Qa'ida trained and recruited fighters to help the Taliban in its struggle to control Afghanistan. The majority of al-Qa'ida's camps in Afghanistan focused on training fighters to help defeat the Northern Alliance, not to conduct sophisticated terrorist attacks against the West. One anonymous US government official declared, "The vast majority of them were cannon fodder."[76] Perhaps 5,000 non-Afghan fighters linked to al-Qa'ida assisted the Taliban's military effort.[77]

Indeed, one of the most important units for the Taliban was Brigade 055, a military unit composed of Arab fighters loyal to Bin Ladin. Although exact numbers are difficult to pinpoint, the unit consisted of perhaps between 300 and 1,000 Arabs. Known for their bravery and

---

[73] Chivers and Rohde, "The Jihad Files: Training the Troops," p. A1. See Biddle, *Afghanistan and the Future of Warfare*.

[74] The Taliban in 1995 received perhaps $120 million from smuggling and taxes on narcotics trafficking. Burke, *Al-Qaeda*, p. 115. The National Commission on Terrorist Attacks Upon the United States reports that the Taliban received between $10 million and $20 million a year from al-Qa'ida, perhaps two thirds of the movement's budget. National Commission on Terrorist Attacks Upon the United States, "Overview of the Enemy," p. 11.

[75] Bartholet *et al.*, "Al Qaeda Runs for the Hills," pp. 20–26 and McGeary, "The Taliban Troubles," pp. 46–50.

[76] Rohde and Chivers, "The Jihad Files: Life in bin Laden's Army."

[77] Sirrs, "The Taliban's International Ambitions," p. 62.

savagery, many members were veterans of the struggle against the Soviets and of conflicts around the Muslim world.

The al-Qa'ida-trained fighters were often given the tougher tasks due to their greater experience, expertise, and commitment. Bin Ladin and Mohammed Atef, his senior military commander, often deployed their forces to the battle at a key moment.[78] A retired Pakistani general who worked with many Afghan groups noted that "The Arabs are the best fighters they have," and that, in contrast to many Afghans, "The Arab fighters cannot be bought."[79]

Al-Qa'ida also used terrorism on behalf of the Taliban. On September 9, 2001, it assassinated Ahmed Shah Masood, the legendary fighter who commanded the troops of the Northern Alliance, the Taliban's only remaining opponent in Afghanistan. Masood's murder, many believed, would lead to the collapse of the Northern Alliance.

Little response to outside pressure

The United States reacted cautiously as the Taliban emerged in the mid-1990s, hoping it would be a force for stability in the region and would be favorable to US interests, such as the construction of oil pipelines from Central Asia across Afghanistan by a US oil company, UNOCAL. The movement at first expressed goodwill to US officials and claimed it would respect human rights, move to eradicate poppy production, and seek an Islamic form of democracy. The Taliban were also pro-Saudi and anti-Iranian, both of which were in harmony with US policy at the time. Initially, US officials portrayed the Taliban as backward but not anti-Western. A perception even emerged in the region that the United States backed the Taliban.[80]

---

[78] Burke, *Al-Qaeda*, p. 171.

[79] Weiner, "'Afghan Arabs' Said to Lead Taliban's Fight." The 055 Brigade, however, was not deployed as a single unit. Rather, its members served as bodyguards or as an elite force to reinforce or encourage other forces. See Eisenberg *et al.*, "Secrets of Brigade 055," p. 63.

[80] US Department of State, "Finally a Talkative Talib"; Rashid, *Taliban*, pp. 164–176; and Maley, *The Afghanistan Wars*, p. 227. In reality, US policy on the Taliban initially vacillated between outrage and concern on one hand, and on the other the hope that it might bring stability to Afghanistan and moderate its harsh ways over time.

As the Taliban consolidated power, the United States tried to sway the movement to respect human rights and favor US interests through diplomacy. Although considerable attention has focused on US attempts to arrange for a Trans-Afghan oil pipeline, the United States also pushed the Taliban on its treatment of women and minorities and Afghanistan's opium production. Terrorism and Bin Ladin initially were lesser concerns.[81]

As al-Qa'ida became more powerful, the presence of its terrorist training camps in Afghanistan became a divisive issue. In December 1997, Assistant Secretary of State Karl Inderfurth pressed the Taliban to pledge that Bin Ladin would not use Afghanistan as a base for conducting attacks.[82] These efforts continued over the years, with the Taliban trying to deflect pressure by denying Bin Ladin was involved in terrorism, claiming they were restricting Bin Ladin's activities, and considering (but not agreeing to) a trial of Bin Ladin by Muslim jurists.[83]

US hopes that the Taliban might prove a benign force were quickly dashed. By 1998, Washington was dismayed by the lack of progress on the pipeline deal, the Taliban's dismal and apparently worsening human rights record (particularly its abysmal treatment of Afghan women), the movement's involvement in narcotics trafficking, and its support for Bin Ladin.

Despite this litany of problems, Afghanistan was largely ignored for most of the 1990s, as it was seen as irrelevant to US interests.[84] This neglect diminished after al-Qa'ida bombed the US Embassies in Tanzania and Kenya on August 7, 1998. The bombings demonstrated al-Qa'ida's impressive capabilities and its determination to strike American targets. The Taliban's support for al-Qa'ida, which before was an irritant in US–Afghanistan relations, now became a major grievance.

---

[81] Coll, *Ghost Wars*, p. 335.

[82] US Department of State, "Summary: A/S Inderfurth Met December 8 with Three Taliban 'Acting Ministers.'"

[83] For a review of US efforts, see US Department of State, "US Engagement with the Taliban on Usama bin Ladin." See also Albright, *Madame Secretary*, p. 369.

[84] Ambassador Robin Raphel, the Assistant Secretary of State for South Asia, was one of the few officials focused on the Taliban but was not able to engage other high-level officials. Coll, *Ghost Wars*, pp. 328–329.

In response to the attacks, the United States bombed four al-Qa'ida training camps in Afghanistan on August 20, 1998. The strikes killed Arab, Afghan, Pakistani, and Kashmiri militants, but failed to kill Bin Ladin himself or other senior leaders.[85] The strikes not only missed their target, but they also backfired in a strategic sense. Outside Afghanistan, the bombings lionized Bin Ladin among Islamists. As Maulana ul-Haqq, a senior Pakistani religious leader, told Peter Bergen, a journalist and expert on al-Qa'ida, the US strikes transformed Bin Ladin into "a symbol for the whole Islamic world. Against all those outside powers who were trying to crush Muslims. He is the courageous one who raised his voice against them. He's a hero to us, but it is America who first made him a hero."[86] As a result, the movement's prestige soared, and al-Qa'ida was able to greatly expand fundraising and recruiting. In addition, the Taliban felt newly committed to protecting their guest, fearing that expelling him would allow the movement to be painted as a US and Saudi stooge. The bombing also led to turbulence in the region. Pakistan in particular experienced street demonstrations against the US attacks. The weak civilian government there tried to appease enraged Islamists by making promises to speed the introduction of Islamic law.[87]

Continued al-Qa'ida plots led the United States to warn the Taliban that it must end its support for terrorism. After the 1998 Embassy bombings, the US Special Coordinator for Counterterrorism Michael Sheehan threatened the Taliban that it would be held responsible for further al-Qa'ida attacks. In July 1999, President Clinton issued an executive order placing US sanctions on the Taliban because of its support for Bin Ladin.[88] Sheehan again warned the Taliban after al-Qa'ida's failed attacks during the millennium celebrations, that "If you have an arsonist in your house, you become responsible for his actions."[89] In 2000 and 2001, the United States was also considering providing covert assistance to the Northern Alliance, though it refrained

[85] Maley, *The Afghanistan Wars*, p. 249.

[86] Bergen, *Holy War, Inc.*, p. 129.

[87] Burke, *Al-Qaeda*, p. 168; Cullison and Higgins, "Strained Alliance"; and Griffin, *Reaping the Whirlwind*, p. 173.

[88] Hufbauer *et al.*, "Using Sanctions to Fight Terrorism."

[89] Cullison and Higgins, "Strained Alliance."

from significant support due to concerns about worsening strife in Afghanistan, angering Pakistan, and backing allies it deemed of dubious reliability and involved in drug trafficking, among other nefarious activities.[90]

The United States also tried to influence the Taliban indirectly by working with its Pakistani and other backers. As early as February 1996, the acting Secretary of State, Strobe Talbott, warned the Pakistanis that their support for the Taliban was destabilizing the region and Pakistan itself.[91] In the years after the Embassy bombings, the United States urged Prime Minister Nawaz Sharif and President Pervez Musharraf both to end their support for the Taliban and to cooperate on efforts to disrupt al-Qa'ida. The United States also asked Saudi Arabia, the United Arab Emirates, and Pakistan – the three countries that had formal relations with the Taliban – to support US demands. These countries at times passed on US warnings to no avail.[92]

International efforts against the Taliban also grew because of its support for terrorism. Russia, India, Uzbekistan, Tajikistan, and Iran all backed the Northern Alliance, in part because the Taliban and al-Qa'ida had worked together to support Sunni radical groups in these countries. With strong US support, the United Nations demanded in October 2000 that the Taliban surrender Bin Ladin to justice. Failure to do so led the UN to demand the cutting of air links to Afghanistan, stopping any form of military assistance to the Taliban, and freezing the Taliban's financial resources in UN Resolution 1333, in December 2000.

US efforts remained limited to sanctions, political pressure, and limited military strikes despite policymakers' growing concerns. Policymakers believed there was little support at home – and none abroad – for various proposals to insert even limited numbers of US troops or otherwise put "boots on the ground." Lacking the intelligence needed to be sure they would kill Bin Ladin in a strike, the Clinton and then Bush administrations did not conduct other military options against al-Qa'ida or the Taliban after 1998. The 1998 cruise missile strikes on Afghanistan have been widely criticized in the United States as a political gambit to distract

---

[90] Coll, *Ghost Wars*, pp. 534–535 and Albright, *Madame Secretary*, p. 370.
[91] US Department of State, "Pak Foreign Minister Asks US Cooperation."
[92] Albright, *Madame Secretary*, pp. 369–370.

attention from President Clinton's troubles over White House intern Monica Lewinsky, and policymakers knew it had raised al-Qa'ida's stature internationally. More robust covert action was actively considered and apparently was in the process of being implemented, but policymakers moved slowly on this due to suspicions of the local proxies in Afghanistan and concerns about widening Afghanistan's civil war.[93] The United States also avoided stronger action in part because it feared angering the Taliban's backers in Pakistan.[94]

Sanctions and isolation proved ineffective for a variety of reasons. As noted above, the Taliban was increasingly committed to al-Qa'ida for ideological reasons. In addition, its continuing war with the Northern Alliance left it dependent on al-Qa'ida's military and financial support. Political isolation meant little to the Taliban, both due to their ideological nature and due to their lack of diplomatic sophistication. Economic punishments mattered relatively little as well. The regime's focus on the community's spiritual as opposed to material status meant that economic growth was not a priority, even though Afghanistan faced drought at the time and had suffered many years of devastation from war. In addition, the sheer poverty of the country and the importance of smuggling and other informal mechanisms meant that limits on trade and investment had little impact.

As with the use of military force, US efforts to isolate the regime and increase economic pressure may have inadvertently pushed the Taliban toward Bin Ladin. The lack of diplomatic recognition and interaction left al-Qa'ida as one of the few organizations in regular contact with Taliban leaders. Moreover, isolation efforts with regard to terrorism made it difficult to provide positive incentives on other issues, such as narcotics. The West's failure to respond to the Taliban's serious effort to ban opium – and subsequent UN sanctions after the ban – strengthened al-Qa'ida's influence, undermining moderates urging reconciliation by

---

[93] National Commission on Terrorist Attacks Upon the United States, *The 9/11 Commission Report*, pp. 126–144; Coll, *Ghost Wars*, pp. 501–502, 534–537 and Albright, *Madame Secretary*, p. 368.

[94] Griffin, *Reaping the Whirlwind*, p. 169. Although Pakistan blatantly violated these sanctions, the United States did not confront Islamabad over this issue until after the September 11, 2001 attacks. Maley, *The Afghanistan Wars*, p. 250.

convincing Taliban leaders that the West indeed was out to destroy the movement and would not respond to any positive steps it took.[95]

Diplomatic pressure also failed in part because of the Taliban's simple lack of diplomatic capacity. One observer compared negotiating with the Taliban to "grasping smoke."[96] As a result, the movement was not able to articulate its objectives to its neighbors or fully appreciate the costs of its continued support for terrorism.

Over the brink

After September 11, the Taliban paid the ultimate political price for supporting terrorism – removal from power. The massive slaughter resulting from the attacks, which dwarfed other attacks in the history of terrorism, made a decisive US military response almost inevitable. In his historic September 20, 2001 speech before Congress, President Bush made a series of demands on the Taliban that his administration almost certainly knew would not be met:

> Deliver to United States authorities all the leaders of al Qaeda who hide in your land. Release all foreign nationals, including American citizens, you have unjustly imprisoned. Protect foreign journalists, diplomats and aid workers in your country. Close immediately and permanently every terrorist training camp in Afghanistan, and hand over every terrorist, and every person in their support structure, to appropriate authorities. Give the United States full access to terrorist training camps, so we can make sure they are no longer operating. These demands are not open to negotiation or discussion. The Taliban must act, and act immediately. They will hand over the terrorists, or they will share in their fate.[97]

Such an ultimatum, demanding unprecedented public concessions, would have humiliated the Taliban leadership, forcing them to openly renounce the teachings and ideas they had promulgated since taking power as well as forsake an ally with whom they had become increasingly intertwined militarily and ideologically.

[95] Burke, *Al-Qaeda*, pp. 173–174. Even after the September 11 attacks, the State Department noted that "the Taliban enforced an effective ban on the cultivation of poppy last year, eliminating approximately two-thirds of the world's annual illicit opium supply." Bach, "The Taliban, Terrorism, and Drug Trade."

[96] Maley, *The Afghanistan Wars*, p. 232.

[97] President George W. Bush, Speech to Congress.

Even before the United States invaded Afghanistan in October, the Taliban had also suffered the loss of its patron and only true ally, Pakistan. Pakistan's previous policy of working with the Taliban (and, indirectly, al-Qa'ida) while seeking to maintain good relations with Washington became impossible once the September 11 attacks necessitated war in Afghanistan. US policymakers emphasized to Pakistan that continued support for the Taliban would transform the country into an enemy, while cooperation would bring a renewed alliance.[98] Faced with the choice between an administration that would provide financial and military aid versus one that would fully support India and allow Pakistan's economy to collapse – and probably work to overthrow the regime – Musharraf gave in and turned on the Taliban.

On October 7, 2001 the US military campaign began with a sustained series of air attacks. US intelligence personnel and special operations forces later entered the country, working with the Northern Alliance and with anti-Taliban Pashtuns. Backed by US air power, these forces quickly routed the Taliban from Afghanistan's major cities, forcing the movement to again become a guerrilla force. Today, the Taliban remain a potent threat to the new Afghan regime of Hamid Karzai but no longer control large swathes of territory on which they can sponsor terrorists.[99]

Al-Qa'ida without a state

Al-Qa'ida did not collapse when the Taliban lost power and a pro-American government took power in Kabul. Indeed, some analysts argued that al-Qa'ida may even have become more powerful. Al-Qa'ida's ideological appeal remains strong, and the movement appears to have inspired Muslims around the world to embrace an anti-US *jihad*. Moreover, its fighters have dispersed, making other groups more lethal.[100] In addition, since September 11 the pace of al-Qa'ida-linked terrorist attacks has remained brisk. This includes bloody attacks in Indonesia, Pakistan, Spain, Kenya, Yemen, Morocco, and elsewhere in the world.

---

[98] Woodward, *Bush at War*, pp. 47, 58–59.

[99] In late 2003, Taliban attacks actually increased over previous periods. Anonymous, *Imperial Hubris*, p. 41.

[100] Tenet, "Worldwide Threat Briefing 2004."

Al-Qa'ida's unusual organizational structure, which involves a dense set of links to groups with a more national agenda, and its presence in dozens of countries, has enabled it to endure despite the loss of Afghanistan. The movement today is far more dispersed than it was on September 11, with local commanders and groups enjoying much more autonomy. As Benjamin and Simon contend: "Virtuality has its own advantages. A dispersed group is harder to locate and attack. Some elements will inevitably be identified and arrested, but other parts of the network will not be affected. With their Macintosh laptops and encrypted communications, stolen credit cards, access to Internet cafes and disposable cell phones, false passports, and comfort with long distance travel, jihadists can be everywhere and anywhere."[101] In addition, the movement no longer spends the majority of its budget supporting the Taliban, freeing up much needed funds.[102]

The loss of a state, however, was a major setback for al-Qa'ida and for the broader *salafi* cause. The one true Islamist state in the eyes of the *jihadists* was no more, replaced by a pro-US regime. As Montasser al-Zayyat, an Egyptian lawyer sympathetic to the *jihadists*, lamented, "Thus bin Laden and Zawahiri lost the Taliban, a government that had protected Islamists for many years."[103] The much-vaunted network structure of al-Qa'ida, while making it easier for the organization to survive, makes it far harder for it to engage in concerted action. Although al-Qa'ida enjoys a presence in Yemen, Indonesia, Western Europe, and elsewhere, it does not have the ability to recruit, train, and plan on the same scale as it did from its base in Afghanistan. Supporting the global insurgency is far harder without control of actual territory.

The rise and fall of the Taliban illustrates many extremes in the annals of state support for terrorism. In contrast to the cautious support Iran and Syria give to their proxies, the Taliban gave al-Qa'ida considerable freedom to conduct attacks and grew increasingly dependent on the movement's support for their own power. Moreover, the terrorist group exercised an increasingly ideological influence on its sponsor,

---

[101] Benjamin and Simon, *The Age of Sacred Terror*, p. 169.
[102] National Commission on Terrorist Attacks Upon the United States. "Overview of the Enemy," p. 11.
[103] Al-Zayyat, *The Road to Al-Qaeda*, p. 97.

helping shape its behavior with regard to a variety of social and diplomatic decisions, such as the destruction of the statues of the Buddha and the regime's decision to turn against the United Nations despite the aid the organization was providing. This remarkable degree of support for al-Qa'ida proved disastrous for the Taliban in the end. The regime's open association with the increasingly lethal movement led directly to its removal after the terrorist organization engaged in a mass casualty attack on US soil – perhaps the only use of massive military force to change a regime solely in response to terrorism in history.

The Taliban's experience thus serves as a cautionary tale for other states considering the support of terrorism, suggesting that if a terrorist group breaches certain limits its sponsor will pay a heavy price. It is also a cautionary tale for the United States and other victims of terrorism. Some state leaders do not act prudently and do not fear escalation. At times, they may go over the brink, backing terrorists even though it brings disaster down on their heads.

8

Passive sponsors of terrorism

The world of state sponsorship cannot be divided simply into good and evil. There are gradations of culpability, and a failure to act can be almost as damning as supporting the wrong side. For many terrorist groups, a state's tolerance of or passivity toward their activities is often as important to their success as any deliberate assistance they receive. Open and active state sponsorship of terrorism is blessedly rare, and it has decreased since the end of the Cold War. Yet this lack of open support does not necessarily diminish the important role that states play in fostering or hindering terrorism. At times, the greatest contribution a state can make to a terrorist's cause is to simply not act against it. A border not policed, a blind eye turned to fundraising, or even the toleration of recruitment all help terrorists build their organizations, conduct operations, and survive.

This passivity in the face of terrorism can be deadly. In conducting the September 11 attacks, al-Qa'ida recruited and raised money in Germany with relatively little interference, enjoyed financial support from many Saudis unobstructed by the government in Riyadh, planned operations in Malaysia, and sent operatives to America. None of these governments are "sponsors" of al-Qa'ida – indeed, several are bitter enemies – but their inaction proved as important as, if not more important, than the haven the group enjoyed in Afghanistan in enabling al-Qa'ida to conduct the attacks. As Deputy Secretary of Defense Paul Wolfowitz testified about the attacks, "even worse than the training camps [in Afghanistan] was the training that took place here in the United States and the planning that took place in Germany."[1]

September 11 highlighted this problem of inaction, but it is not new. Writing just before the September 11 attacks, terrorism expert Paul Pillar described a category of terrorism "enablers": countries that help terrorists indirectly, even if they were not open supporters.[2] Similarly, the National Commission on Terrorism's 2000 report noted that "[s]ome countries use the rhetoric of counterterrorist cooperation but are unwilling to shoulder their responsibilities in practice, such as restricting the travel of terrorists through their territory...."[3] The list of countries that tolerate at least some terrorist activity is long, and is not confined to the Middle East or even to states ruled by aggressive dictators. For example, France allowed various Middle Eastern terrorist groups to operate with impunity in the 1980s, as well as Basque separatists; the United Kingdom tolerated the presence of Islamist radicals who were later implicated in several terrorist attacks; the United States permitted an umbrella group representing the anti-Tehran Mujahedin-e Khalq (MEK) to lobby in the United States until 1997; the Liberation Tigers of Tamil Eelam (LTTE) raised money with little interference in Canada and the United Kingdom; and Venezuela allowed the FARC to operate on its territory.[4]

Passive support appears particularly bewildering because it is often against the strategic interests of a state. Government tolerance often complicates a state's alliances with the victims of terrorism and damages its overall reputation. The terrorist group may even threaten the government in question.

---

[1] Deputy Secretary of Defense Paul Wolfowitz, Testimony before the Joint Inquiry of the House Permanent Select Committee on Intelligence and the Senate Select Committee on Intelligence, "Counterterrorism Center Customer Perspectives."

[2] Pillar, *Terrorism and US Foreign Policy*, pp. 179–185.

[3] National Commission on Terrorism, *Countering the Changing Threat of International Terrorism*, p. 23.

[4] For an overview of the changing French attitude toward support for terrorism on its soil, see Shapiro and Suzan, "The French Experience of Counterterrorism." For an excellent overview of the Tamil diaspora in supporting the Liberation Tigers of Tamil Eelam (LTTE), see Gunaratna, *Dynamics of Diaspora-Supported Terrorist Networks*.

Passive support has a different set of motivations and a different set of solutions than does conventional state assistance. Regimes may turn a blind eye for a variety of reasons, including strong popular support for the terrorist group's cause, a lack of direct threat, and limited costs to the government (including only a limited fear of suffering a damaging attack themselves) that tolerates the terrorists' activities – and at times all three.

Passive support for terrorism can contribute to a terrorist group's success in several ways. Passive support often allows a group to raise money, acquire arms, plan operations, and enjoy a respite from the counterattacks of the government it opposes. Passive support may also involve spreading an ideology that assists a terrorist group in its efforts to recruit new members.

Passive support may be a more intractable problem than open support for terrorism. Passive support introduces new actors beyond the supportive regime into the counterterrorism equation, several of which are not typical interlocutors for states. Diasporas, for example, often play a vital role in passive support. In addition, public opinion often motivates passive support.

Many of the measures used to fight state sponsors, such as sanctions or military strikes, would even prove counterproductive against passive sponsors, alienating an already hostile populace when better solutions might involve wooing popular sympathy. Outside governments can affect these motivations by trying to sway supportive populaces against the terrorist group and by imposing costs on the government for failing to act, as well as for action in support of terrorists. However, it is often difficult for outside governments to convey the necessary sense of threat or to sway domestic opinion sufficiently to change a government's tolerance of terrorism, particularly if the group does not pose an immediate danger to the regime that tolerates its activities.

Lack of counterterrorism capacity is linked to passive support, but it is not identical to it. Some governments simply cannot act. The government of Tajikistan, for example, controls activity in the capital during daylight hours on a good day; expecting it to police its borders with Afghanistan is unrealistic. However, many governments do not develop their police forces, strengthen counterterrorism laws, increase intelligence, or otherwise develop counterterrorism capacity because they do not see terrorism as a serious problem or due to sympathy for the terrorists' cause. Outside powers, however, can have a tremendous impact on counterterrorism capacity, both through direct assistance and by pressing the government to improve its ability to fight terrorism.

This chapter analyzes the vexing issue of passive support for terrorism, first defining passive support, then looking at three countries that can rightly be accused of passive support for, or at least tolerance of, terrorism: Saudi Arabia's backing of radical Islamist causes before 9/11, Greece's tolerance of the 17 November Organization, and the United States' blind eye for Provisional Irish Republican Army (PIRA) fundraising. In each of these instances, the government allowed terrorists to operate, and at times flourish, despite being aware of their activities. The chapter concludes by trying to explain why passive support occurs, how it changes, and its impact.

Definitions

As defined in Chapter 1, state sponsorship is deliberate assistance to a terrorist group. This chapter defines passive support as *knowingly allowing* a terrorist group to raise money, enjoy a sanctuary, recruit, or otherwise flourish without interference from a regime that does not directly aid the group itself. Passive support has the following characteristics:

- The regime in question itself does not provide assistance but knowingly allows other actors in the country to aid a terrorist group;
- The regime has the capacity to stop this assistance or has chosen not to develop this capacity; and
- Often passive support is given by political parties, wealthy merchants, or other actors in society that have no formal affiliation with the government.

At the high end, passive support involves governments that are knowledgeable about a terrorist group and have the capacity to quash it but do not do so; at the low end, it often involves a government that misjudges the level of the threat or deliberately does not develop the capacity to counter it. This definition excludes a regime that deliberately provides government support to a group – such backing would qualify as active support. This definition also excludes governments that try to quash terrorism but fail (e.g., Spain in regard to the Basques) and governments that are not aware that significant support is occurring within their borders (e.g., Indonesia's lack of knowledge about al-Qa'ida before 2001).

Most importantly, this definition excludes countries that lack the capacity to counter terrorism effectively even though they seek to do so. Thus, failed states such as Somalia or Tajikistan would not be considered passive supporters of al-Qa'ida, even though the organization has been active in these countries, because the regimes are far too weak to confront the movement although they wish to do so.

The line between active and passive support easily blurs. Pakistan actively backed various Kashmiri groups fighting against India. In so doing, it tolerated the activities of al-Qa'ida and the global *jihad*, as this assisted its cause in Kashmir indirectly. The government of Pakistan did not support attacks on US forces and officials, but its direct support for other radicals indirectly bolstered anti-American forces.

Three instances of passive support

To flesh out the concept of passive support and illustrate the motivations of the supporters and its impact on the group, this chapter examines three cases: Saudi Arabia's relationship with al-Qa'ida and other *jihadist* causes; Greece's connection to the November 17 Organization; and the United States' experience with the Provisional Irish Republican Army. In all three of these instances, the governments opposed the groups in question, but in all three they often allowed support from within their countries to continue.

These cases were chosen for several reasons. First, the groups receiving passive sponsorship vary considerably, including a religious group, a Marxist one, and an ethnonationalist cause. Second, the problems all three governments encountered offer insight into the interplay between a regime's desire to crush terrorism and a regime's ability to do so. Third, in all three instances the attitude toward the terrorist group changed, leading to a decline in or an end to passive support. Fourth, the regime type of the sponsoring state varies, with two types of democracy being examined along with an authoritarian monarchy. Particular attention is given to Saudi Arabia, given the importance of its relationship with al-Qa'ida, the world's most deadly terrorist group.[5]

---

[5] These three instances of passive support are only the tip of a large iceberg. A larger study of passive support would examine additional regimes, compare the strength of diaspora movements, determine whether passive support varies

Saudi Arabia and Islamic radicalism

Saudi Arabia is often painted as an open patron of Islamic radical groups, including al-Qa'ida. A range of critics in the US Congress and in the American media have lambasted the Kingdom for backing al-Qa'ida and promoting hatred of the United States more generally. Former Central Intelligence Agency (CIA) operative Robert Baer, for example, notes that "Saudis fed the ATM machine for the [9–11] hijackers."[6] In July 2003, 191 members of the House of Representatives supported a bill to add Saudi Arabia to the official US list of state sponsors of terrorism.

Other observers, however, portray the Kingdom as al-Qa'ida's leading target and note the deadly enmity between Saudi Arabia's ruling family, the Al Saud, and Usama bin Ladin. These defenders emphasize al-Qa'ida's repeated denunciations of the Al Saud, attacks on US and Saudi targets in the Kingdom, and reports that Saudi Arabia tried to assassinate Bin Ladin in Sudan.[7] Summing up this perspective, former US Ambassador to Saudi Arabia Charles ("Chas") Freeman declared, "You can be damn sure that any al Qaeda operative is on the Saudi wanted list."[8]

Explaining these seemingly contradictory views requires a closer look at the specifics of the accusations against Saudi Arabia. Both perspectives contain elements of the truth. Al-Qa'ida did draw considerable assistance from the people of Saudi Arabia even as the Saudi regime tried to defeat the movement. The vast majority of support, however, fell into the passive category. Riyadh's tolerance declined after the September 11 attacks, and fell even further after the May 2003 attacks that occurred in the Kingdom itself.

according to the type of terrorist group, and otherwise further develop the variables identified in this chapter.

[6] Baer, *Sleeping with the Enemy*, p. 21.

[7] Michael Scott Doran, for example, argues that Bin Ladin's primary goal is revolution within the Muslim world, with Saudi Arabia being at the top of the list. Attacks on America are designed to weaken regimes such as the Al Saud, not to defeat the United States. Doran, "Somebody Else's Civil War," p. 23. For reports on the supposed Saudi attempt to kill Bin Ladin in Sudan, see Weiser, "Plot to Kill Bin Laden Disclosed" and Weaver, "Blowback."

[8] As quoted (derisively) in Baer, *Sleeping with the Enemy*, p. 202.

THE AL SAUD'S BARGAIN

The modern Saudi regime has worked with religious leaders since its inception. Saudi Arabia's founder, Abdul Aziz ibn Saud, forged an alliance with the followers of Mohammed ibn Abd al-Wahhab, who practiced and sought to spread a puritanical version of Islam. Using fighters from the religiously inspired *Ikhwan* to defeat his enemies, Abdul Aziz ibn Saud conquered what is now modern Saudi Arabia and established a state where the Wahhabis held considerable sway. Wahhabism was used to unite Saudi Arabia's fractious tribes and to legitimate Abdul Aziz ibn Saud's rule.

The relationship, however, was not completely peaceful. In 1929, King Abdul Aziz ibn Saud's forces turned on the *Ikhwan*, and crushed them because they demanded the continuation of *jihad* abroad (particularly against regimes in Jordan and Iraq that were protected by Britain, a Christian power). This broke the *Ikhwan's* power, but Islamic radicals remained a force of opposition to the Al Saud, particularly when it tried to introduce modernizing reforms. In 1979, religious zealots captured the Grand Mosque in Mecca and called for an uprising against the corrupt Al Saud in the name of Islam.[9] In response to the Al Saud's decision to invite US troops into the country in August 1990 to defend it against Iraq, a movement calling itself *Sahwa* (Awakening) emerged and began to criticize the regime harshly for its supposedly un-Islamic decision.[10]

Both to legitimate their role and because of a genuine belief in Wahhabi teachings, the Al Saud made religion a centerpiece of their rule. The Kingdom follows *shari'a* (Islamic law) as interpreted by the Wahhabis, and religious officials have a tremendous say in education and other issues. Religious leaders became important state employees and inter-married with royal family members. King Abdul Aziz ibn Saud and his successors turned to them to legitimate major decisions, such as the 1990 invitation to the United States to send forces to defend the Kingdom against Iraq. The royal family also supported mosques, schools, and preaching in Muslim communities around the world. Throughout the century, the Al Saud drew on this relationship and portrayed themselves

---

[9] Fandy, *Saudi Arabia and the Politics of Dissent*, pp. 21–60; Holden and Johns, *The House of Saud*, pp. 1–109, 511–526; and Vassiliev, *The History of Saudi Arabia*, pp. 139, 201–299.

[10] Kepel, "The Origins and Development of the Jihadist Movement," p. 98.

as a pious Sunni Muslim alternative to rival ideologies such as Arab nationalism, communism, or Iranian-backed Shi'a fundamentalism. The Al Saud would try to increase their identification with religious causes and issues after events that had the potential to discredit their legitimacy, such as the original crushing of the *Ikhwan* in 1929, the 1979 mosque seizure, and the 1990 invitation to US troops.[11]

The Wahhabism of Saudi Arabia today differs somewhat from the *salafi jihadism* of Bin Ladin today.[12] Although both credos endorse a literal reading of Islamic texts and call for conservative social values, they differ in several important ways that are often not recognized. First, Wahhabism in recent years did not see other regimes ruled by Muslims, even ones they regarded as insufficiently pious, as apostate and thus requiring violent resistance. Second, the Wahhabis supported more moderate Islamist movements, such as the Muslim Brotherhood, that attempted to work within the existing political system rather than rejecting it. Third, the Wahhabis did not reject other religious establishment members as corrupt (and in Saudi Arabia the Wahhabis were the religious establishment). Finally, Wahhabis opposed elements of Westernization of Muslim lands, but it did not endorse *jihad* against the United States or other Western powers. The *salafi jihadists*, on the other hand, are far more critical of existing Muslim regimes and other Islamist movements, excoriate the traditional religious establishment, and endorse the idea of violent *jihad* as the proper solution to Islam's problems. The United States is a particular target of their opprobrium.[13] Many *salafi jihadists'* beliefs are similar to the Wahhabism of the early period of Al Saud rule, before the Saudi regime coopted and tempered much of the movement's leadership.

[11] See Lippman, *Inside the Mirage*, pp. 208–209, 303.

[12] As Gause notes, however, the Saudis have been promoting their ideology and religious system for decades, but only recently has it exploded into anti-American violence. Clearly, something else must be at work as well. Gause, "Be Careful What You Wish For," p. 46.

[13] Kepel, *Jihad*, pp. 205–225. Many of the *salafi-jihadist* arguments, however, are more typical of Wahhabist beliefs before the Al Saud consolidated its control. The Wahhabists did legitimate Al Saud attacks on other Muslim principalities by declaring them to be insufficiently pious, and many saw the Shiites as heretics. As Abdul Aziz ibn Saud consolidated control, however, the movement became more moderate.

SAUDI FINANCIAL SUPPORT FOR ISLAMIC RADICALISM

The Saudi largesse that helped secure the Al Saud in power is under intense scrutiny. Many reputable critics see the Saudi regime as turning a blind eye toward support for terrorism, particularly financial assistance, from Saudi citizens. Many private individuals in Saudi Arabia control massive amounts of money: several economists and bankers working in Saudi Arabia estimate that only 85,000 Saudis control perhaps $70 billion. Some of this money is used to spread Wahhabism outside the Kingdom through mosques, schools, and Islamic centers. US officials claim that Saudi Arabia for many years allowed money to flow into the hands of terrorist organizations. The range of causes was wide, ranging from Kashmir and Chechnya to Bosnia, Afghanistan, and of course the Palestinians.[14] David Aufhauser, the Treasury Department's general counsel who also led the Bush administration's interagency process on terrorist financing, declared in June 2003 that Saudi Arabia was the "epicenter" for the financing of al-Qa'ida.

Much of this money flows through charities and other non-governmental organizations (NGOs), which operate on a massive scale. Al-Haramayn, a large charity, claims that it has printed millions of books, founded over 1,000 mosques, and sent over 3,000 missionaries out to spread its message. Tens of millions of dollars have flowed to charities active in the Balkans, in the Palestinian territories, and in other strife-torn areas – the same areas that often witness insurgencies and terrorist groups.[15] Matthew Levitt testified that Saudi Arabia remains the capital of finance for international terrorism, using organizations such as the World Muslim League, the International Islamic Relief Organization (IIRO) and the al-Haramayn Islamic Foundation.[16] These organizations are not entirely private. Charities such as the IIRO or the Muslim World League are overseen by Saudi Arabia's grand mufti and enjoy the patronage of the government and

---

[14] Meyer, "Cutting Money Flow to Terrorists Proves Difficult"; Mintz, "Wahhabi Strain of Islam Faulted," p. A11; and Kaiser and Ottaway, "Enormous Wealth Spilled into American Coffers."

[15] Mintz, "Wahhabi Strain of Islam Faulted"; Kaplan, "The Saudi Connection;" and Beyer *et al.*, "Inside the Kingdom."

[16] Levitt, "Testimony Before the US Senate Judiciary Subcommittee on Terrorism, Technology, and Homeland Security."

many royal family members. Islamic Affairs Bureaus of Saudi Embassies often aid and coordinate the charities' activities.[17]

Much, probably most, of the charities' money went to legitimate humanitarian or standard missionary work, but terrorists diverted some of it. Terrorists used the money to purchase weapons, recruit new radicals, and run training camps. In addition to diverting money, radicals often subverted local branches of these charities. NGOs offer terrorist operatives a legitimate job and identity, as well as access to local communities. The CIA found that one third of the Muslim charities in the Balkans helped various Islamic terrorist groups.[18]

Even when money did not go directly into the hands of terrorists, critics blast the Saudis for supporting charities, mosques, educational institutions, and other activities that provide places for terrorists to recruit, train, and, most importantly, be indoctrinated in a virulent, anti-Western ethos. Although much of the purpose of many of these charities is financial assistance, they also endorse the value of violent *jihad*, a hostile view of US policy, and the sentiment that secular Arab regimes are not legitimate. Such proselytizing enables al-Qa'ida to appeal to recruits already sympathetic to its worldview. Juan Zarate, a Treasury Department official, noted that "Al Qaeda has taken advantage of state-supported proselytizing around the world."[19]

The Saudis also promote ideas that accept violence, particularly against non-Muslims, at home. Sermons praise *jihadist* causes and criticize American and Jewish influence. In Saudi schools, textbooks often denigrated non-believers. In addition, their portrayal of the world echoes that of many *jihadists*, with the texts extolling martyrdom, criticizing imitation of the West, calling for restrictions on non-Muslims, and contending that Islam is on the defensive and that modern trends such as globalization and modern science are undermining Islam.[20]

---

[17] Kaplan, "The Saudi Connection."
[18] The United Nations offers a valuable overview of al-Qa'ida financing, see "Second Report of the Monitoring Group." See also Kaplan, "The Saudi Connection" and Isikoff and Hosenball, "The Saudi–Al Qaeda Connection."
[19] Schmidt, "Spreading Saudi Fundamentalism in US."
[20] Eleanor Doumato, "Manning the Barricades," *The Middle East Journal*, vol. 57, no. 2 (Spring 2003): 233–238. Doumato contends, however, that much of the criticism of Saudi texts is overstated and takes particular lessons out of context.

Indeed, the Kingdom's Foreign Minister noted that a post-September 11 review of curricula revealed that 10 percent of the material in textbooks was questionable and another 5 percent was "abhorrent."[21]

Motivations

Saudi support for radical Islamists may be significant and widespread, but it is far different from the type of backing given by Iran, Pakistan, or other more traditional state sponsors of terrorism. Saudi motivations included a fear of offending domestic support for *jihadist* causes; a sense that the al-Qa'ida threat was limited; and a belief that the danger might actually increase through confrontation. As a result, the regime did not develop its counterterrorism capacity.

STRONG DOMESTIC SUPPORT FOR *JIHADIST* CAUSES

Saudi leaders step gingerly in the world of Islamist politics. *Jihadist* causes, many of which are linked directly or indirectly to al-Qa'ida, are popular in the Kingdom. Islamist insurgencies in Kashmir, Uzbekistan, Chechnya, and elsewhere for many years were viewed as legitimate struggles that deserved the support of fellow Muslims. The Palestinian cause enjoyed particular sympathy. When Islamists champion these issues, they stand with many Saudis behind them. The Saudi regime has backed several of these causes, including supporting Islamic radicals in Afghanistan after the end of the anti-Soviet *jihad*, in part to curry favor with Islamists at home. Riyadh also worked closely with Islamabad for much of the 1990s, providing it with massive financial support and helping it support *jihadists* in Kashmir and, initially, the Taliban and other radical groups in Afghanistan.[22]

The legitimacy of *jihadist* causes was bolstered by the widespread backing given to the anti-Soviet *jihad* in the 1980s. The Saudi regime actively backed this struggle, and it encouraged other Saudis to provide financial support. It also praised many of the Saudis who fought in Afghanistan, while more extreme elements of Saudi society lionized them. Thus, individual participation in *jihad* was widely viewed as admirable.

---

[21] Beyer *et al.*, "Inside the Kingdom," pp. 38–49.
[22] Coll, *Ghost Wars*, pp. 217, 296–297.

Support for al-Qa'ida itself appears strong in much of the Kingdom. Indeed, the Interior Minister Prince Nayif himself declared that "we find in our country those who sympathize with them," an unusually candid reference from a regime that often denies any domestic problems whatsoever.[23] Saudis comprise one of the top nationalities within al-Qa'ida. A leading US observer of the Kingdom, F. Gregory Gause III, contends that "any elections in Saudi Arabia would now be won by people closer to bin Laden's point of view than to that of liberal democrats."[24]

Anti-Americanism in the Kingdom is strong. Polls taken in early 2003 indicated that an astonishing 97 percent of Saudis hold a negative view of the United States, a dramatic increase from previous years. Saudi media, with the tolerance of Saudi officials, regularly criticized the United States, highlighting civilian deaths during the war against the Taliban in Afghanistan and the second Gulf War, and the mistreatment of Arabs in the United States. These specific grievances related to terrorism build on the tremendous hostility toward US support for Israel and perceived mistreatment of the Iraqi people, particularly with regard to the effects of sanctions, during the Saddam Husayn era.[25]

Although the Saudi regime is a monarchy that draws legitimacy from its religious credentials, it does respond to public opinion. Political activism in the Kingdom is modest, but Gause notes that in recent years increased education, urbanization, and high population growth rates have increased political activity in the Kingdom. Until the regime feels directly threatened, it avoids taking steps that would offend the public, preferring instead to coopt dissent. Thus, even as it suppressed religious dissidents, it has tried to coopt their issues, in part by supporting Islamic causes abroad, backing Muslim charities, and otherwise displaying the regime's religious *bona fides*. It was particularly difficult for the Al Saud

---

[23] *Al-Hayat*, pp. 1 and 6. As quoted in Gause, "Be Careful What You Wish For," p. 50 endnote 4.

[24] Gause, "Be Careful What You Wish For," p. 48.

[25] Ibid., pp. 40–41; Dobbs, "US–Saudi Alliance Appears Strong"; and Dobbs, "Saudi Rulers Walk Political Tightrope." Polling data before 2003 are not available. However, numerous observers of the Kingdom contend that anti-Americanism is far stronger than ever before.

to back any initiatives supported by the US government, including those related to counterterrorism.[26]

The result was a measure of tolerance for radical activity in order to avoid public measures that would discredit the regime. This has proven a problem for actions against al-Qa'ida even after the organization's 2003 attacks on the Kingdom. Almost half of the Saudis polled in early 2004 had a favorable opinion of Bin Ladin's sermons and rhetoric.[27]

A LIMITED THREAT?

The Saudi regime has a history of successfully managing dissent. The regime weathered pan-Arabism and the Iranian revolution, both by suppressing sympathizers and by coopting them. Opposition of any stripe is not well organized in Saudi Arabia, making it hard for the Al Saud to be dislodged. The regime also tries to take the wind out of their critics' sails by endorsing, on the surface at least, many of their proposals for change. Moreover, the Saudi regime enjoys support from Saudi religious leaders, who have repeatedly issued decrees backing the regime's controversial decisions such as introducing television, inviting US forces to protect the Kingdom in 1990, and participating in peace talks with Israel.[28]

On the surface, many Islamist causes, even those linked to violent groups, do not appear to pose a direct threat to the Al Saud. Most of these groups have a national focus rather than a global one: HAMAS and the Palestine Islamic Jihad, for example, focus their attacks on Israel (and on rival Palestinian groups), the Harakat-ul-Mujahedin confines its strikes to Kashmir, and so on. Despite the different objectives and theaters of operations of these groups, however, aiding one often results in indirectly supporting another. These groups share a broad ideology that emphasizes anti-Western themes, the value of *jihad*, and hostility

---

[26] Gause, "Be Careful What You Wish For," pp. 41–42; Byman and Green, *Political Violence and Stability in the States of the Northern Persian Gulf*, pp. 29–31; Pollack, "Anti-Americanism in Contemporary Saudi Arabia," pp. 33–39; Yamani, "Saudi Arabia," pp. 145–147; and Anonymous, *Through Our Enemies' Eyes*, p. 145.

[27] "A Measure of Democracy," p. A18.

[28] Gause, "Be Careful What You Wish For," pp. 37–38. For an overview of such techniques, see Byman and Green, *Political Violence and Stability in the States of the Northern Persian Gulf*, pp. 71–94.

toward secular Arab regimes. Moreover, they often share logistics cells, drawing on the same individuals for passports and weapons. Part of al-Qa'ida's mission, moreover, is to knit these disparate causes into a broader struggle.[29]

Because of this superficial calm, the Saudis took many years to realize that some of their friends had become enemies. Thus, coopting the latest threat may have seemed attractive to the Al Saud. Although al-Qa'ida is a vehemently anti-Saudi organization, the threat it posed to the royal family was in many ways quite limited, particularly in the eyes of Saudi leaders. Saudi officials believed that they had eliminated al-Qa'ida in the Kingdom itself in the mid-1990s through their own security efforts. In the early 1990s, Islamist political activists tried to press the regime for reform, but this pressure did not shake the Al Saud's grip on power. Opposition figures submitted petitions, sent faxes denouncing corruption, delivered speeches in mosques, and otherwise tried to incite unrest. The regime, however, clamped down on unrest and arrested various leaders. In 1993 and 1994, it detained militants who criticized the government and coopted others, often through financial support. The regime also pushed many senior religious figures to retire. This limited the contact between dissident religious leaders and the broader population.[30] With these successes in mind, the royal family probably judged that shutting off support for various Islamist causes, including those with close links to al-Qa'ida, was not worth the cost to its self-proclaimed image as the defender of the Muslim faithful.

FEAR OF RETALIATION

The Al Saud may have perceived that the threat from al-Qa'ida would increase if the family confronted the organization. The Al Saud may also

---

[29] Wilshire, "Testimony Before the Senate Foreign Relations Committee."

[30] Fandy, *Saudi Arabia and the Politics of Dissent*, pp. 61–114; Gause, "Be Careful What You Wish For," pp. 39 and 44; and Kepel, "The Origins and Development of the Jihadist Movement," p. 99. There is a small liberal movement in the Kingdom that Crown Prince Abdullah has often tried to work with, although he does not endorse many of their positions. For a review, see Dekmejian, "The Liberal Impulse in Saudi Arabia." For a broader overview of charges against the Al Saud, see Aburish, *The Rise, Corruption, and Coming Fall of the House of Saud*.

have allowed support to go to Al-Qa'ida – and perhaps even provided money directly – to avoid attacks on royal family members and targets within the Kingdom. Critics of the regime repeatedly make this argument. Simon Henderson claims that after the 1995 bombings of the Office of the Program Manager/Saudi Arabian National Guard office bombings in Riyadh, which killed five Americans and two Indians, the Saudi Interior Minister and the Minister of Defense and Aviation paid Bin Ladin and al-Qa'ida to not conduct attacks in the Kingdom. They were willing to offer the terrorists money even though they recognized that they would attack US targets overseas.[31] Dore Gold, a former Israeli Ambassador, claims that Saudi royal family members directly funded Bin Ladin in order to buy protection: in exchange for money, al-Qa'ida would not conduct operations in the Kingdom. He contends, "Saudi Arabia was paying a ransom to be left alone."[32]

Judging these claims is difficult, as evidence is understandably spare. Most who make these claims do so with almost no specifics to support their evidence. Moreover, Bin Ladin funded anti-Saudi causes early on and otherwise directly challenged the Al Saud – activities that usually lead the Al Saud to confront a threat more directly. Indeed, there are numerous accusations that the Saudis tried to kill Bin Ladin in Sudan. The National Commission on Terrorist Attacks Upon the United States reports that it "found no evidence that the Saudi government as an institution or senior officials within the Saudi government funded al Qaeda."[33]

The Commission, however, noted that al Qaeda received considerable financial support from the Kingdom. Moreover, Saudi Arabia did pay protection money to various Palestinian groups that threatened to kill regime members and that challenged its nationalist credentials. In addition, through diplomacy it has tried to buy off or coopt threats from Nasser's Egypt and Saddam's Iraq – but was also willing to confront them directly when cooptation failed.

---

[31] Henderson, "Address before the Washington Institute for Near East Policy."
[32] Gold, *Hatred's Kingdom*, p. 182.
[33] National Commission on Terrorist Attacks Upon the United States, "Overview of the Enemy," p. 10.

INCAPACITY

Given the rather nebulous nature of passive sponsorship, it is often difficult to stop even when a regime aggressively seeks to end it. However, there is tremendous variation in governments' abilities to act decisively on counterterrorism. The Saudi government is highly personalized, with institutions often being little more than a brittle shell surrounding one individual.[34] Decision-making is highly centralized, and the number of competent bureaucrats is low. The Ministry of Foreign Affairs, for example, revolves around Prince Saud al-Faisal; others in the Ministry cannot, and will not, make important decisions. Many Saudi institutions barely function or function poorly. For example, Saudi Arabia's military forces remain inept, even by regional standards, despite having billions of dollars lavished on them over the course of several decades and being trained by US, British, and other Western forces.[35]

Not surprisingly, the Saudi regime was often unable to respond to repeated requests for counterterrorism assistance. Lee Wolosky, a former Bush and Clinton administration staffer on the National Security Council, noted, "You have to be very careful what you ask for from the Saudis because if you have a list of more than one item you frequently don't get to the second."[36]

The Saudis have a limited capacity to crack down on terrorist financing in particular. Former Ambassador to Saudi Arabia Chas Freeman contends the Saudis are guilty of "negligence and incompetence," not complicity.[37] Before September 11, the Saudis lacked a financial regulatory system and did not oversee their charities. Because the Kingdom does not impose taxes on its citizens, it often did not collect basic financial data that allow for the enforcement of financial controls.[38]

Capacity and regime priorities are intimately linked. Many of the problems above are serious, but the Al Saud made few efforts before September 11 to address them. As discussed below, the September 11

[34] For a review of Saudi institutions, see Raphaeli, "Saudi Arabia."
[35] Pollack, *Arabs at War*, pp. 425–446.
[36] Van Natta Jr. and O'Brien, "Saudis Promising Action on Terror."
[37] Kaplan, "The Saudi Connection."   [38] Ibid.

attacks led to improvements, but it really took the May 2003 strikes on the Kingdom itself for the royal family to decide to build capacity.

An end to passive support?

Saudi Arabia's willingness to tolerate support for radicals linked to al-Qa'ida and, to a lesser degree, other Islamist groups ranging from Chechens to HAMAS, fell dramatically in recent years. The September 11 attacks on the United States dramatized the lethality of al-Qa'ida and greatly increased American pressure on the Saudi regime to halt any support for the attacks. Subsequent attacks in May 2003 highlighted the threat even more directly, enabled the regime to gain more domestic support, and compelled the Kingdom to build its counterterrorism capacity.[39]

Saudi Arabia has long depended on the United States for security, and the two governments (but not the two peoples) are very close.[40] This relationship predates the first Gulf War when the United States sent troops to protect the Kingdom from Iraq and, ultimately, to roll back its invasion of Kuwait. In the decades before the war, Riyadh worked with the United States to counter Arab nationalism, to offset Soviet influence throughout the world, to oppose revolutionary Iran, and otherwise to advance their common interests in regional stability.[41] Not surprisingly, the regime responded to the tremendous US pressure after September 11 by stepping up cooperation on counterterrorism and reducing its tolerance for many activities related to violence. A failure to act risked serious costs for the Saudi government, endangering a vital relationship that was at the core of its security. Moreover, it feared the

[39] Even after the May attacks, the Saudi government is split on the danger the attacks pose and the best response – as well as the proper degree of cooperation with the United States. See Doran, "The Saudi Paradox," pp. 39–42.

[40] For an overview of the US–Saudi relationship, see Lippman, *Inside the Mirage*.

[41] For a review of Saudi security policy until the 1980s, see Safran, *Saudi Arabia*. Safran argues that the Saudis relied heavily on the United States in times of crisis but often tried to distance themselves from Washington when the immediate danger subsided. For a detailed review of the early years of the security relationship this century, see Hart, *Saudi Arabia and the United States*.

political embarrassment occurring on a daily basis, as critics around the world blasted the Al Saud for its links to terrorism.[42]

The September 11 attacks also led some members of the Al Saud to recognize that al-Qa'ida posed a direct threat to their own position. The scale and lethality of the attacks demonstrated al-Qa'ida's prowess to even the most skeptical. In response, the Al Saud began to move away from many of the causes it had once embraced. Senior Saudi princes criticized the religious establishment for stepping beyond its traditional role, and the *de facto* ruler, Crown Prince Abdullah, on November 14, 2001 called on religious leaders not to exceed "the proper boundaries in religion" – a strong statement for a leadership that always embraced the role of religion in society. The regime began to investigating terrorist financing, wayward charities, and other forms of support. However, it still did not aggressively confront its Islamist opponents.[43]

Efforts to crack down on support climbed even more dramatically, however, after the May 12, 2003 attacks, where 34 people died in multiple attacks on compounds housing US security personnel in the Kingdom. The November 8, 2003 attacks, where 17 died and another 100 were wounded, kept the momentum going. Because the victims of the November attacks were largely Arab, the attack had little popular support, even among those who might be sympathetic to an anti-Western strike.

The 2003 attacks removed any vestige of hope that the Al Saud could divert al-Qa'ida and focus it outside the Kingdom. The subsequent investigation further dispelled any lingering illusions. Saudi security forces uncovered a large network of radicals in the Kingdom. Many were well armed, and the amount of explosives discovered suggested that they were prepared for a long struggle, not simply a terrorist attack or two. The deaths of several regime security officers in the course of the investigation made the regime even more determined to root out any network and increased popular support for a crackdown.

After these attacks, the Saudis implemented a number of unprecedented measures to fight terrorism, greatly increasing overall counterterrorism

---

[42] US–Saudi relations sunk to perhaps their lowest level ever, with mutual recriminations and widespread public hostility on both sides. See Gause, "The Approaching Turning Point, " pp. 3–6.

[43] As quoted in Gause, "Be Careful What You Wish For," p. 44.

capacity. The Saudis excised much, though not all, of the material denigrating other religions from school textbooks. Aufhauser noted that the Saudis strengthened their regulation of informal money transfers, stepped up fund-management responsibility, and increased prohibitions on charitable donations outside the Kingdom. The regime publicized a list of names and photos of the most-wanted terrorist suspects and visibly increased security – very public measures for a regime that prefers to operate in the background. Crown Prince Abdullah traveled to Russia and condemned Chechen violence. A senior Saudi official also claimed that the regime planned to shut down the Islamic affairs section in every Embassy, reversing decades of official support for Islamic education and missionary work around the world.[44] These measures suggest that the Al Saud now recognize the connections among disparate Islamists, even those not directly attacking the Kingdom, and how their proselytizing bolsters al-Qa'ida.[45]

The May and November attacks also helped the regime work with the conservative religious establishment in the Kingdom. The establishment was highly critical of extremists for attacking fellow Muslims, in contrast to past attacks that targeted Americans primarily. Even former firebrands such as Safar al-Hawali and Salman al-'Awda – shaykhs whom Bin Ladin himself had praised in the early 1990s – condemned the May attacks.[46]

The Kingdom's determination and its ability to work with establishment clerics continued into 2004, even though al-Qa'ida-linked groups in the Kingdom had apparently learned their lesson and focused their attacks on Westerners rather than Saudis. Testifying in March 2004, Ambassador Cofer Black, the US Coordinator for Counterterrorism, declared that the Saudis understood the threat they faced and were closely cooperating with US officials.[47]

Capacity remains a problem for the Kingdom, though it is improving. Saudis are working with American intelligence and law enforcement

---

[44] Aufhauser notes, however, that the Saudis remained reluctant to hold any individuals accountable for financial activity in support of terrorism. Aufhauser, "War on Terror." See also "Saudis List Top Terrorist Suspects" and Schmidt and Murphy, "US Revokes Visa of Cleric at Saudi Embassy."

[45] For a critical review, see Levitt and Henderson, "Waging the War on Terror."

[46] Dekmejian, "The Liberal Impulse in Saudi Arabia."

[47] Black, "Testimony to the House Committee on International Relations, Subcommittee on the Middle East and Central Asia."

officials, who are training them on tracking terrorist financing, investigating techniques, and other aspects of counterterrorism. Despite these improvements, the Kingdom remains a developing nation, where inefficiency is often the rule rather than the exception. Oversight of charitable giving remains incomplete, and many of the Kingdom's new initiatives have not been tested.[48]

Taken together, the main motivations behind Saudi tolerance – domestic sympathy, perceived low risk of attack, limited costs for inaction, and incapacity – all diminished. Although some support, particularly financial support, almost certainly continues, the regime is far more energetic in trying to stop it and is building its capacity to do so. As a result, Saudi Arabia has gone from a major passive sponsor of terrorism to a regime that is committed to crushing it.

Greece and the revolutionary organization November 17

In many ways, Greece is the polar opposite of Saudi Arabia. Fanatical Marxists, not radical Islamists, comprised the Greek terrorism problem for most of the past three decades. In contrast to tens of thousands of radical Saudi Islamists, the number of violent leftists was exceptionally small, probably in the dozens, though many Greeks may have sympathized with their cause. Greek society did not provide the same level of backing as did Saudi society, and the Greek government did not indirectly aid the radicals' cause as did the Al Saud.

Nevertheless, successive Greek governments, like the Al Saud, often failed to act against terrorists and their supporters for many years. The Greek government deliberately took little action to stop the terrorists and did not develop the capacity to act more effectively. The reasons for this inaction are similar to the Saudi experience: a lack of a perceived threat, domestic sympathy for the terrorist cause, and limited capacity. As a result, Greece suffered from one of the worst, and most sustained, terrorism problems in Europe.[49]

---

[48] Harrington, "Saudi Arabia and the Fight Against Terrorism Financing," and Zarate, "Testimony to the House Committee on International Relations, Subcommittee on the Middle East and Central Asia."

[49] Greece's tolerance of terrorists was not limited to November 17. Greece reportedly helped smuggle the PKK's leader, Abdullah Ocalan, to Kenya in an attempt to help him elude Turkish authorities.

On December 23, 1975, three gunmen from the leftist Greek terrorist group Revolutionary Organization November 17 (N17) gunned down Richard Welch, the CIA station chief in Athens. Welch's murder marked the beginning of a violent spree that would last until 2002, when an arrest after a botched N17 attack led to the discovery and collapse of almost the entire group. During this time, N17 committed over 100 attacks, including at least 23 murders. N17 murdered US and other Western officials, Greek politicians of the right and moderate left, and prominent businessmen. Over time, it also conducted remote-controlled bombings and attacked facilities with anti-tank rockets.[50]

N17 took its name after the date in 1973 when the Greek military government bloodily crushed students who had seized the Athens Polytechnic and called for democracy. In its many manifestoes, November 17 trumpeted both socialism and nationalism. It saw force as the only path to victory, rejecting social reform, democratic politics, and other elements of the strong left-wing movement in Greece that had emerged after the seven-year period of military rule ended in 1974. It opposed the Greek establishment of both the left and right and attacked a range of targets that it saw as linked to capitalism, imperialism, and the state. N17 also championed an array of nationalist goals, such as ending Greece's membership in the North Atlantic Treaty Organization (NATO) and expelling Turkey from Cyprus.[51]

The Greek government's effort to halt attacks from N17 met with no success until July 2002, when a botched bombing in the port of Pireaus led to the arrest and trial of most of the group.[52] For almost three decades the group had operated with apparent impunity, with no member of the group ever being captured or killed during this period. As George Kassimeris, a leading expert on N17, notes, "any study of Greece's counter-terrorism effort quickly reveals it to be ramshackle...the ineptitude of the Greek state has been unparalleled."[53]

---

[50] Corsun, "Group Profile," p. 97.
[51] Kassimeris, *Europe's Last Red Terrorists*, pp. 106–151.
[52] For a review, see Szymanski, "Greece: November's Fall?"
[53] Kassimeris, *Europe's Last Red Terrorists*, p. 152.

Explaining Greek inaction

Greece's attitude toward N17 was mirrored by its broader policies with regard to other terrorist groups. Athens was reluctant to extradite terrorists to other European countries, instead allowing them to go to sympathetic countries after their arrest. For example, in 1988 a Palestinian terrorist wanted by Italy was sent – by his choice – to Libya instead. Many Greeks opposed government attempts to crush N17 and other leftist terrorist groups.[54]

Greek history also offers an insight into the seemingly bizarre tolerance of the Greek left and much of the mainstream for political violence. During the years of the military dictatorship, the police and security services focused their activities on suppressing communism, rather than stopping crime. They stifled any form of dissent.[55] Not surprisingly, moderates and leftists were exceptionally sensitive to any bolstering of police power and suspicious of calls to curtail civil liberties in the name of fighting terrorism. A strong state was more of a menace than a few murders. As late as 2000, the US State Department declared that in Greece "Popular opinion makers generally downplayed terrorism as a threat to public order, even as terrorists continued to act with virtual impunity."[56]

In part because of this history, counterterrorism capacity was a tremendous problem. Kassimeris notes that N17's violence "exposed several of the deficiencies of the political system and the state structure: irresolute administrations, unreliable intelligence services, inadequate police forces, and a cumbersome judicial system."[57] The security services took a decade to accept that N17 attacks were not simply the work of disorganized anarchists, but rather part of a coordinated and sustained campaign by a disciplined group. Forensic evidence, which at times was excellent, was not carefully examined. The security services did not properly gather intelligence, let alone disseminate it. The security services often made matters worse by arresting familiar opposition

---

[54] Jongman, "Trends in International and Domestic Terrorism in Western Europe, 1968–1988," pp. 64–65.
[55] Kassimeris, *Europe's Last Red Terrorists*, p. 192.
[56] US Department of State, *Patterns of Global Terrorism 1999*, p. 18.
[57] Kassimeris, *Europe's Last Red Terrorists*, p. 191.

figures whom they said were subversive rather than hunting for the true terrorists.[58]

Such bungling reflects a deliberate design, not incompetence. Security services were deliberately factionalized and kept ineffective in order to limit their political influence. As George Kassimeris lamented in 2000, "For most of the past 25 years, anti-terrorist strategy has been carried out by an under-resourced, under-trained and ill-equipped police force that lacks the motivation, discipline, dedication and expertise to wage an effective war against the professionalism and sophistication of 17N."[59]

The parliamentary debate over counterterrorism highlights the tension between suspicion of government and greater counterterrorism capacity. The Greek government introduced laws as early as 1978 modeled after Italian and German statutes that had proven effective against their own leftist terrorists. The legislation outlawed various forms of terrorism and activities that would support it. However, government attempts to expand police powers and stiffen penalties for political violence met with considerable resistance. Still reeling from seven years of military dictatorship, left-wing political parties denounced proposed laws as a pretext for subverting democracy. In addition, they condemned attempts to gain informers and otherwise reward betrayal. Moreover, they questioned the government's interpretation of the threat level and argued there was no true crisis that demanded harsher measures. As a result, many measures were not properly enforced or were even abolished. When the Panhellenic Socialist Movement (PASOK) took power, it abolished the anti-terrorist legislation passed in 1978. One law passed even prohibited the extradition of a terrorist if he is believed to be fighting for freedom.[60]

In response to another N17 attack in 1989, Greece's Parliament passed another tough anti-terrorism bill in 1990. This bill was even more expansive than the 1978 law, allowing the police to detain individuals without charge for fifteen days, requiring newspapers to

[58] Ibid., pp. 193–194 and US Department of State, *Patterns of Global Terrorism 1999*, p. 19.
[59] Kassimeris, "17N."
[60] Jongman, "Trends in International and Domestic Terrorism in Western Europe, 1968–1988," p. 64 and Kassimeris, *Europe's Last Red Terrorists*, pp. 156–170. The Greek law, however, did not allow additional police surveillance or detention powers.

limit the publication of N17 communiqués, as well as measures to encourage informers and punish supporters of terrorism. The law, however, backfired by polarizing the political debate and harming the consensus that was building against N17's activities. In 1993, PASOK abolished the law. A PASOK deputy argued that tough anti-terrorism laws "lead to the undermining of human liberties and the policing of political life."[61] Participating in a terrorist group was relegated to being a misdemeanor.[62]

Another tough law passed in 2001 gave significantly expanded powers, including an increase in authority for the police to infiltrate groups, nonjury criminal trials, and other measures. Again, much of the governing Socialist party walked out of the vote itself in an attempt to distance themselves from the legislation.[63]

Popular incredulity, and at times sympathy for the general cause, contributed to the problem, making it harder for the government to act. For many years, many mainstream politicians, journalists, and analysts advanced a welter of bizarre conspiracy theories rather than recognize the indigenous nature of N17.[64] Pillar notes that N17 acquired a "Robin Hood aura" and was admired because of its anti-Turkish, anti-NATO, and anti-US activities.[65]

Rumors abounded of links, or certainly sympathies, between leading socialist politicians and the radicals. Many PASOK members and other leftists were part of the Greek student movement and its struggle against military rule, a background shared by more violent leftists. At the working level in many bureaucracies, sympathy for N17 – and thus the potential for police operations to be compromised – was high.[66]

As a result of the popular and elite sympathy and concern over civil liberties, the government was neither able nor willing to make a concerted effort against N17. Counterterrorism capacity was deliberately kept low. Nicholas Burns, the US Ambassador to Greece, noted that "One

---

[61] As quoted in Bakoyannis, "Terrorism in Greece," p. 23.
[62] Kassimeris, *Europe's Last Red Terrorists*, pp. 174, 202 and Bakoyannis, "Terrorism in Greece," p. 26.
[63] Vlahou, "Greece Launches Attack on Terrorism," p. A11.
[64] Kassimeris, *Europe's Last Red Terrorists*, p. 192.
[65] Pillar, *Terrorism and US Foreign Policy*, p. 180.
[66] "November 17, Revolutionary People's Struggle" and Pillar, *Terrorism and US Foreign Policy*, p. 180.

of the problems in the past was the Greek government did not make a concerted effort to track down these terrorists."[67] The State Department's *Patterns of Global Terrorism 1999* report used unusually harsh language for an ally: the report declared Greece's counterterrorism performance to be "feeble."[68]

Sources of change

Over time, public attitudes toward terrorism changed. The widow of the murdered British Defense Attaché led a vigorous public campaign against N17, drawing wide sympathy. After the attack, British police spent two years in Greece, launching a successful effort to involve the community in supporting counterterrorism efforts. Memories of the military dictatorship became more distant, decreasing both sympathy for N17's agenda and the fear of stronger security services. Archbishop Christodoulos Paraskevaides held a memorial service for the victims of terrorism, and Greece in 2000 signed UN counterterrorism conventions and began to work more closely with the United States and Britain.[69]

Greece also faced steady pressure from the United States, the UK, and others regarding N17, and this grew as the United States and others warned that the threat of terrorism could prove a problem for the 2004 Olympics, which would be held in Greece. The government feared both an actual attack and that US concerns would result in fewer tourists traveling to Greece to attend the games. This pressure eventually bore fruit and contributed to a more aggressive government effort to stop November 17, including a greater willingness to work with British and American counterterrorism specialists. Greek security services aggressively and competently followed up on the bungled Pireaus attacks, and the judicial system brought them to trial smoothly.

As with Saudi Arabia, the linked problems of incapacity and popular support for the cause – if not the means – of the terrorists made it hard for the government to act decisively. In Greece, outside pressure and in particular a shift in public attitudes helped change the balance, enabling the government to act more effectively and end the threat posed by N17.

---

[67] As quoted in Vlahou, "Greece Launches Attack on Terrorism," p. A11.
[68] US Department of State, *Patterns of Global Terrorism 1999*, p. 16.
[69] "November 17, Revolutionary People's Struggle."

This shift, however, took several decades in which N17 and its lethal activities continued with little opposition.

The United States and the Provisional IRA

America's self-image as a staunch opponent of terrorism and its closeness to London make it all the more surprising that for many years the United States tacitly allowed Irish republican terrorists to raise money and organize on US soil with relatively little interference. Since the advent of modern terrorism in 1968, President after President has condemned it in the strongest language. Moreover, the United Kingdom is perhaps America's closest ally in the world. A shared history, shared values, and common strategic interests bind the two governments and peoples closely. Nevertheless, the United States, like Greece and Saudi Arabia, allowed terrorists to flourish due to domestic sympathy, limits on capacity (in this case for legal reasons), and little sense of threat.

The United States was long a hotbed of Irish resistance to British rule over the Emerald Isle. Throughout the nineteenth and early twentieth centuries, wave after wave of immigrants left Ireland for America, bringing with them an accumulated hatred of the British for their brutal rule, and a strong sense of Irish nationalism. Over the years various violent resistance movements had branches, or even headquarters, in the United States as they plotted against the British government. The Fenian Brotherhood, formed in the 1850s, helped plan the unsuccessful uprising in Ireland in 1866, providing arms, volunteers, and money. After the rebellion collapsed, a new organization, Clan na Gael, served the cause of independence from the United States. The Friends of Irish Freedom played a similar role, helping to gather money and other aid for the Irish Republican Army (IRA) during its struggle for independence from 1919 to 1921. In addition to these formal organizations, many Irish dissidents lived in the United States, having fled from the British authorities. In addition to plotting resistance, the dissidents raised money and gathered arms.[70]

The Irish cause did not die out after the birth of the Irish Free State in 1921. The Irish Republican Army continued to pursue the armed struggle for five years under Eamon de Valera, and when he rejected violence

---

[70] Holland, *The American Connection*, pp. xv–xvi; Bell, *The Secret Army*, p. 56; and Bell, *The IRA, 1968–2000*, p. 35.

in 1926 and brought his Fianna Fail party into politics, a rump of his movement – the forefather of today's IRA – continued the fight. As the movement faded in the Irish republic, the Irish diaspora in America and elsewhere remained militant. In particular, though many in the new Irish republic reconciled themselves to the partition of Ireland into the Protestant-dominated north and a Catholic south, the small number of diehard irredentists drew on the American diaspora to support their strategy of using military force to reverse the partition of the country.[71]

The modern chapter of the IRA's history began with the so-called "Troubles" in 1969. The causes of the explosion of violence are complex. Catholics in Northern Ireland were fed up with decades of discrimination in housing, voting, jobs, education, and every other facet of life. Led by young leaders, many of whom were part of a new, better-educated group of activists, the Catholic community began agitating for more rights. Initial peaceful demonstrations were brutally put down by local security forces and Protestant mobs rampaged through defenseless Catholic neighborhoods. British troops were deployed to bring order, but they were quickly seen as a prop for the Protestant regime, not as impartial arbiters.[72] The result was widespread violence, with the IRA engaging in a low-level war for almost thirty years.

Initially, the Irish Republican Army itself was at most a minor player in this drama. In the 1960s, it embraced a political strategy, reducing its use of violence in favor of social activism. Its leaders were heavily influenced by Marxist theories of revolution and political action. By 1969, it was neither well armed nor organized for violence. The social explosion and violence of 1969 proved a boon for recruitment, but most of the new recruits favored violence, both to protect their communities and because they believed peaceful means had failed. Angry at the IRA's neglect of self-defense and skeptical of its Marxist bromides, many leaders and new recruits split and formed the Provisional Irish

---

[71] For a history, see Bell, *The Secret Army*, pp. 29–98. Militants among the diaspora had less patience for purely political strategies. In the 1960s, diaspora support for the IRA fell as the movement abandoned its military campaign in favor of a strategy involving peaceful protest. Geraghty, *The Irish War*, pp. 7–8. For more on the role of diasporas, see Shain and Sherman, "Dynamics of Disintegration" and Sheffer, "Ethno-National Diasporas and Security."

[72] Bell, *The Secret Army*, pp. 355–373.

Republican Army (PIRA, also called the "Provos"). The PIRA rather quickly became the dominant nationalist movement, in large part because it could effectively use violence to defend Catholic areas and was eager to bring the war to the British and the Protestant government. Over time, their name became synonymous with the IRA itself.

As the Troubles engulfed Northern Ireland, sympathy from the United States – followed by money and weapons – grew dramatically. Numerous organizations sprang up to advance the Irish cause. The Provisional IRA received considerable funding from the Irish Northern Aid Committee (often known as NORAID), an organization that collected private financial contributions from US citizens. Whether diverted through NORAID or supplied privately, the Irish-American diaspora provided important financial assistance to the IRA. NORAID raised between $3 million and $5 million for the IRA. Contributions were especially high after high-profile British violence, such as the January 30, 1972 killing of fourteen Irish Catholic protesters by British troops, known as "Bloody Sunday."[73]

Much of this money went for weapons, either directly or indirectly. In the 1970s, NORAID played a major role in sustaining the families of IRA prisoners and freed up almost £200,000 to spend on arms each year. NORAID was a major source of money for weapons until the IRA began receiving weapons from Libya in the late 1980s; previously perhaps 80 percent of its weapons came from the United States.[74] By 1970, NORAID had 2,000 members in the New York area and branches in Chicago, Boston, Detroit, and other cities.[75]

---

[73] Geraghty, *The Irish War*, p. 9; Holland, *The American Connection*, pp. 28–29; Holland, *The American Connection*, p. xvii; English, *Armed Struggle*, p. 152; and Guelke, "The United States, Irish Americans and the Northern Ireland Peace Process," p. 524. Bell argues that the impact of diaspora money was important, but that it was overestimated by governments and that the amount given was "never crucial." Bell, *The IRA, 1968–2000*, pp. 187–188.

[74] O'Brien, *The Long War*, p. 121 and Holland, *The American Connection*, p. 61. During the 1970s, much of the IRA's income came from theft.

[75] Holland, *The American Connection*, pp. 29–37. Irish-American support for the IRA occurred despite ideological differences. The New York head of NORAID, for example, was Michael Flannery, an arch-conservative who disapproved of the Marxist tendencies of some IRA leaders in the early 1970s.

The IRA helped midwife this support network. Two senior IRA officers, Daithi O'Conaill and Joe Cahill, came to the United States shortly after the Troubles broke out in order to energize potential donors and restore the arms network that had existed before the IRA focused on social activism. The IRA also sent relatives of the victims of British attacks to publicize their plight in the United States. To avoid offending more conservative American audiences, the US version of *An Phoblacht*, the IRA newspaper, played down the organization's socialist rhetoric.

NORAID tried to emphasize its support for the combatants' widows and children, and its ties to Sinn Féin, the IRA's political wing, rather than its direct connection to the IRA. Sinn Féin, however, was directly controlled by the IRA's army council, and many of the militants occupied senior positions in Sinn Féin. Moreover, the founder of NORAID publicly stated that the organization was created in response to the IRA's requests for help. NORAID members also went to Ireland in 1971 to arrange and finance IRA arms purchases in Europe. Not surprisingly, the US, British, and Irish governments all considered NORAID to be a front organization for the IRA.[76]

NORAID was the most public organization linked to the Irish nationalist cause, but much of the arms procurement and other illicit activities went through low profile organizations. George Harrison, a leading IRA operative in the United States who worked with local Mafioso, procured perhaps 2,500 guns while active, as well as a million rounds of ammunition. The IRA often came to Harrison with a shopping list of requirements, along with money to buy the weapons. Harrison helped procure the IRA's signature weapon, the Armalite, as well as the full-automatic M-16 (and later the M-60) and other weapons. Harrison's network provided several hundred weapons to the IRA a year – a large number, as the number of full-time IRA fighters averaged perhaps 500 in the 1970s and 200–300 in the 1980s. This steady supply was vital, as the British often seized weapons as they disrupted operations or killed IRA members. The US connection was particularly

---

[76] English, *Armed Struggle*, p. 117 and Holland, *The American Connection*, p. 32. NORAID funds went to *An Cumann Cabrach*, which assisted the families of IRA prisoners. Guelke, "The United States, Irish Americans and the Northern Ireland peace process," p. 524.

vital in the early years, as the movement sought to establish itself as a
viable resistance force.[77]

Arms in small batches were relatively easy to acquire in the United States.
In many states, gun laws were lax or non-existent, and civilian versions of
military weapons were often available.[78] Indeed, the signature IRA weapon –
the Armalite – was a civilian version of the US-manufactured M-16.

The diaspora also acted as a haven for IRA fugitives. NORAID helped
IRA operatives find new identities and jobs in the United States, enabling
them to escape justice in Northern Ireland.[79] This sanctuary boosted
the morale of operatives, enabling them to escape and decreasing the
number of demoralizing arrests. Moreover, it frustrated British intelligence by decreasing their ability to gain information from arrested
IRA members.

In addition to money, arms, and a haven, IRA supporters also placed
pressure on the British government through their political influence in
America. Many Irish Americans opposed violence but saw the IRA and
its republican supporters as a key to Northern Ireland's future and
believed it should be part of negotiations over the future of the North.
Lobbying groups like the Irish National Congress helped
persuade Jimmy Carter to express his support for Irish unity and concern
over abuses of human rights in Northern Ireland when he was the
Democratic candidate for President in 1976. In 1977, Congressman
Mario Biaggi established the Ad Hoc Committee on Irish Affairs,
which pushed to have hearings on Northern Ireland (which would
embarrass London) and to press the State Department to give visas to
IRA members. The Ad Hoc Committee had over 100 Congressional
members. NORAID members picketed the British Consulate in New
York for three years following the death by hunger strike of Bobby Sands
in May 1981, creating a visible daily reminder of the unpopular British
occupation of Northern Ireland. The strike appealed to many Irish
Americans who otherwise rejected the IRA because of its use of violence.

---

[77] English, *Armed Struggle*, pp. 116–117, 344. Harrison managed to procure
weapons for several decades before being caught by the FBI. Moloney,
A Secret History of the IRA, p. 16, 421 and Holland, *The American
Connection*, pp. 72–113.
[78] Bell, *The IRA, 1968–2000*, p. 183.
[79] Moloney, *A Secret History of the IRA*, pp. 16, 421.

During the strike, Thomas ("Tip") O'Neill, the Speaker of the House of Representatives, demanded that Prime Minister Thatcher recognize the hunger strikers' demands. Speaker O'Neill, who often denounced the IRA, at times allowed legislation to pass that went against the British position.[80]

The diaspora's pressure served several purposes. Prime Minister Thatcher, for example, often moved away from a hardline position against negotiations with Irish nationalists in response to US pressure or even to offset potential criticism. In addition, US pressure made her and other British leaders more willing to press Protestant opponents of negotiations to make concessions.[81] Constant Congressional scrutiny and criticism also embarrassed the British government and the local administration in Northern Ireland and emboldened the IRA. Finally, this pressure helped generate political protection for IRA fundraising and other activities, making it politically more costly for politicians to crack down on the IRA's support network.

The US government interfered only fitfully with the IRA's efforts to raise money or acquire weapons. Needless to say, the IRA's struggle against the British government posed no direct security threat to the United States. For part of the 1970s, the Federal Bureau of Investigations (FBI) ignored IRA efforts.[82] J. Bowyer Bell declared the arms conduit "blatant."[83] The US government monitored NORAID, watching Cahill,

---

[80] Ibid., p. 209; Holland, *The American Connection*, p. 2; O'Dowd, "The Awakening," p. 67; and Guelke, "The United States, Irish Americans and the Northern Ireland peace process," pp. 527–532. The Irish National Caucus, founded in 1974, by the 1980s had become the primary political organization for lobbying Congress on behalf of the IRA. Guelke, "The United States, Irish Americans and the Northern Ireland peace process," p. 526. One example of anti-British legislation occurred in 1979, when O'Neill allowed a bill to pass that halted arms sales to the Royal Ulster Constabulary from the United States. Holland, *The American Connection*, p. 139.

[81] Holland, *The American Connection*, pp. 145–151 and Guelke, "The United States, Irish Americans and the Northern Ireland peace process," p. 530.

[82] Moloney, *A Secret History of the IRA*, p. 16. The Bureau's very investigation of some NORAID activities, however, did discourage some potential members from joining and led some branches to collapse. Holland, *The American Connection*, pp. 38–39.

[83] Bell, *The Secret Army*, p. 467.

O'Conaill, and other IRA members, but seldom interfered with its activities.[84]

Domestic politics explains much of why the United States did not act to shut down fundraising and other activities. Irish-American political clout in the United States can be considerable. Over 40 million Americans claim at least some Irish heritage, and much of the Catholic Irish population is concentrated in the northeast and north central part of the country.[85] The broader perception among Irish Americans that the British were backing a discriminatory Protestant government made it harder for the US government to crack down on IRA supporters.

Capacity was also a problem, though the lack of capacity took a far different form than that of Saudi Arabia or Greece. US laws allowed some fundraising and support for widows and other dependants, even if this activity was indirectly linked to terrorism. Efforts to stop fundraising immediately led to civil liberties concerns, particularly with regard to freedom of speech. In response to one attempt, the American Civil Liberties Union noted that "The government's attempt to deter and harass such fundraising would still be unlawful" even if the money would eventually be used for terrorism.[86] Similarly, a US judge refused to extradite an IRA member who had killed a British soldier, noting that this act, while deplorable, clearly fell under the "political offense exception" and thus the suspect was not subject to extradition.[87]

The British government put pressure on the United States to end the weapons smuggling and to allow suspects to be extradited for trial. Pressure grew in the 1980s, as British Prime Minister Thatcher made action against the IRA an important issue in the close bilateral US–UK

---

[84] Pillar, *Terrorism and US Foreign Policy*, p. 139; Bell, *The IRA, 1968–2000*, p. 187 and Holland, *The American Connection*, p. 32.

[85] Irish immigrants have intermarried with non-Irish Americans, with the result that only 10 million Americans claim an Irish heritage on both sides of the family. Moreover, half of those with an Irish heritage are Protestant. See Guelke, "The United States, Irish Americans and the Northern Ireland Peace Process," p. 523.

[86] As quoted in Holland, *The American Connection*, p. 40.

[87] Holland, *The American Connection*, pp. 161–163. Subsequent judges, however, had different interpretations of the political offense exception. One found that indiscriminate bombing that killed civilians did not constitute a political act. Holland, *The American Connection*, p. 191.

relationship. IRA fundraising proved an embarrassment to the Reagan administration, which had made a tough stance against terrorism a standard part of administration rhetoric.[88]

British pressure, and the IRA's often brutal attacks, produced results. Starting in the mid-1970s, the United States began to deny visas to prominent Sinn Féin and IRA spokesmen. In the early 1980s, Harrison and other members of his network were arrested, as were several other rings. British pressure also led to changes in US laws. In May 1986, President Reagan helped push the Supplementary Treaty through the Senate. The Treaty excluded violent acts from being treated as political offenses. Because of Thatcher's pressure, the IRA's supporters had little influence with the Reagan administration.[89]

The US government's reinvigorated effort, while incomplete, had a significant impact. Bell argues that "arms procurement was no longer a patriotic lark" but rather a risky endeavor. By the mid-1980s, large-scale arms procurement in America had collapsed. The collapse of the US network was painful for the IRA, reducing the number of weapons in its hands and the level of violence it perpetrated until it could find alternative suppliers – a move that pushed the IRA toward Qaddafi's Libya.[90]

In addition to direct diplomatic pressure on the US government, the British played to the American people, including Irish Americans. London painted the IRA as murderers, stressing that their use of violence actually harmed their efforts to advance the Northern Irish Catholic cause. British counterterrorism excesses often hurt their own campaign. Nevertheless, over time it became clear that London was not simply pushing to ensure Protestant domination and was trying to use force more discriminately. Various IRA blunders that killed innocents reinforced the British claims and convinced many Americans to withhold support from the IRA. Over

---

[88] O'Dowd, "The Awakening," p. 69.
[89] Holland, *The American Connection*, pp. 41 and 194–195 and Moloney, *A Secret History of the IRA*, p. 16. Britain's support for the US bombing of Libya contributed to Reagan's energetic push to have the pro-British legislation passed. However, many of those arrested were found innocent, and much of the network was not unraveled. Bell, *The IRA, 1968–2000*, p. 183.
[90] Moloney, *A Secret History of the IRA*, p. 16; Bell, *The IRA, 1968–2000*, p. 185; Geraghty, *The Irish War*, p. 181; and Holland, *The American Connection*, p. 110.

time, support for the IRA fell and did not increase again until the movement began to embrace peace.[91]

The Irish Republic's condemnation of the IRA and political pressure on its supporters made the British campaign especially credible. Unlike the United Kingdom, Irish Americans felt fondly toward the republic, and its opinion carried considerable weight among Irish Americans. Dublin did not always endorse London's position, but it firmly rejected that of the IRA. Dublin worked to counter Irish-Americans, such as Senator Edward Kennedy, who were initially considered "too green." During the Carter administration, Dublin sought to increase US involvement in the conflict, hoping to have US aid to Northern Ireland conditional on British support for a power-sharing agreement. At the same time, the Irish government actively tried to undermine support for the IRA in the United States. Dublin saw the IRA as an embarrassment, hurting both the chances for peace and more broadly the image of Ireland in America.[92]

As the Irish struggle wore on – and as the perception of the British changed from that of a hostile occupying force to a more positive one – the Irish-American diaspora became a source of pressure for peace. By the 1980s, many Irish Americans no longer saw a British withdrawal and a united Ireland as key to the problem. Leading Irish-American figures, many of whom were not affiliated with NORAID and the armed struggle, pressed Gerry Adams and other IRA leaders to deliver peace in the 1990s. The IRA was willing to disappoint more militant supporters in NORAID to do so.[93]

New Irish-American organizations contributed to this shift. Americans for a New Irish Agenda pushed for the United States to become more active in helping negotiate an end to the violence in Northern Ireland and putting pressure on the British government. The group successfully lobbied Bill Clinton as a candidate for the presidency to support the Northern Irish cause, leading him to endorse several

---

[91] Bell, *The IRA, 1968–2000*, p. 195.

[92] Holland, *The American Connection*, pp. 115–133 and O'Dowd, "The Awakening," pp. 65–66. At the request of London, the Irish government even opposed US efforts to encourage fair employment practices in Northern Ireland.

[93] Moloney, *A Secret History of the IRA*, p. 421 and Guelke, "The United States, Irish Americans and the Northern Ireland peace process," p. 532.

political initiatives in October 1992, just before being elected. In 1994, the group helped convince President Clinton to grant Gerry Adams a visa to speak in the United States over the opposition of the State Department and other parts of the bureaucracy – a decision that helped contribute to the IRA's decision to support a ceasefire and move toward power sharing.[94] Again, domestic politics played a major role in this shift. Niall O'Dowd, an intermediary for Adams with the US government, recalls that before the decision was made he "received a call from the White House asking for the percentage of Irish-Americans in each state of the Union. I took this as a very positive sign that Clinton, the *uber*-politician, was calculating the political odds, and I knew there were no votes whatever in the British position."[95]

The shifting views of the diaspora encouraged IRA leaders to embrace a new direction, and this shift in turn reinforced the more peaceful strains among the diaspora. As the IRA began to abandon the armed struggle in the 1990s, it created a new group to raise money in place of NORAID – the Friends of Sinn Féin (FoSF). NORAID's association with the violent side of the IRA was unwelcome after the ceasefire, as the IRA sought to have its representatives work directly with US political leaders. Moreover, many NORAID members had condemned the IRA's decision to accept a ceasefire in August 1994, and the organization itself appeared ambivalent with regard to the decision to end the armed struggle. The FoSF worked directly with the US Department of Justice to ensure that money raised in the US was not used "for any unlawful purpose," such as helping the IRA directly – a decision taken without the backing of Adams or other IRA leaders. Much of the American money thus went to helping back the peace process and to strengthen Sinn Féin, the IRA's political wing.[96]

---

[94] Clinton did not follow through with many of the Americans for a New Irish Agenda's requests when he became President, only doing so after it became clearer that the IRA was willing to move toward peace. Guelke, "The United States, Irish Americans and the Northern Ireland peace process," pp. 533–534; English, *Armed Struggle*, pp. 304–307; and O'Dowd, "The Awakening," pp. 73–74.

[95] O'Dowd, "The Awakening," p. 74.

[96] Moloney, *A Secret History of the IRA*, p. 460; Holland, *The American Connection*, pp. 256–258; and Bell, *The Secret Army*, p. 656.

The US government's attitude toward the IRA reflects some of the ambivalence found in Greece and Saudi Arabia as they confronted their own terrorist movements. Popular sympathy and lax laws enabled support. Over time, a change in popular attitudes, successful pressure on successive US administrations, and a shift in the movement itself led the United States to act more aggressively and to build its capacity to shut down support for IRA terrorism.

Why does passive support occur?

The Saudi, US, and Greek experiences suggest that passive support usually occurs for three reasons, often in combination: domestic sympathy for the group; a sense that the group poses little threat to the host government itself; and relatively low costs of inaction.

Domestic sympathy for the terrorist group's cause is a common motivation for passive support. Although the level of Saudi domestic support for al-Qa'ida is unclear, the large number of Saudis in al-Qa'ida suggests at least some sympathy. Moreover, support for related Islamist causes that al-Qa'ida supports and draws on – such as Muslim insurgencies in Kashmir, Chechnya, Palestine, and elsewhere – and its anti-US agenda is high. In addition, al-Qa'ida was able to tap into broader Saudi support for spreading its Wahhabi interpretation of Islam, an extremely popular policy and one that the regime repeatedly used to improve its political standing. N17's attacks appeared to have enjoyed some backing from many Greeks, particularly nationalists and leftists. At the very least, many of these did not condemn N17's choice of targets. Much of the Irish-American community at least sympathized with the IRA's objectives if not its methods.

Terrorist groups often play on the perceived legitimacy of their cause (the spread of Islam, Greek nationalism, Irish independence, and so on) even when the supporting populations do not endorse a more violent struggle. When the cup is passed in the name of these causes, supporters often ask few questions.

In particular, providing aid to humanitarian causes linked to the terrorist group is not seen as endorsing violence. In reality, however, NGOs and humanitarian assistance groups play a vital role for terrorist organizations. NGOs are often fronts for operatives to recruit, operate with a legitimate cover, and raise money. Even when the money does not support the operatives themselves, the humanitarian activities enable the group to extend its support base among the population at large by creating a sympathetic community. This enhances the group's appeal beyond violence and gives it access to additional potential recruits.

Because passive support is far more open than active support, often it is viewed as more acceptable internationally, and thus has fewer diplomatic costs. Only when nations make it an important bilateral issue do the costs begin to mount. For example, the US decision to crack down on the IRA's more blatant activities in the United States came only after the British government repeatedly pushed Washington. Similarly, the United States pushed the Saudis after September 11, gaining an increase in their cooperation against violent Islamists. The threat to the Olympic Games in Greece raised the potential costs to the Greek government of a continued terrorist threat, even though the danger to the government and society remained limited.

Passive support appears to require a low level of perceived threat from the terrorist group by the government that hosts it. The IRA, of course, was not a threat to the United States. For many years, N17 was not seen as a danger to the Greek regime – at least not as much of a danger as the increased police powers needed to fight it. Saudi Arabia represents the exception that proves this rule. Although al-Qa'ida was violently opposed to the Al Saud and made this clear in the early 1990s, the Kingdom itself did not see it as a mortal danger until much later, possibly as late as 2003. Until the May 2003 attacks on Saudi soil, the Saudi regime appears to have seen al-Qa'ida more as a nuisance that could be diverted rather than as a direct danger that had to be confronted.

A lack of capacity

A lack of capacity also explains passive support, but it is only partly satisfying.[97] Saudi Arabia's ability to crack down on al-Qa'ida financing was (and remains) limited given the poor financial oversight structure in the Kingdom. The Saudi regime was also handicapped by a lack of skilled personnel. Greece was not able to investigate N17's murders and bombings, in part because its security and intelligence services were factionalized and inept.

---

[97] For a review of the problem of state capacity today, see Fukuyama, *State-Building*.

A lack of capacity can also involve legal restrictions as well as institutional competence. Many activities related to terrorism – proselytizing, fundraising, and even recruiting – are at times protected by laws governing free speech and free association. The IRA's ability to enjoy a haven in the United States and to raise money was bolstered by US laws governing the rights of those engaged in political activity, even if it involved violence. US protection of IRA murderers on the grounds of their political activity was a particularly glaring weakness.

The desire to invest in and build capacity, however, is directly linked to the perceived costs and threat and the level of domestic support for terrorism. In Greece, there was tremendous resistance to improving the capacity of the intelligence and security services, as many Greeks feared that their government would use counterterrorism as an excuse to infringe on civil liberties. For Saudi Arabia, the effort needed to crack down on support for radical groups abroad – and the domestic political costs this would entail – began tentatively after US pressure skyrocketed following the September 11 attacks, but it was not seen as completely worthwhile until after the May 2003 attacks posed a direct threat to the Kingdom itself.

Why does passive support diminish?

In all three of the cases examined, passive support for the terrorist group diminished over time. The United States became a champion of Sinn Féin's (and thus the IRA's) move toward peace, while Saudi Arabia and Greece became dangerous foes of the terrorist movements they once tolerated.

Saudi Arabia's shift occurred in response to the increased costs of tolerating radical Islamist activities and, eventually, the recognition of the grave threat the movement posed to the Kingdom. For many years, the al-Saud were content to let the sleeping dog of Islamic radicalism lie, hoping to exploit rather than confront the movement. The diplomatic costs of such tolerance grew enormously after the September 11 attacks threatened the Kingdom's alliance with the United States. Even more important, the subsequent attacks in the Kingdom in 2003 demonstrated that the movement being tolerated was more dangerous to ignore than to confront.

In both Greece and the United States, a shift in public opinion played a major role in ending passive support. In both cases, the luster of the terrorists' methods diminished, in part due to the lobbying efforts of other governments. As with Saudi Arabia, both governments also feared the diplomatic costs of alienating key allies over their tolerance of terrorism.

Change in passive support is often directly linked to the actions of the terrorist group. The American role – both among the diaspora and in the Clinton administration – shifted in response to the IRA's gradual embrace of negotiations over violence. Al-Qa'ida's decision to attack Saudi Arabia in May 2003 greatly sped up the Saudi shift against the movement.

The impact of passive support

Passive state support for terrorist groups often transformed weak groups into strong ones or made strong ones even more capable. Al-Qa'ida may have raised hundreds of millions of dollars from Saudi Arabia, helping it set up a truly global network and enabling it to back guerrilla movements in Chechnya, Kashmir, Afghanistan, and elsewhere. These dollars reinforced the movement's preeminence, enabling it over time to direct as well as support movements to promote its ideology over more national agendas. IRA fundraising in America enabled the movement to become extremely well armed, making it far harder for Britain to break the back of the movement.

Self-financing groups also face fewer restrictions on their activities. Iran, Syria, and Pakistan all were able to influence their proxies, in part because of their financial support for them. Al-Qa'ida, however, is far less responsive to the desires of even supportive regimes such as the Taliban, as it does not depend on their largesse to survive. As a result, it is able to conduct horrific operations such as the September 11 attacks with less fear of offending its sponsor.

For al-Qa'ida, backing from Saudi Arabia also proved vital for recruitment. Not only did many Saudis join the movement directly, but the activities the Kingdom supported made recruiting Muslims overseas far easier. Saudi-backed NGOs, including several that had close ties to the regime, helped al-Qa'ida operatives find local cover for their activities. Riyadh's efforts to spread Wahhabism created numerous mosques and cultural centers that radicalized local Muslims, making them far more receptive to al-Qa'ida's message.

Passive support also greatly aided actual operations, allowing terrorist groups to strike more effectively or to work with relative impunity. N17 appears to have enjoyed considerable freedom of action for its attacks, being able to strike without fear of arrest. Islamists in the Kingdom ran NGOs such as al-Haramayn that had close links to terrorist groups, helping build a radical network to conduct operations without government interference. For almost two decades, the IRA acquired most of its arms from the United States. This greatly increased the lethality of IRA attacks and helped the movement weather British countermeasures. The IRA was also able to send its operatives to the freedom of the United States, making it easier to encourage more dangerous activities and preserving its institutions in the face of a very aggressive British counter-terrorism effort. In all cases, passive support enabled the movements to survive more easily and discredited the government they opposed – top goals of all terrorists.

Although passive support is superficially less menacing than traditional sponsorship, it plays a major role in helping groups sustain themselves and conduct operations. Indeed, as traditional sponsorship has declined, passive support has emerged as one of the leading problems in counterterrorism today. The experiences of Saudi Arabia, Greece, and the United States all suggested that passive support can be reduced, and even ended, through policy intervention. Success, however, requires reconceptualizing what state sponsorship of terrorism is and reevaluating the means we use to fight it.

9

The difficulties of stopping state sponsorship

Terrorism is a weapon of the weak. Israel has a more powerful military and far larger economy than Syria; the United States is more powerful than Iran; India is more powerful than Pakistan, and so on. Yet these powerful countries cannot, or at least do not, marshal their economic influence and military power to stop terrorism. Indeed, they resemble helpless giants, unable to use their massive strength to defend themselves against an elusive and ruthless adversary.

The previous chapters in this book suggest that stopping state sponsorship involves more than leveraging a state's military and economic power. Rather, the state sponsor's own priorities and limits, and the peculiarities of its embrace with a terrorist group, also are key determinants of whether outside pressure will succeed or fail. Recognizing both the dynamics of the sponsor and the states that oppose it are vital for understanding how to cut the ties that bind states to terrorist groups.

Several problems in particular hinder efforts to coerce sponsors into stopping their support. First, the sponsors of terrorists often anticipate the punishment they will receive for their support. Thus, they are prepared for it or find ways to manipulate their support to avoid it. Second, the stakes are often imbalanced, favoring the state sponsor. Sponsors may see their support for terrorism as linked to vital interests or to the survival of their regime, while the victim state may perceive the threat of terrorism less acutely, despite the lives lost. Third, sponsors often think they have few alternatives in achieving their ambitions, believing that outright war or negotiations would both fail. Fourth, many leading sponsors are ideologically driven, a class of motivations that is particularly hard to affect. Fifth, outside powers seldom recognize the full range of state support, focusing their efforts on too narrow a set of concerns. Finally, the coercing power often has a poor understanding of the problem, a mischaracterization that makes counterterrorism less effective.

This chapter reviews each of these problems. However, these problems are not insurmountable. Thus this chapter also briefly discusses why state sponsors do change their level of support despite these problems. Yet another problem coercing states have – that the policy options available to them are blunt instruments that often are more costly to use than is suffering continued state sponsorship of terrorism – is discussed in Chapter 10.

Weathering the punishment

Before the sponsoring regime begins backing a terrorist group, it often has already considered the feasible range of punishments it may face. In going ahead, the sponsoring state has concluded that support for terrorism is nevertheless valuable and that it can dodge or weather the response of the victim countries. Iran has long understood that a rapprochement with the United States and restored economic relations will not be possible as long as Tehran actively supports a variety of anti-US and anti-Israel terrorist groups. Iranian leaders also recognized that increased support for terrorism might lead to a commensurate increase in US efforts to isolate and weaken the clerical regime. After the 1979 revolution, they welcomed this confrontation. Even today, the clerical regime believes its interests are still served by supporting radicalism. Similarly, Syria and Pakistan recognize that Israel and India respectively might conduct limited military strikes in response to terrorism but have calculated that support for terrorism by itself will not lead to an all-out war. Such costs are accepted, and at times even embraced. In essence, many of the possible punishments are accepted in advance, making it less surprising that the application of these punishments often fails to change the sponsor's behavior.

For the most part, these sponsoring states are correct. The number of casualties inflicted by terrorism is usually low and does not force the victim government to respond with all available means – the September 11 attack being the exception that proves this rule. International support for retaliation is often lacking when the number of victims is small. Israel's 2003 attack on Syria, the 1986 US bombing of Libya, and the 1998 US strike on Afghanistan were criticized, at times vociferously, by foreign governments who saw the strikes as a dangerous escalation. Former Secretary of State George Schultz noted that the Reagan administration wrestled with the problem of how to meet "violent threats that lay between doing nothing or launching an all-out conventional war."[1]

Sponsoring regimes often ratchet down their support for terrorism in the face of unwanted escalation, particularly if the regimes' motivations are strategic. Syria has reined in Hizballah and Palestinian groups when they interfered with Damascus' gambits during the peace process in the 1990s, Tehran halted anti-US terrorism in the Gulf because it feared a repeat of Khobar Towers would lead to a US attack and multilateral sanctions, and Pakistan has forced Kashmiri groups to assume a lower profile in order to appease the United States after September 11. In all three cases, the states did not abandon the terrorists but rather modulated support to meet new political realities.

Some states, of course, do not ratchet down their support but in fact increase it, particularly if the regime depends on supporting the group as part of its domestic legitimacy or for ideological reasons. In such cases, the infliction of any punishment generates additional costs to the regime that make it more likely to escalate and support terrorism, or at least not abandon the group entirely.[2] Indeed, such attacks may transform support for the terrorist group from a minor concern to a vital one linked to the regime's political stature. The Taliban regime probably did not anticipate a US military response to the 1998 al-Qa'ida attacks, but when the strikes came they made it harder politically for Mullah Omar to distance himself from the terrorist group. In addition to having lost an important ally and benefactor, the Taliban would have lost face among nationalistic Afghans, gone against *pashtunwali*'s dictates of hospitality, and enraged those opposed to the United States if it abandoned al-Qa'ida

---

[1] Schultz, *Turmoil and Triumph*, p. 650.

[2] Coercion often imposes "audience costs" on the adversary state. For more on this concept, see Fearon, "Bargaining, Enforcement, and International Cooperation" and Putnam, "Diplomacy and Domestic Politics." For the risk of escalation, see Downs and Rocke, "Conflict, Agency, and Gambling for Resurrection," p. 364.

in the face of US pressure, even though before the US attack the Taliban and al-Qa'ida reportedly had an uneasy relationship.

The fiction of deniability also serves the sponsor well in avoiding punishment. The links of various Kashmiri groups to Pakistan and of the Lebanese Hizballah to Iran are well known. Indeed, Iranian and Pakistani leaders regularly meet with and praise terrorist group leaders. Yet these groups do at times act independently, and critics of escalation are quick to echo the supporting regime's excuse that the group did not act under its sponsor's explicit instruction.

Sponsoring states can also increase their use of terrorism in response to pressure from the targeted state or its ally – a danger that the targeted state often anticipates, and that in turn serves as a deterrent. The limits that states often place on their supported terrorist groups also gives them the option of escalation. Syria and Iran, for example, could use Hizballah to attack US Embassies overseas that the Iranian government has already "cased" or have the group use its long-range rockets to attack major cities in Israel such as Haifa. Any US or Israeli escalation against the group or its sponsors has to take into account these risks. Similarly, Pakistan could increase its support for Kashmiri groups, providing them with more funding or advanced weapons if it chose.[3]

An imbalance of stakes

Another problem for coercers is that the stakes involved usually favor the state sponsor.[4] Terrorism typically poses a grave but not mortal threat to the victim state. Despite the drama of terrorism, the number of casualties inflicted is often low. In contrast, states that sponsor terrorism are often in a strategic bind. States that end their support for terrorism are often, in effect, abandoning what they consider an important strategic objective or at least abandoning an important tool for achieving this end. If Iran abandoned Hizballah and various rejectionist Palestinian groups, Tehran would have at most limited influence in Lebanon and almost none over Israel. Pakistan would have little hope of weakening India or undermining its control over Kashmir if it limited itself to backing non-violent groups in the disputed region.

---

[3] Pillar, *Terrorism and US Foreign Policy*, p. 159.
[4] George and Simons, *The Limits of Coercive Diplomacy*, p. 281.

This bind is often even tighter when regimes support terrorists for domestic reasons. If Damascus abandoned the Palestinian cause it would embolden the Baath regime's critics, a potentially fatal step given the regime's weak legitimacy. Israeli threats and the damage from limited sanctions were secondary concerns. For the Taliban, losing al-Qa'ida's military and financial support would have weakened the movement's control over Afghanistan and hindered its progress against its enemies in the civil war. The damage inflicted by US economic sanctions or cruise missile attacks paled before these concerns.

The impossibility of divorcing counterterrorism from other foreign policy concerns also can play to the advantage of the sponsoring state, further tilting the imbalance of stakes in its favor. Iran and Syria have both exploited their geostrategic position and various Western foreign policy objectives such as counterproliferation and trade to offset pressure on their support for terrorism. Indeed, counterterrorism measures against one group cannot often be divorced from efforts against another. Washington's influence on Pakistan's support for Kashmiri groups is limited in part because the United States needs Islamabad's cooperation against al-Qa'ida. If the United States imposed harsh penalties on Pakistan for its backing of terrorists in Kashmir, it would risk losing Islamabad's help against al-Qa'ida.

Few alternatives to terrorism

An important question for understanding state motivations is not simply why states support terrorists, but why they support terrorists over other options. As is frequently noted, terrorism is war by other means. Such a cliché, however, obscures one of the main reasons states choose to use terrorism: it is usually *not* treated as an act of war. Pakistan-backed Kashmiris can attack the Indian Parliament as they did on December 13, 2001, Iranian-backed Saudis can blow up a US military base as they did at Khobar in 1996, and Syrian-linked Palestinians can bomb an Israeli bus, all without the victim state treating it as an act of war.

Such a distinction is vital for the supporting state, as it is usually too weak for conventional conflict. Indeed, most of the state sponsors learned the hard way that their own conventional forces cannot achieve the regime's objectives. Israel, of course, trounced Syria in every one of their many confrontations over the years. Pakistan tried to use conventional forces and its own irregulars to wrest Kashmir from India upon partition in 1947 and again in 1965, failing both times. Pakistan also suffered a humiliating defeat in 1971 at India's hands, and the conventional gap grew after that. Supporting Kashmiri insurgents was one of the few means available to challenge India. Similarly, Iran was well aware of its conventional inferiority to the United States, having suffered the loss of much of its navy in 1988 when it threatened US-flagged shipping in the Persian Gulf, and having witnessed the US devastation of Iraqi forces in 1991 and 2003.[5] Terrorism is one of the few means available for Tehran to remain on the offensive. In such cases, support for terrorism is one of the few means available to weak states to advance their interests.

Terrorism also offers an advantage because it can be used globally, while the state's conventional military assets are at best regional. By employing Hizballah, Iran can strike at targets in Europe, Latin America, and elsewhere in the world. Its conventional forces, on the other hand, can barely project power near Iran's borders, let alone thousands of miles away.[6]

A third advantage of terrorism over conventional force is that it is cheap. Small numbers of terrorists can wreak havoc, forcing the adversary government to devote thousands of troops or police officers to counterterrorism and to spend millions – at times billions – of dollars in defense. In contrast, the supporting state may be providing only small numbers of light arms, rudimentary training, and a camp in which to train, plan, and take shelter.

Thus, support for terrorism is often deliberately chosen because it walks the line between effective provocation and a direct attack. It is not the ideal choice from a state's point of view. Terrorists are often weak, untrustworthy, or incompetent. However, other options are often off the table because of the state's own weaknesses.

---

[5] For a description of the reflagging operation, see Palmer, *Guardians of the Gulf*, pp. 128–149. For the long-term implications of this, see Byman *et al.*, *Iran's Security Policy in the Post-Revolutionary Era*, p. 90.

[6] Cordesman, *Iran's Military Forces in Transition*, pp. 405–416; Eisenstadt, "The Armed Forces of the Islamic Republic of Iran"; and Byman and Wise, *The Persian Gulf in the Coming Decade*, pp. 19–22.

The dangers of ideological regimes

The importance of ideology as a motivating force poses an additional set of problems. Regimes like the Taliban's Afghanistan, Turabi's Sudan, and Khomeini's Iran are admittedly rarities on the world stage. Nevertheless, they represent a large share of the sponsorship of terrorism since the end of the Cold War.

Such ideologically driven regimes are exceptionally difficult to coerce. The typical cost-benefit calculations that motivate most regimes weigh concerns about strategic advantage, economic growth, control over territory, and other standard issues. Ideological regimes, however, may genuinely care about the advancement of a set of ideas such as communism or Arab nationalism and are willing to sacrifice other, more standard interests on these altars. The costs that pressure imposes often matter less to an ideological regime than to other types of governments, while the rewards of supporting terrorists often involve ineffable, but nevertheless important, objectives such as spreading a particular faith or worldview. Khomeini's Iran, for example, tried to export its religious revolution to numerous countries. In doing so, it managed to turn both the Soviet Union and the United States against it even as it fought a life-and-death struggle with Iraq. It also openly scorned the idea that government policies should focus on advancing economic growth.

Since the end of the Cold War, political Islam has proven the most potent ideology leading to state support for terrorism.[7] Although Iran's revolutionary fervor began declining at the end of the 1980s, spreading the revolution remained a motivation for the clerical regime in the late 1990s and even through today. In Sudan and Afghanistan (both of which hosted al-Qa'ida, among other groups), the advancement of political Islam was reflected in disastrous domestic and social policies as well as in their foreign relations. All three countries were willing to antagonize their neighbors and the United States, even though the response involved sanctions, isolation, and measures to undermine these regimes.

The problem is not just that pressure on ideological states fails to stop support for terrorism. Rather, it is likely to backfire. As Stephen Walt's work has demonstrated, pressure on revolutionary governments often confirms the enmity they perceive and thus redoubles their

---

[7] For reviews of modern forms of political Islam, see Fuller, *The Future of Political Islam*; Roy, *The Failure of Political Islam*; and Kepel, *Jihad*.

determination to confront the source of pressure, creating a "spiral of suspicion."[8] Indeed, outside threats at times may bolster the revolutionary regime, enabling it to consolidate power.

Too narrow a focus

Current analytic categories for understanding state support for terrorism are too limited, failing to take into account the wide range of backing that states can provide. Most descriptions of state sponsorship focus on terrorist operations. As such, they review a state's provision of weapons, logistical support, money, and at times a sanctuary for particular attacks. Although such backing is often vital, it is only part of a much broader picture.

Critics of state support should also highlight the role that states play in legitimating terrorist activities and in providing organizational assistance. Terrorists crave legitimacy. State recognition is an important marker of their role as a, or the, legitimate voice of opposition. Terrorists take heart from such support and are able to increase their recruitment and fundraising. Organizational backing also can be vital. Many causes fail because their self-anointed champions turn on each other. Perhaps Iran's most effective form of support for Hizballah was its active role in helping the movement unite disparate Shi'a militants in Lebanon and focus their activities. States opposed to terrorism must recognize these categories of support, which are not linked to immediate operations but are nevertheless vital for a terrorist group's ultimate success.

Nuances in the provision of sanctuary are often missed, or deliberately overlooked. Sanctuary is usually the most important form of support that states provide, and as such its role deserves close scrutiny. Major reports such as the US State Department's *Patterns of Global Terrorism* do list the role that several states play in providing a sanctuary for various terrorist groups. However, such reports usually ignore the role of client states in providing support, thus allowing various sponsors to "outsource" sanctuary and other forms of backing without suffering any penalties. Syria dominates Lebanon, for example, and has long used that country's soil as a base for terrorist groups that Damascus favors. Pakistan worked closely with the Taliban, in part because the Afghan

---

[8] Walt, *Revolution and War*, pp. 33–37.

movement was willing to arm, train, and shelter various Kashmiri groups, enabling Islamabad to claim that it was not directly sponsoring these militants. The US State Department report and other official international community documents try to preserve the fiction of sovereignty in these pseudo-client states, failing to make the true powers that be assume responsibility.

As a result of this narrow focus, the international response to state support is often skewed. Countries that provide passive support or work through proxies are often able to escape the stigma that comes with sponsoring terrorism, while other regimes that may have a more limited, but more direct, role in sponsoring terrorism are often branded as international rogues.

A poor conceptualization of the problem

A limitation particular to the United States is in how the problem of terrorism is defined and understood – a conceptual problem greatly complicated by politics. The United States maintains several lists ostensibly intended to designate, and then punish, regimes that sponsor terrorism. However, the criteria are vague and the process is exceptionally politicized, allowing some of the most active sponsors in the last decade (such as Pakistan and the Taliban's Afghanistan) to remain off the list, while countries that have cut their involvement in terrorism, such as Libya, Sudan, North Korea, and Cuba remain on the list. As a result, the coercive potential of the list is limited. Politically well-connected states have far less concern about being placed on the list, while those who have been designated have fewer incentives to change their behavior, as getting off the list is almost impossible.

On paper, the US process seems straightforward. The 1979 Export Administration Act authorized the State Department to designate governments that "provided support for acts of international terrorism."[9] In subsequent years, Congress tried to clarify what "providing support" meant, noting that this included offering sanctuary, money, arms, planning assistance, training, and other specific forms of assistance.[10] This designation assumed far greater importance a decade later, when the

---

[9] See Export Administration Act, PL 96–72, 50 U.S.C. App. § 2405 (6) (j) (1979).
[10] Pillar, *Terrorism and US Foreign Policy*, p. 158 and Levitt, *Targeting Terror*, p. 45.

Anti-terrorism and Arms Export Amendments Act required sanctions on the states that appeared on the terrorism list.[11] Related to this list is the State Department's Foreign Terrorist Organization (FTO) designation. This list is reviewed every other year and is required under the 1996 Anti-terrorism and Effective Death Penalty Act. Together, these lists provide the US government's answer to the most basic question: which states are sponsoring which groups?[12]

Congress demanded such a list to ensure that the executive branch took terrorism seriously. Too often, in the eyes of Congress, political expediency or the strategic demands of the moment took precedence over establishing a firm commitment against terrorism. Despite this purpose, the criteria for what constitutes support are extremely vague, giving the executive branch considerable wiggle room. US law authorizes the Secretary of State to designate a regime as a state sponsor if it "has repeatedly provided support for acts of international terrorism."[13] The lack of precision in the words "repeatedly provided support" allows the State Department to use different levels of culpability for different regimes.

At times the list has become a means to blacken the name of an opponent of the United States that is not actively involved in terrorism. For example, Paul Pillar notes that Cuba is on the list due to the US policy of ostracizing Castro's Cuba, not because it is a major sponsor of terrorism. Similarly, Pakistan was left off the list despite being a major sponsor because this would hinder US interests in South Asia.[14] Indeed,

---

[11] Anti-Terrorism and Arms Export Amendments Act, PL 101–222, 22 U.S.C.A. §§ 1732, 2364, 3371, 2753, 2776, 2778, 2780 and 50 U.S.C.A. § 2405 (1989).

[12] The punishments for state sponsors vary. The legislative authority given directs the United States to consider punishments related to arms sales bans, restrictions on sensitive exports, prohibitions on economic and developmental assistance, opposition to World Bank and International Monetary Fund program applications, and various trade restrictions. US Department of State, *Patterns of Global Terrorism 2002*, p. 150. The Anti-Terrorism and Effective Death Penalty Act, PL 104–132, § 327, requires the US to oppose various forms of aid to state sponsors.

[13] US Department of State, *Patterns of Global Terrorism 2002*, p. 150.

[14] Pillar, *Terrorism and US Foreign Policy*, p. 162.

the US government's designation process illustrates Brian Jenkins' claim that terrorism is too often defined as "what the bad guys do."

This inconsistency, in turn, has undermined the effectiveness of the list. When countries like Cuba that have at best marginal involvement in terrorism in recent years are included, while others that are extremely active such as Pakistan are excluded, the "name and shame" power of the list itself suffers. Not surprisingly, other states refuse to see the list itself as proof that the state is involved in terrorism. US officials involved in counterterrorism tried unsuccessfully to change this: Michael Sheehan, the former Special Coordinator for Counterterrorism at the State Department, told critics: "if you have a problem with Cuba on human rights, get your own sanctions, don't use mine."[15] Such efforts were resisted because politicians feared that removing a state from the terrorism list would confer legitimacy on it.

Ironically, because it is so hard to get off the list and because the various punishments (intentionally) interfere with negotiations and bilateral relations, executive branch officials are often reluctant to put states on the list in the first place. Thus, though the Taliban hosted Bin Ladin and al-Qa'ida in 1996 and quickly emerged as the dominant power in the country, the regime was not listed as a sponsor of terrorism. In part this was because sponsorship would require recognition of the government, but it was also felt to tie the executive branch's hands with relatively little benefit. Moreover, the forms of pressure used can often be blunt, hindering the segments of society that might be more pro-American, or otherwise failing to affect the regime properly.[16] Similarly, Pakistan was not designated a sponsor again in part because this was seen as a measure that would do more harm than good.

Getting on the list is often a contentious process, but once on it is difficult to be removed. In theory, the state sponsor list is meant to be flexible. The State Department notes that "The bar for a state or a group being removed from a US terrorism list is and must be high – it must end all involvement in any facet of terrorism, including passive support, and satisfy all US counterterrorism concerns."[17] By including passive

---

[15] As quoted in ibid., p. 172.   [16] Ibid., p. 164.

[17] US Department of State, *Patterns of Global Terrorism 2002*, p. 150. The State Department's *Patterns of Global Terrorism* claims the list is not meant to be immutable.

support, however, the criteria can easily become insurmountable. For example, many states in the Middle East – including almost every US ally – laud the Palestinian terrorist group HAMAS, seeing it as a legitimate resistance movement. Forcing states to end any ties to HAMAS, even the most minimal such as meeting with HAMAS leaders to show solidarity, would damage their legitimacy at home. Similarly, some groups draw on fundraising among a state's citizens (as discussed in Chapter 8); halting this may require US government assistance through financial monitoring training, not US government sanctions.

Because the criteria are so politicized, in reality a state has to go from an adversary of the United States to an ally to get off the list, a move that would require many states to dramatically remake their foreign policy and at times their very government, not just to end their links to terrorism. The inability to get off the list in turn makes the list even less effective. If states fear that a true change in their behavior will only result in the bar regarding terrorism being raised or that other concerns such as human rights will come into play, they have no incentive to reduce support for terrorism.

Another problem with the state sponsor list is that terrorism is often not an important priority for the bilateral relationship. Pillar notes that the presence of North Korea and Cuba on the terrorism list complicates US diplomacy toward these countries, even though their current levels of sponsorship are minor. Moreover, in both cases the United States has other more pressing concerns. In North Korea's case, for example, efforts to achieve a diplomatic solution to the country's nuclear program were complicated by the restrictions that came with being on the terrorism list.[18]

A related problem for the United States is recognizing the distinction between terrorist and insurgent groups. Although the US emphasis on terrorism focuses on a group's attacks on civilians, such attacks are often a logical part of an insurgency strategy. This logic is especially strong when the label "civilians" is used to include intelligence officers, police, and others involved in prosecuting the insurgent operation. In practice, any violent non-state movement is illegitimate according to US policy, even if it only attacked soldiers. States that disagree can easily be labeled as sponsors, even if their proxies primarily conduct

[18] Pillar, *Terrorism and US Foreign Policy*, pp. 161–162.

guerrilla war. Again, there is no incentive to halt attacks on "real" civilians if militarily necessary targets are painted as the equivalent of clear civilian targets.

Why do states change?

Given the unfavorable conditions with regard to halting terrorism, it is legitimate to ask whether states will ever abandon their use of terrorism. Libya, discussed in Chapter 10, offers a dramatic example of a leader renouncing the use of terrorism. Iran has diminished its support for some terrorist groups, as have Pakistan and Syria, though at times only temporarily. What explains such changes and modulation?

Some leaders do respond to a simple calculation of risks and benefits. In 1998, for example, Turkey's military threats posed a credible and immediate danger to Syria. Aiding the PKK, on the other hand, offered Damascus relatively few advantages, particularly when compared with the benefits it gained from backing Hizballah and various Palestinian groups. Backing down clearly was the better option strategically, and it involved few domestic costs. Similarly, after the September 11 attacks Pakistan felt it necessary to turn against the Taliban and al-Qa'ida and to restrict Kashmiri groups, fearing a massive blow to its economy and a US strategic alignment with India.

In many cases, states under pressure seek to split the difference, demonstrating their willingness to make concessions while trying to preserve their strategic or domestic political objectives. Thus, after September 11 Pakistan curtailed the activities of some Kashmiri groups and made some arrests, but it did not engage in a massive crackdown or otherwise make the changes sought by India and the United States. Syria has placed limits on various rejectionist Palestinian groups, having them train in Lebanon or retain operational autonomy in order to keep the regime's hands cleaner. The groups, however, remained active.

Such states, of course, are long-established regimes ruled by level-headed, if not always shrewd, leaders. In contrast, fierce ideologues dominated several of the biggest sponsors of terrorism in recent years: Khomeini's Iran, Turabi's Sudan, and the Taliban's Afghanistan. In all three instances, revolutionary fervor kept support for terrorism high. Only when military leaders purged Turabi and Khomeini died did Sudan and Iran become less eager to sacrifice on behalf of a broader ideological cause. The Taliban defended Bin Ladin until the death of the regime.

When revolutionary fervor declines, other concerns rise to the fore, particularly economics. Iran ended its use of terrorism in Europe in an effort to court European investment to prop up its sagging economy. Similarly, Iran reduced its support for radicals in the Persian Gulf in an attempt to court its neighbors' goodwill.

Taking advantage of these sources of change is not a straightforward task. Nevertheless, it is essential to recognize why states change and the barriers to progress in designing more effective policies. If victim states and the international community can recognize these lessons, they will be better able to force or (more rarely) persuade sponsors into halting their backing.

Halting support for terrorism

State sponsorship of terrorism is a complex problem that cannot easily be solved. Despite diplomatic protests, economic sanctions, and even military pressure Iran, Pakistan, and Syria have supported numerous terrorist groups for decades. The Taliban persisted in its support of al-Qa'ida until US-backed forces toppled it from power. Many other states also backed terrorist groups, at times even risking war to do so. Such persistence in the face of pressure suggests that cutting the deadly connection between states and terrorist groups is difficult at best and impossible at worst. Yet the picture is not entirely bleak. Although there are no perfect solutions, careful policymakers can design better ones and avoid many common mistakes that can make the problem of state sponsorship worse.

States seeking to halt support for terrorism generally use several methods, almost always in combination. They include engaging the state sponsor; using massive military force to change a regime; punitive or coercive uses of military force; threats of military force; varying levels of unilateral and multilateral economic sanctions; backing an insurgency or terrorist group of one's own; and diplomatic isolation. Each of these tools has different benefits, costs, and conditions under which they are effective. All, however, can backfire and actually strengthen the bond between a terrorist group and its supporters.

Because states back terrorists for reasons ranging from a shared ideology to ruthless *realpolitik*, there is no universal policy or simple response that the United States or other concerned countries can take to get state sponsors out of the terrorism business. Where economic sanctions might lead one regime to calculate that its interests are better served by avoiding terrorism, a more ideologically motivated state may take this pressure as proof that its rivals are determined to choke its economic lifeblood and thus increase its support for terrorists.

Supporting states also have different vulnerabilities. Iran, for example, faced at most a limited risk of an Israeli military response to its support for Hizballah and the Palestine Islamic Jihad (PIJ) due to geography: Iran's borders are simply too far from Israel for the Jewish state's military forces to conduct sustained military operations. The Taliban's Afghanistan enjoyed a different kind of protection. Its economy was too weak, and the country's infrastructure too devastated, for trade sanctions to have a significant impact.

Success is often elusive even in the best of circumstances, but the United States and the international community can take several steps that would make coercion more effective. Recognizing that one-size-fits-all punishments do not work is a first step. The coercing power must recognize variations in the motivations of the state sponsor and the type of support it provides as it tailors its counterterrorism policies. At times, sponsors must have a way out if they are to stop their attacks, but other states must also recognize that a carrot without a stick can often make the problem worse. Coercing states, particularly the United States, must also take pains to differentiate "enemies" from "terrorists," separating out countries like North Korea or Cuba that may be hostile regimes but are not terrorism sponsors like Iran or Pakistan. In addition, the international community should work to end the fiction of deniability that state sponsors often enjoy when they use terrorist proxies. This ties the victims' hands unnecessarily. Increasing international support for coercers that escalate against state sponsors is also essential. When possible, states should work multilaterally, as multilateral pressure and support often make coercion far more effective despite the difficulties in gaining this support. Finally, the coercing powers must have realistic expectations. Success will seldom be absolute, but even a marginal decline in a state's support for terrorist groups may save many lives.

This chapter presents the different instruments available to states for ending terrorism, paying particular attention to the use of limited military force and economic sanctions – the two most common means used to halt sponsorship – but also reviewing engagement, political isolation, and support for domestic opponents of a state sponsor. It then reviews perhaps the most remarkable turnaround in the history of state sponsorship: Libyan leader Moammar Qaddafi's decision to go from being one of the world's leading sponsors of international terrorism to an active opponent of it. The various efforts to press Libya to end its support for terrorism, which at times backfired but eventually culminated in Qaddafi's cooperation with the international community, are then reviewed. The chapter concludes by offering recommendations for halting the support of sponsorship.

What instruments are available to states?

Some states seek to engage state sponsors of terrorism, but this often fails to produce the results they want or is rejected on principle. As an alternative to engagement, states have several options for pressing state sponsors of terrorism short of all-out war, ranging from limited military force to political pressure. These instruments, however, are at best imperfect, often ineffective, and at worst counterproductive. Limits on the instruments of statecraft like sanctions or military force compound the many difficulties inherent in stopping state sponsorship. The pressure imposed is often too blunt or too weak. In addition, the use of these instruments often has costs of its own.

States that are victims of terrorism often try to take action against the sponsoring state to persuade or force it to end its support. This pressure is often described as coercion: the threatened use of force, and at times the limited use of actual force to back up the threat, to induce an adversary to change its behavior.[1] By definition, coercion goes beyond the exclusive use of inducements, which try to bribe an adversary into complying. Coercion, however, falls short of the use of a level of military force to remove an adversary from power completely.[2]

---

[1] This definition is also the one I used in my previous work on coercion with Matthew Waxman. See Byman and Waxman, *The Dynamics of Coercion*, p. 1. Classic works on coercion include Schelling, *Arms and Influence*; George and Simons, *The Limits of Coercive Diplomacy*; and Pape, *Bombing to Win*.

[2] Such an effort would fall into the category that Thomas Schelling has labeled "brute force." The distinction is that brute force simply destroys the adversary's capacity to the point where it must give in, while adversaries choose to give in to coercion when they still, in theory at least, could continue to resist. See Schelling, *Arms and Influence*, p. 3 and Pape, *Bombing to Win*, p. 13.

Coercive pressure can convince sponsors to rein in terrorists or, at the very least, place limits on some types of operations. Indeed, coercion "successes" are often difficult to observe, as they are indicated by a reduction in violence from what it might be if the coercion threat were not present – not simply the absence of an attack. Thus, Hizballah's "non-use" of long-range rockets against Israeli cities can be depicted as a coercive success, though Hizballah of course remains active against Israel in a variety of ways. Similarly, Iran's shift from actively urging groups like the Islamic Front for the Liberation of Bahrain to overthrow the Al Khalifa to maintaining limited contacts entails a major shift, though hardly an abandonment of the group. At times, however, coercive pressure backfires. Rather than be intimidated into abandoning terrorists, states may become more willing to back terrorists, treating the pressure as yet another provocation to which they must respond. Such a spiral may stem from psychological factors, as leaders see the coercing state as engaging in unprovoked aggression, or nationalistic pressures as leaders felt compelled to respond to public outrage.[3]

States usually employ some combination of four means to coerce state sponsors: political pressure, economic sanctions, military force, and support for an insurgency or other group (including terrorists) opposed to the state sponsor. As an alternative (or, more rarely, a complement), states may try to engage sponsors of terrorism. Each of these methods works in different ways, and each has its limits.

ENGAGEMENT

Victims of terrorism may try to engage a sponsor, offering concessions in order to reduce the likelihood of further terrorism. Regardless of the morality of "giving in to terrorists," such engagement is often based on a ruthless strategic judgment: by conceding on what a government may deem a minor issue, it can free itself from the scourge of terrorism. Engagement may prove particularly attractive if the victim regime has few alternatives with which to press the sponsoring state.

Until 1986, France had a "sanctuary doctrine," essentially giving terrorists considerable freedom to operate within French borders in the hopes of minimizing international terrorism on French soil. France

---

[3] This concept was best laid out in the seminal work of Robert Jervis. See Jervis, *Perception and Misperception in International Politics*, pp. 58–113.

allowed various Palestinian groups to operate as well as the Basque separatist group ETA. Paris also allowed individuals being investigated for their responsibility for various attacks to leave the country. France also adjusted its foreign policy to win over state sponsors and their proxies. The sanctuary doctrine had several advantages. Some groups, such as the PLO, abided by the bargain and did not conduct attacks in France. Paris was also able to maintain relations with several state sponsors of terrorism.[4]

France suffered several problems with this approach. Most importantly, several groups did not keep their side of the bargain and began not only attacking in France, but attacking French targets (as opposed to US or Middle Eastern ones). In addition, the accommodation with groups and sponsors created both diplomatic and political problems for Paris. Relations with victim countries, such as Spain, suffered considerably. Moreover, domestic audiences in France did not support appeasement. After 1986, France slowly began to move to suppress terrorist groups, recognizing that its efforts to engage were a failure.[5]

Engagement is particularly tempting if the regime in question is not the victim of state sponsorship or does not see it as a serious threat. Thus, it is easy for European states to ignore Iranian-backed terrorism against Israel, which does not directly threaten them. They were often willing to look the other way at Iranian terrorism in Europe in the late 1980s and early 1990s against Iranian dissidents, viewing this as an internecine dispute rather than a true security threat.

As the French experience suggests, engagement suffers from several problems. Naturally, the victim state and its allies are often furious at what they see as appeasement and use considerable diplomatic pressure to stop this. Moreover, appeasement is unpopular politically. Despite government efforts to downplay terrorism, European states repeatedly had to temporarily cut ties to Iran or otherwise take confrontational steps in response to public outrage over Iranian involvement in terrorism. Engagement, of course, also indicates that the government in question will indeed be blackmailed, thus encouraging additional threats or actual attacks. This not only encourages the particular state sponsor, but also sends a message to all potential sponsors that using terrorists can

[4] Shapiro and Suzan, "The French Experience of counter terrorism," pp. 69–73.
[5] Ibid., pp. 70–74.

pay off. Also engagement does not always provide protection from all terrorists. It is far more effective with a group like the PLO, which had little interest in attacking France, than it would be with an Algerian terrorist group that saw France as an enemy.

Engagement is particularly difficult with an ideologically driven state. US attempts to engage the Taliban before the 1998 Embassy bombings often were viewed as unwanted meddling rather than as a gentle alternative to confrontation. As tension heated up, efforts to engage were often overwhelmed by the negative impression created by even limited coercion. The Taliban viewed UN efforts to feed Afghanistan's hungry, for example, as part of a broader effort to subvert their teaching, a misperception encouraged by UN opposition to the destruction of the statues of the Buddha in Bamiyan and other criticism of the regime's human rights record.

Finally, engagement often requires painful policy choices that a state might not otherwise make. Partly in response to terrorism, Israel has engaged Syria over the Golan Heights, and India has engaged Pakistan over Kashmir. For both Jerusalem and New Delhi, the fact of negotiations – to say nothing of the possibility of ceding land or accepting limits to sovereignty – was a painful concession.

Despite these many problems, engagement is at times necessary as long as it is part of a broader effort that involves coercive forms of pressure. Engagement, by itself, tends to make the problem of terrorism worse. However, coercion without any promise that the pressure will relent is not really coercion in the true sense: there must be an incentive to stop the support for terrorism, and the promise of engagement is thus often necessary.

POLITICAL PRESSURE

State efforts to halt support for terrorism almost always involve some form of political pressure. The US state sponsor list's "name and shame" power is one means of getting state sponsors to abandon their support for terrorism. As Edmund Hull, the former acting Coordinator for Counterterrorism, contended about regimes on the list, "Most of these governments are extremely uncomfortable with the stigma that comes attached to being accused of sponsoring terrorism, and they will over time seek ways to escape that stigma."[6] Another common form of

---

[6] Hull, briefing upon release of the report, *Patterns of Global Terrorism 2000*.

pressure is an official *démarche* meant to discourage a particular act in support of a terrorist group, such as Ambassador Inderfurth's warning to the Taliban that it must crack down on al-Qa'ida. The *démarche* and other warnings suggested that relations would be frayed if support continued and that the Taliban would be held accountable for future al-Qa'ida attacks. At times, states may attempt to make a rival regime an international pariah, shunned by its neighbors and the rest of the world. After the attempted assassination of Egyptian President Mubarak in 1995, the United States worked with Sudan's neighbors and the United Nations to isolate Khartoum, which was linked to the attackers.

Political pressure can complicate a state supporter's diplomatic relations, making it harder for it to achieve its goals. Pakistan, for example, has faced political pressure from the United States and other countries due to its support for radical groups in Kashmir. Thus Islamabad's calls for international pressure against India to make concessions on Kashmir have been met with little sympathy. Moreover, Pakistan's reputation has been damaged due to its continued backing of terrorism.

By itself, however, political pressure is a weak instrument. The "punishment" of a damaged reputation, the lack of diplomatic support on other issues, or even near-complete isolation usually pales before the broader strategic objectives, domestic concerns, or ideological agenda that led to the support of terrorism in the first place.

Isolation may also prove ineffective or difficult to establish because of the supporting state's importance for a host of other issues not related to terrorism. The United States, for example, has made relations with Syria a diplomatic priority because of its importance to an Arab–Israeli peace, leading to hundreds of high-level contacts in the 1990s that undermined any efforts to isolate Damascus. Iran, a major player in a vital region, is similarly hard to shun, as many European powers and Japan see it as a major trade and investment opportunity and felt that its critical geo-strategic position made engagement a better option. Libya and Cuba, in contrast, are far easier to isolate as they lack the strategic or economic importance of other sponsors.

Other states also have different threat perceptions, making it harder to present a unified front to a state sponsor. Iran and Hizballah, for example, pose little threat today to the interests of most Western European states. As a result, US calls for these countries to press Tehran often fall on deaf ears. In addition, many states favor dialogue and engagement over political pressure, believing this is the best way to moderate a hostile regime.

Despite these many limits, political isolation offers several advantages for policymakers over other options. Most important is its low cost: it demands few sacrifices and carries few risks. In addition, political isolation is almost always part and parcel of a larger coercive campaign involving economic and military measures. Political pressure can be seen as a first step, or a reinforcing measure, for other forms of coercion. Former Secretary of State George Schultz, for example, argued that "Diplomacy could work these problems [those related to terrorism] most effectively when force – or the threat of force – was a credible part of the equation."[7] Even if the use of massive military force is contemplated, political pressure must be used to signal the adversary as to what is desired. Moreover, obtaining multilateral support for these measures often makes them far more effective.

ECONOMIC PRESSURE

Economic pressure is another common means of trying to persuade sponsors to stop supporting terrorism. States can limit trade, withdraw investment, punish foreign companies, and otherwise use economic means to convince other countries not to support terrorism. Many of the penalties linked to the US list of state sponsors, for example, involve restrictions such as bans on critical technologies and US foreign assistance, including US opposition to support at international financial institutions like the World Bank and the International Monetary Fund. Perhaps wrongly, such pressure is often seen by the public and policymakers as a middle ground between an empty *démarche* and a full-scale invasion in terms of coercive power.[8]

---

[7] Schultz, *Turmoil and Triumph*, p. 650.

[8] See Baldwin, *Economic Statecraft*, for a broad review of different forms of economic tools. Jonathan Kirshner offers a balanced review of how sanctions work, as does Elizabeth Rogers. See Kirshner, "The Microfoundations of Economic Sanctions" and Rogers, "Using Economic Sanctions to Control Regional Conflicts." For other works on sanctions, see Pape, "Why Economic Sanctions Do Not Work," and Hufbauer *et al.*, *Economic Sanctions Reconsidered*. The works of David Baldwin and Jean-Marc F. Blanchard and Norrin M. Ripsman offer nuanced views of how to think about sanctions' effectiveness that are highly relevant for their impact on terrorism. See

Sanctions are imposed on states for a variety of reasons beyond counter-terrorism, a fact that makes them less effective in halting support for terrorism as well as complicating judgments as to their effectiveness. Terrorism scholar David Tucker notes that the United States imposed sanctions on many states that sponsored terrorism as part of an effort to contain their expansionism, to show solidarity with key allies, to force a change in regime, to diminish their military capacity, and to symbolize opposition to their policies. Indeed, for three states that have long been on the list of state sponsors – Cuba, North Korea, and Iraq – counterterrorism was at best a minor reason for the use of sanctions.[9] For Iran, Syria, Libya, and Sudan, however, their support for terrorism was a major reason that sanctions were imposed and sustained over the years.

Economic pressure can be unilateral, multilateral, or, more rarely, comprehensive. Unilateral sanctions are the most common and are often initiated by the stronger, victim state. India has restricted trade with Pakistan, but few other countries have followed New Delhi's lead. The United States has long had a variety of sanctions on Iran, but it has had little success in persuading other countries to go along. Indeed, some countries have rushed in to fill the economic void created by the lack of a US presence.

At times, the United States has orchestrated multilateral sanctions, working with several allies to limit investment, the sale of arms, or other forms of economic punishment. After Iran took sixty-six Americans hostage in 1979, for example, most Western European countries joined the United States and imposed a range of economic penalties (most of which were far stronger on paper than in practice) on the clerical regime. More rarely, near-universal sanctions have been imposed. Examples of near-universal sanctions related to terrorism are the 1996 UN Security Council resolution that imposed limited punishments on Sudan because of its support for radical groups and the 1992–93 sanctions placed on Libya for its non-cooperation with the Pan Am 103 bombing investigation.

In theory, governments may back down in the face of economic pressure, fearing that the loss of trade or other benefits would hurt tourism, hinder economic growth, prevent a military rearmament, or otherwise harm objectives not related to terrorism. This logic suggests

Baldwin, "The Sanctions Debate and the Logic of Choice" and Blanchard and Ripsman, "Asking the Right Question."
[9] Tucker, *Skirmishes at the Edge of Empire*, pp. 89–90.

that the economic costs to a regime (i.e., how much money it would lose) and its vulnerability (i.e., whether it could replace the lost trade or investment) would be key concerns.[10] Such a decision is strictly a cost-benefit calculation: sanctions work when the strategic, ideological, or domestic rewards of backing a terrorist group are outweighed by the economic pain outsiders inflict.

Economic pressure also may affect elite or popular support for a regime, another theoretical potential point of leverage. A regime that fails to deliver economically might be voted out of power or lose the support of key interest groups keeping it in power. A travel ban, for example, undermines one of the perquisites of wealth and power. Leaders and other elites are not given a place on the world stage and worse, for some, no spot on the Riviera. Some policymakers have even argued that sanctions will foster widespread popular unrest due to economic problems. The unrest, in turn, will either lead the regime to make concessions or possibly even lead to its collapse.

Sanctions, however, have several profound limits on their effectiveness. Studies of sanctions have determined that, in general, they succeeded only 17 percent of the time when imposed unilaterally and only slightly more often when imposed multilaterally.[11] What explains this dismal success rate?

The biggest problem for coercers is that it is difficult to use sanctions to increase the level of pain sufficiently to affect a hostile regime's decision-making. As noted above, many state sponsors had already weighed the potential repercussions when they considered supporting terrorism. As such, they were likely to avoid angering a state on which they already depended economically or otherwise feared to offend (ideological regimes being a painful exception to this generalization). Moreover, most state sponsors of terrorism are autocratic regimes and, as such, are less sensitive to the needs of their population than are democracies. The people may grumble, but the ruler can safely ignore them. Popular revolutions have never occurred in response to sanctions.[12]

---

[10] This concept emerged in the work of Robert O. Keohane and Joseph S. Nye. See Keohane and Nye, *Power and Interdependence*, pp. 12–16.

[11] Hufbauer *et al.*, "Using Sanctions to Fight Terrorism."

[12] Pape, "Why Economic Sanctions Do Not Work." Pape contends that sanctions never achieve their maximal objective of toppling a regime. Critics of

Indeed, one widely noted effect of sanctions is that they backfire politically, and adversarial leaders are able to use them to increase their hold on power. Sanctions, by cutting off trade and other channels outside the formal state apparatus, often increase a regime's ability to channel goods to its favorites and weaken potential rivals. When Saddam Husayn held power in Iraq, for example, his regime controlled the food supplies and used this influence to ensure the regime's dominance. The regime also used its control of the economy to allow selective access to the black market, enabling it to shore up support among regime loyalists, particularly in the military and security services.[13]

Sanctions' poor success rate is also explained in part because they are often imposed unilaterally, a less effective form of pressure. The United States had long imposed a series of sanctions on Libya to little effect, in part because Libya had access to investment and markets elsewhere. Unilateral sanctions were particularly irrelevant as Libya's chief export – oil – was not affected by the loss of the US market, as oil is a global commodity.

Gaining multilateral support, however, is often exceptionally difficult. The United States has long tried to convince European states and Japan to back its attempts to sanction Iran with little success. Indeed, it was this frustration that led to the passage of the Iran–Libya Sanctions Act in 1996, as Congress sought to punish other countries, including several close US allies, who refused to sanction Tehran. As with political isolation, other states may not forgo the lost trade and investment opportunities, either because they do not share the same sense of threat as the victim state or because of the state sponsor's political and economic importance on issues not related to terrorism.[14] At other times, they may genuinely believe that sanctions would only backfire and make the supporting regime more hostile or create a humanitarian disaster.

Pape contend that he sets the bar too high for whether sanctions should be considered a success or not.

[13] Gause, "Getting it Backward on Iraq," p. 57. This problem of shifting the impact of sanctions from elites to the people in general is common. See Pape, "Why Economic Sanctions Do Not Work," p. 93.

[14] As Stuart Eizenstadt argues about Iran, for example: "Iran is simply too important a country in the region to isolate, and US sanctions efforts such as ILSA (unilateral in nature and with no international backing) have been ineffective." Eizenstadt, "Do Economic Sanctions Work?" p. 12.

The result is often a weak compromise: multilateral sanctions whose breadth and bite are limited. The UN-mandated sanctions on Libya and Sudan, for example, were limited in scope. For Sudan, they focused primarily on restricting travel and reducing official contact with Khartoum. Libya too was isolated through sanctions, and it faced additional punishments such as having its assets frozen and restrictions on its purchases of oil and gas equipment.[15]

Sanctions are particularly ineffective when a regime is motivated by ideological reasons. Ayatollah Khomeini of Iran famously scorned the importance of economics, declaring that the Islamic revolution was not about "the price of watermelons." The Taliban also cared little about the material well-being of ordinary Afghans in comparison to what they saw as their religious duty to support a range of radical groups, including al-Qa'ida. Limits to economic growth, for such regimes, is a price they often willingly pay. Not until Khomeini died did economic growth become a priority for the regime in Tehran, and thus only then did it become sensitive to economic punishments and incentives on terrorism.

Unsuccessful sanctions do not always simply fail: they can backfire and make a regime more intractable. Attempts to isolate the Taliban helped convince Mullah Omar that, as Bin Ladin argued, the West was attempting to crush the fledgling Islamic state. In Iran, the clerical regime has used sanctions to persuade its people that the United States is hostile to Iran and seeks to harm its people. In Iraq, Saddam Husayn's regime used the comprehensive sanctions to punish parts of the population that did not support his rule.[16] Thus, sanctions can at times increase the supporting regime's popularity, weaken the opposition to it, and raise the overall level of hostility directed at the coercer.

The humanitarian impact of sanctions is another major drawback, both due to the inherent suffering they cause among innocents and because this suffering makes it harder to sustain them. Sanctions on Iraq, for example,

[15] The UN sanctions imposed on Iraq in 1990 were truly comprehensive, limiting almost every aspect of the country's economic activity. These sanctions, however, were imposed after Iraq's invasion of Kuwait and were continued after Iraq's defeat in 1991 because of Baghdad's refusal to abide by various UN resolutions (and because they were seen as a tool that would lead to Saddam's collapse). Iraq's involvement in terrorism was not a major consideration.

[16] For a review see Baram, "The Effects of Iraqi Sanctions."

were roundly condemned as doing little to shake the Baath regime while devastating the lives of innocent Iraqis. The deaths of hundreds of thousands of Iraqi civilians were widely reported, including, famously, a UNICEF report that claimed that sanctions killed 500,000 Iraqi children.[17] F. Gregory Gause III bitterly wrote that, "American policymakers need to recognize that the only 'box' into which sanctions put Iraqis is coffins."[18] John and Karl Mueller echoed this point, lambasting the humanitarian effects of sanctions as "Sanctions of Mass Destruction."[19] Even if these critics overstated the humanitarian impact of sanctions or wrongly pinned responsibility for the suffering on the United States, the sanctions proved a political disaster for Washington. Much of the world saw the United States as deliberately supporting a policy that killed hundreds of thousands of children while doing nothing to harm Saddam's regime – a perception that tarnished America's image worldwide.

THE USE OF FORCE

When political and economic pressure is not promising, states often use their military force to respond to terrorism. At the most extreme levels, this may involve invading another country and trying to change its government by force. A recent example is the 2001 US invasion of Afghanistan, where the United States worked with local Afghan allies to overthrow the ruling Taliban because of its support for al-Qa'ida. (The United States also invaded Iraq in 2003, with Iraq's support for terrorism frequently stated as a reason for the attack – a rationale that before the war was strained and after it seems an ever-weaker reed.[20])

---

[17] Amatzia Baram's review argues that the total death toll of children from sanctions numbered well over 100,000, a far smaller but still staggering number of deaths. See Baram, "The Effects of Iraqi Sanctions." Other reviews put the figure over 300,000, less than UNICEF claimed but still overwhelming. Suellentrop, "Are 1 Million Children Dying in Iraq?"

[18] Gause, "Getting it Backward on Iraq," p. 56.

[19] Mueller and Mueller, "Sanctions of Mass Destruction."

[20] The National Commission on Terrorist Attacks Upon the United States (the "9/11 Commission") found: "We have no credible evidence that Iraq and al Qaeda cooperated on attacks against the United States." National Commission on Terrorist Attacks Upon the United States, "Overview of the Enemy," p. 5.

Far more common is the limited use of force to punish a regime for supporting terrorism and, ideally, deter it from backing future attacks. The United States bombed Libya in 1986 because of Libya's use of terrorism; in 1993, the United States struck Iraq in response to its attempted assassination of former President George H. W. Bush; and in 1998, the United States attacked Afghanistan and Sudan after al-Qa'ida bombed US Embassies in Kenya and Tanzania.[21] The United States, of course, is not the only country that uses force in response to terrorism. Iran repeatedly struck at MEK bases in Iraq, and Egypt sought to attack Sudan in 1995 after Sudanese-based Egyptian terrorists tried to kill President Mubarak in Ethiopia. Turkey used the threat of invasion to compel Syria to end its backing of the PKK. India has long threatened military retaliation for Pakistan's support of Kashmiri groups. Most prominently, Israel has conducted military strikes at various points in its history against Egypt, Syria, Jordan, Lebanon, and Tunisia, either at Palestinian targets directly or on regime targets in order to dissuade them from backing various Palestinian groups.

In these attacks, the coercing governments usually tried to focus on the terrorist group itself or on targets related to its activities – a problematic set of targets. Thus in 1998 the United States bombed an al-Qa'ida camp in Afghanistan, while Israel's attack in Tunisia focused on the Palestinian Liberation Organization (PLO) headquarters there. The reasons for these limits are simple. Military strikes on terrorists based in a sympathetic country face many difficulties. In contrast to conventional militaries, terrorist groups themselves have few assets worth bombing. The "infrastructure" of support for terrorism is often not possible to destroy through bombing: training camps are rudimentary, and the weapons systems involved are small and easy to replace. Terrorists themselves can easily disperse, making them difficult to strike – especially by air strikes or other "standoff" means. Even worse, terrorists often melt back into the civilian population, increasing the likelihood of significant civilian casualties. Many terrorists are also part of a broader insurgent movement. As such, it is relatively easy

---

[21] The attacks on Libya in 1986 and Iraq in 1993 were both in response to the regime's use of its own operatives, not the regime's support for a particular terrorist group.

for the group to replace the cadre lost in a limited military strike with other dedicated recruits.

At times, however, governments try to coerce the sponsoring state in order to force it to end its support and to crack down on the terrorist group. In 1993 and 1996, Israel tried to put pressure on the government of Lebanon to crack down on Hizballah. Israel's strikes went beyond those targets linked directly to Hizballah to include a broader set designed to coerce the government of Lebanon. This was done in order to impose direct costs on the regime by destroying the country's infrastructure and undermining public confidence. In theory, such punishment can impose a tremendous political cost, as a regime unable to defend its people is often viewed as illegitimate.

Despite this potential, military force in limited quantities seldom affects a regime's ability or willingness to support terrorism and often makes the problem worse.[22] Strikes may harden the supporting regime's attitudes for several reasons. Capitulation in the aftermath of a military attack would be a grievous political blow to most governments. For the Taliban to have surrendered Bin Ladin after the 1998 US strikes on Afghanistan, for example, would demonstrate that the movement was abandoning the tradition of Pashtun hospitality for an honored guest. More generally, it would demonstrate to a highly nationalistic people that the regime had caved in in the face of outside pressure. The strikes may even increase the popularity of a group, making it more attractive as a partner. The Israeli attack on Lebanon, for example, actually increased popular support for Hizballah. The devastation of the Israeli attacks made the group's claim that it was only defending Lebanon from an invader more credible.

Military strikes often have little support abroad. Because the terrorist attacks often inflict relatively few casualties, military force is often viewed as a disproportionate response. In addition, the military strikes are often seen as destabilizing and thus jeopardizing a host of other strategic and economic interests.

States and terrorists can also retaliate in response to military attacks, further decreasing international support for the attacks and often

---

[22] For an interesting assessment of this issue that draws primarily on Cold War era data, see Brophy-Baermann and Conybeare, "Retaliating against Terrorism."

leading decision-makers to avoid the use of force in the first place.[23] When Israel attacked into Lebanon, Hizballah shelled Israeli settlements near the borders. As discussed below, the 1986 air strike on Libya led to the Pan Am 103 bombing as well as a host of smaller attacks. These instances painfully demonstrated that states and terrorist groups may increase their attacks in the face of pressure.

Backing radicals of one's own

Another form of pressure is to give a state sponsor a taste of its own medicine. Outside powers can back a terrorist or insurgent group against the sponsor as a form of pressure to convince it to end its support. During the Cold War, the United States supported opponents of Qaddafi's regime in Libya as a way to weaken the Libyan dictator, and after it ended Washington backed Iranian oppositionists and foes of Saddam's regime in Iraq. Sudan's neighbors backed the Sudanese People's Liberation Army (SPLA) and other fighters opposed to Khartoum, in part in response to Sudan's backing of radicals in their own countries, whether directly or through its ties to al-Qa'ida. Iran and Iraq engaged in a constant back-and-forth using terrorist groups as proxies, as each regime supported almost any group that could be used to weaken the other.

Coercion in such cases relies on the same type of pain that the state sponsor sought to inflict in the first place. One means of leverage is damage to lives and property. The Iraq-backed Mujahedin-e Khalq (MEK) killed hundreds of Iranians, including many senior leaders of the regime, in its bloody campaign. Successful terrorist groups and insurgencies can destroy confidence in a regime. In addition, they can make part of a country ungovernable and eventually lead to wars of ethnic secession. When its neighbors backed the SPLA, Sudan risked

---

[23] Judging military force and other forms of pressure, however, is difficult due to the counterfactual nature of the question. The question most often asked – did terrorism increase or decrease after a strike? – is misleading. The best question is really whether terrorism increased or decreased from levels it would have been at without the use of force. For example, the Reagan administration had intelligence before Operation El Dorado Canyon that Qaddafi was planning other attacks on the United States and that a strike would not make things worse. Stanik, *El Dorado Canyon*, p. 147. Thus, if the attack occurred after the strike as planned the strike could not truly be said to have made the situation worse.

losing control over much of the country as it was not able to subdue its opposition by force.

Backing opposition forces as a coercive instrument also offers several political advantages. Support for terrorists or insurgents is often a low-cost option, particularly compared with the use of conventional force. Many vengeful sponsors are also simply instituting a form of payback, demonstrating their own wrath.

Supporting an insurgency or terrorism of one's own, however, has serious drawbacks. Many of these disadvantages are common to support for terrorism in general, such as the danger of escalation, the unsavory and often incompetent nature of many terrorist group partners, the risk of making an otherwise competent opposition appear a pawn of its sponsor, and harming the state's reputation in general. Delegitimating terrorism in general becomes almost ludicrous if the coercing state is also using it – a concern that victims of terrorism feel more acutely than do sponsors. The humanitarian costs are also considerable, as this form of pressure is in essence support for a low-level war. The United States, for example, shied away from backing the Northern Alliance before September 11, in part because it feared that it would worsen Afghanistan's already miserable humanitarian situation. Finally, the support can also rebound on the coercing state, bolstering ethnic divisions or empowering radicals in their own country as the conflict spreads across borders.

Explaining the Libyan success

In 1980, the CIA declared Libya to be the world's biggest sponsor of international terrorism.[24] Twenty years later, Libyan leader Moammar Qaddafi had effectively abandoned terrorism, compensating some of Libya's victims, sending his own intelligence operatives to be tried under Scottish law, and working with the international community against some of the various terrorist groups he once championed. Although Iran, Pakistan, Syria, and other countries have at times decreased their involvement in terrorism, Libya's case represents a fascinating instance of a regime dramatically ending its support for terrorism. What explains this turnaround?

Shortly after Qaddafi took power in a coup in 1969, the Libyan regime established ties to various radical Palestinian groups, many of which

---

[24] Stanik, *El Dorado Canyon*, p. 38.

used terrorism. Qaddafi's regime at times worked with the PLO, and it more steadily backed the Abu Nidal Organization (ANO), the PFLP-GC, the PFLP, and various Fatah dissidents, several of which conducted extremely bloody terrorist attacks in the mid-1980s, such as the December 1985 ANO attacks on the Rome and Vienna airports that killed twenty people.[25] Libya also provided aid to the Black September Organization, which murdered numerous Israelis and moderate Arab regime officials. Libyan operatives themselves also were responsible for two bloody attacks: the December 21, 1988 attack on Pan Am 103, which killed 270, and the September 19, 1989 bombing of the French Air Liner UTA 772 over Niger, in which 171 died.

Qaddafi also supported a variety of causes throughout Africa, aiding what he saw as liberation movements. In 1980, he backed guerrillas fighting the government of Tunisia, and later in the year Libyan forces entered Chad, helping to overthrow the government there. The United States claimed in 1981 that Qaddafi was supporting insurgencies in over thirty countries.[26] Libya also trained several Liberian figures in the 1980s who later became prominent in the successful insurgency that toppled the government there in 1990 and plunged much of West Africa into an exceptionally brutal civil war.[27] Qaddafi also supported several dictators in Africa, such as Idi Amin in Uganda, providing them with soldiers to maintain their rule.[28]

Qaddafi's support went well beyond the Middle East and Africa. In the 1980s, he provided aid to the Sandinista regime in Nicaragua, to the Moro National Liberation Front (MNLF) in the Philippines, to Islamist radicals in Thailand, and to rebels in Guatemala and Bangladesh. He also forged ties to the Provisional IRA, ETA, and other Western European groups, training their operatives and providing the IRA with massive arms deliveries.[29] Libyan operatives and terrorist groups tied to them also murdered Libyan dissidents and moderate Arab and African leaders.[30]

[25] Oakley, "Prepared Statement of Robert B. Oakley," p. 54.
[26] Stanik, *El Dorado Canyon*, p. 24. For a broader review, see Deeb, *Libya's Foreign Policy in North Africa*.
[27] *Online NewsHour*, "Liberia's Uneasy Peace."
[28] Stanik, *El Dorado Canyon*, pp. 20–23.
[29] Oakley, "Prepared Statement of Robert B. Oakley," p. 54 and US Department of State, "Libya under Qaddafi," pp. 63–67.
[30] US Department of State, "Libya under Qaddafi," p. 63.

As this brief discussion suggests, the scale of Qaddafi's activities was daunting. One expert contends that in the 1980s Qaddafi's regime trained several thousand terrorists and guerrillas, spending over $100 million to this end. Libya was second only to Iran at this time in terms of total spending on terrorist groups.[31] President Ronald Reagan declared Libya to be the "mad dog of the Middle East" in 1986 due to its support for terrorism.[32] Even into the 1990s, Qaddafi championed Palestinian reject-ionists and opposed the PLO after it decided to pursue the Oslo peace process in the 1990s.

Terrorism for Qaddafi served several purposes. When he came to power, Qaddafi was a genuine revolutionary who believed in backing other movements that opposed what he saw as oppressive imperial powers. Qaddafi was focused initially in particular on Arab unity, the Palestinian cause, and various "liberation" movements. In addition, ter-rorism extended Qaddafi's reach, enabling him to be a player against Israel or in other causes of concern to him. He also was concerned for geopolitical reasons regarding Libya's neighbors, such as Algeria, Egypt, and Chad. Finally, Qaddafi hoped to use his identification with various revolutionary causes, particularly in the Arab world, as a means of enhanc-ing his stature at home and throughout the revolutionary community.[33]

When Qaddafi took power, the United States hoped that Libya would moderate its policies and it relied primarily on political pressure to change the regime's behavior.[34] The failure of diplomacy in the 1970s led to an increase in other forms of pressure. Sanctions against Libya began in 1979, when Libya was designated a state sponsor of terrorism, and became far more intense during the 1980s. In 1982, the United States banned the import of crude oil from Libya, and in 1986 almost all economic contacts were cut.

Unilateral sanctions by themselves appear to have had little impact on Libya. Although the United States was no longer an oil customer, Germany, Italy, and other buyers quickly bought the Libyan crude, with

---

[31] Davis, *Qaddafi, Terrorism, and the Origins of the US Attack on Libya,* pp. 10–11.

[32] As quoted in Murphy, "Libya Opens Up," p. 8.

[33] Deeb, *Libya since the Revolution*; Deeb, *Libya's Foreign Policy in North Africa*; and Monti-Belkaoui and Belkaoui, *Qaddafi.*

[34] O'Sullivan, *Shrewd Sanctions,* p. 175.

no impact on Tripoli. Indeed, as a result of US sanctions, Libya increased its economic investment in Europe which strengthened its ties to European governments.[35]

A number of other measures meant to isolate and weaken Qaddafi's regime backed up the sanctions. In 1981, the Reagan administration closed the Libyan "people's bureau" (the name of Libya's official diplomatic facilities) in the United States. Washington assisted exiled opponents of the Qaddafi regime in an attempt to remove the Libyan leader from power. The United States also provided Libya's neighbors with military assistance, conducted major military exercises near Libya to intimidate Qaddafi, and pushed European states to impose sanctions – a move that the Europeans resisted. Washington also engaged in several covert options to undermine Qaddafi's proxies and to destroy Libya's military.[36] In addition, Washington backed Hissan Habre in Chad against the Libyan-backed government there, contributing to Habre's victory in 1982.[37]

Military force also played an important role in US policy. In 1981, the United States shot down two Libyan planes over the Gulf of Sidra, when they challenged the US right to navigate near the Libyan coast.[38] Most famously, in 1986 the United States bombed Libya in Operation El Dorado Canyon. The 1986 US raid on Libya was designed to punish Libya for past attacks such as that on La Belle Discoteque in Berlin, to deter Qaddafi from supporting terrorism, to destroy the Libyan infrastructure for supporting terrorism, and to demonstrate US resolve.[39] The strikes were also meant to encourage a coup by hitting targets such as paramilitary units linked to regime security, and avoiding military infrastructure, the destruction of which might anger potential coup plotters.[40]

[35] Ibid., p. 191.

[36] Stanik, *El Dorado Canyon*, pp. 42–44, 73–81 and Woodward, *Veil: The Secret Wars of the CIA, 1981–1987*, pp. 96–97, 157, 366.

[37] Stanik, *El Dorado Canyon*, p. 40.

[38] Libya claimed that its territorial waters extended to include the entire Gulf of Sidra, arguing that it was in fact a bay and thus internal waters. The international standard for a bay, however, is 24 miles wide, while the Gulf of Sidra was 250 miles wide. The United States sent naval forces to deliberately challenge Libya's claim. See Stanik, *El Dorado Canyon*, p. 27.

[39] Tucker, *Skirmishes at the Edge of Empire*, p. 96 and Stanik, *El Dorado Canyon*, p. ix.

[40] Stanik, *El Dorado Canyon*, pp. 148–149.

US military strikes led to an increase in Libyan support for terrorism, particularly in the short term. The initial downing of Libyan planes in 1981 led Qaddafi to explore ways to assassinate President Reagan and his regime's ties to terrorist groups continued unabated.[41] Subsequent clashes that resulted in further Libyan losses led Qaddafi to mount the attack on the La Belle discoteque, which killed three people including two Americans and triggered the 1986 US raid.[42]

The 1986 strikes in particular backfired. Although the strikes were impressive from a logistical and technical point of view, Libyan infrastructure was not damaged significantly, and many targets were missed. Qaddafi's hold on power was not shaken. There was no coup, and the infrastructure for supporting terrorism remained intact.[43] Libya expert Ray Takeyh even contends that the strikes enhanced Qaddafi's power at home and lionized his stature in much of the world.[44]

Violence surged after the attacks. Immediately after the bombing, the British Ambassador's house in Lebanon was attacked because Britain had allowed several of the US airplanes that participated in the attack basing and overflight rights, and several American and British people in Lebanon were killed by a group with links to the Abu Nidal Organization, which was then in Qaddafi's employ. The Central Intelligence Agency also reported that Libya "bought" Peter Kilburn, an American hostage in Lebanon, and executed him.[45] Libya later bombed Pan Am 103 in 1988, killing 270 people. In addition, in 1989 Libya again challenged the US Navy, despite repeatedly having lost aircraft in past confrontations.[46] Nor was the United States the only Libyan target. In 1989,

---

[41] Ibid., pp. 63–71. Qaddafi's reported desire to assassinate Reagan was widely believed in the intelligence community in the mid-1980s, but some in the community came to doubt the extent and seriousness of these plans.

[42] Ibid., p. 143. The attacks were carried out by Libyan agents, not a terrorist group.

[43] Ibid., p. 207.

[44] Takeyh, "The Rogue who Came in from the Cold," p. 64.

[45] Stanik, *El Dorado Canyon*, p. 218.

[46] Stanik, *El Dorado Canyon*, p. 229. For a comparison of the frequency of attacks, see Prunckun and Mohr, "Military Deterrence of International Terrorism," pp. 274–276. Prunckun and Mohr argue that the US attacks did lead to a decrease in Libya's use of terrorism over time, following the initial spike – something they refer to as an "extinction burst." Prunckun and Mohr, "Military Deterrence of International Terrorism," p. 276.

Libya also bombed UTA 772, killing all 170 people on board, in response to France's support for the Habre regime in Chad.

Stephen Collins finds that the number of Libyan attacks fell in the years after the 1986 strikes, but the lethality grew tremendously. In the five years before the US airstrike, Libyan clandestine state attacks and those of Libyan-backed groups killed 91 people, while the figure for the five years after the strike was 491.[47]

Few European states or other allies openly supported the attacks, and many made clear they thought the United States was overreacting. However, their concern about additional US attacks led them to become more aggressive against Libya in other ways. The Europeans expelled Libyan diplomats and students from Europe, some of whom were often involved in supporting terrorism. European states also increased pressure on Syria, which contributed to Damascus' decision to cut its ties to the Abu Nidal Organization.[48] US diplomats claim that the 1986 raid on Libya made many European states more willing to cooperate on isolating Libya, as they feared a failure to act would lead the United States to use additional military force. Thus, several experts categorize the raid as a "success" for deterrence in general, as it successfully communicated US resolve to a host of sponsors and would-be sponsors – one of the main US goals.[49]

After the 1986 strike, the United States returned to economic and political pressure as the primary means of coercing Libya. Sanctions, however, shifted from unilateral to multilateral after the United States and Britain pressed forward with evidence implicating Libyan intelligence officers in the Pan Am 103 and UTA 772 bombings. They persuaded the United Nations to call on Libya to turn over the suspects and, when that failed, impose limited sanctions in 1992.[50] In 1993, the UN also imposed sanctions on the sale of oil and gas equipment to Libya and froze Libyan funds abroad.

By themselves, the sanctions embodied in UN Security Council Resolutions 748 and 883 were not overwhelming and did not have the

---

[47] Collins, "Dissuading State Sponsors of Terrorism," p. 8.
[48] Tucker, *Skirmishes at the Edge of Empire,* p. 97 and Schultz, *Turmoil and Triumph,* p. 687.
[49] Prunckun and Mohr, "Military Deterrence of International Terrorism," p. 270.
[50] Tucker, *Skirmishes at the Edge of Empire,* p. 81.

same level of restrictions as unilateral US sanctions did. Libya was able to export crude oil, by far its most important export. Moreover, punishments such as the travel ban were often honored only in the breach, and as the decade wore on were increasingly violated. Libya's economy stagnated, but this was in large part due to the plunge in the price of crude oil in the 1990s and rampant mismanagement.[51]

Nevertheless, multilateral sanctions packed a bigger wallop than had the varied unilateral US efforts. The sanctions and fears of US escalation scared off foreign investors, fostered economic uncertainty, and hurt tourism. Military imports, already far lower than in the 1980s, fell from $410 million in 1991 to zero in 1993 after sanctions were imposed.[52] Libya was not able to find substitute markets or sources of imports for many goods due to their multilateral nature. In addition, air traffic from Libya fell, as the aviation industry could no longer obtain spare parts. Libya's air force practically rusted on the runways, completing only 85 hours of flight time in total in 1994.[53] Perhaps most importantly, Libya found it difficult to maintain parts of its oil sector due to a lack of spare parts and investment.[54] These contributed to a severe economic crisis that led to 30 percent unemployment, inflation of perhaps 50 percent, and few prospects for growth.[55]

Qaddafi was concerned, moreover, by the impact of sanctions on Libya's economy – a concern that was not present in the 1970s and 1980s. The ideology promulgated by the regime that may have had adherents in the 1970s had long turned stale by the 1990s. Several popular protests occurred, despite the regime's authoritarian policies. Libya had a burgeoning Islamist movement that rejected the regime's legitimacy. Discontent in the army was growing, and several coup plotters emerged. Discontent within the regime and army required purges and other harsh measures to ensure loyalty. Popular expectations, which had soared during the oil boom of the 1970s, also were not being met,

---

[51] O'Sullivan, *Shrewd Sanctions*, p. 184.   [52] Ibid., p. 207.
[53] Collins, "Dissuading State Support of Terrorism," p. 11.
[54] O'Sullivan, *Shrewd Sanctions*, pp. 197–199.
[55] Murphy, "Libya Opens Up," p. 8 and Collins, "Dissuading State Support of Terrorism" p. 12. Murphy gives a lower figure of 25 percent for inflation than does Collins, who puts it at 50 percent.

causing further concern to a regime that had always sought to maintain a high standard of living in order to gain popular support.[56]

The biggest impact of sanctions, however, was political. Sanctions reinforced Libya's isolation in general and curtailed Qaddafi's influence in the Arab world.[57] Mary Jane Deeb contends that Qaddafi sought to be the region's "elder statesman" but that the UN-sanctioned isolation prevented this.[58] Part of Qaddafi's motivation for supporting terrorists and insurgents – to play a major role on the world stage – was countered by the UN travel ban, making sanctions particularly effective.[59] Indeed, because Arab states in general respected the travel ban, while African countries often ignored it, Qaddafi turned away from Arab politics, and with it many of the terrorist groups he supported.[60] The multilateral nature of the sanctions was particularly important, as it prevented Qaddafi from portraying himself as representing Arab, African, or developing nations against the hostile Western imperialist powers.

Several factors that led Libya to change course were not directly linked to sanctions. The collapse of the Soviet Union removed a counterweight to the United States, diminishing any hopes in Tripoli that US pressure might be offset – demonstrated by the UN Security Council resolution against Libya, which the Soviets would have vetoed during the Cold War era. In addition, the failure of Libya's various economic programs made Qaddafi more keen to gain outside economic backing. Finally, the burgeoning Islamist insurgency was linked to economic discontent, but also to Libya's many political maladies and the growing appeal that radical Islam had throughout the Muslim world. Sanctions made these problems more painful and diminished chances that Qaddafi's regime would be able to resolve them successfully.

In response to these pressures, Libya began to shun the terrorist groups it once embraced and even became a voice of moderation in the Arab

---

[56] O'Sullivan, *Shrewd Sanctions*, p. 204; Stanik, *El Dorado Canyon*, p. 12; and Collins, "Dissuading State Support of Terrorism," p. 12.

[57] O'Sullivan, *Shrewd Sanctions*, p. 203.

[58] As quoted and referenced in Collins, "Dissuading State Support of Terrorism," p. 12.

[59] Pillar, *Terrorism and US Foreign Policy*, p. 167.

[60] Indyk, "The Iraq War Did Not Force Gadaffi's Hand" and Stanik, *El Dorado Canyon*, p. 237.

world. Libya no longer sponsored international terrorism, though it initially retained ties to terrorist groups and attacked Libyan dissidents.[61] By the mid-1990s, Libya had largely moved away from radicalism. Libya switched from supporting rejectionist Palestinian groups to backing Yasir Arafat, a decision that would have been anathema to it in the 1970s and 1980s. As early as 1992, Qaddafi tried to use back channels to negotiate with the United States and the United Kingdom to end the pressure.[62] In April 1999, Libya agreed to allow two intelligence officers to stand trial under Scottish law for the Lockerbie bombings.[63] After September 11, Libya began cooperating with the United States on al-Qa'ida. In 2002, Libya supported the Saudi initiative that offered Israel diplomatic recognition and cautioned Arafat not to declare a Palestinian state. In Africa, Libya mediated conflicts in Sudan, Uganda, and Congo.[64]

Qaddafi saw the United States – above other Western powers – as the key to restoring his international position. To this end, he was willing to renounce terrorism and even end his chemical, biological, and nuclear programs. Qaddafi's son and heir apparent, Saif ul-Islam Qadhafi, interpreted his father's thinking, noting that "If you have the backing of the West and the United States, you will be able to achieve in a few years what you could not achieve in 50."[65]

Lessons for coercers

As the experiences of Libya and several other sponsors of terrorism suggest, states can be coerced into halting their support, but the process is arduous and lengthy. Although there are no simple steps that can guarantee that a state will cease its support for terrorism, there are several guidelines that coercing states should recognize when seeking to halt the sponsorship of terrorism (or, more realistically, to reduce it).

---

[61] Tucker, *Skirmishes at the Edge of Empire*, p. 81.
[62] Hart, "My Secret Talks with Libya," p. B05.
[63] In May 1999, Qaddafi's government officially conveyed to the United States a proposal to ends its weapons of mass destruction programs. Indyk, "The Iraq War Did Not Force Gadaffi's Hand."
[64] O'Sullivan, *Shrewd Sanctions*, p. 209.
[65] "Qadhafi's Son Says Libya was Promised Economic, Military Gains for Disarmament."

Equally important, coercers should be aware of the limits of their influence and the potential for pressure to backfire.

UNDERSTANDING THE ADVERSARY

The first set of lessons involves understanding the nature of the adversary. Both support for terrorism and efforts to stop it are embedded issues, part of a regime's overall political trajectory. Revolutionary Iran and the Taliban's Afghanistan backed other radical groups as part of their overall efforts to spread their interpretation of Islam, a goal that was apparent in their domestic as well as foreign policy; their support for terrorists was initially part and parcel of this broader trend. However, if it is possible to reintegrate the state in general, counterterrorism pressure is more likely to succeed. It is no coincidence that Libya began talks regarding ending its support for terrorism at the same time that it proposed giving up its weapons of mass destruction programs – both stood as obstacles to the regime's reacceptance as a "normal" member of the international community.

Undifferentiated pressure almost always fails. The motivations of the supporting state, the type of support provided, and the dynamic of the group it supports all will affect whether coercion succeeds or fails. Nor can pressure be divorced from the broader strategic context. What worked with Libya in the 1990s would probably have failed in the 1970s when the regime was more ideological and faced fewer problems at home.

Efforts to halt sponsorship must recognize, and ideally capitalize on, the reasons why sponsors support terrorism. For example, Pakistan's support for militants in Kashmir is largely (though not entirely) driven by a strategic ambition to weaken India. During the Kargil crisis, the US threat to realign strategically with New Delhi if Pakistan did not withdraw its forces thus had a tremendous impact. Similarly, US pressure after the September 11 attacks also affected the primary reason why Pakistan backed the militants. Limited economic pressure that increased Pakistan's economic pain for much of the 1990s, in contrast, were far less effective. The domestic importance of the Kashmir issue, however, made it impossible for Musharraf to completely cut off support, placing limits on any progress.

Because ideological regimes are so difficult to coerce through the imposition of standard costs or to persuade by offering common benefits, it is often necessary for the revolution to age before these regimes agree to abandon terrorism. Over time, the fervor of all revolutions wanes. Charisma is "routinized" and the petty corruption and ambitions that characterize most politics eventually overcome the initial ardor for a cause. Revolutionary behavior also is punished by other states, which try to weaken, undermine, and contain those that threaten their power and position. Iran today is often described as "post-revolutionary," and Sudan is now far less radical. Qaddafi too has abandoned his revolutionary pretensions. All three have reduced their support for terrorism. This process, however, takes years if not decades.[66]

In essence, the best policy when confronting an ideological regime may be a form of containment.[67] That is to say, coercers should try to limit the spread of the revolutionary ideology by building up vulnerable states, both politically and militarily. Reducing their vulnerability to terrorism may require bolstering the victim states' intelligence services, helping to reduce government corruption, targeting regime largesse to groups or areas most susceptible to the terrorists' appeal, or otherwise reducing opportunities for radicals to exploit.

Coercers must also consider the type of sponsor they face. For "strong" supporters such as Iran with Hizballah, the stakes for the supporting state are often so high that completely stopping support is not a realistic short-term goal. "Lukewarm" supporters, on the other hand, may be far more willing to abandon their proxies. Syria, for example, abandoned the PKK in the face of Turkish threats but comparable pressure by Israel did little to shake its support for Palestinian groups. "Antagonistic" sponsors are yet another class. Again, the stakes involved are often high for this group, but coercers must recognize that the supporting state often weakens the overall movement and cause rather than strengthens it. Removing such support may actually make the group or overall cause more lethal. Truly united Kashmiris or Palestinians who receive little foreign backing would pose a far greater challenge to India or to Israel than would divided groups that enjoy state support.

[66] See Brinton, *The Anatomy of Revolution*, for a classic work on this subject.

[67] For an excellent review of containment's variations and difficulties, see Litwak, *Rogue States and US Foreign Policy*. Most of the discussion in this volume does not directly pertain to terrorism, but rather examines US policy toward states that violate international norms on proliferation among other security issues. Litwak is highly critical of the idea of undifferentiated containment.

Passive sponsors of terrorism pose their own set of challenges. Chapter 8 discussed these in some detail. Nevertheless, it is important to emphasize that many of the measures for halting passive sponsorship – helping the "sponsor's" security services, providing economic support for a weak regime, and so on – are the opposite of the tools states use to coerce active sponsors. Confusing active and passive sponsors, as suggested by calls to put Saudi Arabia on the state sponsor list, may lead to measures that actually weaken the capacity of passive sponsors, further worsening the problem.

In addition to understanding the motive of the sponsoring state, coercers must recognize whether that state is focused primarily on backing an insurgency or on backing a terrorist group. Israel's experience with Hizballah suggests the many difficulties in confronting a skilled terrorist group that is also a popular insurgent movement. Although Hizballah at times kept its cadre for guerrilla operations distinct from its terrorist cadre, the political leadership and many of the key personnel belonged to both groups. Thus it proved impossible for Israel to eradicate Hizballah as a terrorist movement without destroying it as a guerrilla operation as well. Hizballah simply had too many well-trained and motivated people who could be used for both terrorist and guerrilla operations.

In theory, it is possible for a state to support a group's guerrilla activities only but not endorse attacks on civilians, though in practice such a line almost always is crossed. More realistically, coercing states must recognize that counterinsurgency requires a different tool set than does counterterrorism. Traditional terrorist groups are small, and few have deep roots among the population. Insurgencies, in contrast, are far broader movements and often control territory. Fighting an insurgency requires going beyond narrow intelligence gathering and taking measures to reassure, sway, and at times intimidate the general population. In addition, it requires a far more active role for certain types of military forces, which may have to guard remote areas where insurgents might be active, train other forces in how to conduct counterinsurgency operations, win over the population, and so on.[68] Insurgencies also appear under different conditions than do smaller terrorist groups, an important consideration

---

[68] See Shafer, *Deadly Paradigms*; Blaufarb, *The Counterinsurgency Era*; Tanham and Duncanson, "Some Dilemmas of Counterinsurgency"; Odom, *On Internal War*; Eckstein, *Internal War*; Leites and Wolf, *Rebellion and Authority*; and

when trying to understand how to anticipate and counter such violence.[69]

Finally, timing is often vital. The same pressures applied against the same adversary will have different effects depending on the circumstances. Revolutionary fervor may need to wane before many coercive pressures take effect. A change in leadership, a shift in the regional balance of power, a decline in the price of a key export, or other changes may be necessary as well. Such changes may be beyond the control of the coercing power, but these powers should always be aware of potential shifts that might increase the chances of success.

A WAY OUT . . . CONDITIONALLY

One reason states often support terrorism is that they have few if any other options for achieving their strategic ambitions. Demanding that a state end its support for terrorism thus involves far more than the state jettisoning a small group of unsavory thugs. In reality, the coercer is asking the supporting state to abandon a strategic objective or a vital domestic concern. Pushing Syria to unconditionally end its support for Hizballah and Palestinian rejectionists would leave Damascus with few effective means of pressing Israel on the Golan Heights and other disputes and would leave it vulnerable to charges of selling out at home. If Pakistan abandoned Kashmiri militants, its rival India would emerge far stronger. Iran's relationship with Hizballah represents an exception that proves the rule. With Iranian approval, Hizballah did reduce its use of terrorism in the 1990s, but it did so in part because more conventional guerrilla operations against Israel were proving effective in achieving its goal of driving Israel from Lebanon.

As Libya's experience indicates, providing state sponsors with a diplomatic way out thus may make the path to halting sponsorship easier. The promise of negotiations can offer states another means of achieving their objective that does not require terrorism. This approach was the US "answer" to the problem of Syrian terrorism: by forging a Syrian–Israeli peace, Syria would achieve its objectives at the bargaining table rather than through the use of terrorism.

Hoffman and Taw, *A Strategic Framework for Countering Terrorism and Insurgency*.

[69] For an overview of the conditions of insurgency, see Fearon and Laitin, "Ethnicity, Insurgency, and Civil War."

Once again, however, this diplomatic "out" may easily backfire. If they are not careful, outside powers are rewarding the use of terrorism, suggesting to other states that its use pays off diplomatically. Moreover, the supporting state has an incentive to encourage terrorists to step up their activities when talks stall or when it deems the concessions insufficient, at times increasing the incidence of terrorism. Although Damascus at times curtailed the activities of Hizballah and various Palestinian proxies, it never cracked down on them entirely as it sought to keep them strong to preserve its best bargaining chip. Finally, offering ideologically or domestically driven states a way out may accomplish little. Their motives are not linked to the benefits that the victim state or others can provide – often their own politics must change before progress can be made.

If a way out is offered, it must be balanced with strong coercive leverage, ensuring that the state in question does not see support for terrorism as beneficial on the whole. Engagement is at times necessary, but its costs can be considerable if it is unconditional. States must not only recognize there is a penalty for continuing to support a terrorist group, but also that support for terrorism in general is foolish and can only backfire. The US handling of Libya after the mid-1990s represents an almost perfect balance of coercion and engagement. Without the constant US-led campaign, Qaddafi would not have come to the bargaining table. But without the promise of relief, he would never have made concessions.

SETTING PRIORITIES

Too often, the United States makes counterterrorism one goal of many, failing to set priorities. When pressing the Taliban in the 1990s, narcotics trafficking, human rights, and ending the civil war often took precedence over counterterrorism. Libya is again instructive. When beginning talks with Libya, in contrast, the US agenda was appropriately limited. The United States did not press Qaddafi on human rights, elections, or other internal issues despite Libya's dismal record on these scores. Washington initially even held back on Libya's offer to end its weapons of mass destruction program, recognizing that terrorism should be the top priority.

Counterterrorism, of course, should not always be the top priority. For US relations with North Korea, counterproliferation is a far more important goal, and any lingering concerns about Pyongyang's involvement in terrorism should be subordinate to this objective. The key is not always to make counterterrorism a top priority, but rather to have priorities.

Even with regard to the continued terrorism, establishing "red lines" and other priorities is essential. Mass casualty attacks, of course, are of far more concern than less deadly violence. A clear priority should be a state's transfer of weapons of mass destruction (particularly any material for nuclear weapons or viral biological agents) to a terrorist group. Various WMD-armed states have so far refrained from such transfers, probably because they fear escalation from potential victims. Reinforcing such a concern among all potential proliferators is vital.

ENEMIES VERSUS TERRORISTS

One obvious step is to reform the process of designating state sponsors of terrorism. Currently, US definitions of terrorism conflate the difference between attacks on combatants and attacks on non-combatants rather than highlight it.[70] It is ironic that the *majority* of the states on the State Department sponsorship list had only minimal involvement in terrorism in 2003. Cuba and North Korea had long ago ceased to support terrorist groups in any meaningful way. Sudan and Libya, both of which were at times major sponsors of terrorism, have also largely ended their support for terrorist groups. Unfortunately, by lumping them together in the same category as Syria and Iran (and by excluding such egregious sponsors as Pakistan), any "name and shame" power of the list is reduced. In addition, the penalties that go with the sponsorship status remain considerable, making it hard to offer incentives for states that are moving in the right direction already.[71] Ideally, there would be more categories in between the black and white of sponsor and non-sponsor that recognize progress

---

[70] The phrase "war on terrorism" as often mocked as a foolish concept, comparable to a war on a particular tactic rather than a war on a real adversary. Former National Security Advisor Zbigniew Brzezinski caustically noted that, "Terrorism is a technique for killing people. That can't be an enemy. It's as if we said that World War II was not against the Nazis but against blitzkrieg. We need to ask who the enemy is, and what springs him or her to action against us?" Brzezinski, "To Lead, US Must Give Up Paranoid Policies." A broader case can be made, however, that particular methods and tactics are reprehensible and should not be used regardless of the larger conflict. Thus you can have war without deliberately slaughtering civilians, capitalism without slavery, and so on.

[71] Not surprisingly, this has generated complaints from regimes seeking rewards for ending their support of terrorism. See "Sudan Demands To Be Lifted from State Sponsors of Terrorism."

and have fewer fixed penalties. In addition, the sponsorship list would be focused on terrorism, not on broader US concerns about a rogue regime.

Politics now dominates policy. Those seeking change must recognize the political risks they run as they try to create more coherent definitions and categories. Changing the listing of who is a sponsor and what constitutes terrorism, for example, would be criticized as legitimating Castro's noxious regime in Cuba or attacks on US or other soldiers. Continuing the current set of definitions, however, reduces the potency of US political measures such as the state sponsorship list and gives terrorist groups few incentives to avoid attacks on true non-combatants

The United States should also distinguish between civilians and combatants in its definition of terrorism. US policies should encourage even guerrilla groups to avoid clear non-combatant targets, even at the price of recognizing that the chief of police, a soldier, or even a government official at times would be considered a combatant. Such a recognition should in no way imply support for the group. Instead, the United States and other countries must recognize the distinction between enemies and terrorists: a group or state can still merit opposition as an enemy without being a terrorist group.

Encouraging this distinction is particularly important for ending a dispute, as it is easier to negotiate with a "terrorist" group that respects it. A group that focuses only on legitimate combatants rather than on children or other obvious non-combatants indicates that it is, or can be, a more restrained and disciplined actor. Moreover, such attacks are less heinous, diminishing (though hardly eliminating) the hostility that any sort of political violence inevitably brings. Israeli experts, for example, have told me that Hizballah should be treated differently from HAMAS, as the former has become far more professional in its attacks in the last decade, the latter wantonly killing civilians.[72] Such a group thus generates less hatred and can convincingly show that it will abide by promises, in contrast to a less restrained group.

---

[72] Signaling such a distinction is particularly hard. Many groups, particularly those that are not politically sophisticated or that are largely underground, may not recognize that the coercing government makes this distinction.

CHANGING THE RULES OF THE GAME

The international community can make several changes in how it responds to state support that would make coercion more likely to succeed. One change is to end the fiction of deniability. Pakistan's links to Kashmiri militants, the Taliban's connections with al-Qa'ida, Iran's and Syria's ties to Hizballah, and other relations between states and major terrorist groups are usually well known and often publicized by the supporting state itself. Nevertheless, there is often a Talmudic debate over responsibility for a particular attack. For example, former National Security Advisor Samuel ("Sandy") Berger noted about the Khobar Towers attack that, "We know it was done by the Saudi Hizballah. We know that they were trained in Iran by Iranians. We know there was Iranian involvement. What has yet to be established is how substantial the Iranian involvement was."[73] Similarly, the Clinton administration agonized over Bin Ladin's direct role in the bombing of USS *Cole*, even though it knew relatively early on that al-Qa'ida members were responsible. Such hair-splitting gives a sponsor an incentive to offer sanctuary and logistical support to a group while avoiding a direct role in the final decision to strike a particular target. Instead, the burden should be on the accused state to demonstrate it has worked against the terrorist group and did not support its operations in any way, no matter how indirect.

Another fiction serving state sponsors is the respect given to sovereignty in cases where it is not exercised. Syria hides behind Lebanon, and Pakistan hid behind Afghanistan, using these ostensibly sovereign states for their own ends. Again, even though their dominance of these countries is or was widely recognized, they were able to exploit the narrow rules of the system to avoid responsibility for their actions.

A related change is for the international community to lower the bar on legitimate escalation on state sponsors. If states believe that only massive terrorist attacks will provoke international backing for a response, they have fewer reasons to withhold support. On the other hand, if the victim state believes that international support for a response would be forthcoming, it is far more likely to take advantage of its conventional military superiority. The October 2003 Israeli attack on Syria, which has long sponsored a range of rejectionist groups against Israel, was roundly condemned in Europe as escalation, while Syria's

[73] Walsh, "Louis Freeh's Last Case."

continued backing of violent groups was taken in stride. Similarly, condemnation of the US 1998 cruise missile strike on Sudan focused on whether the target hit was indeed a chemical weapons plant or a pharmaceutical factory rather than on Khartoum's longstanding ties to terrorist groups. France criticized the 1986 US strike on Libya as an attack that would lead to an escalation of violence.[74]

International support for escalation, however, is intertwined with the coercing state's overall reputation. US officials, for example, noted that escalation against the Taliban became harder after 1998 because the United States was involved in a war in Kosovo and a low-level conflict in Iraq. Further bombing by the United States in Afghanistan would have reinforced the image of America as a trigger-happy country. Israel has found it difficult to escalate because of its low international standing, despite the rather open and egregious support that several of its neighbors have provided for terrorism over the years. Because of these linkages, counterterrorism policy cannot be divorced from a state's overall foreign policy.

THE EFFECTIVENESS OF MULTILATERALISM

When possible, pressure should be multilateral. Multilateral policies have many problems: they are cumbersome, require concessions to allies, and at times lead to a lowest-common-denominator effect.[75] These problems make it difficult to increase pressure on state sponsors. Despite these weaknesses, gaining the support of allies often means the difference between success and failure.

In large part, multilateral support for coercing state sponsors limits sponsors' options, both in terms of avoiding pressure and with regard to their other objectives. In short, they have no "plan of victory" that enables them to achieve their goals. US unilateral efforts for years failed to move Tripoli. UN sanctions and international isolation of Libya after the Lockerbie and Air France bombings, however, gave Qaddafi few options for gaining much needed foreign investment or for playing the leading role he sought to play in the Arab and broader world.

Even the relative failure of pressure on Iran suggests the importance of multilateralism. When Iran feared in the mid-1990s that the United

[74] Prunckun and Mohr, "Military Deterrence of International Terrorism," p. 270.
[75] Byman and Waxman, *The Dynamics of Coercion*, p. 162.

States would convince European states to join in sanctions, it cut back its support for terrorism in Europe. US power alone proved far less effective. The Iran example indicates that even important regional states still fear escalation.

REDUCING PASSIVE SUPPORT

The recommendations for ending, or at least reducing, passive support are straightforward. Whenever possible, outside governments should try to impose new costs on regimes that tolerate terrorist-related activities, diminish the popular support the group enjoys, and bolster counter-terrorism capacity.[76]

Imposing new costs or increasing existing costs is a time-honored tactic. In general, however, such threats must be part of a broader effort or else they cease to be meaningful. The United States, for example, did not make support for radical Islam a priority in the US–Saudi relationship, giving Riyadh few additional incentives to crack down on this activity.

Simple embarrassment proved surprisingly effective in the cases of passive support examined in Chapter 8, though by itself it was not sufficient to end support. The spotlight held on Saudi Arabia after September 11 humiliated the Al Saud, making them scramble to at least appear cooperative. Greek leaders feared that their hosting of the Olympics would be ruined. Similarly, US leaders recognized that support for the IRA undercut overall attempts to portray the United States as tough on terrorism.

---

[76] The United States has started to recognize the various problems related to passive sponsorship. The *National Strategy for Combating Terrorism* declares, "The strategy to deny sponsorship, support, and sanctuary is three-fold. First, it focuses on the responsibilities of all states to fulfill their obligations to combat terrorism both within their borders and internationally. Second, it helps target US assistance to those states who are willing to combat terrorism, but may not have the means. And finally, when states prove reluctant or unwilling to meet their international obligations ... the United States ... will take appropriate steps to convince them to change their policies." *National Strategy for Combating Terrorism*, p. 17. The *National Strategy* further notes that "legislative assistance, technical aid, investigative help, intelligence sharing, and military and intelligence training are appropriate forms of assistance to improve capacity." Ibid., p. 20.

Diminishing popular support is far more complex. Efforts to play up the terrorist group's missteps and atrocities should be made at the popular level as well as at the governmental level. The effort by a British widow of N17's terrorism helped undercut the image of the group as a "Robin Hood" striking out against imperialism. Similarly, British efforts to play up the IRA's bloodiness (and their own willingness to work with peaceful opposition figures) helped cut support for the IRA among Irish Americans. Propaganda campaigns are notoriously difficult, however, and US efforts to demonize al-Qa'ida have conspicuously failed.[77]

Working indirectly to diminish support may be essential. The Irish Republic's willingness to criticize the IRA made a profound impression on Irish Americans, bolstering the British case considerably. Given the deep unpopularity of the United States in Saudi Arabia, US efforts to diminish al-Qa'ida's luster may only burnish it. It would be more effective if respected Muslim authorities criticized the organization, as these voices have credibility with the key audiences.

Bolstering capacity is a more straightforward task. This can range from technical assistance, such as helping improve databases or information systems that track terrorists and their activities to advice on intelligence reorganization and legal reform. Training can be particularly important, as many skills related to shutting down passive support, such as financial tracking, are relatively rare in government circles, particularly in the developing world. Money can also be provided to boost the size and skills of security and intelligence services. Passive support may also require going beyond the government. Jessica Stern, for example, contends that the United States can help Pakistan tamp down unrest and support for terrorism by strengthening its secular education system, thus weakening the religious schools that are an important base for *jihadists*.[78]

Many regimes in the developing world, however, have only a limited capacity to absorb US or other outside assistance meant to shore up their ability to fight terrorism. In Saudi Arabia, for example, the myriad new

---

[77] For a highly critical review of US capability to influence foreign publics, see the Advisory Group on Public Diplomacy for the Arab and Muslim World, "Changing Minds, Winning Peace."

[78] Stern, "Pakistan's Jihad Culture," p. 126.

programs the Kingdom has introduced in cooperation with the United States suffer from a lack of skilled and experienced personnel. As a result, even the most dramatic turnaround in the regime's intentions to crush terrorism will produce only modest results for many years.

Reducing passive support can transform the struggle against non-state actors like al-Qa'ida. If al-Qa'ida were hounded wherever it tried to set up shop, it would be far harder for the organization to recruit, train, raise money, purchase weapons, protect its leadership, and otherwise survive and prosper. Ironically, the key to success against these non-state actors lies in engaging or coercing their inadvertent hosts to move against them – and helping them gain the capacity to do so.

REALISTIC EXPECTATIONS

Coercion is difficult at the best of times, and success requires anticipating problems and recognizing the possibility of failure. Even modest progress can take years. Libya, for example, suffered unilateral sanctions, a direct military strike, and finally broad (if limited) UN-mandated sanctions before agreeing to end its support – a process that took years. Power shifts that led to the purging of ideologues were necessary for Iran to reduce, and Sudan to end, their support for terrorism, and in Tehran's case the level of activity still remains high. In part, the long time necessary for success stems from the very nature of coercion. Most forms of coercive pressure will initially strengthen a regime, producing a rally "round the flag" effect.[79] The punishment inflicted, in contrast, may take years to sink in.

Coercing states must also be wary of limited uses of force. Often, such gestures are politically necessary, fulfilling a desire to "do something."[80] Ironically, though military force is often depicted as a strong response, its use in a limited way may signal weakness. The 1993 US strike on Iraq's intelligence headquarters after the attempted assassination of former President George H. W. Bush was roundly depicted as a "pinprick" that demonstrated only America's aversion to a strong response. Moreover, in terms of their counterterrorism effectiveness, limited strikes often make

---

[79] Byman and Waxman, *The Dynamics of Coercion*, pp. 34–35.
[80] Pillar, *Terrorism and US Foreign Policy*, p. 101. Baldwin offers a defense of the political use of various tools, noting that appearing to condone offensive or hostile activity is implicit when no action is taken. Baldwin, "The Sanctions Debate and the Logic of Choice," pp. 83–84.

the supporting state more recalcitrant. The US bombing of Libya in 1986, the 1998 attack on Afghanistan, and the various Israeli forays into Lebanon all made the target regime more enthusiastic in its backing of the terrorists. In addition, such attacks can lionize the terrorists among potential supporters, increasing their ability to raise money and to recruit.

At times, states will have to settle for progress rather than for complete success. Cases such as Qaddafi's Libya are rare. Far more common are instances where outside pressure leads states to cut ties to particular groups or reduce their activities. Iran's reduced support for terrorists operating against the United States and the Gulf states, for example, is a step forward even though Iran still has a long road to walk. Similarly, Damascus' decision to abandon the PKK represents progress despite the Baath regime's continued ties to various anti-Israel groups. Demanding an all-or-nothing standard, however, reduces supporting states' incentives to place limits on their proxies or to cut support to select terrorist groups while retaining ties to others.

Final words

It is easier to stop state support for terrorism before it starts than to halt backing after it begins. The back and forth between the coercing state and the state supporter can generate a cycle of hostility and make it difficult for the supporter to back down and lose face, even when the stakes involved are not high. Thus, one of the greatest challenges to the international community is preventing the rise of new Talibans or other regimes that see supporting terrorism as ideologically vital. Similarly, states must be discouraged from following the path of Pakistan, which found strategic advantage by supporting terrorism.

Creating a strong norm against the sponsorship of terrorism both makes states less likely to engage in it in the first place and enables the victim state to respond more easily. Diplomatically, this requires engaging both allies and other states on these issues before the support for terrorism becomes well established. In addition, it demands that the United States and other countries offer would-be sponsors alternatives to terrorism, such as giving them options at the negotiating table.

Creating standards is vital with regard to the problem of passive sponsorship. Passive support today is a grey area in international relations, in part because the international community is reluctant to confront the difficulties of state capacity building and of demanding a higher standard for regime accountability. Passive sponsors have quite different motivations than do active sponsors, and the solutions to this problem differ in turn. Nevertheless, passive support remains vital for many terrorist groups, particularly al-Qa'ida and its affiliates.

Such preventive diplomacy, however, is exceptionally difficult. Often, the bloodshed and carnage terrorists inflict must be manifest before any response occurs. In addition, states inevitably have different interests and different strategies for influencing would-be sponsors of terrorism, making it difficult to forge a common approach. The problem of passive sponsorship in particular will prove difficult to solve. Nevertheless, addressing these issues in advance offers one of the few long-term hopes for reducing the problem of state sponsorship.

Appendix: Major terrorist groups

This appendix briefly describes several of the major groups that are treated at greater length in the main portion of this book. It draws heavily on the US State Department's *Patterns of Global Terrorism* reports and the *MIPT Knowledge Base*, among other sources. The appendix is not meant to present original research or to offer more than the barest description of the groups in question. As the point of the Appendix is to offer concise overviews of the various groups, I have refrained from discussing some of the more contentious issues with regard to particular dates, activities, and so on that would be of concern to specialists but not to a general audience.

Abu Nidal Organization (ANO)

DESCRIPTION
- Palestinian nationalist group split from the PLO in 1974. Led by Sabri al-Banna until 2002, the group operates internationally.[1]
- The Iraqi government claimed that Abu Nidal committed suicide in August 2002. Some believe that Saddam Hussein ordered Abu Nidal assassinated. The ANO has stated that the group is still in operation and will appoint a new leader.[2]

[1] US Department of State. *Patterns of Global Terrorism, 2003* p. 114.
[2] "Terrorist Group Profile: Abu Nidal Organization (ANO)." *MIPT Knowledge Base.* Available at: http://www.tkb.org/Group.jsp?groupID = 1 (accessed on September 17, 2004).

GOALS

Historical goal of the total liberation of Palestine through armed struggle.[3]

MAIN ACTIVITIES

- The group has conducted attacks in twenty countries since 1974 and targeted the US, England, France, Israel, the PLO, and various Arab countries.[4]
- As of October 2004, the group is reportedly responsible for 77 attacks which inflicted 565 casualties and killed 188 persons.[5]

GROUP SIZE

A few hundred individuals.[6]

STATE SPONSORSHIP

Historical aid from Iraq, Syria, and Libya.[7]

AREA OF OPERATIONS

Maintained presence in Iraq at least until 2002. Maintains an operational presence in Lebanon. The group has demonstrated the ability to operate over a wide area, including the Middle East, Asia, and Europe.[8]

KEY LEADERS[9]

Atef Abu Baker (Abu Bakr); Abdel Rahman Issa (Abd-al-Rahman Isa); Sabri l-Banna (deceased).

Al-Qa'ida

DESCRIPTION

- Sunni Islamic fundamentalist umbrella organization. Reportedly operates in approximately sixty-five countries.[10]

---

[3] Ibid.

[4] US Department of State. *Patterns of Global Terrorism 2003*, p. 114.

[5] "Terrorist Group Profile: Abu Nidal Organization (ANO)." *Knowledge Base*, (accessed on October 3, 2004).

[6] US Department of State. *Patterns of Global Terrorism 2003*, p. 114.

[7] Ibid.   [8] Ibid.

[9] "Terrorist Group Profile: Abu Nidal Organization (ANO)" (accessed on October 3, 2004).

[10] "Terrorist Group Profile: Al Qaeda." *MIPT Knowledge Base*. Available at: http://www.tkb.org/Group.jsp?groupID = 6 (accessed on September 19, 2004).

- Founded in 1988 by Osama bin Laden and Dr. Abdullah Azzam in Afghanistan. Successor to the Afghan Bureau Azzam created to funnel Arab recruits to fight the Soviets in Afghanistan.[11]

GOALS

Establishment of a pan-Islamic Caliphate.[12] Overthrow of regimes within the Muslim world it deems un-Islamic. Withdrawal of Western, principally US, forces from the Arabian Peninsula.[13] Destruction of Israel. Punishment of the US for perceived acts of aggression against Muslims.[14]

MAIN ACTIVITIES

- In 2002–03, conducted bombings in Saudia Arabia, Morocco, Turkey, Kenya, Tunisia. Conducted suicide attack on the MV *Limburg* near the Yemeni coast. Attacked US military personnel in Kuwait. Reportedly supported bombings in Indonesia and was involved in attacks in Afghanistan. Attempted to shoot down an airliner in Kenya with a shoulder-fired missile.[15]
- Conducted suicide attacks in the US on September 11, 2001 against the World Trade Center Towers in New York City and the Pentagon in Washington, DC by crashing hijacked airliners into the buildings.[16] A fourth hijacked airliner was crashed near Shanksville, Pennsylvania.[17] An al-Qa'ida associate, Richard Reid, unsuccessfully attempted to detonate a bomb on a transatlantic flight.[18]
- As of October 2004, the group is reportedly responsible for 21 attacks which inflicted 6,327 casualties and killed 3,539 persons.[19]

GROUP SIZE

Estimates vary. The US State Department estimates al-Qa'ida comprises several thousand members.[20] The International Institute of Strategic Studies estimates that al-Qa'ida, in a slightly different formulation, can draw on more than 18,000

[11] Ibid.
[12] US Department of State. *Patterns of Global Terrorism 2003*, p. 131.
[13] Ibid., p. 131.
[14] Robbins. "Bin Laden's War," pp. 354–355. See also Anonymous, *Through Our Enemies' Eyes*, p. 4.
[15] US Department of State. *Patterns of Global Terrorism 2003*, p. 132.
[16] Ibid. [17] Ibid. [18] Ibid.
[19] "Terrorist Group Profile: Al Qaeda." *MIPT Knowledge Base*. Available at: http://www.tkb.org/Group.jsp?groupID = 6 (accessed on October 3, 2004).
[20] US Department of State. *Patterns of Global Terrorism, 2003* p. 132

"potential terrorists" based on estimates that as many as 20,000 terrorists passed through al-Qa'ida training camps in Afghanistan.[21]

STATE SPONSORSHIP
Formerly provided with safe haven by Afghanistan and the Sudan. No known formal state sponsorship currently.[22]

AREA OF OPERATIONS
Global.[23]

KEY LEADERS
Osama bin Laden; Dr. Ayman Zawahiri.

HAMAS

DESCRIPTION
- Sunni Islamist Palestinian nationalist group established in 1987 after the outbreak of the first *intifada*. The group was founded by the Muslim Brotherhood in Palestine.[24]
- In addition to conducting attacks, the group operates social services not provided by the Palestinian Authority within the West Bank and Gaza Strip.[25]

GOALS
To destroy Israel and establish an Islamic Palestinian state.[26]

MAIN ACTIVITIES
- Most notable for suicide bombings and relatively high operational tempo.

[21] "Still Plotting, Still Recruiting." *The Economist*. June 1, 2004. Available at: http://www.economist.com/agenda/displayStory.cfm?Story_ID = 2705024 (accessed on September 19, 2004).
[22] US Department of State. *Patterns of Global Terrorism 2003*, p. 133.
[23] "Terrorist Group Profile: Al Qaeda." *MIPT Knowledge Base*. Available at: http://www.tkb.org/Group.jsp?groupID = 6 (accessed on September 19, 2004).
[24] "Terrorist Group Profile: HAMAS." *MIPT Knowledge Base*. Available at: http://www.tkb.org/Group.jsp?groupID = 49 (accessed September 18, 2004).
[25] Ibid.
[26] US State Department. *Patterns of Global Terrorism 2003*, p. 120.

- As of October 2004, the group is reportedly responsible for 167 attacks which inflicted 2,589 casualties and killed 522 persons.[27]

GROUP SIZE
More than 1,000 members.[28]

STATE SPONSORSHIP
Limited support from Iran and Syria.[29]

AREA OF OPERATIONS
West Bank, Gaza Strip, and Israel.[30]

KEY LEADERS[31]
Mahmud al-Zahhar; Ibrahim Ghousheh; Musa Abu Marzuq; many other leaders deceased.

Harakat ul-Mujahidin (HUM)

DESCRIPTION
Pakistani militant group formed in 1985, split from Harkat-ul-Jihad-al-Islami (HuJI), to combat Soviet troops in Afghanistan. Shifted operations to Kashmir and Jammu following the Soviet withdrawal from Afghanistan in 1989. Merged with HuJI in 1993, at the urging of Pakistan's ISI, to form Harkat-ul-Ansar (HuA) which was designated a Foreign Terrorist Organization (FTO) by the US. HuA was subsequently returned to the name Harakat ul-Mujahidin to avoid sanctions.[32]

GOALS
Liberation of Kashmir and its accession to Pakistan.[33]

---

[27] "Terrorist Group Profile: HAMAS." *MIPT Knowledge Base* (accessed September 18, 2004).
[28] Ibid.   [29] Ibid. (accessed October 3, 2004).
[30] US State Department. *Patterns of Global Terrorism 2003*, p. 120.
[31] "Terrorist Group Profile: HAMAS." *MIPT Knowledge Base* (accessed October 3, 2004).
[32] "Terrorist Group Profile: Harakat ul-Mudjahidin (HuM)." *MIPT Knowledge Base*. Available at: http://www.tkb.org/Group.jsp?groupID = 50 (accessed September 19, 2004).
[33] Ibid.

MAIN ACTIVITIES

- Conducted numerous attacks against the Indian military forces and civilians in Kashmir. Hijacked an Indian airliner in 1999 and is linked to the kidnapping of five Western tourists in Kashmir during 1995. All five were reportedly killed later in the year.[34]
- Information on number of attacks, casualties inflicted, and persons killed is unavailable.

GROUP SIZE

Several hundred members.[35]

STATE SPONSORSHIP

Reportedly, historic support from Pakistan's ISI.[36]

AREA OF OPERATIONS

Kashmir and Pakistan.[37]

KEY LEADERS[38]

Maulana Masood Azhar; Farooq Kashmiri Khalil; Fazlur Rehman Khalil; Maulana Saadatullah Khan

Hizb-ul-Mujahedin

DESCRIPTION

Kashmiri militant group. Hizb-ul-Mujahedin is the militant wing of Jamaat-i-Islami, the Pakistani Islamic political party.[39]

GOALS

To unite Kashmir with Pakistan.[40]

---

[34] US State Department, *Patterns of Global Terrorism 2003*, 2004, p. 147.
[35] Ibid., p. 121.
[36] "Terrorist Group Profile: Harakat ul-Mudjahidin (HuM)." *MIPT Knowledge Base* (accessed September 19, 2004).
[37] US State Department, *Patterns of Global Terrorism 2003*, p. 121.
[38] "Terrorist Group Profile: Harakat ul-Mudjahidin (HuM)." *MIPT Knowledge Base* (accessed September 19, 2004).
[39] US State Department, *Patterns of Global Terrorism 2003*, p. 147.
[40] "Terrorist Group Profile: Hizbul Mujahideen (HM)." *MIPT Knowledge Base*. Available at: http://www.tkb.org/Group.jsp?groupID = 52 (accessed September 19, 2004).

MAIN ACTIVITIES

- Conducts attacks primarily against Indian military, and at times civilian, targets in Jammu and Kashmir.[41]
- As of October 2004, the group is reportedly responsible for five attacks which inflicted four casualties and killed eight persons.

GROUP SIZE

Several hundred members.[42]

STATE SPONSORSHIP

Reportedly, receives significant support from Pakistan. Pakistan's Inter-Services Intelligence agency urged Jamiat-e-Islami to establish Hizb-ul-Mujahedin to counter the secular Jammu Kashmir Liberation Front (JKLF).[43]

AREA OF OPERATIONS

Jammu, Kashmir, and Pakistan.[44]

KEY LEADERS[45]

Abdul Majeed Dar; Syed Salahuddin

Jaish-e-Mohammed (JEM) (Army of Mohammed)

DESCRIPTION

Islamic extremist group based in Pakistan and formed in 2000. The group is associated with the Jamiat-e-Ulema Islam Fazlur Rehman faction (JUI-F), political group.[46] The group was banned by the Pakistani government in 2002.[47]

---

[41] US State Department. *Patterns of Global Terrorism 2003*, p. 147.

[42] Ibid., 147.

[43] "Terrorist Group Profile: Hizbul Mujahideen (HM)." *MIPT Knowledge Base* (accessed September 19, 2004).

[44] US State Department. *Patterns of Global Terrorism 2003*, p. 147.

[45] "Terrorist Group Profile: Hizbul Mujahideen (HM)." *MIPT Knowledge Base* (accessed September 19, 2004).

[46] US Department of State. *Patterns of Global Terrorism 2003*, p. 123.

[47] "Terrorist Group Profile: Jaish-e-Mohammad (JEM)." *MIPT Knowledge Base*. Available at: http://www.tkb.org/Group.jsp?groupID = 58 (accessed on September 19, 2004).

GOALS

Unite Kashmir with Pakistan.[48]

MAIN ACTIVITIES

- Claims to have conducted suicide attacks, later denied by the group, against Jammu and Kashmir legislative buildings. The Indian government claims that JEM was involved in the December 2001 attack on the Indian Parliament.[49]
- As of October 2004, the group is reportedly responsible for two attacks which inflicted sixty casualties and killed thirty-nine persons.[50]

GROUP SIZE

Several hundred members.[51]

STATE SPONSORSHIP

Reportedly received assistance from Pakistan's Inter-Services Intelligence agency.[52]

AREA OF OPERATIONS

Kashmir, Jammu, and Pakistan.[53]

KEY LEADERS[54]

Maulana Qari Mansoor Ahmed; Maulana Masood Azhar; C. Maulana Abdul Jabbar; Sheikh Omar Saeed; Maulana Sajjad Usman

Jammu and Kashmir Liberation Front (JKLF)

DESCRIPTION

Two groups historically operated under the JKLF title, one led by Amanullah Khan and the other by Yasin Malik. JKLF was established by Khan in 1977

---

[48] US Department of State. *Patterns of Global Terrorism 2003*, p. 123.

[49] Ibid., p. 123.

[50] "Terrorist Group Profile: Jaish-e-Mohammad (JEM)." *MIPT Knowledge Base* (accessed on October 3, 2004).

[51] US State Department. *Patterns of Global Terrorism 2003*, p. 123.

[52] "Terrorist Group Profile: Jaish-e-Mohammad (JEM)." *MIPT Knowledge Base* (accessed on September 19, 2004).

[53] US State Department. *Patterns of Global Terrorism 2003*, p. 123.

[54] "Terrorist Group Profile: Jaish-e-Mohammad (JEM)." *MIPT Knowledge Base* (accessed on October 3, 2004).

following the effective destruction of the Jammu and Kashmir National Liberation Front (JKNLF) by Indian forces. Malik split from Khan in 1995 over a difference in tactics; the Malik faction had renounced violence. The Khan faction was effectively destroyed by the Indian military in two separate attacks in 1996. The Malik faction, the only surviving JKLF group, is a member of the All Party Huriyat Conference.[55]

GOALS

To establish an independent Jammu and Kashmir.[56]

MAIN ACTIVITIES

- The group engaged in propaganda supporting a plebiscite on independence in Jammu and Kashmir during the 1970s. In the 1980s, the group engaged in terrorist attacks, including the hijacking of an Indian Airlines aircraft and the killing of the Indian Deputy High Commissioner.[57]
- Beginning in 1991, the group was increasingly marginalized and actively suppressed by the Pakistani ISI and allied insurgent groups. Initially, the ISI used the JKLF to establish a network within Kashmir and recruit insurgents. ISI used those recruits to establish pro-Pakistani groups (e.g., Hizb-ul-Mujahedin) which supported Pakistani control over Kashmir, rather than Kashmiri independence.[58]

GROUP SIZE

Unknown.[59]

STATE SPONSORSHIP

Historically, Pakistan through the ISI.[60]

AREA OF OPERATIONS

England and Kashmir.[61]

---

[55] "Jammu and Kashmir Liberation Front (JKLF)." Globalsecurity.org. Available at: http://globalsecurity.org/military/world/para/jklf.htm (accessed on October 4, 2004).

[56] Ibid. [57] Ibid. [58] Ibid. [59] Ibid.

[60] Ibid. [61] Ibid.

KEY LEADERS

Yasin Malik[62]

Kurdistan Worker's Party (PKK) (currently the Kongra-Gel (KGK))

DESCRIPTION

Kurdish Marxist-Leninist group established in 1982 within Turkey.

GOALS

- Historically, establish an independent, democratic Kurdish state.[63]
- Following the 1999 arrest of the PKK's leader, Abdullah Ocalan, by Turkey and his subsequent declaration of a unilateral ceasefire, the group was significantly weakened. In 2002, the group changed its name to the Kurdistan Freedom and Democracy Congress (KADEK) and then to the Kurdistan People's Conference (KHK) in 2003. Later in 2003 the group changed its name once more to the Kongra-Gel (KGK).[64] The group has asserted that it has eschewed violence, yet continues military training.[65]

MAIN ACTIVITIES

- In the 1990s, the group attacked Turkish governmental and commercial organizations in Western Europe, as well as bombing tourist sites and kidnapping foreigners within Turkey.[66]
- As of October 2004, the group is reportedly responsible for 84 attacks which inflicted 214 casualties and killed 38 persons.[67]

GROUP SIZE

Approximately 5,000 members.[68]

---

[62] Ibid.

[63] US Department of State. *Patterns of Global Terrorism 2002*, p. 112.

[64] US Department of State. *Patterns of Global Terrorism 2003*, p. 125.

[65] "Terrorist Group Profile: Kurdistan Workers' Party." *MIPT Knowledge Base*. Available at: http://www.tkb.org/Group.jsp?groupID = 63 (accessed on September 16, 2004).

[66] US Department of State. *Patterns of Global Terrorism 2002*, p. 112.

[67] "Terrorist Group Profile: Kurdistan Workers' Party." *MIPT Knowledge Base* (accessed on September 16, 2004).

[68] US Department of State. *Patterns of Global Terrorism 2002*, p. 112.

STATE SPONSORSHIP
Historically received aid from Syria, Iran, and Iraq.[69]

AREA OF OPERATIONS
Turkey, Europe, and the Middle East.[70]

KEY LEADERS[71]
Abdullah Ocalan; Cemil Bayik; Duran Kalkan; Osman Ocalan; Kemal Pir.

Lashkar-e-Tayyeba (LeT)

DESCRIPTION

- Militant arm of Markaz-ud-Dáwa-wal-Irshad, a Pakistani Sunni Muslim religious organization.
- LeT is a member of the International Islamic Front for Jihad against the US and Israel formed by Osama bin Ladin.[72]

GOALS
To establish an Islamic state that includes all Muslim majority regions surrounding, and including, Pakistan.[73]

MAIN ACTIVITIES

- Since 1993, conducts attacks in Jammu and Kashmir. The Indian government believes that the LeT was involved in the December 2001 attacks on the Indian Parliament.[74]
- Abu Zubaydah was captured in Pakistan at an LeT safe house in 2002. It is believed that the LeT is assisting al-Qa'ida.[75]

---

[69] Ibid., p. 113. [70] Ibid., p. 112.
[71] "Terrorist Group Profile: Kurdistan Workers' Party" (accessed on September 16, 2004).
[72] "Terrorist Group Profile: Lashkar-e-Taiba (LeT)." *MIPT Knowledge Base.* Available at: http://www.tkb.org/Group.jsp?groupID = 66 (accessed on September 17, 2004).
[73] Ibid.
[74] US Department of State. *Patterns of Global Terrorism 2003*, p. 126.
[75] Ibid., p. 126.

- As of October 2004, the group is reportedly responsible for 10 attacks which inflicted 217 casualties and killed 98 persons.[76]

GROUP SIZE

Several thousand members.[77]

STATE SPONSORSHIP

Historical support from Pakistan's Inter-Services Intelligence agency.[78]

AREA OF OPERATIONS

Pakistan, Jammu, and Kashmir.[79]

KEY LEADERS[80]

Abdullah Azam; Maulana Abdul Wahid Kashmiri; Hafiz Mohammed Saeed; Saifullah; Zaki ur Rehman Lakhwi.

Lebanese Hizballah

DESCRIPTION

Radical Shi'ite organization established in 1982 following the Israeli invasion of Lebanon.[81]

---

[76] "Terrorist Group Profile: Lashkar-e-Taiba (LeT)" (accessed on September 17, 2004).

[77] US Department of State, *Patterns of Global Terrorism 2003*, p. 126.

[78] "Terrorist Group Profile: Lashkar-e-Taiba (LeT)." *MIPT Knowledge Base.* (accessed on September 17, 2004).

[79] US Department of State, *Patterns of Global Terrorism 2003*, p. 126.

[80] "Terrorist Group Profile: Lashkar-e-Taiba (LeT)." *MIPT Knowledge Base.* (accessed on September 17, 2004).

[81] "Terrorist Group Profile: Hezbollah." *MIPT Terrorism Knowledge Base.* Available at: http://www.tkb.org/Group.jsp?groupID = 3101 (accessed September 16, 2004). "Over the last 20 years, however, Hezbollah has become increasingly integrated into the government of Lebanon. The group holds seats in the Lebanese parliament and its political wing runs a variety of social programs, including schools and hospitals, augmenting those of the state. Its military wing serves as a *de facto* security force in southern Lebanon. The group's spiritual leadership officially denies links to al Qaeda."

GOALS

Historically, establish a Shi'ite theocracy in Lebanon, destroy Israel, and eliminate Western influences from the region.[82]

MAIN ACTIVITIES

- From 1982 until 2000, Hizballah waged a guerrilla campaign against Israel to drive it out of Lebanon and weaken it in general.
- In 2003, the group established a sizeable presence, an approximately 90 person "security team," among Shi'ia in Southern Iraq.[83]
- Among many notable attacks are the 1994 bombing of a Jewish cultural center in Buenos Aires, the 1992 bombing of the Israeli Embassy in Buenos Aires, the 1984 suicide bombing at the US embassy in Beirut, and the 1983 bombing of the multinational force barracks in Beirut.[84]
- As of October 2004, the group is reportedly responsible for 189 attacks which inflicted 1,150 casualties and killed 851 persons.[85]

GROUP SIZE

- Several hundred active members and several thousand part-time fighters, activitists, and supporters.[86]
- Receives significant financial, military, and diplomatic aid from Syria and Iran.[87]

AREA OF OPERATIONS

Primarily Lebanon, however, maintains cells in Europe, Africa, South America, North America, and Asia.[88]

KEY LEADERS[89]

Hassan Nasrallah; Naim Qassem; Mohammad Raad; Imad Mugniyah.

---

[82] Ibid.
[83] James Risen, "Hezbollah, in Iraq, Refrains From Attacks on Americans." *The New York Times*, November 24, 2003.
[84] "Terrorist Group Profile: Hezbollah." *MIPT Terrorism Knowledge Base* (accessed September 16, 2004).
[85] Ibid.
[86] US Department of State. *Patterns of Global Terrorism 2003*, p. 122.
[87] Ibid.   [88] Ibid.
[89] "Terrorist Group Profile: Hezbollah." *MIPT Terrorism Knowledge Base* (accessed September 16, 2004).

The Palestine Islamic Jihad (PIJ)

DESCRIPTION
Sunni Islamist Palestinian Movement founded in the late 1970s.[90]

GOALS
Destroy Israel and establish an Islamic Palestinian state.

MAIN ACTIVITIES
- Notable for large-scale suicide bombings.[91]
- As of October 2004, the group is reportedly responsible for 44 attacks which inflicted 618 casualties and killed 122 persons.[92]

GROUP SIZE
Approximately 1,000 members.[93]

STATE SPONSORSHIP
Iran and Syria.[94]

AREA OF OPERATIONS
Israel, the West Bank, and Gaza Strip.[95]

KEY LEADERS[96]
Sheikh Abd al-Aziz Awda; Bashir Musa; Ramadan Abdullah Shallah.

---

[90] See US State Department, *Patterns of Global Terrorism 2003*, p. 130. "Terrorist Group Profile: Palestinian Islamic Jihad (PIJ)." *MIPT Knowledge Base*. Available at: http://www.tkb.org/Group.jsp?groupID = 82 (accessed September 18, 2004).

[91] US State Department, *Patterns of Global Terrorism 2003*, p. 130.

[92] Ibid., p. 130. "Terrorist Group Profile: Palestinian Islamic Jihad (PIJ)." *MIPT Knowledge Base* (accessed September 18, 2004).

[93] US State Department, *Patterns of Global Terrorism 2003*, p. 130. "Terrorist Group Profile: Palestinian Islamic Jihad (PIJ)." *MIPT Knowledge Base* (accessed September 18, 2004).

[94] US State Department, *Patterns of Global Terrorism 2003*, p. 130.

[95] Ibid.

[96] Ibid. "Terrorist Group Profile: Palestinian Islamic Jihad (PIJ)." *MIPT Knowledge Base* (accessed September 18, 2004).

Palestine Liberation Organization (PLO) and al Fatah

DESCRIPTION

The PLO is an umbrella organization composed of Palestinian nationalist groups. The PLO was founded in 1964 under the guidance of Egypt.[97] Al-Fatah, led by Yasir Arafat, aligned itself with the PLO in 1967. By 1969, Arafat was serving as the PLO's Chairman and Fatah had established itself as the dominant faction within the broader organization. Since the 1993 Oslo Accords, the PLO has transformed itself into the quasi-governmental Palestinian Authority. Elements within Fatah continue terrorist attacks against Israel.[98]

GOAL

Establish a Palestinian state.

MAIN ACTIVITIES

- The PLO carried out attacks against Israel from Jordan in the mid- to late 1960s until expelled in September 1970. The group then moved to Lebanon and continued to conduct attacks against Israel until the Israeli invasion of Lebanon in 1982 and subsequent expulsion of the PLO.[99]
- Al-Fatah, operating under the name "Black September," held hostage, and killed or caused the deaths of eleven Israeli athletes, members of the 1972 Israeli Olympic team during the Munich Olympics.[100]
- Elements of al-Fatah including the al-Aqsa Martyrs Brigades and the Fatah-Tanzim conducted attacks against Israel prior to, and especially after, the start of the second *intifada*.[101]
- The PLO conducted over 8,000 terrorist or other attacks between 1969 and 1985, primarily against Israeli citizens.[102]

[97] Rubin, *Revolution Until Victory?*, p. 2.
[98] "Al-Fatah Terrorist Group Profile." *MIPT Terrorist Knowledge Base.* Available at: http://www.tkb.org/Group.jsp?groupID = 128 (accessed on September 18, 2004).
[99] Rubin, *Revolution Until Victory?*, p. 25.
[100] The Council on Foreign Relations, *Terrorism: Questions & Answers; Israel.* Access to online encyclopedia available through: http://www.cfr.org/reg_issues.php?id = 13 | | | 1 (accessed on October 3, 2004).
[101] "Al-Fatah Terrorist Group Profile." *MIPT Terrorist Knowledge Base* (accessed on September 18, 2004).
[102] Rubin, *Revolution Until Victory?*, p. 25.

Appendix

GROUP SIZE
More than 10,000 members for al-Fatah alone.[103]

STATE SPONSORSHIP
Historic support for terrorist activities from Egypt, Iraq, Jordan, Lebanon, Syria, and various other Arab states.[104]

AREA OF OPERATIONS
Gaza, West Bank, Israel, Lebanon, and Western Europe.[105]

KEY LEADER[106]
Yasir Arafat (deceased). As of this writing, it is unclear who will emerge as the preeminent leader of the PLO.

Popular Front for the Liberation of Palestine (PFLP)

DESCRIPTION
A Marxist-Leninist Palestinian nationalist group formed in 1967. Joined the PLO in 1968.[107]

GOALS
To destroy Israel and establish a Palestinian state. The PFLP believes the Palestinian nationalist movement is an element in a larger class struggle and seeks to replace conservative Arab regimes with Marxist-Leninist states.[108]

MAIN ACTIVITIES
- Committed numerous terrorist attacks during the 1960s and 1970s, most notably a series of airline hijackings. The group continues to conduct limited operations, but is increasingly marginalized.[109]

[103] "Al-Fatah Terrorist Group Profile." *MIPT Terrorist Knowledge Base* (accessed on September 18, 2004).
[104] Rubin, *Revolution Until Victory?*, pp. 2–10.
[105] "Al-Fatah Terrorist Group Profile." *MIPT Terrorist Knowledge Base* (accessed on September 18, 2004).
[106] Ibid.
[107] US State Department, *Patterns of Global Terrorism 2003*, p. 130.
[108] "Terrorist Group Profile: Popular Front for the Liberation of Palestine (PFLP)." *MIPT Knowledge Base*. Available at: http://www.tkb.org/Group.jsp?groupID = 85 (accessed on September 18, 2004).
[109] Ibid.

- As of October 2004, the group is reportedly responsible for 89 attacks which inflicted 594 casualties and killed 148 persons.[110]

GROUP SIZE

Approximately 800 members.[111]

AREA OF OPERATIONS

Syria, Lebanon, Israel, West Bank, and Gaza Strip.[112]

STATE SPONSORS

Syria.[113]

KEY LEADERS[114]

George Habash, Abdel Rahim Mallouh, Ahmed Saadat.

Popular Front for the Liberation of Palestine – General Command (PFLP-GC)

DESCRIPTION

A splinter group of the PFLP which left the larger organization in 1968. The group is strongly opposed to the PLO.[115]

GOAL

To destroy Israel and establish a Palestinian state.

MAIN ACTIVITIES

Most active during the 1970s and 1980s. Conducted attacks in Europe and the Middle East. Notable for novel methods (e.g., use of hot air balloons, and of hang gliders) to mount cross-border attacks into Israel.[116]

---

[110] Ibid.   [111] Ibid.
[112] US State Department, *Patterns of Global Terrorism 2003*, p. 131.
[113] Ibid., p. 131.
[114] "Terrorist Group Profile: Popular Front for the Liberation of Palestine (PFLP)." *MIPT Knowledge Base* (accessed on September 18, 2004).
[115] US State Department, *Patterns of Global Terrorism 2003*, p. 131.
[116] Ibid.

Appendix

GROUP SIZE
Several hundred members.[117]

STATE SPONSORSHIP
Syria and Iran.[118]

AREA OF OPERATIONS
Southern Lebanon, Israel, West Bank, and Gaza Strip. Offices and bases located in Damascus and Lebanon.[119]

KEY LEADER[120]
Ahmad Jabril

Provisional Irish Republican Army (PIRA)

DESCRIPTION
The IRA was established in 1919 during the Anglo-Irish War (1919–21). The Provisional Irish Republican Army (PIRA) assumed effective political control of the IRA in 1969.[121]

GOAL
Unification of an independent Ireland.[122]

MAIN ACTIVITIES
- The IRA has conducted bombings, assassinations, and kidnappings in Northern Ireland and England throughout its history.[123]
- The IRA committed itself to non-violent methods in pursuit of its political goals following the ceasefire in July 1997 which was reaffirmed in July 2002. Splinter groups such as the Continuity IRA and Real IRA continue to employ violence, however.[124]

---

[117] Ibid. [118] Ibid. [119] Ibid. [120] Ibid.
[121] "Terrorist Group Profiles: Irish Republican Army (IRA)." *MIPT Knowledge Base*. Available at: http://www.tkb.org/Group.jsp?groupID = 55 (accessed September 18, 2004).
[122] Ibid.
[123] US State Department, *Patterns of Global Terrorism 2003*, p. 148.
[124] "Terrorist Group Profiles: Irish Republican Army (IRA)." *MIPT Knowledge Base* (accessed September 18, 2004).

- As of October 2004, the group is reportedly responsible for 82 attacks which inflicted 124 casualties and killed 26 persons.[125]

GROUP SIZE

Several hundred members.[126]

STATE SPONSORSHIP

Historical support from Libya and the Palestine Liberation Organization.[127]

AREA OF OPERATIONS

Northern Ireland, Republic of Ireland, Great Britain, and Europe.[128]

KEY LEADERS (SINN FÉIN)

- Sinn Féin, an Irish Republican political party, is widely considered the political wing of the Provisional Irish Republican Army.
- Gerry Adams (Sinn Féin); Martin McGuinness (Sinn Féin)

Revolutionary Organization 17 November (N17)

DESCRIPTION

- Greek Leftist group established in 1975. The group is named for the date of a student protest in November 1973 against the Greek dictatorship.[129]
- Nineteen core members were arrested in 2002 following a failed bombing. It is believed the group was effectively broken by the arrests and has been inactive since the arrests.[130]

GOALS

Removal of US military bases from Greece, the removal of the Turkish military from Cyprus, withdrawal of Greece from the North Atlantic Treaty Organization (NATO), and withdrawal of Greece from the European Union (EU).[131]

---

[125] Ibid.

[126] US State Department, *Patterns of Global Terrorism 2003*, p. 148.

[127] Ibid.   [128] Ibid.   [129] Ibid., p. 135.   [130] Ibid.

[131] "Terrorist Group Profile: Revolutionary Organization 17 November (RO-N17)." *MIPT Knowledge Base.* Available at: http://www.tkb.org/Group.jsp?groupID = 101 (accessed on September 18, 2004).

MAIN ACTIVITIES

- During the 1980s, conducted assassinations and bombings against US officials and Greek politicians. During the 1990s the group also conducted attacks against EU facilities and foreign firms.[132]
- As of October 2004, the group is reportedly responsible for forty-five attacks which inflicted forty casualties and killed seven persons.[133]

GROUP SIZE

Believed to be inactive. Members claim an additional ten members (beyond the 19 arrested in 2002) are still at large.[134]

AREA OF OPERATIONS

Greece.[135]

KEY LEADER[136]

Alexandros Giotopoulos

Supreme Council for Islamic Revolution in Iraq (SCIRI)

DESCRIPTION

Shi'ite Muslim umbrella organization of Iraqi factions opposed to Saddam Husayn. The group was established in Iran in 1982 and initially included some elements of the Da'wa party. After the 2003 overthrow of Saddam Husayn's regime, several SCIRI leaders have entered politics and are part of the government.

GOAL

Islamic-based democracy in Iraq.[137]

---

[132] US State Department, *Patterns of Global Terrorism 2003*, p. 148.
[133] "Terrorist Group Profile: Revolutionary Organization 17 November (RO-N17)." *MIPT Knowledge Base* (accessed on September 18, 2004).
[134] Ibid.
[135] US State Department, *Patterns of Global Terrorism 2003*, p. 135.
[136] "Terrorist Group Profile: Revolutionary Organization 17 November (RO-N17)." *MIPT Knowledge Base* (accessed on September 18, 2004).
[137] "IRAQ: Iran's Involvement." *Council on Foreign Relations.* May 15, 2003. Available at: http://www.cfr.org/background/background_iraq_iran.php (accessed on September 17, 2004).

MAIN ACTIVITIES

- Elements of what became SCIRI conducted a variety of attacks against Saddam's regime and other opponents of Iran.
- Elements of the SCIRI militia known as the Badr Brigade which was trained by Iran reportedly entered Iraq after the US invasion.[138]

GROUP SIZE

Several thousand.[139]

STATE SPONSORSHIP

Iran.[140]

AREA OF OPERATIONS

Iraq and Iran.[141]

KEY LEADER

Ayatollah Mohammed Bakr Hakim.[142]

---

[138] "IRAQ: Iraqi Opposition Groups." *Council on Foreign Relations*. April 29, 2003. Available at: http://www.cfr.org/background/background_iraq_opposition.php (accessed on September 17, 2004).

[139] Ibid.   [140] Ibid.

[141] See ibid. and The Supreme Council for Islamic Resistance in Iraq, "About Us." Available at: http://www.sciri.btinternet.co.uk/English/About_Us/about_us.html (accessed on October 3, 2004).

[142] The Supreme Council for Islamic Resistance in Iraq. "About Us." Available at: http://www.sciri.btinternet.co.uk/English/About_Us/about_us.html (accessed on October 3, 2004).

Bibliography

Aburish, Said. *The Rise, Corruption, and Coming Fall of the House of Saud.* New York: St. Martin's Press (1995).

Nasser: The Last Arab. Thomas Dunne Books (2004).

Agha, Hussein. "The Syrian–Iranian Axis in Lebanon." In *Lebanon on Hold: Implications for Middle East Peace*, ed. Rosemary Hollis and Nadim Shehadi. London: Royal Institute for International Affairs (1996), pp. 24–30.

Ajami, Fouad. *The Vanished Imam.* Ithaca, NY: Cornell University Press (1993).

Albright, Madeleine. *Madam Secretary: A Memoir.* New York: Miramax Books (2003).

Alikhani, Hossain. *Sanctioning Iran: Anatomy of a Failed Policy.* London: I.B. Tauris (2000).

Al-Zayyat, Montasser. *The Road to Al-Qaeda*, trans. Ahmed Fekry. London: Pluto Press (2004).

Andrew, Christopher and Vasili Mitrokhin. *The Sword and the Shield: The Mitrokhin Archive and the Secret History of the KGB.* New York: Basic Books (1999).

Anonymous. *Imperial Hubris: Why the West Is Losing the War on Terrorism.* Washington, DC: Brassey's (2004).

Through Our Enemies' Eyes. Washington, DC: Brassey's (2002).

Anti-Terrorism and Arms Export Amendments Act, PL 101–222, 22 USCA §§ 1732, 2364, 3371, 2753, 2776, 2778, 2780 (1989).

Arjomand, Said Amir. *The Turban for the Crown: The Islamic Revolution in Iran.* New York: Oxford University Press (1988).

Armitage, Richard L. "Testimony before the Senate Foreign Relations Committee." US Congress (October 28, 2003). Available at http://www.state.gov/s/d/rm/25682.htm (accessed December 12, 2003).

335

Aufhauser, David. "War on Terror: Follow the Money." *Policywatch, no. 812.* Washington Institute for Near East Policy (December 8, 2003).

Bach, William. "The Taliban, Terrorism, and Drug Trade." Testimony before the Committee on Government Reform, US House of Representatives (October 3, 2001).

Baer, Robert. *Sleeping with the Devil.* New York: Crown Publishers (2003).

Bakhash, Shaul. *Reign of the Ayatollahs.* New York: Basic Books (1986).

Bakoyannis, Dora. "Terrorism in Greece." *Mediterranean Quarterly*, no. 6 (Spring 1995), 17–28.

Baldwin, David. *Economic Statecraft.* Princeton, NJ: Princeton University Press (1985).

"The Sanctions Debate and the Logic of Choice." *International Security*, vol. 24, no. 3 (Winter 1999–2000), 80–107.

Baram, Amatzia. "The Effects of Iraqi Sanctions: Statistical Pitfalls and Responsibility." *Middle East Journal*, vol. 54, no. 2 (Spring 2000), 194–223.

Barkey, Henri. "Turkey and the PKK." In Robert Art and Louise Richardson, eds., *Democracy and Counterterrorism.* Washington, DC: US Institute of Peace (forthcoming).

Bartholet, Jeffrey, *et al.* "Al Qaeda Runs for the Hills," *Newsweek* (December 17, 2001), pp. 20–26.

Bell, J. Bowyer. "The Armed Struggle and Underground Intelligence: An Overview." *Studies in Conflict and Terrorism*, vol. 17 (1994), 115–150.

The IRA, 1968–2000: Analysis of a Secret Army. Portland, OR: Frank Cass (2000).

The Secret Army. New Brunswick, NJ: Transaction Publishers (2003).

Benjamin, Daniel and Steve Simon. *The Age of Sacred Terror.* New York: Random House (2002).

Bergen, Peter. *Holy War, Inc.: Inside the Secret World of Osama Bin Ladin.* New York: Simon & Schuster (2002).

Beyer, Lisa *et al.* "Inside the Kingdom," *Time* (January 15, 2003), 38–49.

Biddle, Stephen. *Afghanistan and the Future of Warfare: Implications for Army and Defense Policy.* Carlisle, PA: Strategic Studies Institute (2002). http://www.carlisle.army.mil/ssi/pubs/pubResult.cfm/hurl/PubID=109/.

Black, Ian and Benny Morris. *Israel's Secret Wars: A History of Israel's Intelligence Services.* New York: Grove Press (1991).

Black, J. Cofer. "Syria and Terrorism." Testimony before the Senate Foreign Relations Committee (October 30, 2003).

"Testimony to the House Committee on International Relations, Subcommittee on the Middle East and Central Asia" (March 24, 2004). http://wwwc.house.gov/international_relations/108/blac032404.htm.

Blanchard, Jean-Marc and Norrin M. Ripsman. "Asking the Right Question: When Do Economic Sanctions Work?" *Security Studies*, vol. 9, no. 1 (Autumn 1999), 219–253.

Blanford, Nicholas. "Hizbullah Attacks Force Israel to Take a Hard Look." *Jane's Intelligence Review*, vol. 11, no. 4 (April 1, 1999), electronic version.

"Diplomats Say Israel Set to Continue Overflights Over Lebanon." *Washington Report on Middle East Affairs*, vol. 22, no. 8 (October 2003), electronic version.

Blaufarb, Douglas. *The Counterinsurgency Era: US Doctrine and Performance.* New York: Free Press (1977).

Brand, Laurie A. *Jordan's Inter-Arab Relations: The Political Economy of Alliance Making.* New York: Columbia University Press (1994).

Brinton, Crane. *The Anatomy of Revolution.* New York: Vintage Books (1965).

Brophy-Baermann, Bryan and John A. C. Conybeare. "Retaliating against Terrorism: Rational Expectations and the Optimality of Rules versus Discretion." *American Journal of Political Science*, vol. 38 (1994), 196–210.

Brumberg, Daniel. "Khomeini's Legacy." In *Spokesmen for the Despised*, ed. R. Scott Appleby. Chicago, IL: University of Chicago Press (1997).

Reinventing Khomeini: The Struggle for Reform in Iran. Chicago, IL: University of Chicago Press (2001).

Brzezinski, Zbigniew. "To Lead, US Must Give up Paranoid Policies." *International Herald Tribune*, (November 13, 2003).

Buchta, Wilfried. *Who Rules Iran?* Washington, DC: Washington Institute for Near East Policy (2000).

Burke, Jason. *Al-Qaeda: Casting a Shadow of Terror.* New York: I.B. Tauris (2003).

Burns, William J. "Statement before the Senate Foreign Relations Committee" (October 30, 2003).

Bush, President George W. "Address to a Joint Session of Congress and the American People," United States Capitol, Washington DC (September 20, 2001) http://www.whitehouse.gov/news/releases/2001/09/20010920-8.html (accessed July 7, 2004).

"President Bush Calls for New Palestinian Leadership" (June 24, 2002). Available at http://www.whitehouse.gov/news/releases/2002/06/20020624-3. html (accessed on May 7, 2004).

Byman, Daniel. "The Logic of Ethnic Terrorism." *Studies in Conflict and Terrorism*, vol. 21, no. 2 (April–June 1998), 149–169.

Byman, Daniel and Jerrold Green. *Political Violence and Stability in the States of the Northern Persian Gulf.* Santa Monica, CA: RAND (1998).

Byman, Daniel and Matthew Waxman. *The Dynamics of Coercion: American Foreign Policy and the Limits of Military Might.* New York: Cambridge University Press (2002).

Byman, Daniel and John R. Wise. *The Persian Gulf in the Coming Decade: Trends, Threats, and Opportunities.* Santa Monica, CA: RAND (2002).

Byman, Daniel, Shahram Chubin, Anoushiravan Ehteshami, and Jerrold Green. *Iran's Security Policy in the Post-Revolutionary Era.* Santa Monica, CA: RAND (2001).

Byman, Daniel, Peter Chalk, Bruce Hoffman, William Rosenau, and David Brannan. *Trends in Outside Support for Insurgent Movements.* Santa Monica, CA: RAND (2001).

Central Intelligence Agency. *Palestinian Organizations.* Document LDA 92–12531. Washington, DC: Central Intelligence Agency (1992).

CIA World Factbook 2003. Washington, DC: Central Intelligence Agency (2003) http://www.cia.gov/cia/publications/factbook/geos/in.html#Econ.

Guide to the Analysis of Insurgency. Washington, DC: Central Intelligence Agency (n.d.).

Chaliand, Gerard. *Terrorism: From Popular Struggle to Media Spectacular.* London: Saqi Books (1987).

Chalk, Peter. "Pakistan's Role in the Kashmir Insurgency." *Jane's Intelligence Review* (September 1, 2001).

Chivers, C. J. and David Rohde. "The Jihad Files: Training the Troops." *New York Times* (March 18, 2002), A1.

Cohen, Eliot, Andrew Bacevich, and Michael Eisenstadt. *Knives, Tanks, and Missiles: Israel's Security Revolution.* Washington, DC: The Washington Institute for Near East Policy (1998).

Cohen, Stephen. *The Idea of Pakistan.* Washington, DC: Brookings Institution Press (2004).

Coll, Steve. *Ghost Wars: The Secret History of the CIA, Afghanistan, and Bin Laden: From the Soviet Invasion to September 10, 2001.* New York: Penguin Press (2004).

Collins, Stephen D. "Dissuading State Support of Terrorism: Strikes or Sanctions? (An Analysis of Dissuasion Measures Employed Against Libya)." *Studies in Conflict & Terrorism,* no. 27 (2004), 1–18.

Cordesman, Anthony. *Iran's Military Forces in Transition: Conventional Threats and Weapons.* Westport, CT: Praeger (1999).

Council on Foreign Relations. "The Northern Alliance," http://cfrterrorism.org/afghanistan/alliance.html (accessed April 1, 2004).

"November 17, Revolutionary People's Struggle." available at: http://cfrterrorism.org/groups/rps.html

Council on Foreign Relations and the Asia Society. "Afghanistan: Are We Losing the Peace?" New York (June 2003).

Cowell, Alan. "Syria and Iran Agree Militias Can Remain in Parts of Lebanon." *New York Times* (April 30, 1991).

Crenshaw, Martha. "How Terrorism Declines." *Terrorism Research and Public Policy*, vol. 3, no. 1 (Spring 1991), 69–87.

"How Terrorism Ends." *US Institute of Peace* (May 25, 1999), 1–4.

Cronin, Audrey Kurth. "Foreign Terrorist Organizations." *Congressional Research Service* (February 6, 2004).

Cullinson, Alan and Andrew Higgins. "A Computer in Kabul Yields a Chilling Array of al Qaeda Memos." *Wall Street Journal* (December 31, 2001), A1.

"Strained Alliance: Al Qaeda's Sour Days in Afghanistan." *Wall Street Journal* (August 2, 2002), A1.

Dabashi, Hamid. *Theology of Discontent: The Ideological Foundation of the Islamic Revolution in Iran*. New York: New York University Press (1993).

David, Steven R. "Israel's Policy of Targeted Killing." *Ethics & International Affairs*, vol. 17 (Spring 2003), 111–126.

Davis, Brian L. *Qaddafi, Terrorism, and the Origins of the US Attack on Libya*. New York: Praeger (1990).

Deeb, Mary Jane. *Libya Since the Revolution: Aspects of Social and Political Development*. New York: Praeger (1982).

Libya's Foreign Policy in North Africa. Boulder, CO: Westview Press (1991).

Dekmejian, Richard. "The Liberal Impulse in Saudi Arabia." *The Middle East Journal*, vol. 57, no. 3 (Summer 2003), 400–413.

DeSutter, Paula A. "Testimony before the US–Israeli Joint Parliamentary Committee." US Congress (September 17, 2003). Available at http://www.state/gov/t/vc/rls/rm/24494.htm (accessed December 12, 2003).

Dobbs, Michael. "Saudi Rulers Walk Political Tightrope." *Washington Post* (March 14, 2003), A23.

"US–Saudi Alliance Appears Strong." *Washington Post* (April 27, 2003), A20.

Doran, Michael. "Somebody Else's Civil War." *Foreign Affairs* (January–February 2002), 22–42.

"The Saudi Paradox." *Foreign Affairs* (January–February 2004), 35–51.

Doumato, Eleanor. "Manning the Barricades: Islam According to Saudi Arabia's School Texts." *Middle East Journal*, vol. 57, no. 2 (Spring 2003), 230–247.

Downs, George W. and David M. Rocke. "Conflict, Agency, and Gambling for Resurrection." *American Journal of Political Science*, vol. 38, no. 2 (May 1994), 362–380.

Drumbl, Mark A. "The Taliban's 'Other' Crimes." *Third World Quarterly*, vol. 23, no. 6 (2002), 1121–1131.

Eckstein, Harry, ed. *Internal War: Problems and Approaches*. New York: Free Press (1964).

Ehteshami, Anoushiravan. *After Khomeini*. New York: Routledge (1995).

Eisenberg, Daniel, *et al.* "Secrets of Brigade 055." *Time Europe*, vol. 158, no. 19 (November 5, 2001), 63.

Eisenstadt, Michael. *Iranian Military Power*. Washington, DC: The Washington Institute for Near East Policy (1996).

"The Military Dimension," in *Iran under Khatami: A Political, Economic, and Military Assessment*. Washington, DC: Washington Institute for Near East Policy (1998), 71–98.

"The Armed Forces of the Islamic Republic of Iran: An Assessment." *Middle East Review of International Affairs*, vol. 5, no. 1 (December 2000).

Eizenstadt, Stuart E. "Do Economic Sanctions Work? Lessons from ILSA & Other US Sanctions Regimes." Washington, DC: Atlantic Council (February 2004).

English, Richard. *Armed Struggle: The History of the IRA*. New York: Oxford University Press (2003).

Ergil, Dogu. "Aspects of the Kurdish Problem in Turkey." In *Turkey Since 1970: Politics, Economics, and Society*, ed. Debbie Lovatt. New York: Palgrave Macmillan (2001).

Eshel, David. "Counterguerrilla Warfare in South Lebanon." *Marine Corps Gazette*, vol. 81, no. 7 (July 1997), 40–45.

Evans, Alexander. "The Kashmir Insurgency: As Bad as it Gets." *Small Wars and Insurgencies*, vol. 11, no. 1 (Spring 2000), 69–81.

"The Explosive Arrest of an Ambassador." *The Economist* (August 30, 2003).

Export Administration Act, PL 96–72, 50 USC App. § 2405 (6) (j) (1979).

Fair, C. Christine. *Militants in the Kargil Conflict: Myths, Realities, and Impacts*. Santa Monica, CA: RAND (forthcoming).

Fandy, Mamoun. *Saudi Arabia and the Politics of Dissent*. New York: Palgrave Macmillan (2001).

Fearon, James D. "Bargaining, Enforcement, and International Cooperation." *International Organization*, vol. 52, no. 2 (April 1998), 269–305.

Fearon, James D. and David Laitin. "Ethnicity, Insurgency, and Civil War." *American Political Science Review*, vol. 97, no. 1 (2003), 75–90.

Fukuyama, Francis. *State-Building: Governance and World Order in the 21st Century*. Ithaca, NY: Cornell University Press (2004).

Fuller, Graham. *The "Center of the Universe": The Geopolitics of Iran*. Boulder, CO: Westview (1991).

The Future of Political Islam. New York: Palgrave Macmillan (2003).

Gambill, Gary C. "The Balance of Terror: War by Other Means in the Contemporary Middle East." *Journal of Palestine Studies*, vol. 28, no. 1 (Autumn 1998), 51–66.

"The American–Syrian Crisis and the End of Constructive Engagement." *Middle East Intelligence Bulletin*, vol. 5, no. 4 (April 2003). http://www.meib/org/articles/0304_s1.htm (accessed May 17, 2004).

Ganguly, Sumit. *The Crisis in Kashmir: Portents of War, Hopes of Peace*. New York: Cambridge University Press (1997).

Conflict Unending: India–Pakistan Tensions since 1947. New York: Columbia University Press (2001).

Gasiorowski, Mark. "Iran: Can the Islamic Republic Survive?" In, *The Middle East in 2015: The Impact of Regional Trends on US Strategic Planning*, ed. Judith S. Yahphe. Washington, DC: NDU Press (2002), 119–141.

Gause, F. Gregory. "Be Careful What You Wish For: The Future of US–Saudi Relations." *World Policy Journal* (Spring 2002), 37–50.

Gause III, F. Gregory. "Getting it Backward on Iraq." *Foreign Affairs*, vol. 78, no. 3 (May/June 1999), 54–65.

"The Approaching Turning Point: The Future of US Relations with the Gulf States." Washington, DC: The Saban Center for Middle East Policy at the Brookings Institution (May 2003).

Geertz, Clifford. *The Interpretation of Cultures.* New York: Basic Books (1973).

George, Alexander and William Simons, eds. *The Limits of Coercive Diplomacy.* Boulder, CO: Westview (1994).

Geraghty, Tony. *The Irish War.* Baltimore, MD: Johns Hopkins University Press (2000).

Gill, K. P. S. "Khalistan in Waiting." *The Pioneer* (India) (February 21, 2004).

Gold, Dore. *Hatred's Kingdom: How Saudi Arabia Supports the New Global Terrorism.* Washington, DC: Regnery Publishing (2003).

Goodson, Larry P. *Afghanistan's Endless War: State Failure, Regional Politics, and the Rise of the Taliban.* Seattle: University of Washington Press (2001).

Government of India, Ministry of Home Affairs. "Annual Report, 2002–2003" (2003). http://mha.nic.in.

Griffin, Michael. *Reaping the Whirlwind: Afghanistan, Al Qa'ida and the Holy War.* Sterling, VA: Pluto Press (2003).

Griswald, Eliza "Where the Taliban Roam." *Harper's Magazine*, vol. 307, no. 1840 (September 2003), 57–66.

Guelke, Adriane. "The United States, Irish Americans, and the Northern Ireland Peace Process." *International Affairs*, vol. 72, no. 3 (1996), 521–536.

Gunaratna, Rohan. "Dynamics of Diaspora-Supported Terrorist Networks: Factors and Conditions Driving and Dampening International Support." Ph.D. thesis, University of St. Andrews, Scotland (October 1999).

Hajjar, Sami G. "Hizballah: Terrorism, National Liberation, or Menace?" (August 2002), available at http://www.carlisle.army.mil/usassi/welcome.htm

Hamzeh, A. Nizar "Lebanon's Hizbullah: From Islamic Revolution to Parliamentary Accommodation." *Third World Quarterly*, vol. 14, no. 2 (1993), 321–337.

"Islamism in Lebanon: A Guide." *Middle East Review of International Affairs*, vol. 1, no. 3 (Spring 1997), electronic version.

Harik, Judith. "Between Islam and the System: Sources and Implications of Popular Support for Lebanon's Hizballah." *Journal of Conflict Resolution*, vol. 40, no. 1 (March 1996), 41–67.

Harrington, Thomas J., FBI Deputy Assistant Director. "Saudi Arabia and the Fight Against Terrorism Financing." Testimony before the House Committee on International Relations, Subcommittee on the Middle East and Central Asia (March 24, 2004), http://wwwc.house.gov/internaitonal_relations/108/harro32404.htm

Hart, Gary. "My Secret Talks with Libya, and Why They Went Nowhere." *Washington Post* (January 18, 2005), B05.

Hart, Parker T. *Saudi Arabia and the United States: Birth of a Security Partnership*. Bloomington, IN: University of Indiana Press (1998).

Henderson Simon. "Address at the Washington Institute for Near East Policy." (May 20, 2003). http://www.ciaonet.org/pbei/winep/policy_2003/2003_759.html

Hewitt, V. "An Area of Darkness, Still? The Political Evolution of Ethnic Identities in Jammu and Kashmir, 1947–2001." In *Ethnonational Identities*, ed. S. Fenton and S. May. London: Palgrave Macmillan (2002).

Higgins, Andrew and Christopher Cooper. "CIA-Backed Team Used Brutal Means to Break Up Terrorist Cell in Albania." *Wall Street Journal* (November 20, 2001).

Hinnebusch, Raymond. *Syria: Revolution from Above*. New York: Routledge (2001).

Hiro, Dilip. *Iran under the Ayatollahs*. New York: Routledge (1985).
Lebanon: Fire and Embers. New York: St. Martin's Press (1992).

Hoffman, Bruce. *Inside Terrorism*. New York: Columbia University Press (1998).
"The Modern Terrorist Mindset." In *Terrorism and Counterterrorism: Understanding the New Security Environment*, ed. Russell Howard and Reid Sawyer (McGraw Hill, 2002).
"Rethinking Terrorism and Counterterrorism Since 9/11." *Studies in Conflict & Terrorism*, vol. 25 (2002), 303–316.

Hoffman, Bruce and Kim Cragin. "Four Lessons from Five Countries." *Rand Review*, available at http://www.rand.org/publications/randreview/issues/rr.09.02/fourlessons.html

Hoffman, Bruce and Jennifer Morrison Taw. *A Strategic Framework for Countering Terrorism and Insurgency*. Santa Monica, CA: RAND (1992).

Holden, David, and Richard Johns. *The House of Saud: The Rise and Rule of the Most Powerful Dynasty in the Arab World*. New York: Holt, Rinehart, and Winston (1981).

Holland, Jack. *The American Connection: US Guns, Money, and Influence in Northern Ireland*. Boulder, CO: Robert Reinhart Publishers (1999).

Hroub, Khaled. *HAMAS: Political Thought and Practice.* Beirut: Institute for Palestine Studies (2000).

Hudson, Michael. "The Breakdown of Democracy in Lebanon." *Journal of International Affairs*, vol. 38 (Winter 1985), 277–82.

Hufbauer, Gary Clyde, Kimberly Ann Elliott, Jeffrey Schott. *Economic Sanctions Reconsidered.* Cambridge, MA: MIT Press (1985).

Hufbauer, Gary Clyde, Jeffery J. Schott, and Barbara Oegg. "Using Sanctions to Fight Terrorism." Institute for International Economics (November 2001) http://www.iie.com/publications/pb/pb01-11.htm

Hull, Edmund. "Briefing Upon the Release of the Report." *Patterns of Global Terrorism* 2000 (April 30, 2001), http://www.state.gov/s/ct/rls/2001

Human Rights Watch. *Civilian Pawns: Laws of War Violations and the Use of Weapons on the Israel–Lebanon Border* (1996). Available at: http://hrw.org/reports/1996/Israel.htm

"Israel/Lebanon: 'Operation Grapes of Wrath.'" (September 1997) available at: http://www.hrw.org/reports/1997/isrleb/Isrleb.htm#P54_1377 (accessed on March 24, 2005).

"Behind the Kashmir Conflict: Abuses by Indian Security Forces and Militant Groups Continue" (1999), http://www.hrw.org/reports/1999/kashmir/mil-abuses.htm (accessed January 6, 2004).

Afghanistan – Crisis of Impunity: The Role of Pakistan, Russia and Iran in Fuelling the Civil War. New York: Human Rights Watch (2001).

Indyk, Martin. "The Iraq War Did Not Force Gadaffi's Hand." *Financial Times* (March 9, 2004).

International Crisis Group. "Kashmir: The View from Srinagar." *Asia Report*, no. 41 (November 21, 2002).

"Hizbollah: Rebel Group without a Cause?" (July 30, 2003). Available at: http://www.crisisweb.org/projects/showreport.cfm?reportid=1070.

"Iraq's Shiites Under Occupation" (September 2003). Available at: http://www.crisisweb.org//library/documents/report_archive/A401120_09092003.pdf (accessed October 13, 2003).

"Kashmir: Learning from the Past." *Asia Report*, no. 70 (December 4, 2003). http://www.crisisweb.org//library/documents/asia/070_kashmir_learning_from_the_past.pdf

"Kashmir: The View from New Delhi." *Asia Report*, no. 69 (December 4, 2003). http://www.crisisweb.org//library/documents/asia/069_kashmir_new delhi. pdf

"Kashmir: The View from Islamabad." *Asia Report*, no. 68 (December 4, 2003). http://www.crisisweb.org//library/documents/asia/068_kashmir_islamabad.pdf (accessed 2004).

"Unfulfilled Promises: Pakistan's Failure to Tackle Extremism." *Asia Report*, no. 73 (January 16, 2004). http://www.crisisweb.org//library/documents/asia/south_asia/073_unfulfil_promises_pakistan_ extr.pdf

"Syria under Bashar (I): Domestic Policy Challenges." Amman/Brussels (February 11, 2004).

"Syria under Bashar (II): Domestic Policy Challenges." Amman/Brussels (February 11, 2004).

Isikoff, Michael and Mark Hosenball. "The Saudi–Al Qaeda Connection." *Newsweek* (September 11, 2003).

"The Islamists' Drug Connection." *Jane's Islamic Affairs Analyst* (June 1, 2000) (electronic version from database).

Jaber, Hala. *Hezbollah: Born With a Vengeance*. New York: Columbia University Press (1997).

Jaffee Center for Strategic Studies, "Syria." In *The Middle East Military Balance 2002–2003*. Tel Aviv: Jaffee Center (2003). http://www.tau.ac.il/jcss/balance/Syria.pdf

Jamal, Arif. "The Hizbul Mujahedin Once Again Breaks Up." *The News* (January 5, 2003).

"Back to Square One." *The News* (January 12, 2003).

Jankowski, James. *Nasser's Egypt, Arab Nationalism, and the United Arab Republic*. Boulder, CO: Lynne Rienner Publishers (2001).

Jenkins, Brian M. "The Study of Terrorism: Definitional Problems." In *Behavior and Quantitative Perspectives on Terrorism*, ed. Yonah Alexander and John M. Gleason. New York: Pergamon Press (1981).

Jervis, Robert. *Perception and Misperception in International Politics*. Princeton, NJ: Princeton University Press (1976).

Jervis, Robert, Ned Lebow, and Janice Gross Stein, eds. *Psychology and Deterrence*. Baltimore, MD: Johns Hopkins University Press (1985).

Johnson, Scott, and Evan Thomas. "Mullah Omar off the Record." *Newsweek* (January 21, 2002), 26–28.

Jones, Clive. "Israeli Counter-Insurgency Strategy and War in South Lebanon, 1985–1997." *Small Wars and Insurgencies*, vol. 8, no. 3 (Winter 1997), 82–108.

Jones, Owen Bennett. *Pakistan: Eye of the Storm*. New Haven, CT: Yale University Press (2002).

Jongman, A. J. "Trends in International and Domestic Terrorism in Western Europe, 1968–1988." In *Western Responses to Terrorism*, ed. Schmid and Crelisten. London: Frank Cass (1993).

Jouejati, Murhaf. "With Syria, Use Carrots." Statement before the Senate Foreign Relations Committee (October 30, 2003).

Judah, Tim. "The Center of the World." *New York Review of Books*, vol. 49, no. 1 (January 17, 2002), 10–12.

Kaiser, Robert G. and David Ottaway. "Enormous Wealth Spilled into American Coffers." *Washington Post* (February 11, 2002), A17.

Kakar, M. Hassan. *Afghanistan: The Soviet Invasion and the Afghan Response, 1979–1982*. Berkeley, CA: University of California Press (1995).

Kaplan, David. "The Saudi Connection." *US News and World Report* (December 15, 2003).

Karmon, Ely. "Syrian Support to Hizballah: The Turkish Lesson." Institute for Counter Terrorism (November 27, 1998). http://www.ict.org.il/articles/articledet.cfm?articleid=68 (accessed April 22, 2003).

"Kashmiri Terrorism on the Rise." *Jane's Terrorism and Security Monitor* (February 1, 2000).

"Kashmiris Don't Want to Join Pak: Survey." *Times of India* (September 27, 2002). http://timesofindia.indiatimes.com/cms.dll/articleshow?artid=23409600 &sType

Kassimeris, George. "Europe's Last Red Terrorists: The Revolutionary Organization 17 November, 1975–2000." *Terrorism and Political Violence*, vol. 13, no. 2 (Summer 2001), 67–84.

Europe's Last Red Terrorists: The Revolutionary Organization 17 November. New York: New York University Press (2001).

"17N: Greece's Secret Socialist Spectre." *Jane's Intelligence Review*, 11 (September 1999): 23–28.

Katzman, Kenneth. *The Warriors of Islam: Iran's Revolutionary Guard*. Boulder, CO: Westview Press (1993).

Keohane, Robert O. and Joseph S. Nye. *Power and Interdependence*. Boston: Little, Brown (1977).

Kepel, Gilles. *Jihad: The Trail of Political Islam*. Cambridge, MA: Harvard University Press (2002).

"The Origins and Development of the Jihadist Movement." *Asian Affairs*, vol. 34, no. 2 (July 2003), 91–108.

Kerr, Malcolm. *The Arab Cold War*. Oxford: Oxford University Press (1971).

Kessler, Glenn. "Pakistan Fails to Rein in Guerrillas." *Washington Post* (April 18, 2003), A14.

Khan, Akbar. *Raiders in Kashmir*. Karachi: Pak Publishers (1970).

Khan, Ilyas. "Business as Usual." *The Herald* (July 2003), 38–40.

"The Waiting Game." *The Herald* (July 2003), 36–38.

Khoury, Philip. *Syria and the French Mandate: The Politics of Arab Nationalism*. Princeton, NJ: Princeton University Press (1987).

Kimmerling, Baruch and Joel S. Migdal. *Palestinians: The Making of a People*. Cambridge, MA: Harvard University Press (1994).

345

Kirshner, Jonathon. "The Microfoundations of Economic Sanctions." *Security Studies*, vol. 6, no. 3 (Spring 1997), 32–64.

Kitfield, James, "The Iranian Connection," *National Journal*, May 17, 2002, p. 1469.

Klovens, Dean. "The CIA Role in the Peace Process." *Middle East Intelligence Bulletin*, vol. 3, no. 1 (January 2001), electronic version. Available at http://www.meib.org/articles/0101_ip1.htm (downloaded May 30, 2004).

Kramer, Martin. "The Moral Logic of Hizballah." In *Origins of Terrorism: Psychologies, Ideologies, Theologies, States of Mind*, ed. Walter Reich. Cambridge: Cambridge University Press (1990), pp. 131–157. Electronic version available at http://www.geocities.com/martinkramerorg/MoralLogic.htm (downloaded August 31, 2004).

"Hizbullah: The Calculus of Jihad." In *Fundamentalisms and the State: Remaking Polities, Economies, and Militance*, ed. M. Marty and R. S. Appleby. Chicago: University of Chicago Press (1993), pp. 539–556. Electronic version available at http://www.geocities.com/martinkramerorg/Calculus.htm (downloaded August 31, 2004).

"The Oracle of Hizbullah: Sayyid Muhammad Husayn Fadlallah." In *Spokesmen for the Despised: Fundamentalist Leaders of the Middle East*, ed. R. Scott Appleby. Chicago: University of Chicago Press (1997), pp. 83–181. Electronic version available at http://www.geocities.com/martinkramerorg/Oracle1.htm (downloaded August 31, 2004).

Kux, Dennis. *The United States and Pakistan, 1947–2000: Disenchanted Allies*. Baltimore, MD: Johns Hopkins University Press (2001).

Landis, Joshua. "Syria and the Palestine War: Fighting King 'Abdullah's 'Greater Syria Plan.'" In *The War for Palestine: Rewriting the History of 1948*, ed. Eugene L. Rogan and Avi Shlaim. Cambridge: Cambridge University Press (2001), pp. 178–205.

Lane, Charles. "Clinton Pardoned Castro's Terrorists." *Wall Street Journal* (November 19, 1999).

Leites, Nathan and Charles Wolf, Jr. *Rebellion and Authority: An Analytic Essay on Insurgent Conflicts*. Chicago, IL: Markham (1970).

Leverett, Flynt. "Syria–US Policy Directions." Testimony before the US Senate Committee on Foreign Relations (October 30, 2003).

Levitt, Matthew. *Targeting Terror: US Policy toward Middle Eastern State Sponsors and Terrorist Organizations, Post-September 11*. Washington, DC: Washington Institute for Near East Policy (2002).

"Prepared Statement of Matthew Levitt." Hearing before the Subcommittee on the Middle East and South Asia of the Committee on International

Relations, House of Representatives (September 18, 2002). http://www.house.gov/international_relations (accessed on May 3, 2004).

"Confronting Syrian Support for Terrorist Groups." *Middle East Intelligence Bulletin* (May 2003). Available at http://www.meib/org/articles/0305_s1.htm

"Hezbollah's West Bank Terror Network." *Middle East Intelligence Bulletin*, vol. 5, no. 8–9 (August–September 2003). http://www.meib.org/articles/0308_13.htm

"Subversion from Within: Saudi Funding of Islamic Extremist Groups Undermining US Interests and the War on Terror from within the United States." Testimony Before the US Senate Judiciary Subcommittee on Terrorism, Technology, and Homeland Security (September 10, 2003).

"The Hizballah Threat in Africa." *Policywatch* 823 (January 2, 2004).

Levitt, Matthew and Simon Henderson. "Waging the War on Terror: Are the Saudis Starting to Turn the Corner?" The Washington Institute for Near East Policy *Policywatch*, no. 822 (December 31, 2003).

Lippman, Thomas W. *Inside the Mirage: America's Fragile Partnership with Saudi Arabia*. Boulder, CO: Westview Press (1994).

Litwak, Robert S. *Rogue States and US Foreign Policy: Containment after the Cold War*. Washington, DC: Woodrow Wilson Press (2000).

Lotrionte, Catherine, "When to Target Leaders." *Washington Quarterly*, vol. 26, no. 3 (Summer 2003), 73–86.

Luft, Gal. "All Quiet on the Eastern Front? Israel's National Security Doctrine after the Fall of Saddam." Analysis Paper no. 2. Washington, DC: The Saban Center for Middle East Policy (March 2004).

Ma'oz, Moshe. *Syria and Israel: From War to Peace-making*. New York: Oxford University Press (1995).

Maley, William. *The Afghanistan Wars*. New York: Palgrave Macmillan (2002).

Mann, Hillary "Iranian Links to International Terrorism – the Khatemi Era," *Policywatch* 296, January 28, 1998.

Markey, Daniel. "Prestige and the Origins of War: Returning to Realism's Roots." *Security Studies*, vol. 8, no. 4 (Summer 1999), 126–73 .

Marsden, Peter. *The Taliban: War, Religion, and the New Order in Afghanistan*. New York: St. Martin's Press (1998).

McCormick, Gordon H. "Terrorist Decision Making." *Annual Review of Political Science*, vol. 6 (2003), 473–507.

McCormick, G. H. and G. Owen, "Security and Coordination in a Clandestine Organization." *Mathematical and Computer Modeling*, vol. 31 (2000), 175–192.

McGeary, Johanna. "The Taliban Troubles." *Time Europe* (October 1, 2001), 46–50.

Bibliography

McGirk, Tim and Massimo Calabresi. "Is Pakistan a Friend or Foe?" *Time* (September 29, 2003). http://www.time.com/time/archive/preview/ 0,10987, 1101030929-488779,00.html (accessed January 9, 2004).

McGirk, Tim, Hannah Bloch, Andrew Goldstein, Ghulam Hasnain, and Andrew Purvisa. "Smack in the Middle." *Time Europe*, vol. 158, no. 21 (November 19, 2001), 38.

"A Measure of Democracy," *The Washington Post* (June 8, 2004), A18.

Meyer, Josh. "Cutting Money Flow to Terrorists Proves Difficult." *Los Angeles Times* (September 28, 2003).

Mickolus, Edward F. "How Do We Know We're Winning the War Against Terrorists? Issues in Measurement." *Studies in Conflict and Terrorism*, no. 25 (2002), 151–160.

Milani, Mohsen. *The Making of Iran's Islamic Revolution: From Monarchy to Islamic Republic*. Boulder, CO: Westview Press (1994).

Miller, Judith. "Faces of Fundamentalism: Hassan al-Turabi and Muhammed Fadlallah." *Foreign Affairs* (November/December 1994), 123–142.

"Global Islamic Awakening or Sudanese Nightmare?" In *Spokesmen for the Despised: Fundamentalist Leaders of the Middle East*, ed. R. Scott Appleby. Chicago: University of Chicago Press (1997), 182–224.

Mintz, John. "Wahhabi Strain of Islam Faulted." *Washington Post* (June 27, 2003), A11.

Mishal, Shaul and Avraham Sela. *The Palestinian HAMAS: Vision, Violence, and Coexistence*. New York: Columbia University Press (2000).

Moloney, Ed. *The Secret History of the IRA*. New York: W. W. Norton and Company, 2002.

Monti-Belkaoui, Janice and Ahmed Riahi Belkaoui. *Qaddafi: The Man and His Policies*. Aldershot, UK: Ashgate Publishing (1996).

Morris, Benny. *Israel's Border Wars, 1949–1956: Arab Infiltration, Israeli Retaliation, and the Countdown to the Suez War*. New York: Oxford University Press (1997).

Mueller, John and Karl Mueller. "Sanctions of Mass Destruction." *Foreign Affairs*, vol. 78, no. 3 (May/June 1999), 43–53.

Murphy, Edward. "Libya Opens Up." *Harvard International Review*, vol. 22, no. 3 (Fall 2000), 8–9.

Murphy, Richard W. "Syria–US Policy Directions." Statement submitted to the Committee on Foreign Relations of the United States Senate (October 30, 2003).

Nasr, Seyyed Vali Reza. *The Vanguard of the Islamic Revolution: The Jama'at-i Islami of Pakistan*. Berkeley, CA: University of California Press (1994).

Nasr, Vali. "Military Rule, Islamism, and Democracy in Pakistan." *Middle East Journal*, vol. 58, no. 2 (Spring 2004), 195–211.

Nasrallah, Hassan. "Peace Requires Departure of Palestinians." *Middle East Insight* (March–April 2000), 32.

National Commission on Terrorism, *Countering the Changing Threat of International Terrorism*. Washington, DC: National Commission on Terrorism (2000).

National Commission on Terrorist Attacks Upon the United States. "Overview of the Enemy." Staff Statement no. 15 (June 16, 2004). http://www.9-11commission.gov

"Outline of the 9/11 Plot." Staff Statement no. 16 (June 16, 2004). http://www.9-11commission.gov

The 9/11 Commission Report (New York: W. W. Norton: 2004).

Norton, Augustus Richard. *Amal and the Shi'a*. Austin: University of Texas Press (1987).

"Hizballah and the Israeli Withdrawal from Southern Lebanon." *Journal of Palestine Studies*, vol. 30, no. 1 (Autumn 2000), electronic version.

Nye, Joseph. *Bound to Lead: The Changing Nature of American Power*. New York: Basic Books (1991).

O'Brien, Brendan. *The Long War: The IRA and Sinn Féin, 1985 to Today*. New York: Syracuse University Press (1993).

O'Dowd, Niall. "The Awakening: Irish-America's Key Role in the Irish Peace Process." In *The Long Road to Peace in Northern Ireland*, ed. Marianne Elliott. Intl Specialized Book Service Inc. (2002), 64–74.

O'Sullivan, Meghan L. *Shrewd Sanctions: Statecraft and State Sponsors of Terrorism*. Washington, DC: Brookings (2003).

Oakley, Robert B. "Prepared Statement of Robert B. Oakley." Presented in the hearing, "Libyan-Sponsored Terrorism: A Dilemma for Policymakers." Hearing before the Subcommittee on Security and Terrorism of the Committee on the Judiciary. United States Senate (February 19, 1986), 52–62.

Odom, William. *On Internal War: American and Soviet Approaches to Third World Clients and Insurgents*. Durham, NC: Duke University Press (1992).

Olson, Robert. "Turkey–Syria Relations, 1997 to 2000: Kurds, Water, Israel, and 'Undeclared War'." *Orient*, vol. 42, no. 1 (2001), 101–117.

Online NewsHour. "Liberia's Uneasy Peace" (October 24, 2003). http://www.pbs.org/newshour/bb/africa/liberia.html (accessed May 25, 2004).

Oren, Michael B. *Six Days of War: June 1967 and the Making of the Modern Middle East*. New York: Oxford University Press (2002).

Palmer, Michael A. *Guardians of the Gulf: A History of America's Expanding Role in the Persian Gulf, 1883–1992*. New York: Free Press (1999).

Pape, Robert. *Bombing to Win*. Ithaca, NY: Cornell University Press (1996).

"Why Economic Sanctions Do Not Work." *International Security*, vol. 22, no. 2 (Fall 1997), 90–136.

Parachini, John. "Putting WMD Terrorism into Perspective." *The Washington Quarterly*, vol. 26, no. 4 (August 2003), 37–50.

Perthes, Volker. *Syria under Bashar al-Asad: Modernization and the Limits of Change*. London: International Institute for Strategic Studies (forthcoming).

Peters, Philip. "Cuba, the Terrorism List, and What the United States Should Do." *The Lexington Institute* (November 20, 2001). http://www.lexingtoninstitute.org/cuba/cubaterrorism.htm (accessed on August 27, 2003).

Peterson, Don. *Inside Sudan: Political Islam, Conflict, and Catastrophe*. Boulder, CO: Westview Press (2003).

Pillar, Paul. *Terrorism and US Foreign Policy*. Washington, DC: Brookings Institution Press (2001).

Pollack, Josh. "Anti-Americanism in Contemporary Saudi Arabia." *Middle East Review of International Affairs*, vol. 7, no. 4 (December 2003), 30–43.

Pollack, Kenneth. *Arabs at War: Military Effectiveness, 1948–1991*. Lincoln, NE: University of Nebraska Press (2002).

"Powell Urges End to Hezbollah Border Presence." *Ha'aretz* (May 5, 2003).

Pressman, Jeremy. "The Second Intifada: Background and Causes of the Israeli-Palestinian Conflict." *Journal of Conflict Studies*, vol. 22, no. 2 (Fall 2003), 114–141.

Prunckun Jr., Henry W., and Philip B. Mohr. "Military Deterrence of International Terrorism: An Evaluation of Operation El Dorado Canyon." *Studies in Conflict and Terrorism*, no. 20 (1997), 267–280.

Prunier, Gerard. *The Rwanda Crisis*. New York: Columbia University Press (1997).

Putnam, Robert D. "Diplomacy and Domestic Politics: The Logic of Two-Level Games." *International Organization*, vol. 42, no. 3 (Summer 1988), 427–460.

"Qadhafi's Son Says Libya was Promised Economic, Military Gains for Disarmament." *Agence France-Press* (March 10, 2004). http://www.nti.org/d_newswire/issues/2004/3/10 (accessed March 11, 2004).

Quandt, William B. *Peace Process: American Diplomacy and the Arab–Israeli Conflict since 1967*. Washington, DC and Berkeley, CA: Brookings Institution and University of California Press (1993).

Quillen, Chris "A Historical Analysis of Mass Casualty Bombers." *Studies in Conflict and Terrorism*, vol. 25, no. 5 (September–October 2002), 279–292.

Rabinovich, Itamar. *The War for Lebanon, 1970–1985*. Ithaca, NY: Cornell University Press (1989).

Waging Peace: Israel and the Arabs, 1948–2003. Princeton, NJ: Princeton University Press (2004).

Rajaee, Barham. "Unraveling the Iranian Connection." Unpublished paper 2004.

Ramazani, R. K. *Revolutionary Iran: Challenge and Response in the Middle East*. Baltimore, MD: Johns Hopkins University Press (1985).

Rana, Mohammad Amir. *Gateway to Terrorism*. London: New Millennium (2003).

Ranstorp, Magnus. *Hizb'allah in Lebanon: The Politics of the Western Hostage Crisis*. New York: St. Martin's Press (1997).

Raphaeli, Nimrod. "Saudi Arabia: A Brief Guide to its Politics and Problems." *Middle East Review of International Affairs*, vol. 7, no. 3 (September 2003).

Rashid, Ahmed. *Taliban*. New Haven, CT: Yale University Press (2000).

    Jihad: The Rise of Militant Islam in Central Asia. New Haven, CT: Yale University Press (2002).

    "The Mess in Afghanistan." *New York Review of Books* (February 12, 2004), 24–27.

Reidel, Bruce. "American Diplomacy and the 1999 Kargil Summit at Blair House." Center for the Advanced Study of India (2002). http://www.sas.upenn.edu/casi/reprots/RiedelPapero51302.htm (accessed December 31, 2003).

Report of the Advisory Group on Public Diplomacy for the Arab and Muslim World. "Changing Minds, Winning Peace: A New Strategic Direction for US Public Diplomacy in the Arab and Muslim World." Washington, DC: US Department of State (October 1, 2003).

Robbins, James S. "Bin Laden's War," in *Terrorism and Counterterrorism: Understanding the New Security Environment*. Guilford, CT: McGraw-Hill/Dushkin (2003).

Robinson, Emily. "Liberia's Uneasy Peace." *Online Newshour* (n.d.) http://www.pbs.org/newshour/bb/africa/liberia/blah-bio.html (accessed August 3, 2004).

Rodman, Peter. *More Precious than Peace: The Cold War and the Struggle for the Third World*. New York: Scribner's (1994).

Rogers, Elizabeth. "Using Economic Sanctions to Control Regional Conflicts." *Security Studies*, vol. 5, no. 4 (Summer 1996), 43–72.

Rohde, David and C. J. Chivers. "The Jihad Files: Life in Bin Laden's Army." *New York Times* (March 17, 2002), electronic version.

Ross, Dennis. *The Missing Peace: The Inside Story of the Fight for Middle East Peace*. New York: Farrar, Straus, and Giroux (2004).

Roy, Olivier. *The Failure of Political Islam*. Cambridge, MA: Harvard University Press (1996).

Rubin, Barnett. *The Search for Peace in Afghanistan*. New Haven, CT: Yale University Press (1995).

Rubin, Barry. *Revolution Until Victory? The Politics and History of the PLO*. Cambridge, MA: Harvard University Press (1994).

The Transformation of Palestinian Politics: From Revolution to State-Building. Cambridge, MA: Harvard University Press (1999).

Saad-Ghoreyeb, Amal. *Hizbu'llah: Politics and Religion.* Sterling, VA: Pluto Press (2002).

Safran, Nadav. *Saudi Arabia: The Ceaseless Quest for Security.* Cambridge, MA: Harvard University Press (1985).

Sahliyeh, Emile. *The PLO after the War in Lebanon.* Boulder, CO: Westview Press (1986).

"Saudis List Top Terrorist Suspects." *Associated Press* (December 7, 2003).

Schbley, Ayla H. "Religious Terrorists: What They Aren't Going to Tell US." *Terrorism*, vol. 13 (1990), 237–241.

"Torn Between God, Family, and Money: The Changing Profile of Lebanon's Religious Terrorists." *Studies in Conflict and Terrorism*, no. 23 (July–September 2000), 175–196.

Schelling, Thomas. *Arms and Influence.* New Haven, CT: Yale University Press (1996).

Schmidt, Susan. "Spreading Saudi Fundamentalism in US" *Washington Post* (October 2, 2003), A1.

Schmidt, Susan and Caryle Murphy. "US Revokes Visa of Cleric at Saudi Embassy." *Washington Post* (December 7, 2003).

Schofield, Victoria. *Kashmir in Conflict: India, Pakistan, and the Unending War.* New York: I.B. Tauris (2003).

Schultz, George P. *Turmoil and Triumph: My Years as Secretary of State.* New York: Charles Scribner's Sons (1993).

Schweitzer, Yoram. "Hizballah: A Transnational Terrorist Organization" (September 1, 2002). http://www.ict.org.il/articles

Seale, Patrick. *Asad: The Struggle for the Middle East.* Berkeley, CA: University of California Press (1990).

Shafer, D. Michael. *Deadly Paradigms: The Failure of US Counterinsurgency Policy.* Princeton, NJ: Princeton University Press (1988).

Shain, Yossi and Martin Sherman, "Dynamics of Disintegration: Diaspora, Secession and the Paradox of Nation States." *Nations and Nationalism*, vol. 4, no. 3 (July 1998), 321–346.

Shapira, Shimon. "The *Imam* Musa al-Sadr: Father of the Shiite Resurgence in Lebanon." *Jerusalem Quarterly*, no. 44 (1987).

"The Origins of Hizballah." *Jerusalem Quarterly*, no. 46 (Spring 1988).

Shapiro, Jeremy and Benedicte Suzan. "The French Experience of Counter-terrorism." *Survival*, vol. 45, no. 1 (Spring 2003), 67–98.

Sheffer, Gabi. "Ethno-National Diasporas and Security." *Survival*, vol. 36, no. 1 (Spring 1994), 60–79.

Sick, Gary "Iran: Confronting Terrorism," *Washington Quarterly* (Fall 2003), available at http://www.twq.com/03autumn/docs/03autumn_sick.pdf

Simon, Steven N. and Jonathan Stevenson. "Declawing the 'Party of God': Toward Normalizing in Lebanon." *World Policy Journal* (Summer 2001), 31–42.

Sirrs, Julie. "Lifting the Veil on Afghanistan." *National Interest*, no. 65 (2001).

"The Taliban's International Ambitions." *Middle East Quarterly* (Summer 2001), 61–71.

Slater, Jerome. "Lost Opportunities for Peace in the Arab–Israeli Conflict." *International Security*, vol. 27, no. 1 (Summer 2002), 79–106.

Slavin, Barbara. "Officials: US 'Outed' Iran's Spies in 1997." *USA Today* (March 30, 2004), electronic version.

Small Arms Survey 2003. New York: Oxford University Press (2003).

Snyder, Glenn. *Deterrence and Defense*. Princeton, NJ: Princeton University Press (1961).

Sofaer, Abraham D. "Statement to the National Commission on Terrorist Attacks Upon the United States." *National Commission on the Terrorist Attacks Upon the United States* (March 31, 2003). http://www. 9-11commission.gov/hearings/hearing1/witness_sofaer.htm

South Asia Terrorism Portal. "Annual Casualties in Terrorist Violence, 1988–2003." *South Asia Terrorism Portal* (2004). http://www.satp.org/ satporgtp/countries/india/states/jandk/data_sheets/annual_casualties.htm (accessed January 23, 2004).

Stanik, Joseph. *El Dorado Canyon: Reagan's Undeclared War with Qaddafi.* Annapolis, MD: Naval Institute Press (2002).

Stein, Yael. "By Any Name Illegal and Immoral: Response to 'Israel's Policy of Targeted Killing.'" *Ethics & International Affairs*, vol. 17 (Spring 2003). 127–137.

Stern, Jessica. "Pakistan's Jihad Culture." *Foreign Affairs*, vol. 79, no. 6 (November–December 2000), 115–126.

"Sudan Demands To Be Lifted from State Sponsors of Terrorism." *Agence France Presse* (April 24, 2003). http://www.sudan.net/news/posted/ 6698.html

Suellentrop, Chris. "Are 1 Million Children Dying in Iraq?" *Slate* (October 9, 2001). http://slate.msn.com/id/1008414/

Szymanski, Tekla. "Greece: November's Fall?" *World Press Review*, vol. 49, no. 9 (September 2002), 29.

Takeyh, Ray. "The Rogue Who Came in from the Cold." *Foreign Affairs*, vol. 80, no. 3 (May–June 2001), 62–72.

Tanham, George K. and Dennis J. Duncanson. "Some Dilemmas of Counterinsurgency." *Foreign Affairs*, vol. 48 (January 1970), 113–122.

Tellis, Ashley J., C. Christine Fair, Jamison Jo Medby. *Limited Conflicts Under the Nuclear Umbrella: Indian and Pakistani Lessons from the Kargil Crisis.* Santa Monica, CA: RAND (2002).

Tellis, Ashley, Janice Bially, Christopher Layne, and Melissa McPherson. *Measuring National Power in the Postindustrial Age.* Santa Monica, CA: RAND (2000).

Tenet, George. "The Worldwide Threat in 2003: Evolving Dangers in a Complex World." Statement to the Senate Select Committee on Intelligence (February 11, 2003). Available at www.cia.gov

"The Worldwide Threat 2004: Challenges in a Changing Global Context." Statement to the Senate Select Committee on Intelligence (February 24, 2003). Available at www.cia.gov

"Terror in America (14): Syria's Position: Define Terrorism Not Fight It." The Middle East Media Research Institute (October 7, 2001). http://www.memri.org

Tessler, Mark. *A History of the Israeli–Palestinian Conflict.* Bloomington, IN: University of Indiana Press (1994).

Tucker, David. *Skirmishes at the Edge of Empire: The United States and International Terrorism.* Westport, CT: Praeger (1997).

"The United States and Counterterrorism, 1993–1998." Unpublished paper, March 5, 2004.

"United Jihad Groups." *Jane's World Insurgency and Terrorism – 13* (November 28, 2001).

United Nations, "Report of the Secretary General's Military Advisor Concerning the Shelling of the UN Compound at Qana on 18 April 1996." United Nations, Document S/1996/337 (May 7, 1996).

"Second Report of the Monitoring Group." Available at: http://www.motleyrice.com/911_victims/Report%20of%20UN%20Security%20Council%2020120103pdf.pdf

"United States of America *v.* Enaam M. Arnaout. Government's Evidentiary Proffer Supporting the Admissibility of Coconspirator Statements." No. 02 CR 892, United States District Court Northern District of Illinois Eastern Division (January 6, 2003).

"United States of America *v.* Mohamad Youssef Hammoud *et al.*" United States District Court, Western District of North Carolina, Charlotte Division (July 2000).

"United States of America *v.* Usama Bin Ladin *et al.*" Government Exhibit 300B-T (May 1, 2001).

"United States of America *v.* Usama Bin Ladin *et al.*" (May 1, 2001).

US Committee for Refugees, "Displacement from Kashmir." US Committee for Refugees. http://www.refugees.org/world/articles/kashmir_displaced_india.htm (accessed January 6, 2004).

US Congress, Joint Inquiry Staff Statement. "Hearings on the Intelligence Community's Response to Past Terrorist Attacks against the United States from February 1993 to September 2001" (October 8, 2002), 11. http:// intelligence.senate.gov/0210hrg/021008/hill.pdf (accessed September 6, 2003).

US Department of State, "Cuba's Renewed Support for Revolutionary Violence in Latin America." Research paper submitted to the Subcommittee on Western Hemisphere Affairs of the Senate Foreign Relations Committee by the Department of State, December 14, 1981.

Special Report no. 90 (December 14, 1981). Submitted as Exhibit A in the Appendix of US Congress, Committee on the Judiciary, Subcommittee on Security and Terrorism. "The Role of Cuba in International Terrorism and Subversion." US Congress, Appendix, Exhibit A (February 26, March 4, 11, and 12, 1982).

"Syrian Support for International Terrorism: 1983–1986." Special Report no. 157. US Department of State: Washington, DC (December 1986).

"Finally, a Talkative Talib: Origins and Membership of the Religious Students' Movement." Cable from Islamabad, 01792 (February 20, 1995). http://www.gwu/edu/~nsaarchiv/NSAEBB97/index.htm (accessed February 20, 2004).

"Libya under Qadhafi: A Pattern of Aggression" (January 1986). Presented in the hearing, "Libyan-Sponsored Terrorism: A Dilemma for Policymakers." Hearing before the Subcommittee on Security and Terrorism of the Committee on the Judiciary. United States Senate (February 19, 1986), pp. 63–70.

"Pak Foreign Minister Asks US Cooperation in Afghanistan." State 34053 (February 21, 1996). http://www.gwu/edu/~nsaarchiv/NSAEBB97/index.htm (accessed February 20, 2004).

Patterns of Global Terrorism 1995. Washington, DC: US Department of State (1996).

Patterns of Global Terrorism 1997. Washington, DC: US Department of State (1998).

Patterns of Global Terrorism 1998. Washington, DC: US Department of State (1999).

Patterns of Global Terrorism 1999. Washington, DC: US Department of State (2000).

Patterns of Global Terrorism 2000. Washington, DC: US Department of State (2001).

Patterns of Global Terrorism 2001. Washington, DC: US Department of State (2002).

Patterns of Global Terrorism 2002. Washington, DC: US Department of State (2003).

Patterns of Global Terrorism 2003. Washington, DC: US Department of State (2004).

"Summary: A/S Inderfurth Met December 8 with Three Taliban 'Acting Ministers,' Plus the UN 'Permrep Designate.'" State 231842 (December 11, 1997) http://www.gwu/edu/~nsaarchiv/NSAEBB97/index.htm (accessed February 20, 2004).

"Scenesetter for Your Visit to Islamabad: Afghan Angle." Islamabad 000436 (January 16, 1997). http://www.gwu/edu/~nsaarchiv/NSAEBB97/index.htm (accessed February 20, 2004).

"US Engagement with the Taliban on Usama Bin Laden" (July 16, 2001). http://www.gwu/edu/~nsaarchiv/NSAEBB97/index.htm (accessed February 20, 2004).

"Background Note: Iran." US Department of State (June 2003). http://www.state.gov/r/pa/ei/bgn/5314.htm#relations (accessed December 12, 2003).

"Background Note: Syria." US Department of State (October 2003). http://www.state.gov/r/pa/ei/bgn/3580.htm (accessed on May 27, 2004).

US House of Representatives. "Statement by Philip Wilcox before the House Committee on International Relations." In "Syria: Peace Partner or Rogue Regime." Hearing before the Committee on International Relations of the House of Representatives (July 25, 1996). Washington, DC: US Government Printing Office (1996).

Van Dam, Nikolaos. *The Struggle for Power in Syria: Politics and Society under Asad and the Ba'th Party*. New York: I.B. Tauris (1996).

Van Natta, Jr., Don and Timothy O'Brien. "Two Years Later: The Arab Connection: Saudis Promising Action on Terror." *New York Times* (September 14, 2003), 1

Vassiliev, Alexei. *The History of Saudi Arabia*. London: Saqi Books (1998).

Vlahou, Toula. "Greece Launches Attack on Terrorism." *Boston Globe* (June 26, 2001), electronic version.

Vollman, William T. "Across the Divide." *The New Yorker* (May 15, 2000), 58–73.

Walsh, Elsa. "Louis Freeh's Last Case." *The New Yorker* (May 14, 2001), 68–79.

Walt, Stephen. *Revolution and War*. Ithaca, NY: Cornell University Press (1994).

Watson, Paul and Mubashir Zaidi. "Militant Flourishes in Plain Sight." *Los Angeles Times* (January 25, 2004), electronic version.

Weaver, Mary Anne. "Blowback." *Atlantic Monthly*, vol. 277, no. 5 (May 1998), 24–36.

Wedeen, Lisa. *Ambiguities of Domination: Politics, Rhetoric, and Symbols in Contemporary Syria*. Chicago, IL: University of Chicago Press (1999).

Wege, Anthony. "Hizbollah Organization." *Studies in Conflict and Terrorism*, vol. 17, no. 2 (April–June 1994), 151–164.

Weiner, Tim. "'Afghan Arabs' Said to Lead Taliban's Fight." *New York Times* (November 10, 2001), electronic version.

Weiser, Benjamin. "Ex-Aide Proposed Plot to Kill Bin Laden." *New York Times* (February 21, 2001).

The White House, *National Strategy for Combating Terrorism* (2003). Available at: http://www.whitehouse.gov/news/releases/2003/02/counter_terrorism/counter_terrorism_strategy.pdf

Wiley, Joyce. *The Islamic Movement of Iraqi Shi'as*. Boulder, CO: Lynne Reinner (1992).

Wilshire, Thomas. "Testimony before the Senate Committee on Foreign Relations, Subcommittee on International Operations and Terrorism" (December 18, 2001).

Wirsing, Robert G. *India, Pakistan, and the Kashmir Dispute*. New York: St. Martin's Press (1998).

Wolfowitz, Paul, Deputy Secretary of Defense. "Testimony before the Joint Inquiry of the House Permanent Select Committee on Intelligence and the Senate Select Committee on Intelligence on Counterterrorism Center Customer Perspectives" (2002).

Woodward, Bob. *Veil: The Secret Wars of the CIA, 1981–1987*. New York: Simon & Schuster (1987).

Bush at War. New York: Simon & Schuster (2002).

Yamani, Mai. "Saudi Arabia: The 'Arab Street', the Media, and Popular Agitation since September 11." *Asian Affairs*, vol. 34, no. 2 (July 2003), 143–147.

Yousaf, Mohammad and Mark Adkin. *Afghanistan, The Bear Trap: The Defeat of a Superpower*. Havertown, PA: Casemate Publishers and Book Distributors (2001).

Zabriskie, Phil. "Mullah Omar." *Time Europe* (December 31, 2001).

Zarate, Juan C. "Testimony to the House Committee on International Relations, Subcommittee on the Middle East and Central Asia" (March 24, 2004). http://wwwc.house.gov/internaitonal_relations/108/zara032404.htm

Zisser, Ayal. "Appearance and Reality." *Middle East Review of International Affairs* (May 1998).

Assad's Legacy: Syria in Transition. London: C. Hurst & Co. (2001).

Zonis, Martin. *The Political Elite of Iran*. Princeton, NJ: Princeton University Press (1971).

Index

Index

Index